COIMISIÚN LÁIMHSCRÍBHINNÍ NA HÉIREANN
IRISH MANUSCRIPTS COMMISSION

REGISTRY OF DEEDS DUBLIN

ABSTRACTS OF WILLS

VOL. I

1708 - 1745

EDITED BY

P. BERYL EUSTACE

CLEARFIELD

Originally published
Dublin, 1956

Reprinted for
Clearfield Company, Inc. by
Genealogical Publishing Co., Inc.
Baltimore, Maryland
1996

International Standard Book Number: 978-0-8063-5508-5

Made in the United States of America

CONTENTS

INTRODUCTION

It took ten years for the Lords and Commons to deliberate on the setting up of the Registry of Deeds.[1] An Act of Parliament (6 Anne, Chap. 2) entitled "An Act for the Public Registering of all Deeds Conveyances and Wills that shall be made of any Honours, Manors, Lands, Tenements, or Hereditaments" enacted "that one public office shall be established and kept in the city of Dublin" and thus led to the creation in the year 1708 of the Irish Registry of Deeds. In this Act is included provision for the registration of all Wills and devises in writing where "the devisor or testatrix shall die after the said 25th March 1708." The registration or otherwise of Deeds was a matter of choice for the party or parties concerned, a minor compulsion lying in the stipulation that Deeds not registered "were deemed and adjudged fraudulent and void." This proviso has since been much modified by various decisions of the Courts.

In the initial period of the Registry's existence the words "Deeds, Conveyances and Wills" enjoyed a wide interpretation, and many Deeds which would not now be considered acceptable were registered. This catholicity of the subject matter of the Deeds has been of the greatest value to those interested in the family history of the period. For the genealogist the Wills registered have now a special importance because they replace some of those destroyed in the Record Office, Dublin, in 1922, when virtually all the original Irish Prerogative and Consistorial Wills perished.[2] The existence of the Wills at the Registry of Deeds has been almost unknown outside the limited number of persons engaged in research there. In order to find the Wills for

---

[1] *Commons Journal*, 1697-1707.

[2] Before 1857, Wills were proved in the Consistorial Court, that is, the Court of the Bishop or Ordinary, within whose diocese or jurisdiction the testator dwelt ; but if there were effects to the value of £5 (called *bona notabilia*) in two or more dioceses the Will had to be proved in the Prerogative Court of the Archbishop of Armagh, Primate of All Ireland, which was the Supreme Court in matters of which the ecclesiastical jurisdiction had cognisance. The jurisdiction of the Ecclesiastical Courts was abolished and transferred to the Probate Court by the Court of Probate Act, 1857 (20 and 21 Vict., c. 79).

Sir William Betham, Ulster King of Arms, compiled his valuable Will Pedigrees from the Prerogative Wills up to the year 1800. His volumes of these pedigrees, now at the Genealogical Office, Dublin Castle, have been used in checking many doubtful points met with in Wills recorded at the Registry of Deeds.

this Volume alone it was necessary to read through the two entire *Index of Grantors* series 1708–1729, 1730–1745, covering references to over eighty-three thousand recorded Deeds of all kinds. If any Wills remain undetected the laborious nature of this essential preliminary work must be my excuse. By continuing this search through the *Index of Grantors* series over two thousand Wills have already been traced. No official Index of these has ever been compiled.

Wills are recorded at the Registry of Deeds in one of three ways, which, for the sake of brevity, I have termed " Full," " Narrate " and " Précis." A Will described as " Full " in the following abstracts is one which was registered in the testator's own words. While proof that every clause was set down is seldom available, the fact that trivial matters are recorded would imply that nothing of importance was omitted during registration. A Will recorded in the third person singular, that is a " Narrate," was probably read through clause by clause and the testator's provisions registered. Relationships are often difficult to follow in Wills recorded in the narrative form, the use of the third person singular leading to confusion between the testator and the other persons mentioned in the Will. A " Précis " of a Will is not infrequently very short.[1] The testator's lands are generally referred to as his real estate in a given county, and there is usually little further information other than the names of the persons, trustees or executors to whom the lands are assigned. In all three forms of registration the names and addresses of the witnesses to the Will are recorded, together with the names of the persons who witness the signing and sealing of the memorial registered. Registered Wills and Deeds are therefore documents of undoubted authenticity.

Transcripts of the memorials of Wills and other Deeds may be inspected at the Registry of Deeds, Henrietta Street, Dublin, on payment of a small fee.[2] Transcripts, written in the eighteenth century on vellum and thereafter on vellum or good parchment, are bound into large heavy Books measuring about 22 inches by 17 inches. The original memorials, signed and sealed by the person registering the Will or Deed, and often with interesting seals attached, are stored in files in a fireproof vault. The original memorials should always be examined when there is any doubt as to the accuracy of the copies transcribed into the Books. Signatures are often distinctive and

---

[1] See Appendix for copy of a Will registered in précis form.
[2] See Appendix for lists of fees chargeable for searches made at the Registry of Deeds. One shilling per day covers a search made personally on any one surname for Deeds of any period not exceeding ten years.

comparison of them may help to establish the identity or otherwise of persons of the same name—this is a particularly useful method of distinguishing between a father and son with the same address. A word of warning is, however, necessary about the seals attached to the original memorials. Some, it is true, are armorial, but fancy seals abound. Before deciding that an armorial seal belonged to the person beside whose signature it appears the memorials placed in the file before and after the Deed in question should be examined. It sometimes happened that when several Deeds were registered at the same time the one seal was used on all.

Method adopted in making abstracts

The abstracts were made from the transcripts of the Wills, doubtful points in many cases having been checked with the original memorials. The abstracts are numbered in chronological order of registration. Following the *name* and *address* of the testator is his *occupation*, if mentioned in the Will. After the *date of signing* the Will comes the description of *how it is recorded* at the Registry of Deeds, (that is, whether in " full," " narrate " or " précis " form), the *length of the memorial* registered and the *date of registration*.[1] The *relatives* are listed next as they are described by the testator. Ambiguous descriptions are, unfortunately, often used, particularly in the case of Wills recorded in the third person singular. In order to give every possible clue to the correct identity of the persons named all surnames have been copied. Following the relatives come the names and address of all other *legatees, trustees, executors*, etc. and any outstanding legacy of general interest. Less important legacies to charities have been omitted from the abstracts but bequests to churches are included as this information is sometimes helpful to the research worker. The *lands* detailed by the testator are then listed, and the name and address of any *tenants* mentioned. (Long accounts of the history of the holding of lands are often recited by testators, too long to appear in these brief abstracts. The names of grantors are, however, always given in the abstracts in cases where the exact localities of the lands are either not mentioned at all by the testator or are not clearly stated ; a search under the names of these grantors in the Names

---

[1] In this volume of Abstracts all dates are Old Style, that is according to the Old Style official year which commenced on Lady Day, 25th March. Some dates would seem to imply that a Will was registered before it was written by the testator. In such cases the date of registration has been amended.

Index of Grantors at the Registry would probably bring further facts to light.) The names of the *witnesses* to the signing of the Will are next shown, followed by the names of those who witness the registration of the memorial of the Will after the testator's death. One of these, usually an executor named in the Will, signs and seals the memorial. By quoting *the number of the Book, page and memorial*, which are given at the end of each abstract, a certified copy of the Will from which the abstract was made can be obtained.[2]

Personal and place names in abstracts

The indexing of personal names presented many difficulties and it was decided to err on the side of over-indexing rather than under-indexing. For instance A . . . B . . . names "my daughter Mary" without giving her a surname. She could be his own daughter, his daughter-in-law or his step-daughter. In some cases, of course, the correct surname can be inferred from a reference to grandchildren. In order that the daughter Mary may appear in the *Index of Persons* at all it is necessary to include her under the testator's surname. The fact, therefore, that a surname appears in the Index of Persons does not imply that it should be read into the abstract. Married daughters are indexed under both their maiden and married surnames.

More difficult still was the indexing of place names. All too often a testator lists place names without any indication of county or barony. Where it has been possible to ascertain the precise location of any particular place the county has been inserted within square brackets in the abstracts. Place names have been copied as they were found in the transcripts of the Wills ; when, as sometimes occurs, a place name is spelled in various ways in the same transcript I have inserted the alternative in round brackets after the form which is first found. Again, it must not be forgotten that the names of many townlands have altered in the course of the last two centuries. Sometimes the change is radical, the earlier name being replaced by a later one ; in other cases anglicisation has almost obliterated the original form of the Irish name. The difficult—though fascinating—task of identifying places referred to or of furnishing the modern equivalent of eighteenth century place names is, of course, outside the scope of this work. Nevertheless I could not accept without

---

[2] Application should be made to the Assistant Registrar of Deeds, Henrietta Street, Dublin. The Office can supply certified copies of given Deeds but cannot undertake research work on behalf of correspondents.

some investigation a place name which seemed particularly unusual in sound or spelling, and where I have considered the result of this topographical research worthy of incorporation—as a suggestion—it is to be found in square brackets after the doubtful place name.

It will be noticed that a testator occasionally makes a bequest of his real estate; he may mention the county or counties in which his lands lie, or even detail the lessees or tenants, but he, or the persons who registered the memorial of the Will, fails to supply the actual place names. In these cases the testator's place of residence is probably some indication of where his lands were situated.

In conclusion I must stress the importance, from the genealogical point of view in particular, of the vast mass of material other than Wills at the Registry of Deeds. Provided the members of a family owned property in Ireland something is sure to be found on record about them; for in the early eighteenth century though other forms of investment were becoming available, money was still largely tied up in land. Searches can be made by working on the Names Index of Grantors for any period after 1708, or Deeds for any given townland can be traced through the Lands Index series for the county concerned.[1] Wills, marriage settlements, leases and releases, mortgages, declarations of trust, proposals and acceptances (dealing with business matters, not matrimony), conveyances and other forms of recorded Deeds all yield their quota of genealogical data. These documents are not all necessarily of historical value, but they are useful in supplying corroborative evidence.[2] Mr. Weir emphasises this in a paper on the subject.[3] He points out that to the student of history the Deeds indicate the growth of various places such as Belfast and Dublin, and the decline of corporate towns such as Swords and Fethard which

---

[1] There is, unfortunately, no Index of Grantees. For some counties, Lists of Freeholders, compiled during the last half of the eighteenth century, exist; they supply the name of the freeholder and the name of the landlord, or failing that the name of the townland held by the tenant. Several of these valuable lists of Freeholders, collected by Thos. U. Sadleir, Deputy Ulster King of Arms to 1943, are now at the Genealogical Office, Dublin Castle. (See "Forgotten Sources of Irish Genealogy," T. U. Sadleir, *The Irish Genealogist*, Oct. 1938, Vol. 1, No. 4). Griffith's *Primary Valuation of Rateable Property in Ireland* published in the middle of the nineteenth century, lists townlands, occupiers and immediate lessors. These sources provide clues which may be pursued at the Registry of Deeds.

[2] Research must be undertaken either personally or through an agent. The organisation and rules of the Department preclude the transaction of such business by correspondence.

[3] "The Registry of Deeds, Ireland" by Samuel Weir, *Bulletin of the Irish Committee on Historical Sciences*, No. 26, April, 1943; summary of a paper read to the Conference of Irish Historians, 21 March, 1943.

were once flourishing communities. The growth of Limerick and Galway, he says, gives further evidence of the trend from country to city. The social historian will find interest in the transactions of such notable people as Swift and his friends, Charles J. Fox, Grattan, Wolfe Tone, Maria Edgeworth, Robert Emmet, the Duke of Wellington, and Daniel O'Connell.[1]

I am indebted to the Registrar of Deeds, Mr. J. M. O'Byrne, B.L., for his kind permission to make these abstracts. Work was commenced under the guidance of the late Mr. Samuel S. Weir, whose enthusiasm and patient help in preparing plans I shall ever remember with gratitude. Thanks are due to Dr. Edward MacLysaght, Chief Herald of Ireland and Keeper of Manuscripts, National Library, for permission to use the MSS. at the Genealogical Office, Dublin Castle, for purposes of checking doubtful points in some Wills,[2] to Mr. Gerard Slevin for his advice about place names, and to Prof. J. Otway-Ruthven for her assistance. Finally, I must express my best thanks to the officials and staff at the Registry of Deeds for their unfailing help and courtesy.

P. BERYL EUSTACE

January, 1954.

---

[1] See Appendix for list of some interesting signatures.
[2] Square brackets enclose fresh pedigree information from MS sources—usually taken from Betham's Will Pedigrees. I have also checked many points with statements in such authorities as *The Complete Peerage* by G. E. C., printed, and MS. indices of Wills, *Reports of the Deputy Keeper of the Records, Ireland, Alumni Dublinenses* by Burtchaell and Sadleir, Diocesan *Parish and Clergy* histories by Leslie, etc.

REGISTRY OF DEEDS DUBLIN
ABSTRACTS OF WILLS
VOL. I
1708 - 1745

1 ROHD, NICHOLAS, parish of St. Mary's, Dublin.
   22 April 1708. Precis, ½ p., 4 June 1708.

Wife Rachell Rohd. Mr. Robert Mollyneux. Rev. Andres Calenhoosen the Dutch Minister. Rev. Stafford Warren. Letitia Smith. Mr. Patrick Callen. Mr. Simon Anyon and William Anyon his son. Mrs. Frances Courcey. Niece of Mrs. Courcey. Walter Vantreat.

Real and personal fortune. To Blew Boys £5.

Witnesses : Thos. Thompson, Strand St., Dublin, innkeeper, Simon Anyon of same city, gent., Catherine Crimble of same city, widow.

Memorial witnessed by : John Glew, John Price.

1, 52, 29   Rachel Rohd (seal)

2 SULLIVAN, DARBY, Gortnecrehy, parish of Clouncagh, B.[1] of Conelloe, Co. Limerick. 22 July 1708. Narrate, 1½p., 4 Nov. 1708.

Wife Catherine Sullivan. Sons John and Thomas Sullivan. Third son Daniel, fourth son Dennis Sullivan. Daughter Catherine Sullivan.

John Collins, Ballynoe, parish of Clouneilty, B. Conelloe, Co. Limerick, exor.

His real and personal estate in kingdom of Ireland.

Witnesses : Teige Sullivan, Clouny, Co. Cork, Maurice Nash, Ballyhahill, Daniel O'Bryan, Curraghnageare, Richard Cantilon, Morenane, Daniel Sullivan, Gortncreghy, John FitzGerald, Greenhill, Timothy Sullivan, Ahadagh, Derby Sullivan and Matthew Sullivan both of the same, all in the Co. Limerick.

Memorial witnessed by : Daniel Sullivan, John Connell.

1, 247, 151   Tho. Sullivan (seal)
                                                 a devisee

---

[1] The following abbreviations are used in the Abstracts : "Als." for *otherwise* " B " for *Barony*, " exor." for *executor*, " p." for *page*.

3 GRACE, OLIVER, Shanganagh, Queen's Co., gent.
   29 March 1708, (proved 31 July 1708). Précis, ¾ p., 4 Jan.
   1708/9.
   Elizabeth Grace, extx.
   Clonagh, Coolenagh, Shanganaghbegg, Graige, Kilmulrony, Shan-
   ganaghmore, Queen's Co.
   Witnesses : Oliver Weston, Nicholas Keating, Patrick Russell,
   gents.
   Memorial witnessed by : Oliver Weston, Dublin, gent., Wm. Eagan.
   1, 403, 244.   Eliz. Grace (seal)

4 CUPPAIGE, THOMAS, Lambstown, Co. Wexford, gent.
   5 Dec. 1708. Full, 4 pp., 8 Jan. 1708/9.
   Wife Elizabeth Cuppaige. Said wife's mother Sarah Mathews.
   "My brother Amos Strettell." Robert, eldest son, Amos the younger,
   second son, Thomas, third son, and Benjamin, fourth son of said
   Amos Strettell. Ann, Elizabeth and Lydia Strettell, daughters of
   said Amos the elder. "My brother Henry Hillary" and Samuel
   Hillary his son. Robert, Cuppaige, Henry the younger, and Joshua
   Hillary [? sons of said Henry Hillary]. Mary and Elizabeth Hillary,
   daughters of said Henry Hillary the elder.
   Exors. : Brother Amos Strettell, brother Henry Hillary, and Abel
   Strettell, Dublin, merchant.
   Overseers : John Watson, John Barcroft, Thomas Wilson, John
   Bowles.
   Stephen and Thomas Valentine, Elizabeth Willis, Anne Eaves,
   Mary and Experience Valentine, sons and daughters of George and
   Mary Valentine, both deceased. Hanah, wife of William Sandwith.
   Nicholas Lock. Alexander Seaton. "My poor tenants" Edmond
   and Michael Brady, Henry Franklin, Owen Daniel and James Clinchy.
   "Philip Roch and his brother Owen Delane." John Doyle, William
   Murphy, John Whitly, Edmond Kavanagh, Thomas West, Jeffry
   Lace, David McEve. £20 to Quakers in Co. Wexford.
   Lehnich, King's Co. Dunmaghan, Co. Cork. Knocknokeon, Lam[b]s-
   town, Blackhall, Ballinclea, Corlickan, Davidstown, Three Balgans,
   Barrymoney, Taughmond, Ballyclumoge, Co. Wexford. Colcor, Co.
   Meath. Kilknock, Ballybrumell, Co. Carlow.
   Witnesses :   Christopher English, Dublin, linendraper, John

Farbrother, of same, founder, Bruen Worthington, of same, public notary.

Memorial witnessed by : Christopher English, Edmd. Dalton.

1, 405, 247   Anne (Anna) Eves (seal)

5 WALSH, MARY, als. ROURK, Dublin, widow.

3 Nov. 1703. Précis, 1½ p., 15 Jan. 1708/9.

Son Mathias Walsh, Dublin, cordwainer (heir). Son Patrick Walsh. Her lands and tenements etc.

Witnesses : Thomas Lynch, Dublin, baker. Thomas Dollard, taylor, and William Bermingham, gent., both of Dublin.

Memorial witnessed by : John Connell, Henry Buckley.

2, 48, 252   Mathias Walsh (seal)

6 BILLINGTON, DAME DEBORAH, Dublin, widow.

7 July 1708. Précis, 1 p., 7 Feb. 1708/9.

Late husband Sir William Billington.

Eldest son Daniel Cooke.

House, brew house, etc. in St. James's Street, Dublin.

Witnesses : Benjamin Bentley, John and Samuel Dickinson, all servants of testatrix.

Memorial witnessed by : Hen. Buckley, John Connell.

1, 429, 293   Daniel Cooke (seal)

7 SPENCE, GEORGE, Upper Combe, Dublin, brewer.

16 Dec. 1708. Full, 2 pp. 26 Feb. 1708/9.

My mother Elizabeth Spence. Wife Dorothy. Daughter Sarah Falkiner, son-in-law Daniel Falkiner. Brother Godfry Spence. Nephew Abell Spence, under 21 years.

Lewis Edge. James Smith, under 21 years. Rev. Joseph Boyse, clerk. Simon Anyon. £5 to poor of Woodstreet Congregation.

Skinner's Alley. Wood Mills near Harold's Cross, and rest of real and personal estate.

Witnesses : Cornelius Delaney, Dublin, clothier, John Helme, clothier, Simon Anyon, gent., both of Dublin.

Memorial witnessed by : Tho. Trotter, Cornelius Delaney.

2, 139, 338   Dan. Falkiner (seal)

8   BECHER, THOMAS, Sherkin, Co. Cork, Esq.,
21 Aug. 1705. Full, 10 pp. 11 March 1708.
" Brothers-in-law Henry Turner Richard Turner and John Roberts
Esqrs." trustees and exors. Wife Elizabeth Becher. Sons Edward
and Michael Becher (both married). Sons Henry, John and Lionell
Becher. Daughter Susan Becher. Kinsman Francis Becher, Tallough,
Co. Waterford, clerk. Legacy to parish of Ballymoodan.

Ardentane, Cahiroleckeny, Ratooragh, Gortioen, Baneatonacane,
Kiltomane, Maudadinny and Coomfarna in parish of Skull, Bally-
risode, Dunkilly, Callirisoughtra, Baltenoughtra, Killean, Lynane,
Cahir, Quorisk, Cloghane, Co. Cork. Baneaknocksane and Quolaigh,
parish of Skull, Co. Cork. Old Court, Kilfenan, Glaunaroura. Leasehold lands of Aghadowne, Kilkilleene, Callitrumore, Callitrumbegg,
Drumnacahara, Lysheenoughtra, Kilmoonagh, Cluddagh, Smoorane,
Quoscurrine, Rinedrolane, Gortnaclough, Skibbereene als. New-
stapleton, Coronea [? all in Co. Cork].

Witnesses : Dive [Downes], Lord Bishop of Cork and Ross, Robert
Conran, Kinsale, Co. Cork, Esq., Benjamin Weekes, Cork, public
notary, James Russell, servant to said Bishop of Cork.

Memorial witnessed by John Connell, P. G. P. Skynner.

1, 456, 356   John Roberts (seal)

9   PLUNKETT, PATRICK, Drogheda, merchant.
10 Feb. 1708. Full, 2½ pp., 16 March 1708.
Wife Margaret Plunkett als. Cheevers. Eldest son Alexander and
second son Christopher Plunkett. Daughter Mary Plunkett. Daughter
Anne Austin als. Plunkett. Son-in-law Nicholas Austin.

My beloved friend Mr. Michael Moore. Mrs. Northup, Mrs. Accling,
" Yorkshire the porter ", tenants. Henry Nicholas, Drogheda,
deceased, late tenant.

Cannonstowne, Balledonell, parish of Termonfeckin, Co. Louth.
St. Peter Street als. Pillery Street, and Batcheller's Lane, Drogheda.
Justice's Parks in Liberties of Drogheda.

Witnesses : Henry McArdle, Robert Conly, George Warren, all of
Drogheda, gents.

Memorial witnessed by : John Connell, P. G. P. Skynner.

2, 176, 265   Alexandr. Plunkett (seal)

10 KIERNAN, JAMES, Dublin, gent.

2 March 1708. Full, 3 pp., 3 May 1709.

Wife Elizabeth. Son Robert Kiernan. My two younger daughters Honoria and Elizabeth Kiernan. Eldest daughter Sarah Mountford als. Kiernan, her husband Mr. Mountford. Granddaughter Elizabeth Mountford, under 18 years.

John Smith, Edmond Curtis, Bruen Worthington, friends. £10 to repair Balrothery Church.

King Street and Church Street, Dublin. Little Balbriggan, Blackhall, Lusk, Leatown, Ballymad, Gibbonstown, Balrothery, all in Co. Dublin. Kilturkin, Derryneheney, Knocktopher, Deans Rath, Killcollome, Rices Land and wood of Knocktopher, Co. Kilkenny. "The Great Stone House in the city of Kilkenny" and two houses adjoining.

Witnesses: Pan Gran Parabow Skynner and John Connell, clerks to Bruen Worthington, Dublin, notary public.

Memorial witnessed by: John Connell, Hen. Buckley.

2, 219, 421   Elizabeth Kiernan (seal)

11 BLENERHASSETT, JOHN, Ballyseedy, Co. Kerry, Esq.

24 Jan. 1708. Full, 3 pp., 10 May 1709.

Wife Margaret Blenerhassett. Eldest son John Blenerhassett. My younger children—sons Arthur, Thomas, Piercy, Robert, William. Son-in-law Robert Rogers. Sister Ruth Blenerhassett.

Edward Denny, senr. and Edward Denny, junr., Wm. Crosby, Esq., Thomas Blennerhassett, attorney, Francis Barnard, Esq., and Robert Blenerhassett, Esq., to be exors. till testator's son John is 21 years. George Bastable, (mortgagee).

Ballyseedy, Currans, Urroghroghall [Urrohogal], Curraghmore, Killmurry [? all in Co. Kerry]

Witnesses: Rev. Dean John Richards, Tralee, Co. Kerry, Eusebius Chute, Tullygarron, Esq., Barry Denny, Ballyvelly, Esq., Robert Rogers, Cork, merchant, Thomas Crosbye, Ballyheige, Co. Kerry, Esq.

Witnesses to codicil: Eusebius Chute, Robert Rogers, Joseph Rogers, Cork, Doctor of Physick, Ruth Blenerhassett, Tralee, Co. Kerry, widow.

Memorial witnessed by: Henry Parr, Edwd. Herbert, Eusebius Chute.

2, 224, 423   M. Bl.Hassett (seal)

12 SYNGE, SAMUEL, Dean of Kildare.

   9 Aug. 1706. Died 30 Nov. 1708. Narrate, 2 pp. 28 May 1709
Mother Mrs. Barbara Synge. Wife Margaret Synge. Son Michael
Synge. Brother Edward Synge and said brother's son Edward, and
second son Nicholas Synge. Daughter Mary Synge.

   Ballybrickan, Rinskiddy, Ballinrea, Ballinresig, Co. Cork. Bally-
macody, Ballyoughtra, Ballyglassen, Co. Cork. Rawleighstown,
Ballingooley, Co. Limerick. Thomas Court near Dublin, Lands etc.
near Finglas, Co. Dublin. Lands near Kildare.

   Witnesses : John Stearne, John Jones, Dublin, John Doherty,
Cashell.

   Memorial witnessed by : Tim. Dunne, Ro. Collins.

   2, 291, 461   Edw. Synge (seal)

13 COUGHLAN, JOHN, Bandonbridge, Co. Cork.

   24 Jan. 1708. Narrate, 3 pp. 15 July 1709.

   Wife Dorothy Coughlan alias. Gookin. Daughter Dorothy, under
18 years. Eldest son John Coughlan. Son Vincent Coughlan.

   Roger Luffkin, Richard Bermingham, Thos. Bearnish, Thomas
Deane, and Lieut. Abell Harris, tenants.

   Kilmeen and Lissivoaning als. Adesses Land, in B. Kinallmeaky,
Co. Cork. Raharoon in Cantridge of Killbritain, Co. Cork. Lissbralett,
B. Carbry, Co. Cork. Drombofinny, Aghayohiller [situation not
mentioned].

   Witnesses : Katherine Gookin, James Martin, John Jones, all of
Bandon, Co. Cork.

   Memorial witnessed by : Kath. Gookin, Jas. Lucas, John Jones.

   2, 433, 550.   Dorothy Coughlan (seal)

14 HAWKINS, ROGER, Mountmellick, Queen's Co., innkeeper.

   10 March 1708. Full, 1½ p. 1 Aug. 1709

   Mother Joan Hawkins. Wife Hannah Hawkins. " John Wheatley
my wife's son." Brothers John, Thomas and Maurice Hawkins.
Sister Mary Crean and her son. Joan Belshar, Elizabeth Stephens.

   House in Mountmellick. Real and personal estate.

   Witnesses : Hopton Harris, gent., Henry Sumner, apothecary,
Thos. Boneson, gent., all of Mountmellick.

   Memorial witnessed by : Ed. Folio, John Connell.

   2, 493, 587   John Wheatly (seal)

15 FORWARD, JOHN, Castle Forward, Co. Donegal, Esq.

14 Feb. 1708. Full, 4pp. 6 Sept. 1709.

Wife Anne Forward. Son William Forward (a minor). Daughters Isabella, Leticia, Eleanour and Elizabeth Forward. Exors. : Andrew Hamilton, clerk [? *Archdeacon of Raphoe*], testator's wife Anne, " my brother Michael Sampson, Dublin, merchant ", Henry Wray, Castlewray, Esq., and John Stuert, Dairick, gent., both in Co. Donegal.

Bertt (Birt, B. Inestowne), Taughboyne. Coulurletraine, Portlagh, Co. Donegal. Woodestowne, Co. Meath. Estate of inheritance in Counties Donegal and Meath.

Witnesses : John Gee, Robert Houston, William Paterson.

Memorial witnessed by : Alexr. Nesbitt, John Montgomery, Dublin.

2, 579, 644   Isabella Forward (seal)

16 HOWELL, THOMAS, Dublin, joyner.

27 Jan. 1708. Narrate, 1 p., 28 Sept. 1709.

"My wife." Daughter Jane Jacob.

Premises on Blind Key, Dublin.

Witnesses : William Smith, Dublin, vintner, Laurence Luttrell and William Gernon, drawers to said William Smith.

Memorial witnessed by : Bruen Worthington, notary public, John Connell his clerk.

3, 68, 672.   Jane Jacob (seal)

17 NICHOLSON, GILBERT, Dublin.

11 Nov. 1707. Full, 2 pp., 25 Oct. 1709.

To be buried in St. Mary's Chapple, Christ Church, by body of wife. Son John Nicholson. Son Thomas Nicholson (sole exor. and guardian of grandchildren). Granddaughters Christian and Mary, daughters of testator's son John. Grandsons James and Gilbert, sons of said John. " My grandchildren " Anne, Christian, John and Thomas " sons and daughters of my son Thomas." Grandsons Christopher, eldest son, and Gilbert, Thomas and John sons of said son Thomas.

St. Thomas Street, Dublin. St. George's Lane.

Witnesses: Christopher FitzSymons, Dublin, merchant, Edward Verdon, Dublin, joyner, George Merefield, Dublin, scrivener.

Memorial witnessed by : Hen. Buckley, John Connell.

4, 46, 709.   Thos. Nicholson (seal)

18 JAQUESS, WILLIAM, Rossmecarty, parish of Killnerath, B.
of Owny and Arra, Co. Tipperary. 10 Jan. 1705. Précis, 1 p.,
20 Oct. 1709.

Wife Katherine Jaquess. Sons : William, eldest, John, second,
and Luke Jaquess. 1/– each to daughters Katherine, Joan and
Margaret. Rev. Henry Jenings, clerk.

Land and real estate.

Witnesses : Richard Phillipps, Jonas Humbles, Henry Jenings.

Memorial witnessed by : Richd. Phillips, Murroo, Co. Limerick,
Joseph Robinson.

3, 107, 717.   John Jaquess (seal)

19 HANSARD, MARY, suburbs of city of Dublin, widow.
2 Feb. 1708. Précis, ¾ p., 2 Nov. 1709.

Son Ralph Hansard, under 25 years. Daughters Patience Sterling
and Jane Hansard. Cousin Mary Bennett.

Roscommon Row. College Green [? Dublin].

Witnesses : Sarah Lady Gethin, Mary, wife of Nathaniel Marshall
of Dublin, merchant, Edward Butler of same, gent.

Memorial witnessed by : Centen. Lamotte Bellew, John Connell,
P. G. P. Skynner.

3, 116, 726.   J. Hansard (seal)

20 RANSFORD, SIR MARK, Knt., Alderman of Dublin.
10 Aug. 1709. Narrate, 2¾ pp., 28 Nov. 1709.

His wife . . ." her two children." Son Edward and daughter
Ann Ransford, both minors. Sons Mark and Giles Mee Ransford.
1/– each to issue of Mary Burrows, wife of Giles Mee Ransford.
Daughters Forrest, Henrickan and Bowles. " Son " Forrest. Ransford
Henrickan and "his younger brother " [grandchildren ?]. Grand-
daughters Isabella Bowles and Jane Forrest.

Col. James Hamilton, Ald. John Page, trustees for said minors,
or Charles Forrest and Isaac Edward and "their ant Hamilton "
(guardian). Isaac Ward, Charles Forrest and James Hamilton to be
exors. till testator's sons Mark and Edward come to 21 years.

Tenants : Widdow Smith, Walter Maglue, William McDanell, and
Warren Dyer, Thomas Street. William Tracy, Aron Street. Mr.
Miller, Thomas Court. Mr. Iridell, —Connelly and Mr. Byrn, Francis

Street. Mr. Hayes, on the Pottle. — Dalton, on the Pipe. David Elwood, High Street. Mr. Meas, Ransford Street, John Brown, [? Ransford Street], "Parsons the Brewer" and — Pilkington, Ransford Street. "His son Forrest," Little Thomas Court.

"The estate he had by Ald. Gyles Mee." "The great silver tankard given him by the Brewers."

Aron Street, Thomas Court, Brownlows Alley, The Comb, Francis Street, The Pottle, Thomas Street, all in city of Dublin. Kilmainham, Dolphin's Barn, St. James's Street, The Pipe, High Street, Ransford Street, Little Thomas Court [situation either in city of Dublin or not mentioned]. Land in Co. Wicklow.

Witnesses : Richard Blair, Dublin, upholster, Christopher Leonard, Dublin, victualler, Peter Archdekin of same, gent.

Memorial witnessed by : Christopher Leonard, Thos. Trotter.
4, 123, 781.   Barbara Forrest (seal)
                                              a devisee.

21 SAUNDERS, ROBERT, Dublin, Esq., Her Majesty's Privy
Sergt. at Law. 8 March 1707. Narrate, 1½ p., 20 Dec. 1709.

His wife. Sons Morley, Joseph and Robert Saunders. Grandson Anderson, son of Robert Saunders. Brother Anderson Saunders, Dublin, Esq.

Mrs Carroll, grantor of Co. Wicklow lands.

Manor of Tonagh, Co. Cavan. Lovettstown, Ballyg[a]navagh, Reaganstown, Ratheogh, Grany and Coletown, Co. Kildare. Grangecon, and Griffinstowne, Co. Wicklow. Eskaroon, Co. Meath. Houses etc. in Swift's Roe, Strand Street, Church Street, and Ormond Quay [situation not mentioned, ? Dublin]. Lands of inheritance in King's Co., Queen's Co., Co. Cavan and Co. Fermanagh. Iron works etc. at Swanlinbar, Counties Cavan and Fermanagh.

Witnesses : William Westgarth, Dublin, Esq., Samuel Martin, James Nixon, of same, gents.

Memorial witnessed by : James Nixon, Isa. Dobson. Timothy Rourk, Dublin, gent.
4, 183, 853.   Joseph Saunders (seal)

22 FRENCH, PATRICK, Duras, Co. Galway.
In two parts dated 15 and 18 May 1708. Died 5 June 1708.
Narrate, 8 pp., 27 Jan. 1709.

His wife. Son and heir Robuck French (unmarried). Second son Hyacinth French and Surna Blake his wife. Third and youngest son Patrick French—a legacy to him if "he study the Law of England." Sister-in-law Margaret Lynch als. French als. Blake. Grandson Patrick French Fitz Hyacinth, son of testator's son Hyacinth. Sister Ellinor Blake. "Brother" Oliver Martin. Exors. "Brother Turlogh O'Bryan," Andrew Blake, cousin Stephen Lynch FitzNicholas and Dominick Blake FitzPeter.

Charles and John Morgan, debtors. George Gerry, tenant. Patrick Lynch and his wife Margaret, annuitants. John Ormsby, Dublin, Esq. Robert Shaw, Newford, Co. Galway. Nicholas Donellan.

Cloghballymore, Mongane, Gortroe, Killinyvarra, Knockballyclery, Lissinduff, Sessireagh, Duras, Corboy, Kinturlagh, Knockellan, Mullaghardee, Tannaugh, Muniseribagh, Crosnoly, Kinvarra, Lessingerby, Loghcorra, Clonissee, Moish, Trelick, Tunshinbegg, Gortinglogh, Cappaghmore, Cappaghbegg, Gortgowne, Carrowkillin, Cahircunna, Drummun, Pollevalla and Ballygillgea, B. Kiltarton, Co. Galway. Keinsellagh, Cloghbally, Moih, Gortroe, Knockballyclory, Killmearra, Ballyglara and Drinharsna, B. Dunkellin, Co. Galway. Houses etc. in High Street, Kirwan's Lane, Broughmaker's Lane, town of Galway.

Witnesses : Turlogh Hyne, Michael Hyne, William McDanaugh, Redmond Burke.

Memorial witnessed by : Wm. McDonogh, Lastaragg, Co. Galway, gent., aged about 43, S. Lynch, Cloghballymore, Co. Galway, gent.

4, 234, 914.   Hyacinth French (seal)

23 FRENCH, PATRICK. Additional Will. Dated 18 May 1708. Narrate, 1 p., 4 Feb. 1709.

[Repeats last portion of memorial No. 914 above].

John Ormbsy of Dublin, Robert Shaw, Newfoord, Co. Galway, Esq.

Ballygilgea, B. Killtartan, Co. Galway.

Witnesses : Torlagh Heyne, Killoveragh, Co. Galway, clerk, Michael Heyne of same, gent, William McDonnagh, Duras, said Co., gent. "the last two have been servants to the said Patrick French."

Memorial witnessed by : Stephen Lynch, Esq., aged about 40 years, Michael Dalton.

4, 260, 937.   Robert Shaw (seal)

24 CARNEY, LADY LETTICE, Dublin, widow.

  26 Dec. 1709. Précis, ¼ p., 7 Feb. 1709/10.

Granddaughter Lettice Moland, wife of Joseph Moland of Dublin, gent. Exors. said Lettice and Joseph Moland.

All her lands, tenements, houses, estate of inheritance and real estate.

Witnesses : Rev. Charles Carr, minister of St. Paul's Church, Dublin, John Smith and James Meade of Dublin, gents., John Connell, clerk to Bruen Worthington, public notary.

Memorial witnessed by : Tho. Dixon, Hen. Buckley clerk to Bruen Worthington.

4, 262, 938.   Lettice Moland (seal)

25 SHARP, THOMAS, Dublin, gent.

  24 Jan. 1709. Narrate, 1 p., 9 Feb. 1709.

Only son Thomas Sharp. Daughters Mary Gavan and Jane Bradwell. Brother Robert Sharp. Children of nephew William Sharp. Grandson Thomas Oates and his mother. Grandson Thomas Bradwell and his mother. " Other grandchildren." Exors. son Thomas Sharp, Thomas Gavan and George Bradwell.

Andrew Gold, tenant. Joan Gavan.

Bigg Sheep Street, Dublin. "Lands and estate of inheritance in South Brittain." 40/- to parish of Gosford in Great Brittain.

Witnesses : John Write, Dublin, barber, Mary, wife of Rupert Barbor, Dublin, merchant, Thomas Cooke, Dublin, notary public.

Memorial witnessed by : Mary Barbor, John Connell.

3, 285, 948.   Thos. Gavan (seal)

26 HAMILTON, JAMES, Court Hills, Co. Meath, Esq.

  7 Jan. 1708. Narrate, 1 p., 6 May 1710.

His wife. Edward Hamilton [? son]. "Children of his sisters Margaret Mary and Jane Hamilton." Brother Col. Andrew Hamilton.

Andrew Teate, Richard Dudgeon.

His real and personal estate.

Witnesses : John Christian, Dublin, gent. Hugh Gillespry and William Henderson, both of Court Hills, yeomen.

Memorial witnessed by : Wm. Hogan, Hugh Gillespry.

3, 424, 1173.   Richard Dudgeon (seal)

27 DENNY, EDWARD, "Traly," Co. Kerry, Esq.
6 Sept. 1709. Narrate, 1 p., 19 June 1710.
Wife Mary Denny. Brother Barry Denny. Son Edward [? son of testator's brother Barry]. Brothers-in-law Samuel and Barry Baynard. Cousin Barry Denny. Daughter Jane (a minor). Sons-in-law Thomas Crosby, William Sprigge, Esq.
Tythes of parish of Donnerayle, Rossa, Co. Cork. Barrow, Abbey House in Traly.
Witnesses : Thomas Sheiriliff, Richard Keefe, Derby Sulevan, all of Traly.
Memorial witnessed by : B. Denny, Thos. Crosbie, Thos. Connor, Dublin, Esq.
3, 494, 1306.   Mary Denny (seal)

28 AYLMER, CATHERINE, Ballrath, Co. Meath, spinster.
26 March 1709. Full, ¾ p., 10 July 1710.
To visit brother and uncle in England. Brother Sir John Aylmer. Sister Jane Aylmer als. Bath. "Brother" Nicholas Bath. Brother Andrew Aylmer. [No lands mentioned].
Witnesses : John Bath, Monknewtown, Co. Meath, gent., his son John and daughter Elizabeth Bath, both of Co. Meath.
Memorial witnessed by : Patrick Gillmer, Greenoge, Co. Meath, yeoman, Fra. Carbery.
5, 100, 1373.   Jean Bath (seal)

29 ROGERS, GEORGE, Ashgrove, Co. Cork, Esq.
18 Nov. 1709. Codicil 30 Nov. 1709, and another 19 May 1710.
Narrate, 4¾ pp., 21 July 1710.
Wife Mary Rogers. Sons Francis and William Rogers. Grandson George, son of said Francis Rogers. Son Joseph Rogers and his wife. Son Robert Rogers and his wife Agnes Blenerhassett. Daughters Catherine and Lucy Rogers, unmarried. Daughter Mary, wife of Edward Webber. Grandson George Webber. Granddaughter Anne Farmer. Brother Robert Rogers.
Katherine Knowles. Jane Ruddock. William Cox.
Wife not to cut down any trees at Ashgrove.
Lands bought from Trustees of Irish Forfeitures, the property of Edmond Barry, an annuity payable to said Barry's wife. Ashgrove,

Great Island, Knockmandcffe, Killgobnett, Glanelogh, Oughteherris-beg, Oughterherismore, Knockrawes, Carrigacounagh [situation not mentioned]. Ballynahinny, Lady Smith's Lott, and other premises in Liberties of city of Cork. Golds Weyres and Marsh, North Weyr and Fishing [situation not mentioned]. Aghadoe, Co. Kerry.

Witnesses : George Bennett, William Lukey, Rowland FitzGerald, all of Cork. Witnesses to second codicil : Rowland Davies, Dean of Cork, Robert Rogers, Cork, merchant, and Mary Webber of same.

Memorial witnessed by : Walter Gould, Cork, John Connell.

6, 51, 1403.   Edward Webber (seal)

30 SHAW, WILLIAM, Ballygonway, Co. Down, Esq.

1 July 1707. Narrate, 2½ pp., 25 Aug. 1710.

His wife. Son John Shaw. Daughter Rose Haven. Daughter Frances Shaw, wife of Patrick Shaw. Daughter Anne, wife of Cornelius Crimble. Grandson Ganaway Crimble, son of Cornelius Crimble. Granddaughter Jane Crimble. Sister Elizabeth Gillespie. Nephew Hugh Gillespie.

William Shaw, Bush, Co. Antrim. The children of William Catherwood of Newtown.

Ballygonway, Ballywhiskan in parish Donaghadee. Carradoran, BallyMcCraveny, Cahard, and tythes in parish of Tonaghnive, Co. Down. Ballygaley, Tulleigh als. Racavan, Clogoneneriny, B. Antrim, Co. Antrim. Lands in Baronies of Belfast, Carey and Dunluce, Co. Antrim.

Witnesses : John O'Neill, Dunmore, Co. Antrim, Esq., William Catherwood, Newtown, Co. Down, gent., William Colvill, Dublin, gent.

Memorial witnessed by: Edward Dempster, William Colvill.

6, 74, 1444.   Pat. Shaw (seal)

31 FITZSYMON, CHRISTOPHER, Dublin, merchant.

15 July 1710. Proved in Prerogative Court 29 Aug. 1710. Précis, ½ p., 2 Sept. 1710.

Wife Barbara FitzSymon als. White.

St. Stephen's Green [? Dublin].

Witnesses : Oliver Weston, Dublin, gent., Paul White of same, apothecary, Darby Liskin of same, yeoman.

Memorial witnessed by : Oliver Weston, Nic. Peters.

5, 146, 1463.   Bar. FitzSymon (seal)

32 BULKELEY, SIR RICHARD, Old Bawn, Co. Dublin, Bart.
26 July 1706. Précis, 1 p., 9 Sept. 1710.
Died at Elwell, Surrey. Francis Bulkeley, Portamell, Anglesey,
exor. and devisee.
Old Bawne als. Shanbawne, Staghnavan als. Staghnawayn, Cappoge,
Loghanstowne, Killowan als. Kiltalowan, Baghercullen als. Bolene-
managh, and commons in parish of Tallagh, Co. Dublin. Dunlavan,
Marquistowne, Milltowne, Ternant, Loughmoig, Tubber, Logatrine, in
counties of Wicklow, Dublin and Kildare. Houses etc. including " one
small castle within Monastery of Blackfryers of Kilkenny," Goosehill
(near) Irish Towne of Kilkenny, in city of Kilkenny. Impropriate
Rectoryes etc. of parishes of Bananogh als. Castle Dough, Dysert and
Killferagh, Co. Kilkenny.
Witnesses : Em. Echersall, Dublin, Thomas Bulkeley, Old Bawne,
Richard Fitzpatrick.
Memorial witnessed by : Hugh Owen, Arthur O'Neile, Inner
Temple, London, Gent.
6, 111, 1519.   Fran. Bulkeley (seal)

33 MOORE, MARGARET, Dublin, spinster.
24 Oct. 1710. Précis, ½ p., 31 Oct. 1710.
William Harford, Dublin, legatee.
Aghederryetragh, B. Trugh, Co. Monaghan.
Witnesses : Anne Brady, Dublin, widow, Edward Moore of said
city, yeoman, and Catherine his wife, Will. Stagg, Dublin, gent.
Memorial witnessed by : Wm. Stagg, Ben. Lord.
6, 125, 1559.   William Harford (seal)

34 IVIE, JOSEPH, Waterford, Esq.
17 April 1710. Précis, ¾ p., 4 Nov. 1710.
Nieces Sarah Ivie, Hannah Ivie and Susanna Ivie, and nephew
Joseph Ivie, children of testator's late brother Daniel Ivie. Nephew
John Mason, Esq. Cozen Alexander Alcock. Brother-in-law Richard
Christmas, Esq.
£200 to Mayor Dean and Recorder of Waterford for roofing and
repairing St. Michael's Church.
His real and personal estate. His lands in Co. Tipperary.
Witnesses : Thomas Ivie, living near town of Waterford, farmer,

John Young, Dublin, gent., Edward Burk a menial servant to said testator, Richd. Thomson, Dublin, gent.

Memorial witnessed by : John Young, John Connell.

7, 39, 1567.   Richard Thomson (seal)

35 PERRY, JOHN, Woodroffe, Co. Tipperary.

In month of Feb. 1709. Narrate, 2 pp., 17 Nov. 1710.

His wife. Sons John, Micajah and Samuel Perry. Sons Edward and Richard. Daughters Elizabeth, Anne, Grace, Rebecca Pyke and Sarah Perry. Nephew John Low.

Mathew Jacob, Esq., and Mr. John Minchin of Shangarry, trustees. Mat. Jacob, Esq., Humphry Minchin, Esq., Nathaniel Lucas, Esq., Mr. Andrew Roe and Mr. Robert Long to settle any differences over Will. Mrs. Reddish, Alexander Harman (Clonmell tenants).

Testator's wife, " Brother Pyke, Brother Jacob, Brother Minchin " exors. of concerns in Ireland, " his brother Perry " and testator's son John Perry exors. of concerns in England and elsewhere. Killmolash and Mullaghnony, parish Newchappel and Inislonaghty. Garryroe and Grangrobin, parish Inislonaghty. Woodroofe, parish Derrygrath, all in B. Iffa and Offa, Co. Tipperary. Garrantemple, Monks Grange, Carroconeen, Grange Robbin, Currinstowne and Black Castle, in parish Inislonaghty. Graigmoclear and Clasinottin, parish Newchappel. Killtallynemony, parish Inislonaghty. Corless, parish " Derryrath." Killunny, parish Derrygrath. Glankerin and Graige in parishes Ballyclenehan and Newchappell. Houses in parish and town of Clonmell, B. Iffa and Offa, Co. Tipperary. West Jersey [situation not mentioned].

Witnesses : John Shaw, Clonmell, Co. Tipperary, clerk, Henry Cleare of same, merchant, Samuel Gordon of same, merchant, James Keating of same, tallow chandler.

Memorial witnessed by : James Keating, Saml. Gordon.

7, 60, 1611.   John Perry (seal)

36 MAGAN, THOMAS, Togherstown, Co. Westmeath, Esq.

3 Sept. 1710. Full, 3½ pp., 28 Nov. 1710.

Wife Sarah Magan. Only brother Morgan Magan, and Elizabeth his wife. Nephew Thomas Magan, junr., son and heir apparent of said Morgan. Hubert, second son, and William third son of said Morgan Magan. Niece Susanna, eldest daughter of Morgan Magan. Nieces Elizabeth and Sarah Magan. Cousin Richard Magan.

Francis Fetherston, Rath, Co. Westmeath, Esq. James Dillon, son of Robert Dillon of Ballmecallin, Co. Westmeath, and the wife of said James Dillon. Luke Dillon, son of said Robert. John Gaffy, Athlone, merchant. Overseers, Andrew Wilson, Peirsefield, Co. Westmeath, Esq., Thomas Fetherston, Ardagh, Co. Longford, gent., and Cutbord (Cuthbert) Fetherston, Rath, Co. Longford, gent.

Togherstown, Glaneward, Lockardstowne, Lalystown, Irishtown, Cloonkeen, Crieve, Conranstown, Moate, Adamstown, Larragh, Ballintue, Taghboyne, Up. and Lr. Milltowne, Croughowne, Loghane-valla, Gneivestown, Ardbranan, Gibstown, Lisikillin, Cloghtompan, Rowans, Co. Westmeath. Killinsonacan and Rahuff [situation not mentioned]. Other lands of inheritance etc. in Ireland.

Witnesses : Thomas Daly, Killcleagh, Co. Westmeath, Esq., Edmond Byrne, Dublin, gent. and John Kelly his clerk, Michael Dunne, Killare, Co. Westmeath.

Memorial witnessed by : Hen. Buckley, John Connell.

6, 148, 1637.   Morgan Magan (seal)

37 WRAY, WILLIAM, Fore, Co. Donegal, Esq.

12 June 1710. Full, 1½ pp., 1 Dec. 1710.

To be buried in church of Clandahorkae.

Wife Angel Wray. Son Humphrey Wray. "Articles made on the marriage of my son Humphrey with Mrs. Ann Brooke." "Articles of marriage of my son Henry Wray with Mrs. Joan Jackson." Sons-in-law James Sinclaire, gent., and George Knox. Daughter Rebecca Babington. Grandsons William and Henry Babington.

The heirs of Richard Porter, deceased. John Richardson, Kill. My servant Samuel Densmoore. Servant Thomas Blaire, Fore. Mrs Ann Sinclaire. Capt. Henry Hart. William Finlay, Drumnatinny. Estate purchased by Hugh Hamill and William Sampson, Esqrs. Sale of Grenforth estate from Willaim Godfry, Benjamin Galland and "my son-in-law Captain William Babington decd." with payments to Mr John Humble, John Evans, and Capt. George Hamilton.

Trinamulland, Greenforth (Grenforth) [? Greenfort, Co. Donegal], Urny, Raymunterdawny, Brunleck and Glassagh. Castlewray, Clandormont [situation not mentioned]. Fore, Co. Donegal.

Witnesses : George Knox, Pattrick Densmoore, Samuel Densmoore.

Memorial witnessed by : Hum. Wray, Geo. Knox, Thos. Knox.

8, 14, 1659.   Samuel Densmoore (seal)

38 ANGLESEY, RT. HON. JOHN, EARL OF.
    14 June 1708. Précis, ½ p., 22 Jan. 1710.
Died 18 Sept. 1710. Brother Arthur Annesley.
His real and personal estate in England or Ireland.
    Witnesses : Francis Annesley, Inner Temple, London, Esq., Vincent
Oakley, Middle Temple, London, gent., Jean Meades, Michael Cassady
and John Thompson, of parish of St. Giles in the Fields, Middlesex.
    Memorial witnessed by : R. Stewart, Arthur O'Neill, Inner Temple,
London, gent.
8, 58, 1766.   Arthur Annesley now Earl of Anglesea (seal)

39 VAUGHAN, HECTOR, Knocknamease, King's Co., Esq.
    11 Nov. 1710. Narrate, 1½ p., 12 Feb. 1710/11.
Son William Peasley Vaughan, sole exor., and the present wife of
said son William. Son John Vaughan. Second daughter Mrs. Jane
Grant, her husband Mr. Jasper Grant, her eldest sister (married).
Brother Richard Vaughan to live free in the house with exor.
"Lawrence Oxburgh, brother and heir to John Oxburgh, son and
heir of Collonell Hewar Oxburgh," and Mr. Joseph Moland, debtors.
James Dingin, and William Dulchanty of Upper Ballyshane, servants.
Overseers, his good friends Thomas Sadleir and Humphrey Minchin,
Esq.
    Castletown, B. Ballybritt, King's Co., Ballenclough, Clonbegg and
Forelack, said B. and Co., Rathinbroge, Ballyegill and Ballyroane, B.
Cullenagh, Queen's Co.
    Witnesses : Humphrey Minchin, Ballynekill, Co. Tipperary, John
Connor, steward to said Humphrey Minchin, Richard Meara, school-
master at Knocknamease, John Dobson, servant to said Mr. Minchin.
    Memorial witnessed by : Hen. Buckley, John Connell.
8, 87, 1825.   William Peisley Vaughan (seal)

40 EVANS, GEORGE, Ballygrenane, Co. Limerick, Esq., the elder.
    26 Feb. 1705 Narrate, 3 pp., 15 Feb. 1710.
Eldest son George Evans, exor. Son John Evans. "William Evans
the son of Jane Teale wife of Thomas Martin." Mr. Jonathan Perry
and Mr. Thomas Wills, overseers.
    The house testator lived in when in city of Cork. Killmallock Lane

and Cross Street, parish of St. Peter, city Cork. Ballinvarrigg, Kill-cully, Carrow, Raghenisky, Killcronane, Garranboy, Gortrikinokannter als. Westgortinockane, and Laghardane, North Liberties, city of Cork. Milltown, B. Orrery and Kilmore, Co. Cork, purchased from Edward Reyley, gent.

Witnesses : Francis Willmoth, Ballygrenane, George Riggs, Mill-town, Nathaniel Evans, Carassy, Thomas Clancy and Edmond Bourke, both of Ballygrenane, all in Co. Limerick.

Memorial witnessed by : Nathaniel Evans, John Branville.

8, 96, 1836.   George Evans (seal)

41 PIERS, HONORIA LADY, Dublin, widow.

11 March 1707. Précis, ½ p., 26 Feb. 1710.

Son William Piers and daughter Constance Piers, exors. Daughter Honoria Piers.

Julia Connor, wife of Charles Connor, Dublin, gent.

Morenstown, Co. Westmeath.

Witnesses : William Westbery, Dublin, gent. Honora McCarthy, servant to testatrix, Richard Daniel, junr., Dublin, gent

Memorial witnessed by : Will. Westbery, William Smith, clerk to Samuel Cotton, Dublin, notary public.

8, 112, 1874.   Constance Piers (seal)

42 BARRY, EDMOND, city of Cork, Doctor of Physick.

27 May 1710. Narrate, 1½ p., 13 April 1711.

Wife Jane Barry (then enceinte). Sons : William, Edward second, Nathaniel third, Robert fourth, Richard fifth, John sixth. His two daughters Jane and Mary Barry.

Trustees : William Andrews, Cork, alderman, William Masters of same, merchant.

Rearaures [Rearour], Knockan[e]leigh and mountain, B. Muskery, Co. Cork, purchased from Hollow Sword Blade Company.

Witnesses : William Brown, merchant, Garrett Barry, cloathier, Thomas Barry, scrivener, all of Cork.

Memorial witnessed by : Wm. Brown(e), Thos. Andrews.

7, 146, 1948.   Jane Barry (seal)

43 WALLER, EDWARD, Cully, Co. Tipperary, gent.
27 April 1711. Full, ½ p., 9 May 1711.
"My three sisters and my dear mother." Only brother William
Waller.
Alderman Quayle and his daughter. Mr. James Bayly. Symon
George. Legacy to poor of Cully. Legacy to poor of St. Warboroughs
to be distributed by Mr. French, curate there.
" All my lands tenemts. and herediamts, which I am seized possessed
or interested in."
Witnesses : Mathew French, Dublin, clerk, James Bayly, same,
gent., Thomas Cooke, same, notary publick.
Memorial witnessed by : John Connell, Will. Parry.
7, 170, 2046.   William Waller (seal)

44 LEEDS, MICHAEL, Dublin, merchant.
22 June 1708. Codicil 23 Feb. 1708. Full, 1 p., 14 May 1711.
My wife[1]   My mother. Son Nathaniel, and daughters Sarah and
Nancy, under age. Cousins Katherine Aldrich, William Aldrich, Thos.
Meagher. Nephew William Aldrich.   " My cousen Michael Leeds in
London." Aunt Langham. £10 to my cousin John Jackson for
the use of Santry Church. Codicil says wife then enceinte.
Real and personal estate.
Witnesses : Aldn. William Gibbons, Edward Butler, gent., and
Jane Gibbons, spinster, all of Dublin. Witnesses to codicil : Avis
Castleton, Katherine Meagher, Katherine. Martin, all of Dublin.
Memorial witnessed by : Hen. Buckley, John Connell, clerk to
Bruen Worthington.
6, 244, 2065.   ,   Wm. Aldrich (seal)

45 DEMARCON, LEWIS DUBAY, Wad[d]ingstown, Co. Kilkenny,
a French Protestant. 9 March 1710. Précis, ½ p., 1 June 1711.
Wife Jane Piguenit.   "Testator's two sons and daughters."
Held Wad[d]ingstown, Co. Kilkenny in fee simple. A mortgage
due to Mr. Peter Chelar.
Witnesses : Peter Derante, Waterford, chirurgeon, Simon Vashon,
Waterford, merchant, and Peter Chelar, Waterford, gent.

---

[1] Anne Leeds als. Castleton. See a lease 6, 247, 2068.

Memorial witnessed by : Simon Vashon, aged about 46, Arthur Keating.
6, 265, 2110. Jeanne Piguenit (seal)

46 WEEKES, JOHN, Knockstevenogh, Co. Limerick, gent.
17 July 1708. Narrate, 1½ p., 2 June 1711.
His wife. Son Nicholas under age. Daughter Anne (unmarried). Father-in-law George Chinnery, brother-in-law John Chinnery, and Nicholas Lysaght of Kilmallock, Esq., trustees. Brother Nicholas Weekes. Sister Elizabeth Weekes.
Cahirgyllimore, Ballynanties, Co. Limerick. Knockbrack, B. Duhallow, Co. Cork.
Witnesses : Alphonsus Cullen, Ballygrenan, clerk, John FitzGibbon, Fort, Doctor of Physic, Moses Wilmott, late of Knockstevana, gent., all in Co. Limerick.
Memorial witnessed by : Hen. Buckley, John Connell, clerk to Bruen Worthington.
6, 267, 2114. Nich. Lysaght (seal)

47 WRAY, Colonel CHRISTOPHER.
8 July 1710. Narrate, ¾p., 4 June 1711.
Father Sir Drury Wray, Bart. Sisters Frances Wray, Bridget Howard, Eliz. FitzGerald, Diana Twigg, and Mary Whitacre. Niece Mary Kerr. Brother Cecil Wray. John Pigott Coleclough, trustee. John Dowdall, Middle Temple, London, Esq., legatee.
Knockihernane, Co. Limerick. Lands tenements and hereditaments in Great Britain and Ireland.
Witnesses : Nicholas Westby, Ennis, Co. Clare, Esq., John Higgins, Limerick, apothecary, John Dowdall, Middle Temple, London.
Memorial witnessed by : John Connell, Hen. Buckley, clerk to Bruen Worthington, Dublin.
6, 269, 2115. Cecil Wray (seal)

48 CLINCH, WILLIAM, Loughtown, Co. Dublin, Esq.
2 April 1705. Narrate, ¾ p., 20 July 1711.
Leaves all to James Clinch then in France " if the law would permit him to live in Ireland." Appoints William Clinch, son of John Clinch

a butcher in Oxmantown near Dublin, his heir if said James cannot enjoy legacy. Grandchild Thos. Connor. Kinswoman Margaret Hickey. Charles Fagan and Ferdinando Hickey, kinsmen, and Richard Nowlan, overseers.

William Clinch, son of Lawrence Clinch of Killdonane, Co. Dublin. The son of Simon Clinch, Grange, Co. Antrim. Domestic servants Maurice Tarran and Nicholas Tarran. A legacy to Christian Clinch, a widow in Newcastle, she to pay two hens yearly to Loughtown House as an acknowledgement.

Loughtown, Hanistowne, and Newcastle, Co. Dublin.

Witnessed by : John Balthurst, Coolentragh, Co. Wexford, farmer.

Memorial witnessed by : Mich. Doyle, John Connell, Dublin, gent.

6, 336, 2227. Margarrett Hickey (seal)

49 LEONARD, STEPHEN, Carha, Co. Galway, gent.
18 Dec. 1710. Full, ¾ p., 17 Nov. 1711.

To be buried in the Abby of Kilkonnell. Eldest son John Leonard. Sons Alexander and Mic. Leonard. Daughters Hellen, Mary and Peggy Leonard. Youngest daughter Onnor Leonard. A settlement previously made on George Leonard.

John Tobyn of Killuktour, and his eldest son David Tobyn, James Lewis of Killticackie, Richard Marnale and James Blake, debtors. William Donelan, Edward Butler, Robert Mason, Redmond Archdeckne.

Carha, Caramalow, Shanballiroe, Carnentobber, Lackarne, Leckinavinka, Gortmore, Gortimane, Cloonegarry, Clonnectloncane [? Cloonagh, B. Ballymoe, parish Dunmore], Capintreehane [Cappantruhaun], Co. Galway. Cloonefinine, Mulickroe, Cloonesinough, Coolicame, Co. Roscommon. Rents of Buoly.

Witnesses : Joseph Donelan, Edmund Boland, Michael Kelly, all of Co. Galway, gents.

Memorial witnessed by : Thos. Daly, Dublin, gent., Hen. Buckley.

8, 159, 2480. Alex. Leonard (Seal)

50 DAVIS, THOMAS, city of Dublin, merchant.
9 May 1711. Précis, ½ p., 8 Dec. 1711.

My wife Martha Davis.

" My lands tenements " etc.

Witnesses : Peter Kelly, Spanish leather dresser, George Fleming,
Dublin, turner, Isaac Rabotran, Dublin, gent.

Memorial witnessed by : Peter Kelly, Davis . . . . .[1], Si. Anyon.
8, 182, 2539   Martha Davis (seal)

51 ST. GEORGE, SIR GEORGE, Dunmore, Co. Galway, Knt.

7 Feb. 1709. Codicil 29 Sept. 1710. Narrate, 2 pp., 19 Jan. 1711.
Wife Dame Elizabeth. Son Richard St. George, and Anne St.
George, als. Eyre, his wife, second daughter of John Eyre, deceased
[? married 1686], they had no issue. Daughter Emilia St. George.
Daughter Elizabeth.

Sir Robert Newcomen, Mostowne, Co. Longford, Bart., and William
Caulfield, Dunnamon, Co. Galway, Esq., trustees. Francis Muxley,
tenant.

Dun(e)more als. Culterneneene, Leah, Clonkeene, Adergoolebegg
and other lands off Castle side of River of Dunmore, Co. Galway
Shanesaghnassy [? Sheeaun, B. Tiaquin, parish Clonkeene], Killuney,
Co. Galway. Ballaghabranoge.

Witnesses : Hon. Chidley Coote, Rev. Dillon Ashe, D.D., John
Ormbsy, gent., Roger Cloud. Witnesses to codicil : George Gore,
Dublin, Esq., aforesaid John Ormbsy and Roger Cloud.

Memorial witnessed by : Charles Cloyne[2], Roger Cloud, Geo.
Gillcrist.
6, 472, 2613   Eliz. St. George (seal)

52 HUTCHINSON, JOHN, city of Dublin, smith.

10 March 1706/7. Full, 1½ p., 31 June 1711.
Son John Hutchinson, exor. Daughter Rachel Francis, wife of Elisha
Francis of Temple Bar, Dublin, tallow chandler. Daughter Sarah
Studdart, wife of John Studdart, tailor. Daughter Rebekah Hutch-
inson. Sister Jane Webb. Cousins Thos. Rose, John Rose and Jane
Rose, and Thos. Hutchinson (under 21 years).

Amos Strettell, Dublin, merchant, exor. Job Byar, tenant. Mary
Studdart. John Whiting, cabinet maker, and Charles Whiting, baker,
both of London. £5 to Samuel Whiting " if he prove a hopefull youth."

---

[1] Illegible. ? Davis Prytherik.
[2] possibly Charles Crow, Bishop of Cloyne.

Mary Peel, wife of Joseph Peel, carpenter. £5 "to poor Friends called Quakers belonging to the Mens Meeting of Dublin."

Premises at Temple Barr, city of Dublin. A mill, house etc. in Dame Street. Houses etc. in Essex Street, Fleet Street, Lazy Hill.

. Witnesses: Nathaniel Bradford, Dublin, gent., Mary Caddow, wife of John Caddow, Dublin, shoemaker, Thos. Banckes and Thos. Fox, both of Dublin, gents., Daniel Forrest, Dublin, gent.

Memorial witnessed by: John Connell, clerk to Bruen Worthington, Dublin, notary public, Hen. Buckley.

8, 213, 2632   Rebekah Waker (als. Hutchinson) (seal)

53 JACKSON, JAMES, Newtowne, Co. Down.

13 Nov. 1711. Full, ½ p., 18 Feb. 1711/12.

Brother John Jackson of Ballygregin, and his son (testator's nephew) James Jackson. "Nephew Gilbert son to John Jackson of Ballyskeagh." £5 to nephew John Teat "to encourage him to follow his studies."

James Neill, tenant of Ballymasea. John Thompson, John Jackson, both in parish of Newtown. Eliz. Cord, her sisters and brothers. My servants James Sloane and Martha Wither.

"My proportion of the barge commonly called the William and John." Ballymasea. Tan yard, house etc. at Newtown.

Witnesses: Thos. Jackson, Newtowne, innkeeper, John Thomson, of same, merchant, John Mairs, minister in Newtown.

Memorial witnessed by: John Thomson, James Orr.

8, 241, 2687   Gilbert Jackson (seal)
                    James Jackson (seal)

54 HARTLEY, JOHN, Dublin, merchant.

12 Dec. 1709. Narrate, 1 p., 29 Feb. 1711.

Wife Sarah Hartley als. Ashhurst. Daughter-in-law Eliz. Hartley.

Trusty friends Mr. Samuel Card and his son Mr. Ralph Card, Dublin, merchants, trustees and exors.

Ormond Markett, city of Dublin.

Witnesses: James Carnachan, shoemaker, James Robinson, junr., joiner, Thos. Cooke, notary public, all of Dublin.

Memorial witnessed by: Will Sumner, Thos. Cooke, notary public.

8, 258, 2719   Ralph Card (seal)

55 MOTTLEY, WALTER, Dublin, merchant.

9 Feb. 1711. Précis, ½ p., sworn 1 Mar. 1711.

Brothers Edward and Charles Mottley.

His real and personal estate.

Witnesses : George Forbes, Thos. Rush, Thos. Cooke, notary public.
Memorial witnessed by : Geo. Forbes, alderman, Dublin, Mich.
Harborne.

8, 260, 2725   Ch. Mottley (seal)

56 CUPPAIDGE, REBECCA. Died 5 Jan. 1711.

19 Aug. 1707. Précis, ½ p., 17 March 1711.

" Her estates " to Sir Francis Hamilton of Castle Hamilton, Co.
Cavan, Bart., and Dame Anne Hamilton his wife.

Witnesses : Rev. Benjamin Span, clerk, Rev. Maurice Neligan,
clerk, Alexander Brock, Gortnashamer, Co. Longford, gent.

Memorial witnessed by : Richard Young, Lagher, Co. Cavan, gent.,
W. R. Rankin.

7, 399, 2752   Sir Francis Hamilton (seal)
                                      Dame Anne Hamilton (seal)

57 KING, ROBERT, Dublin, Esq.

27 Aug. 1711. Narrate, 1 p., 11 April 1712.

His wife. His mother. Daughter Mary King. Brothers James
King, John King of Gola, and Charles King. Grandsons Robert and
Hamill Ross. Granddaughters Mary and Anne Ross.

His Grace William Lord Archbishop of Dublin, brother James
King and testator's wife, exors. Brigadier Nicholas Price (owes sums
by mortgages on lands in Co. Down).

Estate in Co. Down " not long since purchased in the name of
Robt. Ross, Esq., his son-in-law." Lands in B. Magheraboy, Co.
Fermanagh, and in B. Magherestaffanagh [Magherastephana], Co.
Fermanagh. Corrard and Gola, Co. Fermanagh. Ballyboggan, Bally-
last and Garvary, Co. Donegal. Lands in Co. Donegal and Co. Down.
Skinner Row [? Dublin].

Witnesses : Robert Sherrard, James Nixon of Dublin, gent.,
Robert Cliferley, Dublin, vintner.

Memorial witnessed by : Thos. Somervell, Geo. Hamill, Dublin, gent.

8, 310, 2811   James King (seal)

58 EDWARDS, JOHN, city of Dublin, clerk.

28 Feb. 1709.   Partly in full, ¾p., 29 April 1712.

My honoured father and mother. My late dear wife. Son Eleazer Edwards. My eldest daughter Elizabeth. "All my children." Brothers Abdiell and Eleazer Edwards, exors.

James Carroll, Esq., Mr. Jonathan Sisson, exors. Mr. John Falkiner. Mrs. Bevans. Mrs. Hopkins.

Real and personal estate.

Witnesses : John Meare, weaver, George Ramsay, weaver, and Peter Rice, weaver, all of Dublin.

Memorial witnessed by : Robt. Wallis, William Barry, Dublin, scrivener.

8, 322, 2832   Jonathan Sisson (seal)

59 JACKSON, ROBERT, Crooked Staff, Liberty of Donore, Dublin, tanner. 23 Feb. 1711. Narrate, 1 p., 13 March 1712.

Wife Joyce Jackson. Eldest son Robert Jackson. Sons William, John and Thomas Jackson. Son-in-law Jeremiah Vickers. "His brother Samuel Card." ·

Exors. Samuel Card, and Joseph Marriott, Dublin, gent.

His dwelling house, tan yard, tan house, mill etc. Tenement in Crooked Staff, ground etc. in Chambre Street, and between Cork Street and Chambre Street [Dublin].

Witnesses : Abraham Spence, Dublin, brewer, David Carton, of same, clothier, John Bland, servant to said Joseph Marriott.

Memorial witnessed by : Rich. Cradock, Wm. Barry, John Bland.

7, 464, 2897   William Jackson (seal)

60 ORMSBY, JOHN, Alacca, Co. Limerick, Esq.

13 Oct. 1705. Narrate, 3 pp., in May 1712.

(son of Arthur Ormsby, the elder, of Ballyvinoge, Co. Limerick, Esq.).

Wife Elizabeth Ormsby. Son John Ormsby [? the testator—son of Arthur]. Eldest daughter Jane Ormsby and younger daughter Katherine Ormsby (both under 18 years). ·

Mentions "the great debts the said John Ormsby the Testator was necessitated to contract in England for the support of him and his family during the late rebellion in this kingdom."

Robert Ormsby, the younger, son and heir apparent of Robert

Ormsby, Dublin, counsellor-at-law. Gilbert Ormsby, Esq. Lands mortgaged to Mr. Joseph Damer, Mr. Nathaniel Weld and George Evans, Esq. Recites indenture of 29 May 1686, deed poll 15 Jan. 1688, and a settlement, mentioned in deed of 20 April 1688, of Postume Ormsby, Esq., deceased.

Ballyvinoge, Ballincolla, Clogher, Carhow, Ballysallogh, Millagh, Ballybegg, Knockballinebough, Clonbryan, Coulraversy Land, Knock-ballintorliss, Ballyvoymana, Dromin als. Fansland als. Faranoula, Fox Acre, Rawleighs Acre, Scoalls, Ballinclony, Ballinity, Carrogh-begg, Ballinlee, Ballinguyraur, Gortneraughny, Coolreah, Carroghbegg, Ballincurre, Clondruma, in B. Coshma. Milltown als. Ballymullin, Ballyneguyly, Feehedes, in B. Conello, Co. Limerick. Rosstemple, Rosstemplebegg, Ballycullen, Finiterstowne, Killtenane, Garranboy, Gortnegrewer als. Gertincore, Co. Limerick.

Witnesses : Hugh Gough, Kilfinny, Co. Limerick, clerk, Lewis Geness, Ballyneycleour, Co. Limerick, gent., William Taylor, Alacca, yeoman.

Memorial witnessed by : Fra. Fling, Ja. Hill, Hugh Gough, Lewis Geness.

8, 363, 2918   Jane Ormsby (seal)

61 INGOLDESBY, Lieut. General RICHARD,
       29 Jan. 1711. Full, 1½ p., 12 July 1712.

Wife Frances Ingoldesby. Son Henry. " Sister Mrs. Barbara Ingoldsby." Cousin Sir William Ingoldsby, Bart. Cousin Richard Ingoldesby, Esq., eldest son of Sir Richard Ingoldesby, late of Wald-ridge, Bucks., deceased.

Dr. Bryan Robison. My dear wife's woman Mrs. Elizabeth Higgins. Jacob Donnellan "whom my dear wife hath taken into her care." Servant Anthony Walsh. Symon Purdon, James Naper and testator's wife, exors.

House in Mary Street, Dublin. House in Golden Street, London. Lands etc. in England and Ireland and elsewhere.

Witnesses : Brent Smith, gent., Rev. Jonathan Wilson, clerk, Edmund Shuldham, gent., all of Dublin.

Memorial witnessed by : Anthony Walsh, Carrtown, Co. Kildare, gent., Jonathan Wilson, clerk.

9, 27, 3105   Frances Ingoldesby (seal)

62 HENDRICK, JOHN, Dublin, alderman.
5 Jan. 1711. Précis, ½ p., in Aug. 1712.
Wife Mary Hendrick. Daughter Hawkins, Robert Hawkins her husband. Son Robert. Daughter-in-law Margery Hendrick. Grandchildren Mary, John, James and William Hendrick. Brother Anthony Hendrick.
Alderman John Page, Anthony Hendrick, merchant, trustees. James Allen, Francis Street, tenant. Jeremy Reynolds, Francis Street, tenant.
Dwelling house, Brew House, malt house, mill, etc. [situation not mentioned]. Houses etc. in Francis Street, Lilles Lane, Dublin.
Witnesses : James Allen, pipemaker, Wm. Adaire, gent., and Samuel Cotton, notary public, all of Dublin.
Memorial witnessed by : William Adaire, Dublin, gent., Thos. Trotter.
9, 44, 3189   John Page (seal)

63 DOWDALL, MARY, Gaskinstowne, parish of Duleeke, Co. Meath, widow. 9 Aug. 1712. Précis, ½ p., 19 Sept. 1712.
Sons Philip and George Dowdall.
Ballrath, Co. Meath.
Witnesses : John Tyrrell of the Kernes, Co. Meath, gent., Edward Langan, Sheoge, Co. Meath, farmer, George Dowdall, Gaskinstowne, gent.
Memorial witnessed by : Ol. Weston, Edward Langan.
9, 64, 3267   George Dowdall (seal)

64 CARROLL, JAMES, Baltinglass, Co. Wicklow, Esq.
28 Nov. 1711. Narrate, 1 p., 30 Sept. 1712.
Wife Catherine. Daughter Anne Griffith. Grandson James, and granddaughter Deborah Griffith. His wife's daughter Elizabeth Travers. Children of his sister Lydia. Cousin Mary Clark, widow.
Trustees : Duncan Cumyng, Dublin, doctor of Physic, Joseph Henry, gent., and Caleb Thomas of Dublin, merchant. Exors. the said trustees, and testator's wife, and John Flower, Dublin, merchant. John Travers, son of Samuel Travers late of Dublin, deceased, William, brother of said John, and Samuel the youngest brother of said John Travers. Mary Frakerly als. White. Esther Hughes als. Fakerly.

Mrs. Abdiall Edwards. Mr. Joseph Pettit. Mr. John Hanna. Mr. Peter Cribb. Mr. Richard Forster. To poor of congregation meeting in Swift's Alley £20.

Puckstowne. House in Golden Lane.

Witnesses : Walter Stephens, Dublin, Esq., John Heron, Roger Gough, Dublin, gent.

Memorial witnessed by : Roger Gough, Sil. Pepyat.

9, 71, 3280   Jos. Henry (seal)

65 BACON, DOROTHY, Rathkeany, Co. Tipperary, widow.
   18 Feb. 1707. Narrate, 1 p., 1 Oct. 1712.

Eldest son William Bacon, his two sons George and William Bacon. Her second son Edward Bacon. Her two daughters Dorothy Tily (or Tyly) and Anne Stephens. Grandson Charles, and granddaughter Dorothy Skinner. Grandchild Dorothy Stephens, eldest daughter of her son-in-law Henry Stephens, gent. Grandchildren John, Popham, Mary, Elizabeth and William Stephens. Granddaughters Dorothy and Elizabeth Tyly, grandsons John and Joseph Tyly.

Rathkeany, Co. Tipperary.

Witnesses : Edmund Heydon and John Sparrow, both of St. John-towne, Co. Tipperary, yeomen, Mathew Jacob of same, Esq.

Memorial witnessed by : Ed. Heydon, Math. Jacob, Saml. Jacob.

9, 72, 3281   Edward Bacon (seal)

66 PERRIE, JONATHAN, Cork, Esq.
   30 May 1709. Narrate, ¾ p. 13 Jan. 1712.

Wife Anne Perrie. Only daughter Anne Cooke, widow. Grand-daughters Anne and Mary Cooke, grandson John Perrie Cooke.

Tenants, Baptist Smith, brewer, Robert Hill, Esq., Dutch Consull, Robert Pelitan, clothier, Dennis Leary, the widow of Patrick Stanton, joiner and Thos. Hodder, Esq.

His dwelling house on North East Marsh in Parish Christ Church and South East Quarter of city Cork. Meadows of Parkealmore and Parkekealbeg, in South Suburbs of Cork. Premises in N.E. Quarter of city Cork.

Witnesses : Quintin Osburne, physician, Isaac Anbere, merchant, Thos. Browne, gent., James Reburne, schoolmaster, all of Cork.

Memorial witnessed by : Thos. Browne, Wm. Lane.

9, 235, 3562   Anne Pirrie (seal)

67 JORDAN, ROBERT, Crumlín, Co. Dublin, gent.

14 May 1712. Précis, ½ p., 14 April 1713.

Sister Alson Jordan. Richard Fenner, Dublin, Esq., legatee.

St. Michael's Lane, city of Dublin. His real and personal estate.

Witnesses : Patrick Christy, James Hackett, Richard Reddy, all of Dublin, gents.

Memorial witnessed by : Hen. Buckley, clerk to Bruen Worthington, Dublin, notary public, Will. Westbery.

9, 346, 3796   Rich. Fenner (seal)

68 BLOOD, THOMAS, senr., Bohersalta, Co. Clare, gent.

14 April 1713. Précis, ¾ p., 22 June 1713.

Son Thomas Blood of Cahirnemohir, Co. Clare, gent. Son Neptune Blood of Bohersalta, Co. Clare, gent.

Bohersalta, Cahurgrenane, Cahunemohir [? Cahirmohir], and Dorode, all in parish of Rathon, B. Inshign [Rath, B. Inchiquin], Co. Clare.

Witnesses : Edmond O'Hogan, John Hogan and Thomas Wise.

Memorial witnessed by : Edm. O'Hogane, Thos. Wise.

9, 396, 4031   Nept. Blood (seal)

69 KENNEDY, SIR RICHARD, Co. Wicklow, Bart.

22 May 1707. Narrate, 1 p., 26 June, 1713.

Wife Lady Katherine Kennedy, Daughter Elizabeth Kennedy, (under 14 years). Brother Mr. Howard Kennedy. " One hundred pounds to his grandmother Mrs. Katherine Howard which he desired her to accept of in token of his gratitude for the Great care and tenderness she had for him in his education."

Humphrey Mathews, Co. Wicklow, Esq., Rev. Dr. Claudius Gilbert of Trinity College, trustees. William Domvile, Co. Dublin, Esq. Mr. John Eldwood of Trinity College. Sir Francis Blake, debtor. His real estate.

Witnesses : Peter Blanchvile, servant to testator, Joseph Townsend, servant to said William Domvile, John White, servant to said John Elwood.

Memorial witnessed by : Theo. Bolton, Thomas Jackson, Dublin, gent.

10, 433, 4055   Will. Domvile (seal)

70   JENNINGS, SAMUEL, city of Kilkenny, gent.

     11 May 1708. Précis, ½ p., 7 July 1713.

Wife Penellope Jennings.

Henry Roades, Pallis, Co. Tipperary. His beloved friend John Russell of Ballydavid, Co. Tipperary. His real and personal estate.

Witnesses : Henry Roades, Pallis, Co. Tipperary, gent., Thomas Lanphier, Parkstowne, and Edward Harmer, Coolekennedy, both in Co. Tipperary.

Memorial witnessed by : Francis Lodge, Dublin, gent., Benj. Gale.

9, 418, 4106   Henry Roades (seal)

71   LEE, HENRY, city of Dublin, merchant.

     28 May 1713. Partly in full, 2 pp., 8 July 1713.

My wife Elizabeth Lee. Eldest son William Lee. My two younger sons James and Benjamin Lee. My two daughters Jane Lee and Hester Lee. Sister Mrs Anne Norton.

£10 to put Henry Norton out apprentice. Walter Welsh, John Rourke, James Doyle, George Ord, tenants at Meryoung. My good friends Mr. Simon Anyon and Mr. William Burne, Dublin, gents., exors. Stephen Conditt (Conduitt).

Stafford Street, Jervis Street, Fleet Street. Dawson Street. House at Meryoung. Brickfields, with the horses, carts and other conveniences.

Witnesses : John Rathborne, Dublin, merchant. Hugh Shaw, apothecary, Thomas Cooke, gent., both of Dublin.

Memorial witnessed by : John Rathborne, Stephen Conduitt.

9, 419, 4108   Si. Anyon (seal)

                            Wm. Burne (seal)

72   BENKIER, JAMES, city of Cork, merchant.

     2 Dec. 1712. Narrate, 17 Oct. 1713.

His five nieces the daughters of his brother Patrick Benkier. Nephew James, son of said Patrick. His niece the daughter of his brother Thomas. His two nephews, sons of his brother Thomas.

His friends Mr. William Boyle and Mr. Hugh Mitchell, exors. George Evans, junr., Esq., James Morrison, Cork, merchant, mortgagees.

Lands in Co. Limerick and city of Cork.

Witnesses : William Roberts, merchant, William Chartres, junr., Esq., and Thomas Barry, scrivener, all of Cork.

Memorial witnessed by : Thos. Barry, Wm. Lane.

11, 196, 4331   Wm. Boyle (seal)

73 PYKE, JOHN, Woodinstown, Co. Tipperary, Esq.
  6 June 1713.   Narrate, 2½ pp., 25 Nov. 1713.
His grandson John Pyke. "His said grandson he continuing him
the surname of Pyke and leaving of the surname of Palmer." Grand-
daughter Rebecca Palmer.   Cousin John Pyke, senr., of Apledore,
Devon, mariner, son of his uncle Joseph Pyke of same, deceased.
Cousin Joseph Pyke of Barnestaple, second son of said uncle.   Cousin
George Pyke of Braunton, Devon, third son of said uncle.   Cousin
Samuel Pyke of Apledore, fourth son of said uncle.
  Exors.: Brothers-in-law Mr. John Minchin of Shanagarry and
Mr. Mathew Jacob of St. Johnstown and cousin John Perry of Wood-
roffe, all in Co. Tipperary, gents.
  Woodinstown, Donnegall, Ballygarrolds, Carrigeeniviegh, Knock-
aneiviegh, Chamberlinstowne, Caddleston, Lower Loughkent, Temple-
hill als. Templequarter, Cooleagh, Clorane, Gortnapissy, Carrantubber
Bogg, all in B. Middle Third, Co. Tipperary.   Liskevin, B. Eliogerty,
Co. Tipperary.   Maganstown, Knockine, B. Iffa and Offa, Co. Tip-
perary.   Ballytarsney, Ballycommin, Sal[l]squarter and Ga[i]le, B.
Middle Third, Co. Tipperary.   Coolecat, parish of Fremington, Devon.
  Witnesses: John Burgess, Cashel, Doctor of Physic, Benjamin
Vize, James Atchison, Chamberlinstown, Co. Tipperary, gents.
  Memorial witnessed by: William Connor, gent., Rich. Perry.
11, 239, 4428   John Perry (seal)

74 BELL, THOMAS, Newmarket, Liberty of Donore, Co. Dublin,
      carpenter. 8 Feb. 1710. Narrate, 1¾ p., 5 Dec. 1713.
Wife Jane Bell.   Cousin Jonathan Bell.
  George Rooke, Abel Strettell, Joseph Fade, Joseph Maddock,
trustees. All his working tools of Peter Wenright, he to make himself
Free of the Corporation of Carpenters of the city of Dublin. Thomas
Johnson, Dennis Bennett and Thomas Gore, tenants, Dun[s]combs
Lane. George Rooke, tenant. Thomas Wilkinson, Mary Earle, Thomas
Wilson, Mary Barton, John Thickett, Elizabeth Jacob, Joseph
Thickett, Jane Bell, Esther Bell, John Bell, bricklayer, Elizabeth and
Alexander Wilkinson. £40 to his friends at the Mens Meeting House
called Quakers. Field near Roper's Rest to George Rooke for life,
and afterwards to Dublin Quakers "to be made use of in grazing the
horses of their Friends travelling to and from Dublin."
  Newmarkett, Skinner's Alley, houses in Meath Street including a

house the sign of the Three Compasses ;   Dun[s]combs Lane als. Garden Lane in Liberties of Thomas Court, Dublin.

Witnesses : John Elliott, Dublin, gent., Thomas Merefield, Dublin, gent., Thomas Sisson, Dublin, notary public.

Memorial witnessed by : Ralph Wakfield, Henry Burrows, John Wakfield, Dublin, gent.

11, 262, 4479   Jonathan Bell (seal)

75 DILLON, RT. HON. HENRY VISCOUNT
    10 Jan. 1713. Précis, ½ p., 4 Feb. 1713.

His late father. Wife Rt. Hon. Frances Lady Viscountess Dillon.

Denis Kelly, Agharane, Co. Galway, Esq., (to be agent). Rt. Hon. Elizabeth Lady Baroness of Strabane.

Drumraney, Co. Westmeath, and lands, tenements and hereditaments in Counties Westmeath, Roscommon and Mayo.

Witnesses : Edmund Malone, Esq., James Mellaghlin, Doctor of Physic, Dominick Ryan, apothecary, Garret Dillon, grocer, all of Dublin.

Memorial witnessed by : Garret Dillon, Hen. Buckley.

12, 154, 4674   D. Kelly (seal)

76 HAMILTON, SIR FRANCIS, Castlehamilton, Co. Cavan,
    Bart. 19 Jan. 1713. Précis, 1 p., 25 Feb. 1713.

Wife Dame Anne Hamilton. Father Sir Charles Hamilton, deceased. Nephew Arthur Cecill.

Castle Hamilton, the market town of Killyshandra with customs of fairs and marketts, Kirilagh, Portnaqueen, Inchsonakeile, Gollan, Cordeale, Derrigid, Gortanoule, Portalosse, Killytowna, Corragh, Dysart, Drumellies, East and West Tomlogh, Drumboe, Gortenagerie, Drumerin, Clonnie, Gorteneclogh, Port, Drumines with the Corn Mill, the Bawne als. Dirrindrehett, Aghnecloy, Aghanadran, Deroskert, Cappagh, Drumransk, Aghahulikie, Drumconlister, Ardra, Dirandcrosse, Drumgoe, Drumgoone, Loghard, Drumhillagh, Drumbesse, Garragher, Drummamrie, Drumwhilan, Corr, Gortenardris, the Two Tenenseiris, Drumcon, Corralisse, Mills of Cloghie, Pole of Cloghie, Drumcaghall, the Two Aghasnox, Shancorr, Bruse, Lassall, Sollaghies, Dingans, Knocknecoghie, Gortnatiriffe, Drumcarry, Baye, Shancarr, Drumkirrin, Quinie, [? Quivvy], Drumroe, Drumkirinemore, Cortober,

Aghavains, Corrfrie, the Two fishing Weirs, Portanare, the Pole of Scrabagh, the town of Scrabagh with the market, fairs, customs and mill, Cloone, Mulrek, Arrnagh, Dirrinacapell, Cornegrane, Cornemucklagh and Carfrie, all in B. Tullahuncha [Tullyhunco], Co. Cavan. Advowsons of the parish church of Killshandra, lands of Leitrim, Toome, Kilmore, Aghaconny, Clonagh, Aghakilmore, Innis, Danagh, Lisrorty, Farmolagh, Drumard and Ballyduffe, all in B. Granard, Co. Longford. Drumaker, Co. Leitrim. Letterkenny, Co. Donegal. And all other lands in the Co. Cavan, Longford and Leitrim.

Witnesses : Charles Stewart, Dublin, Esq., Rev. Hugh Skellern, Killyshandra, clerk, Charles Sempkill, near Killyshandra, gent., Alexr. Brock, Co. Longford, gent.

Memorial witnessed by : Richard Young, Dromgoone, Co. Cavan, gent., Will. Hamilton.

20, 200, 4791   Anne Hamilton (seal)

77 MURRAY, CHARLES, Muckross, B. Boylagh and Bannagh, Co. Donegal, gent. 2 Nov. 1708. Sworn at Lifford 4 April 1711. Full, ½p., 9 Mar. 1713.

Wife Frances Murray als. Nesbitt. "No issue of my own." Exors. Alexander Murray, Broughton, Esq., Thomas Knox, Mountcharles, Esq., Capt. Thos. Knox, Lougheaske, and Capt. Albert Nesbitt my brother-in-law.

Under great obligations "to the family of Broughton . . . as my father also was." Leaves freehold of Gortnisillagh, Par. Inniskeell, B. Boylagh and Banagh, Co. Donegal, to Alexander Murray of Broughton, Esq., or Laird of Broughton.

Witnesses : Thos. Knox, John Donnell, Robert Steen.

Memorial witnessed by : Alex. Nesbitt, John Taylor.

11, 415, 4863   Frances Murray (seal)

78 ROE, ANDREW, Tipperary town, gent. 1 Oct. 1713. Narrate, 2¾ pp., 15 March 1713/14.

Wife Mary Roe. Eldest son William, second son James, third son Andrew, youngest son John Roe, a minor. Daughters Mary Roe, Margrett Roe and Anne Sophia Roe.

Mathew Jacob, St. Johnstowne, Nathaniel Lucas, Clonmell and John White, Shrouell, all in Co. Tipperary, gents., trustees. A rent charge payable to Richard Chadwick [? and his wife Mary].

D

Boytonsrath, Grantstowne, Killoge, Rathmacarty, Rathsallagh, Rathduffe, Temple Quarter als. Knockanetemple, Ballynemoght, Ballycry, and Baunrenny, Co. Tipperary.   Ballymacdonoghfeen, Co. Wexford. Houses in Dublin. The house near his dwelling house in town of Tipperary commonly called the Meeting House.

Witnesses : John Burgess, city of Cashell, Dr. of Physic, John Lutherborrow, Tipperary, Dominick Burke, Clonmell, gent.

Memorial witnessed by : Dominick Burke, Robert Ashbrooke.

12, 247, 4909   N. Lucas (seal)

79 BROWNLOW, STANDISH, Louth.

12 May 1713. Précis, ½ p., 15 March 1713/14.

Brothers John and Philemon Brownlow. George Taif, legatee.

Niselaragh, Lisculra, Drumgoaling [? Drumgoolan], " his intermixt lands in and about the town of Louth," Clanbarron, Carrickhoodan, Reth, Loblough, Pinfold, Castlecarrick, Mulincross, Richardstown.

Witnesses : John Meade, counsellor-at-law, James Moore, testator's servant, Charles McQuillin servant to Felix McCartan, Dublin, peruke-maker.

Memorial witnessed by : Roth Jones, John Connell, clerk to Bruen Worthington, Dublin, notary public.

11, 436, 4910   John Brownlow (seal)

80 LANGFORD, THEOPHILUS, Kinsale, Esq.

18 Sept. 1712. Précis, ½ p., 10 May 1714.

Kinsman Hercules Rowley, Esq. "Mrs. Rebecca Britton, daughter of Mary Britton" and Oliver Plunkett, legatees. Mr. Thomas Leasy [? Lacey], Mr. John Suxbery, friends.

Ballincurry, Liberties of Kinsale. House in Cork held by Ald. Crone. Mill Street, Cork, held by Joseph Studdert and John Kelly. Ground etc. in Cork Street, Low Street, without Cork gate, and Low Fish Street joining the Old Key in Kinsale ; a lease in Church Lane near Freer Street, Kinsale, held by William Murphy.

Witnesses : Thomas Lacey, said John Suxbery, James Jones, Kinsale, John Walton, late servant to testator, Robert Williams, Kinsale, shipwright.

Memorial witnessed by : William Barry, Dublin, scrivener, Will. Simpson.

14, 35, 5110   Her. Rowley (seal)

81 BRABAZON, WILLIAM, Co. Louth, Esq.

9 Dec. 1713. Codicil 5 April 1714. Précis 1 p., 26 May 1714.

Wife Elizabeth Brabazon. Sons Wallop, Ralph, Ludlow, William and James Brabazon. Daughter Alice Brabazon. Daughters Barbara and Jane. Brother James Brabazon. Nephew William Brabazon. George Lambert, an exor.

Termonfecken, Nicholstown, Lurganbuoy, parts of Painstown one held from Stephen Ludlow, Esq., Salterstown, Belrobin held from Earl of Dartmouth in B. Dundalk, Corbollis, Whitestown, Ballyhitch, two Kinneliskys, Ballytrasney, Pucksland, lands [situation not mentioned] leased from Major Theobald Throckmorton, Kilronan, Stancorr, Mullaghtee, Mullaghbawn, tenement in Carlingford being the house where the Barrack now stands, Mullatinny, Rath, Killaly, Smithstown and Clonmore, all in Co. Louth.

Witnesses : Rev. John Leavens, Clonmore, Co. Louth, clerk, William Mathews of [blank] near Dundalk, Doctor of Physic, James Hoey, then parish clerk of Clonmore. Witnesses to codicil : said John Leavens, Bryan Lurcan, then servant to said testator, Alice Brabazon, daughter to testator.

Memorial witnessed by : John Connell, Will. Parry, clerk to Bruen Worthington, Dublin.

14, 53, 5154   Geo. Lambert (seal)

82 BAIRD, ROBERT, St. Johnston, Co. Donegal, gent.

19 Dec. 1713. Précis, ½ p., 21 June 1714.

Son Thomas Baird. Grandson Charles McFarland.

Archibald Woods, Transallagh, Co. Donegal, Archibald Coningham, Londonderry, gent, exors. Wm. Cowan, son of John Cowan. Tenants or lessors of houses in Strabane : Patrick Bedlow, Church Street, Andrew Park, Castle Street, Alexander Jameson and Claud Scott.

Salt Pans of Monihiben [? Moniluben], and leases in parish of Deserteignie. Salt Pans of [?] Urras, Co. Donegal. Tithes of parish of Killcah, the Glebe and lease of Altakaskin at town end of St. John-towne, belonging to the Deanery of Raphoe. Premises in Strabane, Co. Tyrone. Freehold in [? Upper] Cloghogle, parish of Donoghedie, B. Strabane, Co. Tyrone.

Witnesses : Alexr. Park, Londonderry, innkeeper, John Harvey, Drumore, Co. Donegall, gent., James Cockran, Londonderry, merchant.

Memorial witnessed by : Alexr. Richardson, Dublin, gent., David Wilson.

12, 316, 5237   Charles McFarland (seal)

83 BILLOP, JOHN, Pimlico, Liberty of Thomas Court and Donore, city of Dublin, merchant. 12 June 1713. Précis, ½ p., 30 July 1714.

Wife Katherine Billop. Son Josiah Billop. Bartholomew Rivers, Dublin, tobacconist, overseer.

His real and personal estate.

Witnesses : Michael Jackson, Dublin, weaver, John Rankin, of same, clothworker, and Cornelius Donnevan, of same, gent.

Memorial witnessed by : William Hogan, Dublin, gent., Robert Sherlock.

13, 105, 5341   Josiah Billop (seal)

84 BROCKLESBY, THOMAS, city of Cork, clothier.

14 March 1712. Partly in full, 2 pp., 4 Aug. 1714.

Wife Mary Brocklesby. Son Richard Brocklesby. Youngest son Thomas Brocklesby, junr.

Trustees, Edward Barwicke, Cork, tanner, and Samuel Watson, Dublin, linendraper.

Real estate in city of Cork purchased from the late Trustees of Forfeitures in Ireland. Leasehold lands : Part of Farrenpheris, Commons in North Liberties of city, and other lands, Rathmore in North Liberties, city Cork, and the house, etc. " part of Farrenpheris wherein formerly my mother dwelled." Ballyneneligh, B. Barrymore, Co. Cork. Lands and premises in Bs. Barrymore and Muskery, Co. Cork, held from Thos. Putland, Esq.

Witnesses : Robert Henderson, city of Cork, linendraper, William Prior of same, silk throster, Thomas Barry of same, gent.

Memorial witnessed by : Thos. Barry, Si. Weldon, ·

13, 109, 5348   Thomas Brocklesby (seal)

85 KEVAN, JOHN, Grovebegg, Co. Kilkenny, gent.

22 April 1712. Narrate, ¾ p., 24 Nov 1714.

Daughter Martha, wife of Mr. James Collier, testator's son-in-law.

Kevan Collier, their son. Grandchild Elizabeth Cochrane als. Izod, daughter to said Martha.

Grovebegg, Haggart, Shortallstown, Vinsgrove and Raheen, B. Kells, Co. Kilkenny.

Witnesses : Jeremiah Ryan and John Ryan, both of Dunganmore, Co. Kilkenny, gents., Roger Hogan, Grovebegg, said Co., yeoman, Martha Comerford, of same, spinster.

Memorial witnessed by : Jeremiah Ryan, Jn. Collier, Jo. Ryan, Will. Hamilton.

13, 240, 5661   Ja. Collier (seal)

86 BINGHAM, SIR HENRY, Castlebarr, Co. Mayo, Bart.

10 May 1712. Précis, 1 p., 27 Nov. 1714.

Wife Lettice Bingham als. Vesey. Nephew John Byngham, Esq., eldest son and heir of testator's brother George Byngham of Foxford, Co. Mayo. Henry Byngham, second son of said George.

Francis Byngham, Levalley, Co. Mayo, gent. Richard Bingham of Bynghams Melcom, Dorset. Trustees : Lord Archbishop of Tuam (John Vesey), Gerald Cuffe, Elmehall, George Browne, the Neal, Martin Blake, Cooleen, Co. Mayo, Esq., and Robert Kearney, Ballinvilly, Co. Mayo, gent.

The Castle, manor, town and lands of Castlebarr and all fairs, markets, mills, etc., Co. Mayo. Cloonegashell, Manor of Clooncashill, Clonecashill, B. Killmaine, Brockagh, Fahy and Rosnemrahir, B. Burresoule, Co. Mayo.

Witnesses : Rev. James Gordon, Castlebarr, clerk, Rev. Andrew Semple, of same, clerk, Henry Byngham, Levalley, Co. Mayo, gent.

Memorial witnessed by : Robt. Wallis, Hen. Buckley, clerk to Bruen Worthington, Dublin, notary public.

12, 423, 5683   Tho. Vesey (seal) guardian
                                                to Jo. Byngham (Rt. Rev.
                                                Sir Thos. Vesey, Bp. of
                                                Ossory).

87 MASON, SARAH als. ALAND, wife of John Mason of Waterford, Esq. 24 June 1714. Narrate, 1¼ p., 17 Dec. 1714.

Husband John Mason. Eldest daughter Sarah Mason. Second daughter Jane Mason. " Mother " Mary Mason. £5 each to her brother and sister. Cousins Margaret and Hannah Mason. Rev. Alexr. Alcock, Chancellor of Cathedral Church of Waterford, and William Alcock, said city, Esq., special trustees for child " wherewith she was then ensient." Trustees : Rev. John Ecles, Dean of Cathedral Church of Waterford, Rev. Thomas France, chanter of said church.

Ballyvony, Faghagh, Rathmeskilloge als. Rathnasculloge, Williamstowne, Garrantortin, Kilmumue, Carryheen, Londony, Dromlohane, Carrigdenehaghy als. Carrigeenehahy, Addermon, Robertstowne, Cottin, North Ballyattin, Coolenelingiddy, and Coolenehorny, Co. Waterford. Tymolin als. Tymolinbegg, Porterseize, Shean als. Shyon, " Tubberkeigh als. Le Blindwell," Burne Church, Collinstowne, Coolreak, Kilkea als. Kilkeagh, Knockbrack, Tomins als. Caminstowne, Gortinabrackan and Killelan, Co. Kildare. Gragavois, Killinebegg, Killynemore, Knockangrasse als. Knocknagrawly, Shanbally, Tomiroe, Rathquill, Graiganossy, Levally als. Longvally, Banabellymore als. Bawneball, Edmond, Ballybug, Crohallagh, Cloneeke als. Clonebe, Harristowne als. Ballyhenry, Coolcoly, Brennon, Castle Fleming, Shianderry, Cooletrim, Brokerry, Knockkea, Knocknair, Derinemorishagh, Rathelnagh, Ballygauly, Garryduffe, Two Ballintaggarts, Kelvestine, Castletowne, Kilreedymore, Benoge als. Leigarrag, Bennogge and Kilnesire, Queen's Co.

Witnesses : James Reynet [? Reyner], Waterford, Doctor of Physic, Michael Tonnery of same, apothecary, Henry Alcock, Joseph Cooke, Daniel Taylor, all of Waterford, gents.

Memorial witnessed by : Hen. Buckley, clerk to Bruen Worthington, Dublin, notary public, Will. Parry.

12, 446, 5772.   John Mason (seal)

88 SMITH, WILLIAM, Waterford, alderman.
        18 Dec. 1714. Narrate, 1¼ p., 5 Feb. 1714/15.

Sons-in-law William Hayden and Margaret, testator's daughter, his wife, Benjamin Morris and Ann, testator's daughter, his wife, John Moore and Isabella his wife. Kinswomen Mrs. Ann West, Mrs. Jane Taylor. Grandson William Morris, son to Benjamin Morris. Brother Ald. Thomas Smith.

Mrs. Sarah Hull, money "lent to her son at his going to Dublin." Mrs. Catherine Batty. Elinor Brenock seven years his servant. Elizabeth Read [or Reed], servant, John Reed, junr., Kill McOliver. Anthony Birk, Kilkenny, weaver. Mary Collercock. Richard Christmas

Esq., and Alderman William Jones, two overseers. £20 to Protestant poor of Waterford.

St. Patrick's Gate, premises without Barristrand's Gate, Barristrand Street, houses in Michael's parish, leases from Corporation of Waterford. Killenleagh, Knockmore, Co. Kilkenny. Ballymakill, Monoohogy.

Witnesses : Robert Backas, gent., Edward Tonnery, apothecary, Joseph Cooke, gent., all of Waterford.

Memorial witnessed by : Jacob Stone, Thomas Roch, Joseph Cooke.

14, 138, 5922. Jane Taylor (seal)

89 CHAMBERS, WILLIAM, Kilboine, Co. Mayo, gent.

19 Aug. 1714. Précis, ¾ p., 12 Feb. 1714/15.

Wife Susanna Chambers. Brother John Chambers of Cloonenrea, B. Gallen, Co. Mayo, gent., Thomas Chambers the eldest son, William Chambers the younger second son, John Chambers the younger, third son, and Edward Chambers the youngest son of said brother John. His other brother Thomas Chambers, Abergaveny, Monmouthshire in Wales.

Exors. Rev. Thomas Quarterman, Dunmore, clerk, John Ormsby, Dublin, Esq., Mathew Bell, Streamstown, Co. Mayo, Esq., and Daniel Surradge, Dunmore, Co. Galway. A rent charge of £26 for ever for Protestant poor of parish of Ballyhean, B. Carrow, Co. Mayo.

A house in Ballinrobe, Co. Mayo. Real estate in counties of Mayo and Galway and elsewhere in Ireland.

Witnesses : Richard Delamer, Dublin, gent., John Sloper, Cloondeasy, B. Carrow, Co. Mayo, gent., Thomas Tarry, Dublin, merchant.

Memorial witnessed by : Robt. Ormsby, Wm. Dick, servant to Samuel Cotton.

14, 161, 5963. Jno. Chambers (seal)

90 NEWTON, Major General JOHN.

22 April 1714. Narrate, ¾ p., 14 Feb. 1714/15.

His sister Singelton. Sister Graham. Nephew William Graham, son of Alderman John Graham, Drogheda. Nieces Sarah Graham, Charity Graham and Christian Graham, daughters of said John. Aunt Martha Thompson als. Newton. Nephews William Newton of Dublin, gent., Lieut. Thomas Newton, and Robert son of said Alderman John Graham. Nieces Mrs. Mary Newton, Mrs. Elizabeth Singleton,

wife of Rev. Rowland Singleton.   Cousins Patience Singleton and
Charity Singleton, daughters of said Rowland Singleton.   Cousins
John Newton and . . . [blank] Newton, sons of said nephew William
Newton.

Mary Hunter, Dublin, widow.   Elizabeth Pickering, Drogheda,
widow.

Carlingstown, BallyMcKenny, in Liberties of town of Drogheda,
and real estate of testator.

Witnesses : William Colvill, Dublin, gent., Henry Buckley, clerk
to Bruen Worthington, Dublin, notary public, William Barry, Dublin,
scrivener.

Memorial witnessed by : Henry Buckley, Robt. Wallis.

13, 361, 5974.   Wm. Newton (seal)

91 FOSTER, DANIEL, Dublin, weaver.
        26 Feb. 1714. Full, ¾ p., 30 April 1715.

My wife. Son-in-law James Gilespye, Dublin, wig-maker. Daughter
Elizabeth [Gilespye].   Daughter Sarah, wife of George Saunders.
Granddaughter Martha, daughter of said Sarah.

Pimlico, in Liberties Thomas Court and Donore. Personal estate.

Witnesses : Seneca Hazor, Downpatrick, Co. Down, gent., Hugh
Gilespye, Dublin, gent., David Gilespie of Downpatrick, Co. Down,
gent.

Memorial witnessed by : Tho. Richardson, Hugh Gillespye.

14, 267, 6203.   James Gilespye (seal)

92 WYNNE, Rev. HUGH, Master of Arts, Rector of Aberfraw,
        Anglesey. 7 Jan. 1713. Précis, ½ p., 11 July 1715.

Wife Margaret. Sister Frances Barry. Nephew Henry Barry. Niece
Frances Barry.

Messuages, lands, tenements and hereditaments in counties of
Anglesey and Carnarvon and elsewhere in Great Britain and Ireland.

Witnesses : Richard Edmonds, curate of Aberfraw, John Hughs,
Glanurravan, gent., Richard Price, Aberfraw, all in Co. of Anglesey.

Memorial witnessed by : William Parry, Dublin, gent., David
Lhoyd.

14, 444, 6543.   Margaret Wynne (seal)

93 WEST, THOMAS, Corleagh, parish Mastrim, Co. Longford, gent. 10th June 1713. Précis, ½ p., 26 Aug. 1715.

Wife Mary West. Sons John and George West. Grandson Thomas West. Sons James West and George West, exors.

Camlisk [situation not mentioned]. Corleaghmony, lease from Col. Henry Edgeworth. Lebard, Cranelaghmore, Rining, Lisanore, Aghmody, Curraghbeg, Aghnacretty als. Aghnecroe, Ballanagoshana, Derrycasan, Dran, Glin, and Lisnecearagh, Co. Longford. Millcastle, Co. Westmeath. Ballybreagh and Mulelelish [Mullalelish], Co. Armagh.

Witnesses : James Bradshaw, Killuky, Co. Westmeath, gent., Edmond Dowd and William Rolet, yeomen.

Memorial witnessed by : James Finin, servant to said George West, Will. Parry.

15, 38, 6696   George West (seal)

94 SHAW, PATRICK, British, parish of Killaid, B. of Masereen, Co. Antrim, gent. 5 July 1715. Précis, ½ p., 29 Aug. 1715.

Daughter Mary Shaw (a minor). Her guardians " his father William Shaw of Bush, Patrick Agnew of Killwaughter and his brother John Shaw of Bush." Estate etc. " which his father-in-law William Shaw of Ganway [? Ganaway, Co. Down] Esq., bequeathed by his Will and which he the said Patrick [the testator] purchased from his son John Shaw before his death." Brother John Shaw of Bush. Brother-in-law John Shaw of Glanway. Brother Thomas Shaw. Kinsman William McCullock of Grogan.

His real and personal estate, and purchased in Counties of Down and Antrim.

Witnesses : Francis Iredell, Dublin, gent., Victor Ferguson, Belfast, Co. Antrim, Doctor of Physic, John Crafford, Bush, Co. Antrim, yeoman.

Memorial witnessed by : Victor Ferguson, Rob. Donnaldson.

15, 39, 6698.   Will. Shaw (seal)
                                               W. McCullock (seal)

95 IRVING, ALEXR., Dublin, plumber.

12 Oct. 1709. Précis, ¼ p., 3 Sept. 1715.

Legacies " to his sisters and other relatives and friends." Trustees his loving friends William Burne and Joseph Love both of Dublin, gents.

Winetavern Street, city Dublin.

Witnesses : John Nash, Dublin, distiller, Edward Doyle, Dublin, plumber, John Connell, Dublin, gent.

Memorial witnessed by : John Connell, James Rose.

15, 51, 6717.   Wm. Burne (seal)

96 STRAUGHAN, JAMES, Radufinore, Co. Wicklow.

7 Jan. 1714. Précis, ½ p., 3 Nov. 1715.

Brother William Straughan. Natural son Charles Straughan. £150 divided among his illegitimate children Ann, James, Richard, Bridget and William.

Winifred Kavanagh, his maid. £5 to Archdeacon Neile for preaching his funeral sermon. Exors. : Rt. Hon. Philip Savage, Chancellor of H.M. Court of Exchequer in Ireland, Capt. William Eustace, Cradockstowne, Co. Kildare, Patrick Kavanagh, Dublin. His real and personal estate.

Witnesses : Denis Byrne, Ballybrack, Co. Wicklow, gent., Michael Kavanagh, Ballyedmond, Co. Carlow, farmer, John Fleming, Balymaghrow, Co. Wicklow, farmer.

Memorial witnessed by : Denis Kavanagh, Hen. Buckley.

15, 81, 6841   Patrick Kavanagh (seal)

97 LINDSEY, ANDREW, Drumenan, Co. Donegal.

28 Oct. 1712. Précis, partly in full, ½ p., 14 Nov. 1715.

Wife Margaret Lindsey. Daughter Susanna Lindsey als. Patterson. Son-in-law Robert Patterson.

Freehold land in St. Johnston. Lower Drumenan, Co. Donegal.

Witnesses : John Lindsey, John Cadow, Tullyowen, Co. Donegal, gents., and Henry Solsberry, Maymore, said Co., shoemaker.

Memorial witnessed by : Henry Solsberry, John McClintok, George Luke.

16, 56, 6891   Robert Patterson (seal)
                                            Susanna Patterson (seal)

98 WILSON, ROBERT, Bukcomera, parish of Sego [Seagoe], Co. Armagh. 14 Dec. 1714. Précis, ¾ p., 16 Nov. 1715.
Wife Elizabeth Wilson. Son Robert Wilson. Sons Thomas and Ralph. Daughter Judith. 5/– each to sons William and Francis, daughters Margaret, Ann and Elizabeth. 6/2 each to son John's three children. Brother-in-law Wm. Mathers.
Bukcomra [Bocombra], Parish Sego [Seagoe], and An[n]agh, parish Dromnee [? Drumcree], Co. Armagh.
Witnesses : Thos. Mathers, Lylow, Francis Mathers, Edenderry, deceased, Miles Reilly, Lurgan, and John David, Bukcomra, all in Co. Armagh.
Memorial witnessed by : John David, Richard Robinson.
16, 58, 6894 Robert Wilson (seal)

99 POWELL, CHARLES.
20 Oct. 1715. Précis, ½ p., 12 Dec. 1715.
Wife Elizabeth Powell, her brother William Nelson and his wife Mary Nelson who is sister to testator. His well beloved kinsman James Fenner. Testator's wife, and friend James Agar, Esq., exors.
Corrstown, Davidstown, Cloghpooke and Cloghrank [situation not mentioned]. St. Patrick Street, Kilkenny.
Witnesses : John Davis, Martin Bluette, William Egan, all of city of Kilkenny, gents.
Memorial witnessed by : Robert Wallis, Dublin, John Robinson.
16, 96, 7003 James Fenner (seal)

100 CREICHTON, JOHN, Crum, Co. Fermanagh, Esq.
14 Nov. 1715. Narrate, 2¼ pp., 14 Jan. 1715/16.
All his real estate, land, tenements etc. in Kingdom of Ireland to David Creichton of Lifford, Co. Donegal. Abraham Creichton, eldest son of said David. Sister Mary Creichton. Aunt Mariana Willoughby.
Sir Gustavus Hume, Sir Ralph Gore, Brigadier David Creichton, Hugh Willoughby, Esq., exors. James Hamilton, Brownhall, Esq., his brother Abraham Hamilton.
Witnesses : Robert Hamilton, Robert Richardson, William Armstrong.
Memorial witnessed by : Charles Crenar, Dublin, Tho. Burgh, Abr. Hamilton.
16, 129, 7098 David Creichton (seal)

101 MEREDYTH, HENRY, Newtown, Co. Meath, Esq.
　　27 June 1715. Full, ¾ p., 16 Feb. 1715/16.
　Uncle Arthur Meredyth. Brother Thomas Meredyth. Nephew
Charles, son of said Thomas Meredyth. "My uncle Smithwick's
daughters." Cousins Alice Smithwick, Sarah Smithwick als. Jones,
and Catherine Smithwick.
　William Birch, servant. Lands and tenements in Co. Meath.
　Witnesses : Duncan Cumyng, William Smith, Edward Worth, all
of Dublin, Doctors of Physic.
　Memorial witnessed by : Edward Worth, Will. Barry.
15, 200, 7204.　　　　　　　　　　　　Thos. Meredyth (seal)

102 KELLY, DANIEL, Dublin, gent.
　　14 Dec. 1715. Précis, ⅛ p., 24 March 1715/16.
　Sister Ann Kelly, extx.
　Witnesses : Robert Jenkins, barber, William Graves, joiner,
Patrick Lawles, joiner, all of Dublin.
　Memorial witnessed by : William Graves, Mark Flood.
15, 231, 7334.　　　　　　　　　　　　Ann Kelly (seal)

103 LANGFORD, SIR ARTHUR, Summerhill, Co. Meath, Bart.
　　1 Dec. 1715. Full, 3¾ pp., 9 May 1716.
　To be buried in my chapel at Summerhill. Brother Henry Langford.
Nephew Hercules Rowley. Sister Susanna Langford. Niece Letitia
Lady Viscountess Loftus of Ely. Cousin Susanna Clements and her
children. Cousin Francis McNeale and children. " My cousins William
Jenny and his sister Mary Usher." Children of my cousin Hercules
Burleigh. Cousin Theophilus Burleigh. Cousin Arthur Burleigh and
his children. Cousin Hercules Courtney, Esq., senr., his sons Hercules
and Francis and his four youngest daughters. Cousins Hercules and
Thomas Upton. Cousin Susanna Carey and her four sisters.
　Thomas Upton, Dublin Esq., trustee. Lady O'Neill, former
annuitant. John Curtis, Dublin, Esq. Dr. Duncan Comyng (Cumyng).
Mr. Joseph Boyse. Walter Stephens, Esq. Mrs. Ann Couse. Mr. Cheney.
Mr. Oliver Bomford and Mr. John Charles, tenants. George Dennis
trustee, and his son Arthur. Mr. Benjamin Pratt, trustee. Geo. Granger,
John Fagan and George Baasman, servants.
　Bequests to Presbyterian Meeting Houses in Dublin, and £30 per
annum for ever for a Presbyterian Minister at Summerhill.

The Manors of Killmakevett, Killelaugh, Massareen, Co. Antrim. Ederaowen in Manor Killulta, Co. Antrim. Carnegraney, Barony Ballaliney and other lands in Co. Antrim. Summerhill, Rahainstowne, Baconstown, Ballanderry, Jordanstowne, Ballygortogh, Iffernock, Agher Pallace, Adrams, Baldwinstown, Newtowne, Tobergregan, Adamstowne and other lands in Co. Meath. Merchant's Key, Skipper's Lane, city of Dublin, and lands in the county, city and suburbs of Dublin, and all other real and personal property etc.

Witnesses : William Tyrrell, Minister of Rathmullion, Henry Shields, Ballygortagh, gent., and Benjamin Pratt, Agher Pallace, gent., all in Co. Meath.

Memorial witnessed by : Ja. Wilde, Hen. Buckley.

16, 284, 7505.   Hercules Rowley (seal)

104 DEVEREUX, MABEL als. HINDE, city of Kilkenny, widow.

7 April 1716. Précis, ¼ p., 16 May 1716.

" Her only daur. Frances Hinde and her husband William Hinde of Galway alderman." " Her said son-in-law William Hinde." Niece Anne Carter.

James Myhill, Esq. Rev. Thomas Martin, Minister of St. Mary's Kilkenny. Her real estate.

Witnesses : Anthony Blunt and Samuel Biddock, burgesses, and Charles Byrne, yeoman, all of Kilkenny. Terence Brenan, servant to said William Hinde.

Memorial witnessed by : Thomas Ringwood, clerk to William Barry, Dublin, scrivener. Thos Power.

15, 296, 7535.   Willm. Hinde (seal)

105 RAWDON, BRILLIANA, Dublin, spinster.

21 Aug. 1712. Précis, ¼ p., 17 May 1716.

Father Sir George Rawdon. Uncle late Earl of Conway. Brother Sir Arthur Rawdon. Nephew Sir John Rawdon. Nieces Lady Dorothy Forbes, Lady Jane Champagnie, Isabella Radon [? Rawdon].

Witnesses : Mary, Countess of Granard, Thos. Prior, Dublin, Esq., Anne Clarke, then servant to testator.

Memorial witnessed by : Thomas Prior, Ja. Wilde.

16, 298, 7540.   John Rawdon (seal)

106 HAMILTON, JOHN, Callidon, Co. Tyrone, Esq.
20 Jan. 1713. Narrate, 1 p., 19 May 1716.

His wife, extx. " He hath but one son and one daughter." Daughter Margarett Hamilton. His three sisters Elizabeth Leslie, Agnes and Magdelan.

William, Archbishop of Dublin, Rt. Hon. Saml. Dopping of Dublin, Esq., and Francis Bernard, Dublin, Esq., trustees.

Carranaghs, Co. Armagh, and other lands, tenements and hereditaments.

Witnesses : Saml. Dopping, Dublin, Esq., Rev. Andrew Hamilton, clerk, Thos. Molyneux, Dublin, Doctor of Physic, David Wilson, Dublin, gent.

Memorial witnessed by : Edward Madden, Dublin, gent., Jane Dopping.

16, 304, 7559.   Lucy Hamilton (seal)
                                  the widow and extx.

107 LOWTHER, GEORGE, Kilrue, Co. Meath, Esq.
9 June 1716. Précis, ½ p., 16 June 1717.

Wife Jane Beresford als. Lowther. Son and heir George Lowther. Daughter Nicola Sophia. Second son Marcus Lowther.

Sir Marcus Beresford his brother-in-law, Richard Berford his brother-in-law, and Thomas Forbys, Minister of Dunboyne, exors.

Kilrue, Co. Meath. Glascarn, Tankerstown, Ratoath, both the Greggs, Kilberry, Glans [? Glan Great and Glan Little, Co. Meath], Balrasny [? Baltrasna, Co. Meath], Raystowne, Harlockstown, Dunsoghlin, Cappoge, Newtown, Trim [situation not mentioned, ? Co. Meath]. Fee farm leases in the Co. Cavan, and other real estate.

Witnesses : Dominick Daly, Dublin, gent., James Fanning, Dublin, one of the servants of testator, and John Nowland, servant to Sir Marcus Beresford.

Memorial witnessed by : Matt. Pennefather, Dominick Daly.

15, 334, 7674   Jane Lowther (seal)

108 BUNBURY, BENJAMIN, Killerick, Co. Catherlogh, Esq.
26 Dec. 1715. Précis, 1 p., 21 June 1716.

His father-in-law Edmd. Huband, Dublin, gent. Wife Hester Bunbury. Son Benjamin Bunbury (a minor). His daughters. His brothers Joseph Bunbury, Thos. Bunbury, William Bunbury and Mathew Bunbury. Sister Diana Barnes. Joseph Bunbury, Johnstown, Co. Catherlogh, an exor.

Butlersgrange, Mortarstown, the Glebe lands and other lands of Killimaster, Tythes of Killerick, Kneestown and Mordstown, Co. Catherlogh.

Witnesses : John Bignall, Isaac Spring, James Powell.

Memorial witnessed by : John Bignall, Dublin, gent., Hen. Buckley.

16, 357, 7709   Edmd. Huband (seal)

109 SAVAGE, JOHN, Dublin, merchant.

5 March 1710. Narrate, 1 p., 9 July 1716.

Wife Katherin Savage [? als. Audley or Andley]. Eldest son William and second son Hugh Savage, both minors. Son William Savage to pay £100 to William Savage of Dunturkin, Co. Down. Remainder to Patrick Savage of Portaferry, Co. Antrim "during life of Hugh Savage of Drumrode, gent. paying to James Savage his brother " £5.

Lands, tenements and premises in B. Lecale, Co. Down. Phenix Street, city of Dublin, and personal estate in city and county of Dublin.

Witnesses : Rowland Savage, Portaferry, Co. Down, Esq., William Cochran, Dublin, victualler, Hugh Savage, Drumaroade, Co. Down, gent., James Rogers, Dublin, gent.

Memorial witnessed by : James Rogers, Ja. Wilde.

16, 386, 7784   Wm. Savage (seal)

110 CRAFFORD, WILLIAM, Belfast, Co. Antrim.

22 May 1716. Narrate, 1¾ p., 11 Oct. 1716.

Wife Jenat Crafford. Only son and heir David Crafford. Grandson William Crafford, granddaughter Anne Crafford. Daughter Helenor Haddock, Roger Haddock her husband. Grandson John Haddock. Sister Grisdall McCologh, widow.

George Macartney, Belfast, Co. Antrim, Esq., Rev. Mr. John Kirpatrick, Mr. Robert Donnaldson, attorney, and testator's wife, exors. Robert Stevenson and Hugh Moore, lessees.

Ballybundon, Dromreagh, Killmood, Manor of Florida, Co. Down, Derryleryderey, Co. Down. The Fall of Malone [situation not mentioned].

Witnesses : John Chalmers, Benj. Paterson, merchants, William King, servant to Samuel McClinto[n], innkeeper, all of Belfast.

Memorial witnessed by : John Chalmers, John Jameson.

17, 37, 8105   David Crafford (seal)

111 THORNTON, GEORGE, Finglas, Co. Dublin, Esq.

16 Sept. 1714. Précis, ½ p., 7 Nov. 1716.

Eldest son William Thornton. Son Thomas Thornton.

Baltinglass [situation not mentioned]. A lease from my Lord Shelburne in the Co. of Meath. Church Street, Dublin. Liberties in town of Kildare. He[d]gestown, parish of Lusk, [Co. Dublin].

Witnesses : Henry Taylor, Finglass, dairyman, Richard Joice, servant to said testator, Thomas Rice, Finglass, gent., John Milner, same, mason.

Memorial witnessed by : John Cooke, junr,. Dublin, Thomas Cooke, notary public.

17, 66, 8177   Will Thornton (seal)

112 SADLEIR, THOMAS, Killnelagh, Co. Tipperary, Esq.

28 Oct. 1715. Précis, ¾ p., 13 Nov. 1716.

Second son Charles Sadleir, third son Robert Sadleir. Daughter Bridget Sadleir.

John Boote, Mota, lessee. Michael Walsh, Thady, Mathew and William Cahalane, Daniel and Darby Costelloe, lessees of part of Scryboge.

Cowlebane (Coolebane), Castletown, Glanbowre, Raheene, Ballindeary als. Ballingyder, Gortnamungagh, Mota, Scryboge, Ballyscanlane, Scriboge als. Knockanaleagh, ClonMcGillyduffe, Cavanstown, Brockaghbegg, all in parish of Kilbarrane, B. Lower Ormond, Co. Tipperary.

Witnesses : Daniel Rogers, Ballyknavin, Theophilus Legg, Rodeen, and William Hayes, Dromanure, all in Co. Tipperary, gents.

Memorial witnessed by : Charles Moony, gent., Will. Carroll.

15, 477, 8230   Rob. Sadleir (seal)

113 WALLACE, HUGH, Ballyobikin, Co. Down, gent.

20 June 1716. Précis, ½ p., 29 Nov. 1716.

Wife Beatrix Wallace. Brother-in-law John Hutcheson, Ballyrea, Co. Armagh. Eldest son Alexander Wallace. Son Hans Wallace. Eldest daughter Beatrix Wallace. Daughters Jane and Sarah Wallace. His town and lands of Ballyobikin.

Witnesses : William Alexander, Doctor of Medecine, Belfast, Co. Antrim, Hugh Catherwood, surgeon, Kirkistown, Co. Down, Hugh McWilliam, Ballyrea, Co. Armagh, servant to said John Hutcheson.

Memorial witnessed by : John Brennand, Ardmagh, gent., James Reed.

18, 57, 8333   John Hutcheson (seal)

114 ROBINSON, RICHARD, town of Monaghan, Co. Monaghan.
7 Sept. 1715.   Précis, ¾ p., 1 Dec. 1716.

Wife Anne Robinson. " His father Nicholas Thettford." Brother James Robinson. Son William, daughters Elizabeth and Ann. Brother William deceased. Sisters Catherine, Sarah and Mary.

Mr. Edward Owen, a trustee. John Litle, lessor of testator's house in Monaghan. " Richard Pockrich and John Barlow Esqrs., his father John Forster and his brother-in-law Nicholas Thetford overseers."

His leases etc. Tydawnett or Tyhollan Lands. Dwelling house in Monaghan.

Witnesses : James Hamilton, Dublin, gent., John Wright, same, perukemaker, Ralph Barlow, Aughnamallagh, Co. Monaghan, gent.

Memorial witnessed by : Ralph Barlow, William Scott, John McCall.

18, 58, 8336   James Robinson (seal)

115 YEEDEN (YEEDON), THOMAS, junr.
7 Nov. 1716.   Précis, ½ p., 11 Dec. 1716.

Wife Rebecca Yeeden. Thomas Yeeden, senr. [father]. Uncle Mathew Yeeden. Mary Yeeden, daughter to his uncle Mathew Yeeden. Uncle John Bollingbrooke.

Casper Wills, Esq., and Owen McDermott, Boyle, overseers.

Gortgrossagh, Kinkellew and Lisscahill, B. Boyle, Co. Roscommon. " His father's estate " [situation not mentioned].

Witnesses : Dominick Daly, Dublin, gent. and John Harford and Toby Allcock, Dublin.

Memorial witnessed by : Dominick Daly, Wm. Harford.

18, 73, 8388.   Rebecca Yeeden (seal)

E

116 ˙WESTBY, NICHOLAS, city of Dublin, Esq.
    18 June 1716. Précis, ½ p., 18 Dec. 1716.
"Brother" Joseph Stepney, Abington, Co. Limerick, and Henry
O'Bryan, Stonehall, Co. Clare, exors. All his lands, tenements etc.
    Witnesses : Ambrose Upton, gent., Ambrose Upton, junr., clerk,
and Daniel Grady, gent., all of Dublin, Charles Stepney, Ballgriffin,
Co. Dublin, gent., and Dominick Burke, clerk to Nathaniel Lucas,
Esq.
    Memorial witnessed by : Fras. Duggan, gent., Chas. Melvill.
17, 138, 8417.   Joseph Stepney (seal)

117 HEAD, MICHAEL, city of Waterford, alderman.
    21 May 1709. Précis, ½ p., 22 Dec. 1716.
  Son Thomas Head. Grandson Michael Head. Trustees : Alexander
Alcock, Richard Christmas, John Jackson.
    Lop of Woodstock, Castlemitchell, B. Riban and Nara [Narragh and
Reban], Co. Kildare. Kilbermeaden, Co. Waterford. Farnog, Co.
Kilkenny.
    Witnesses : Thomas Christmas, Waterford, Esq., Rev. Hugh
Bolton, late of said city, clerk, and Thos. Smith of said city, alderman.
    Memorial witnessed by : Thos. Smith, Joseph Cooke.
17, 145, 8431.   A. Alcock (seal)

118 COLE, ROBERT, Ballymackey, Co. Tipperary, Esq.
    29 Sept. 1716. Précis, 1½ p., 22 Jan. 1716/17.
  Wife Mary Cole. Only daughter Jane Cole[1] (exor. with George
Jackson). Nephew Robert Cole. Thomas Cole, junr., second son to
Thos. Cole, senr. the testator's brother. Michael Cole, third son of
said Thos. Cole, senr.
    George Jackson, Knockanglass, Co. Tipperary, gent., a trustee and
exor. Thomas Ottway, Lissenhall, Co. Tipperary, Esq., and William
Woodward, Cloghprior, Co. Tipperary, gent., trustees. Debts due
"by two severall decrees in Chancery obtained by Thos. Whitney,
Esq., and the Lady Anne Cole his wife in their respective lifetimes
both payable on the death of the said Lady Cole."

---

    [1] A lease and release, 12 and 13 Sept. 1718, Bowen to Oliver, recites the
marriage settlement 28 Jan. 1716 between the above Jane Cole and Henry
Bowen. *Registry of Deeds*, Book 38, page 45, No. 23204.

Ballymackey, Knockaneglass, Cappagh East and Cappagh West, Knockane, Pallice, Clagh, Curragheene, Clonalea, Ballyveny als. Ballyheny, in B. Upper Ormond, Co. Tipperary. A mortgage on said estate held by Stephen Ludlow, Esq.

Witnesses : Mansell Andrews, Rath, King's Co., gent., Joseph Jones, Ballymackey, yeoman, then servant to said testator, John Scott, Emell, King's Co., gent.

Memorial witnessed by : John Scott, notary public, Patrick Hogan.

18, 87, 8508.   George Jackson (seal)

119 SIMONS, HENRY, Donegal (signed Henry Symon).

Not dated. Full, 7 lines only. Sworn at Lifford 10 Jan. 1716/17. Registered 6 Feb. 1716.

My wife and my mother. Saunders, Frank, Thomas [? sons]. Stepdaughter Nelly. George Brown, exor.

Witnesses : George Brown, Connor Mulcheran.

Memorial witnessed by : Ralph Walker, Tho. Knox.

17, 219, 8598.   Nelly Heenson [? Steenson] her mark (seal)

120 FORSTER, WALTER, Inner Temple, London, Esq.

28 Feb. 1715. Narrate, ¾ p., 8 March 1716.

Mother Mary Forster of Belfast, widow. Uncle Thomas Dawson, Armagh, Esq. Cousin John Forster senr. of Tullaghon, Co. Monaghan and his eldest son John Forster, junr. Cousin Francis Forster, Kilmore, Co. Monaghan, "eldest son of Long John Forster, gent. as he is commonly called." Trustees : his mother, and Joseph Dawson, Dublin, Robert Maxwell, Falkland, Co. Monaghan, Edward Dixie, Drogheda, Esq.

Freehold estate in Co. Monaghan : Closagh, Edenbrown, Drombeer, Quigl[o]ugh, Mullaghmore, Dromdeske, Coolkill, Aghlemeen, Forvash als. Forvace, and leasehold etc. property in Co. Monaghan and elsewhere.

Witnesses : John Macqueen, Minister of St. Margaret, Dover, John Forster, Dover, gent., Thomas Mallan, London, gent., and Thomas Dawson, Armagh, Esq.

Memorial witnessed by : Thomas Dawson, John Podmore.

18, 177, 8791.   Joshua Dawson (seal)

121 HARTSTONGUE, JOHN, BISHOP OF DERRY.
5 March 1715. Codicil 6 Jan. 1716. Narrate, 2 pp., 8 March 1716.

His wife [Isabella]. His daughter. Nephew Sir Standish Hartstongue. Price Hartstongue, the eldest son, and John the other son of said nephew. Trustees : Hon. Dr. Henry Brydges and Sir Constantine Phipps, Knt. Hartstongue Martin, a legatee.

Lands etc. in Kingdom of Ireland, Wales and Herefordshire. House in city of Waterford. Estate in the County of the city of Kilkenny.

Witnesses : Margaret Jeffreys, London, spinster, George Jeffreys, same, Esq., Cuthbert Dakin, servant to Beata Danvers, Thomas Alderne, Middle Temple, gent., clerk to Sir Constantine Phipps.

Codicil witnessed by : Frances Freeston, Dublin, Thos. Breviter, Dublin, clerk, and said George Jeffreys.

Memorial witnessed by : Francis North, gent., Geo. Jeffreys.
17, 272, 8795.   Isabella Hartstongue (seal)

122 MOUNT ALEXANDER, HUGH EARL OF.
21 Jan. 1716. Full, 2 pp., 23 March 1716.

Brother Henry Montgomery and his son Thomas. Cousin James Montgomery of Rosement and his son William. Cousin Edmundston Montgomery, brother of said James. Cousin Mrs. Jane Shaw and her daughter Sarah Shaw als. Montgomery. Cousin Mr. Justice Caulfield and my very good friend Charles Campbell, Esq., to assist extx.

My faithful servants Mrs. Jane Meredith (extx.) and Mr. John Meredith. James Johnston, mariner, tenant of a house in Donoghadee, John Hepperson, glover, another tenant.

Lands held from the Primate, and from the Bishop of Down [situation not mentioned]. Land in parish of Kilmore. Mount Alexander, and lease of land adjoining, held from Mr. Ross of Portovo. Rent out of Cherryvally " with the Horse Course reserved to me." Privileges etc. of Manor of Cumber als. Mount Alexander. Ballyhays, Ballymony, Carnyhill. Rents of Manor of Donoghadee. House etc. in Dublin.

Witnesses : Patt. Hamilton, Hugh Clement, Alex. Laing and John Meredith.

Memorial witnessed by : Will. Parry, Dublin, gent., John Gregson.
18, 207, 8855.   Jo. Meredith (seal)

123 ASHTON, THOMAS, of Kevan's Street, suburbs of city of
Dublin, glover. 13 Nov. 1716. Codicil, 28 Dec. 1716. Narrate,
½ p., 12 Ap. 1717.

Wife Susanna Ashton. Only son Isaac Ashton. His granddaughter.
Brothers Joseph Fade and Joshua Willcocks, merchants, overseers.

New Row, liberties of Thomas Court and Donore. Glebe in Thomas
Street. Caven Street [Dublin].

Witnesses : John Rea, Kevan Street, smith, Abraham Clarke of
same, gardener, William Alkin of same, gent. Witnesses to codicil :
Said William Alkin, John Roberts, Kevin Street, malster, Isakar
Wilcocks, son of said Joshua Wilcocks.

Memorial witnessed by : Robert Wallis, John Dowdall, clerk to
William Barry, Dublin, scrivener.

18, 238, 8936.   Isaac Ashton (seal)

124 ROTHERY, GEORGE, city of Dublin, mariner.
27 Jan. 1714. Précis, ½ p., 13 April 1717.

Wife Elizabeth. Only son George. Daughter Martha. Houses and
holdings in Dublin.

Witnesses : Moses Cheatham, late clerk to Mr. Thomas Cooke,
public notary in Dublin, Thomas Cooke, junr., clerk to said Thomas
Cooke.

Memorial witnessed by : William Sumner, clerk to Mr. Thomas
Cooke, Thomas Cooke.

18, 239, 8938.   Geo. Rothery (seal)

125 SHEARES, THOMAS, city of Cork, gent.
27 Sept. 1712. Codicil, 22 April 1717. Narrate, 2 pp., 8 May
1717.

Kinsman Henry Sheares, exor. " The children of the several
brothers and sister of his father Humphrey Sheares decd." Aunt
Jane. Aunt Mary Lye. Cousins Charles Newman and Mary Wright.
Kinsman Sheares Olliffe.

Charles Newman, Cork, gent., and Thomas Browne, Cork, apothecary, trustees. Godson Richard Browne (under 10 years). God-
daughter Sheares Browne (under 10 years), daughter of Richard

Browne, junr. of Dundarricke. £20 to Ellinor Sweeny who attended him in his sickness. William Love, Christopher Love. Elizabeth Dickson. Mary Olliffe. Elizabeth Wade. Dorothy Skippon. Thomas Deane, servant. Exor. to build a tomb in St. Peter's Church, Cork. Magolin and Ballyburden als. Burdenstown, B. of Barrets, Co. Cork.   Coundrommy, Caherdagh, Knockshahan, Killmacranoge, Clontikerteen in B. of Muskry. Coolevolty and other lands in B. of Duhallow. Dunscomb's Marsh [Cork].

Witnesses : John and Francis Roche, James Crooke. Witnesses to codicil : William Chartres, junr., Nathaniel Barry, Charles Callaghan.

Memorial witnessed by : Francis Roche, William Chartres, junr., Cha. Whiting, Cha. Callaghan.

18, 270, 9022.   Henry Sheares (seal)

126 LYNCH, PHILIP, formerly of Parish of St. Katherine's, Island of Jamaica, late of Parish of St. James, Westminster, Middlesex.
28 Jan. 1716. Précis, ½ p., 9 May 1717.

Uncle John Ormsby, Dublin, Esq. Nephew Philip Athy, son of his sister Margaret Athy. Nephew John Athy. Brother-in-law Edmond Athy, Esq. Friends Edmond Kelly and Andrew Archdeckne, Esq.,

Newharbour als. Rinvile, Co. Galway.

Witnesses : Rev. Samuel Hawes, city of Westminister, William Stephens of same, brazier, and Mary Stephens his wife.

Memorial witnessed by : William Dick, Thomas Londry.

17, 337, 9037   Jo. Ormsby (seal)

127 PURCELL, RICHARD, Dublin, gent.
22 July 1715. Précis, ¼ p., 20 May 1717.

Wife Anna Maria Purcell als. Carr, daughter to Mrs O'Hara. Brother Toby Purcell.

" His fortune." [No lands mentioned].

Witnesses : Toby Purcell, Susanna Morris, wife of Hon. Col. Richard Morris.

Memorial witnessed by : Susanna Morris, Tho. Merefeild.

17, 366, 9131   Anna Maria Purcell (seal)

128 MADDOCK, JOSEPH, Dublin, linendraper.
21 Nov. 1713. Full, 4½ pp., 27 May 1717.
To be buried among our Friends called Quakers.
Wife Hannah Maddock. Eldest son Joseph Maddock, second son
Abraham, third son Jacob, fourth son Isaac, fifth and youngest son
James Maddock. My four daughters Hannah, Elizabeth, Amy and
Sarah Maddock. Overseers "my three Brothers, viz. Abraham
Fuller, Jacob Fuller, Josebath Madock and my loving Friends Amos
and Abell Strettle."
My trusty and well-beloved friends William Roberts, Cullinswood,
Co. Dublin, gent. and James Forbes, Dublin, merchant, exors. Henry
Russell, lessee of Hodges Town. Charles Lestrange, lessee of Lisniskey.
Abraham Fuller, senr., and George Ramsbottom, lessees of Ballick-
nehee etc. Henry Fisher, lessee of Mason's Farm. £20 to poor Friends
belonging to Dublin Meeting.
Cupidstowne, Cholmondley's Farm als. Bryams Farm, B. of Salt,
Co. Kildare. Hodges Town and Mason's Farm, Co. Kildare, Lisniskey,
Ballicknehee and part of Kilbride, King's Co.
Witnesses : John Smith and William Sumner, clerks to Thos.
Cooke, Dublin, notary public, and said Thos. Cooke.
Memorial witnessed by: William Parry, Dublin, gent., John Gregson.
17, 383, 9190   Joseph Maddock (seal)

129 JONES, THOMAS, Osberstown, Co. Kildare, Esq.
4 July 1714. Précis, partly in full, ¼ p., 28 June 1717.
His wife. Brother Lewis Jones. My estate, lands, tenements and
hereditaments.
Witnesses : Sir Richard Meade, Ballintober, Co. Cork, Bart.,
Wentworth Harman, Dublin, Esq., and William Moreton, Dublin,
Esq.,
Memorial witnessed by : John Moffitt, Dublin, gent., Ralph Leland.
17, 440, 9374   Lew. Jones (seal)

130 DUIGIN, RICHARD, Palmerstown within the Liberties of
the city of Kilkenny, gent. 30 Oct. 1704. Proved (Ossory
will) 27 July 1708. Précis, ½ p., 5 Aug. 1717.
Wife Elizabeth Duigin als. Floyd. Natural son Philip Duigin.
Niece Ellin Aubary als. Bourke.
Irishtown, Kilkenny. Palmerstown and Carrick.

Witnesses : Rev. Giles Clarke, Kilkenny, clerk. Stephen Haycocke, of same, alderman, and William Stanley of same, wigmaker.
Memorial witnessed by : William Dick, Wm. Lyon.
19, 19, 9536   Phil. Duigin (seal)

131 WHITE, ABRAHAM, Dublin, gent.
11 June 1717. Narrate, 1½ p., 10 Aug. 1717.
Wife Ann. His mother. Son Thomas White, second son Abraham, third son William White. Daughter Mary, second daughter Honoria, third daughter Anna, fifth daughter Frances, sixth daughter Elizabeth, daughter Martha Betty Anna Maria. Sister Elizabeth White. " Brother " Paul Howell. Trustees his wife, John Usher, Esq., Doctor of Laws, and Paul Howell, gent.
Land in Co. Kilkenny. Ardrass in B. of Salt, Co. Kildare. Inheritances in city and Liberties of Dublin, leases in Co. Dublin. Tincurry, Co. Wexford. Aghavana and the rest of his concerns in Co. Wicklow. Lands bought from Patr. White in Co. Galway.
Witnesses : Rev. Stafford Lightburn, Dublin, clerk, Moses Cahill, Dublin, surgeon, Elizabeth Piers, wife of Thomas Piers of Commonstown, Co. Westmeath, Esq.
Memorial witnessed by : Francis Glascock, Dublin, gent., Hugh Maguire.
18, 463, 9546   Anna White (seal)

132 OSBORNE, SIR THOMAS, Tickincor, Co. Waterford, Knt.
13 Oct. 1713. Précis, ½ p., 17 Sept. 1717.
Wife Dame Ann Osborne als. Usher. Son Nicholas. Grandson John Osborne.
Edward Hubbart, lessee of Winsland als. Farrinbullin near White Church Rock. Edmond Power, lessee of the lands in B. Glannehiry. William Rony, Widow Gough, Widow Bull, Susanna Cox, John Fling, Joseph Thomas, William Hore of Caraine, Widow Ronane, Wm. Fies, Thomas Morrisy, Morrish Houlighane and Gerald Gibbon, tenants in parish of Dungarvan.
Cullenagh, Coolepeasoone [? Coolnabeasoon], Knockmeale, Barneshangannagh in B. of Glannehiry ; Cooleporsilly, Parknecorry, Clynskie, Parkeirsheal, Clynegonniny and Garrystroppie, Parish

Dungarvan, B. of Decies; Winsland als. Farrinbullin, all in Co. Waterford.

Witnesses : William Browning, Affane, Co. Waterford, Esq., James Usher, Ballintaylor, Co. Waterford, Esq., and Robert Carew, Tickinure, Co. Waterford, gent.

Memorial witnessed by : Peter Molloy, Dublin, gent., Cha. Browne.

20, 63, 9749   Ann Osborne (seal)

133 CROSBIE, DAVID, Ardfert, Co. Kerry, Esq.

30 Aug. 1717. Précis, ¾ p., 28 Sept. 1717.

Son Sir Maurice Crosbie. Son-in-law Maurice FitzGerald, Esq., of Dingle commonly called the Knight of Kerry. Trustees and exors. : Sir Maurice Crosbie, William Crosbie of Tubrid, Co. Kerry, Esq., and Henry Ross of Conigar, Co. Limerick, Esq. Money due from Dennis McGillycuddy of Karnleck, Co. Kerry, gent., a lessee.

Ballymacqueen [situation not mentioned]. Estates in Leinster, Counties of Kerry and King's Co. His freehold and leasehold messuages lands, tenements, etc.

Witnesses : Revd. Francis Lauder, Ballingoun, Co. Kerry, clerk, Thos. Parsons, Darby Lawler and Mary Cullen, all then servants of testator.

Memorial witnessed by : Francis Lauder, Thos. Bindon.

20, 71, 9803   Mau. Crosbie (seal)

134 MOLAND, JOSEPH, Dublin, gent.

27 Aug. 1717. Précis, ½ p., 2 Oct. 1717.

Wife Lettice Moland. Sister Mrs. Elizabeth Richardson. Sister Mrs. Mary Moland. Cousin german Thomas Moland, Dublin, gent. William Alcock, Dublin, Esq., his good friend, an overseer.

Kilmore, Brannagh and Rahine, Co. Kildare, purchased from the late Trustees for the sale of Forfeited Estates in Ireland. All other real and personal estate.

Witnesses : Bartholomew Wybrants, Dublin, gent., Edward Moland of same, apothecary, and John Moland of same, gent.

Memorial witnessed by : Robert Wallis, Dublin, gent., Thos Dixon.

20, 74, 9812   Lettice Moland (seal)

135 HEATH, JOHN, Finglas, Co. Dublin, gent.
   8 Oct. 1715. Full, 1½ p., 7 Oct. 1717.
To be buried in Finglas Church. My well-beloved cousin Mr. Stephen
Heath of London, eldest son of my uncle Mr. Henry Heath. Mary
Heath, sister of said Stephen.
   A rent charge to Elizabeth St. Leger on condition " that she be
bred up and continue a Protestant." My very good friend Mr. Thomas
Hand. James Barry, Esq., Rev. Mr. Thomas Dawson, Elinor Brookes,
Margaret Appleby, legatees. "All my rarities of shells, foreign stones,
medalls and coins " to Trinity College, Dublin. £10 towards a public
well and clock in the town of Finglas.
   Estates in King's Co. Lands etc. in Dublin and in Co. Tipperary.
   Witnesses : John Scott, John Edge late of Finglas, Thomas Cooke,
Dublin, notary public.
   Memorial witnessed by : Thomas Ringwood, clerk to Wm. Barry,
Dublin, scrivener, and Peter Walker.
19, 138, 9840   Stephen Heath (seal)

136 BOLTON, THOMAS, Dublin, gent.
   1 July 1717. Précis, ½ p., 21 Oct. 1717.
His adopted daughter Ann Bolton. His adopted daughter Tamasin
als. Mary Bolton. Brother William Bolton.   Grandson Thomas
Bolton.
   Mary Thompson. Mr. Harvey Sale. Mr. James Ryan. Edmond
Ryan, (residuary legatee).
   His real and personal estate in Ireland and elsewhere.
   Witnesses : William Craford, merchant, Edward Hyland, inn-
keeper, and Edmond Keating, gent., all of Dublin.
   Memorial witnessed by : Edward Hyland, John Gregson.
20, 91, 9886   Edmd. Ryan (seal)

137 BULKELEY, RICHARD, Dublin, brewer.
   23 May 1716. Précis, ¼ p., 22 Oct. 1717.
Nephew John Jones to take name of Bulkeley, exor.
   Witnesses : John Donnellan, Hugh Hall, John Williams, all of Dublin,
gents.
   Memorial witnessed by : John Williams, Robt. Tomlinson.
20, 94, 9905   Jno. Bulkeley (seal)

138 WILCOCKS, JOSHUA, Dublin, merchant.

23 July 1717. Précis, ¾ p., 7 Nov. 1717.

Wife Elizabeth Wilcocks. Brother-in-law Joseph Fade merchant, and Abell Strettell, merchant, both of Dublin, exors. John Hayes, Dublin, merchant, and Thomas Robins of same, merchant, trustees. His real and personal estate.

Witnesses : William McCullagh, Dublin, merchant, Henry Buckley, clerk to Bruen Worthington, Dublin, notary public, and William Barry, Dublin, scrivener.

Memorial witnessed by : John Gregson, clk. to Bruen Worthington, Will. McCullagh.

19, 187, 9945   Jno. Hayes (seal)

139 LUTTRELL, HENRY, Dublin, Esq.

22 Oct. 1717. Précis, ½ p., 9 Nov. 1717.

Wife Elizabeth Jones als. Luttrell. Son Robert Luttrell. Second son Simon Luttrell. Natural son Henry Luttrell. Sister Margaret Luttrell. Niece Barbara Delamar. Nephew Simon Slingsby. Sister Ellis Slingsby. Exors. : Wife Elizabeth Luttrell, Rt. Hon. the Lord Cadogan, Rt. Hon. the Lord Gowran and William Strickland. His real estate.

Witnesses : Henry Segrave, Esq., Nicholas Plunkett, gent. and James Tisdall, Esq , all of Dublin.

Memorial witnessed by : James Tisdall, N. Plunkett, Hen. Segrave.

20, 102, 9956   Barbara Delamar (seal)

140 MEADE, DOMINICK, Tullaheady, Co. Tipperary, Esq.

4 Nov. 1717. Précis, ½ p., 21 Nov. 1717.

Wife Dame Alice Meade als. Aylmer als. Brown, extx. Aunt Margaret Meade. Cousins Elinor and John Meade. His mother [? mother of cousin John Meade].

Rt. Hon. Lord Viscount Mayo, Martin Blake, Coolkeen, Co. Mayo, Esq., trustees. Debts due to George Brown, the Neale, Co. Mayo, Esq., and Cornelius Maghan, Dublin, Esq.

Tullaheady, Garran and Cloncrokin, Co. Tipperary, and his real and personal estate.

Witnesses : James Carroll, gent, and Denis Swiny, gent., both of Dublin, John Crosthwaite of Phoenix Park near Dublin, gent.

Memorial witnessed by : John Crosthwaite, Jo. Browne.

20, 130, 10049   All. Aylmer (seal)

141 SMITH, EDWARD, Clonlough, Co. Monaghan, gent.
6 Aug. 1715.   Narrate, ¾ p., 28 Nov. 1717.
Brother Henry Smith, Dublin, merchant.   Sisters, Kath., Mary,
Sarah and Eliza ; their children.   Children of his sister Houghton als.
Jones.   Aunts Barlow and Smith.   Cousins Mr. John Barlow and Mr.
Henry Evatt.   Rev. John Gill.[1]
   Clonlough, Gortmore, Corcallan, Annamartin, Fogan and Drum-
gariah [? Drumgarve], all in parish Drumsnatt ; Milladoo als. Black-
hill, Coolesalah, Mullabrack, Coolatty, Annya [? Annayalla], and
Machry, in parish Clownish ; Formoyle ; Corn and Gortenagh, in
parish Kilmore :   Corenure in parish Clontibret ; Caranbane als.
Belnekinty, all in B. of Monaghan, Co. Monaghan.
   Witnesses : Rev. John Twigge, John Holmes, John Twigge, junr.
   Memorial witnessed by : John Twigge, clerk, John Christell.
20, 149, 10109   Hen. Smith (seal)

142 BILLOP, KATHERINE, city of Dublin, widow.
29 March 1717.   Précis, ¾ p., 23 Dec. 1717.
   Exors. : Richard Hannah, Dublin, butcher, Michael Jackson,
Patrick Warren.   Patrick Warren, tenant in High Street, Dublin.
Rev. Joseph Boyse's son.   William and James, sons of Michael
Jackson, clothier.   A legacy to her old servant Rebecca Lambert
without the intermedling of her husband.
   Witnesses : Roger Parker, gent., Samuel Cooper, shoemaker, and
John Smith, public notary, all of Dublin.
   Memorial witnessed by : John Smith, Luke Wall.
                                   Patrick Warren (seal)
19, 313, 10250   Michael Jackson (seal)

143 O'BRIEN, SIR DONAT, Dromolan, Co. Clare, Bart.
16 Nov. 1717.   Full, 5¼ p., 21 Jan. 1717/18.
   To be buried in Parish church of Killeenasulagh, Co. Clare.   Son
Lucius O'Brien.   Son Henry O'Brien, and Henry O'Brien, eldest
son of said Henry.   Susanna, wife of said Henry O'Brien testator's
son.   My grandchildren, daughters of Henry O'Brien.   Grandsons :
Edward O'Brien, son of Lucius ; Thomas O'Brien, brother of said

---

[1] Vicar of Drumsnatt 1707–1725.

Edward ; and Donat O'Brien second son of Henry O'Brien. Mary O'Brien, daughter of my brother Teige O'Brien. Appoints guardians for grandchildren Thomas and Ann O'Brien.

Tenants : Conor McDonagh, Barbara McDonagh, widow, Donagh McNemara, Sarah Kindall and her son. Capt. John Davis, lessee of Cahirscoley. Mr. Richard Wilson "who hath for many years served me faithfully " (tenant of Sixmilebridge). Mathew Bryan my old servant. Bridgett McNemara, servant. Martha Kelly. Thomas Amory, Esq. A debt due to Mr. David England from Capt. Charles McDonagh, and a legacy to said David England "for his faithful services." Exors. : Henry O'Brien, Esq., Thos Amory and David England.

£18 per annum for ever, £6 per annum to a teacher to instruct in reading and writing and £12 per annum to 24 boys of Killenasulagh parish and neighbourhood. £10 per annum " for the support of the Horse Race established at Turlaghmore."

Cratelaghkeall, Carrownekelly, Rathfolanbegg, Cahirscoley, Cahirscoby Lysaght, Ballynecraggy, Mughane, Beallaghboy, Knockneskibbole and Gortglass, all in B. Bunratty, Co. Clare. Cahirserkin, Fyenna, Dromsillagh, Cappaghercan, Ballymacravan, Cahiricousane, Mohordenis, Lisigorane, Killcarragh, Ballykeal East, Lacamore, Lackamanagh, Ballykeal West, Ballyhanna East, Ballyhanna West, and Glassnane, all in B. Corcamoroe [Corcomroe], Co. Clare. Coskeam, Rannagh, Mogowhy, Beanroe, Ballymoghney, Poulbane, Ballyconree, Cheshymore [Sheshymore and] Ballyline, all in B. Burren, Co. Clare. Ballynora, South Liberties of city of Cork. Shally Coghlan and Shallyworth, Co. Tipperary. Shanavo als. Knockshanavo, Finish Island, Bealenalicky, Tyronan, Kilkee als. Lisnarrivaghall, Ballaboy, Ballykinnecorra South, Carrowkeale, Cahircorcane, Fanore, Cahircullen, Lisnahow, Scraput, Moyglassmore, Moyglassbegg, Carrunagry, Ballagh, Gorteeniard and Sixmilebridge, all in Co. Clare. Farms of Derrine (Jeremy Thyn, lessee), Rosawly, Sheas Acres in Ballycullina and Cahirserkin, Ballymacdonellbane, Ballykinverga, Ballyroughane, Mogohy, Ballyhumulta and Kiltenane. Castle of Ennis. Ballykilty, Glan, Bealrahin, Clonnegilrine, Ballykinnecorra North, Agherim, Ross, Cullrenemacooge (Mr. Walter Taylor, tenant), farms from Lord Allen, Major William Moore, etc. [situation not mentioned].

Witnesses : John Grady, Collreagh, Co. Clare, Esq., William Carrige and M. McMahon, both of Co. Clare, Doctors of Physic.

Memorial witnessed by : John Grady, Thos. Connor.

19, 366, 10372   Hen. O'Brien (seal)

144 BERRY, WILLIAM, Lieut. Col. of Brig. Wolseley's Regt. of
       Horse. 3 May 1717. Précis, ½ p., 15 Feb. 1717/18.
Wife Mary Berry. Son Richard Berry, Esq.   Granddaughter
Mary Berry. William Plumer, son of his sister Frances Plumer. Trus-
tees : Richard Berry, Esq., Thomas Nesbitt, Esq., and William
Alcock of Dublin. His real and personal estate.
  Witnesses : Arnold Cosbye, Lismore, Co. Cavan, Esq. Jane Nesbitt,
of Lismore, wife of Thomas Nesbitt, Esq., and Katherine Whittle,
Wardenstown, Co. Westmeath, spinster.
  Memorial witnessed by : James Wilde, clerk to Bruen Worthington,
Dublin, notary public, Thomas Gullevan.
19, 449, 10542   Richd. Berry (seal)

145 VAUTEAU, ISAAC, of Dublin.
       4 April 1711. Narrate, ¾ p., 3 March 1717.
Wife Mary Magdelen Vauteau. Eldest son John Jacob Vauteau.
Second son Isaac Vauteau. Son Peter Vauteau.
  Pimlico, Great Ship Street and Little Ship Street in suburbs of
city of Dublin. Mill Street.
  Witnesses : John Smith, John Cooke, clerks to Thos. Cooke,
notary public, Dublin.
  Memorial witnessed by : Christr. Downes, clerk to Thos. Cooke,
Geo. Moore.
20, 291, 10655   Marie M. Vauteau (seal)

146 FARRELL, ANN als. BEERS, wife of James Farrell, Dublin,
       Esq. 19 April 1716. Précis, ½ p., 5 March 1717.
James Farrell (husband), exor.
  Her estate and fortune in Co. of Down and Monaghan, Bally-
makconnachy, Ballynehatty, Ballinvally, Co. Down.   Fawgullier
[? Figullar], Drumcorragh [? Drumcondra, B. Trough, parish Errigal
Trough] and Derrynehinch, Co. Monaghan.
  Witnesses : Shea Farrell and Robert Farrall, both of Dublin.
  Memorial witnessed by : James Gregson, clke. to Bruen Worthing-
ton, notary public, James Wilde.
20, 297, 10675   James Farrell (seal)

147 BROWNE, THOMAS, Cork, gent.
28 Dec. 1713. Narrate, 1 p., 8 March 1717.
Daughter Mary, wife of Hugh Millerd the younger. Grandson
Thomas, son of said Hugh Millerd. Sister Sarah Humpston. Grandson William Kingsmill. Grandson Thomas, son of Edward Browne.

Evan Davis, clerk, tenant in Browne Street. A rent charge formerly granted to St. Peter's Parish, Cork. Brown Street, North East Marsh of Cork.

Witnesses : William Olliffe, Theodore Rheda, merchant, and William Lane, gent., all of Cork city.

Memorial witnessed by : William Olliffe, Ed. Barns.

21, 30, 10695   Hugh Millerd (seal)

148 DILLON, EDMOND, Billogh, parish of Ragharoe, B. Athlone,
Co. Roscommon, gent. 18 July 1708. Full, 1 p., 13 March 1717.
My daughters Winifred, Mary and Bridget (heir).

My beloved friend Mr. Joseph Sproule, Gortmacassaughy, Co. Roscommon, gent., and Garrett Dillon, Athleag, said county, merchant, exors. Lands in Co. Roscommon.

Witnesses : Henry Magawly, Ballynahome, Co. Westmeath, gent., Peter Chamberlain, Maynooth, Co. Kildare, gent., Simon Smith, same, gent.

Memorial witnessed by : John Gregson, clerk to Bruen Worthington, notary public, Dublin, Hen. Buckley.

21, 38, 10714   Bridget Dillon als. Kavanagh
                      her mark (seal)

149 SAUNDERS, ANDERSON, Newtownsaunders, Co. Wicklow,
Esq., 24 Jan. 1717. Narrate, part in full, 1 p., 13 March 1717.
Only son Anderson Saunders. Nephews Richard Saunders, Isaac Dobson, Esq., Morley Saunders, Esq., Robert Saunders Esq., Jeffry Paul, Rathmore, Esq., and Francis Hardy (who is to take name of Saunders if he inherits). Exors. Isaac Dobson, Esq., and Mr. Rowland Bradstock.

Newtownsaunders, and lands in Co. Wicklow. Lands of inheritance in Kingdom of Ireland. Lands in Tipperary.

Witnesses ; Phillip Cooley, Dublin, leather dresser, John Trindale, Dublin, linendraper, and Robert Burrell of same, grocer.

Memorial witnessed by : Robert Burrell, Richard Bouland.

Isa. Dobson (seal)

20, 310, 10715   Rowl. Bradstock (seal)

150 ASHE, ST. GEORGE, BISHOP OF DERRY.

31 Jan. 1717. Full, 1 p., 14 March 1717.

Wife Jane. Son St. George Ashe. Daughter Elizabeth Lady Gore. Son-in-law Sir Ralph Gore and Robert Clements of Dublin, Esq., exors. with Mrs. Jane Ashe.

Rev. Richard Hill of Richmond, legatee. My Mathematical books to the Library of Trinity College, Dublin.

Endrum, King's Co. Ballycullane, Co. Limerick, and other lands in said counties. Two leases of lands in Monaghan and county of Fermanagh.

Witnesses : Rev. Anthony Bury, Finglass, Co. Dublin, clerk, John Singleton, servant to testator, Bruen Worthington, Dublin, notary public.

Memorial witnessed by : Henry Buckley, Dublin, gent., Mathew Hudson.

21, 40, 10718   Jane Ash (seal)

151 MASSEY, SAMUEL, Dublin, Doctor of Physic.

– April 1709. Narrate, ½ p., 7 April 1718.

His wife Ann. Nephews William and Charles Massey. Niece Alice Massey. Sister Mary Wrightson.

Donore, B. Lune, Co. Meath. South Carraghkillbranagh, parish Galbally, B. Clanwilliam, Co. Limerick.

Witnesses : Robert Livesley, Dublin, weaver, Edwd. West of same, pattinmaker, Richard Delamer, Dublin, Esq., and Elizabeth Handcock, Dublin, spinster.

Memorial witnessed by : James Henly, Dublin, gardener, Robt. Livesley.

21, 88, 10837   ·   Ann Livesley (seal)

152 RICHISON, WILLIAM, Dublin.
21 June 1717. Full, ½ p., 21 April 1718.
Wife Margaret Richison. Sons John and Richard. Daughters
Mary Franklin and Sarah. Granddaughter Margaret Franklin.
Cozen Jane.
Houses lately built [situation not mentioned].
Witnesses : Alice Pilkington, Dublin, widow, Alice Brownlow,
wife to James Brownlow, Dublin, gent., and by said James Brownlow.
Memorial witnessed by : James Wilde, clerk to Bruen Worthington,
Dublin, notary public [who swears that he saw John Richison sign
memorial], John Gregson.
21, 102, 10894   John Richardson (seal)

153 SHELLY, JOHN, Dublin, brewer.
13 Aug. 1716. Précis, ½ p., 26 April 1718.
Wife Ann Shelly. Eldest daughter Mary Bonham, wife of Francis
Bonham, Dublin, brewer. Three other daughters Rebecca Raynor,
Anne Butler and Sarah Shelly.
A house purchased from Richard Orson who held it from Sir John
Temple [situation not mentioned]. Mill etc. at Bloody Bridge.
Flagarty meadow etc. an estate held from Henry Lord Baron Barry
of Santry (off St. James Street, Dublin).
Witnesses : James Hewetson, Dublin, gent., Elizabeth, wife of
Patrick Grinley of Dublin, victualler, and Charles Hawkins, servant
to testator.
Memorial witnessed by : James Hewetson, Mary Porchey.
20, 364, 10927   Mary Bonham (seal)

154 DENNISTON (or DENISTON), GEORGE, Dublin, merchant.
20 March 1717. Précis, ½ p., 8 May 1718.
Wife Jane Deniston als. Craig(e). Son William Denniston. £10 to
each of his children. His real and personal estate in North Britain or
Ireland.
Witnesses : Wm. Johnston, lives at Finglass Bridge, Co. Dublin,
Margaret Deniston, one of the daughters of testator, and Barnaby
Rider, testator's servant, now dwells on Ormond Quay, Dublin.
Memorial witnessed by : Barnaby Rider, Eu. Lavery.
20, 404, 11044   Jean Denniston (seal)

F

155   ALCOCK, WILLIAM, Dublin, gent.

12 April 1717. Codicil 16 Jan. 1717.   Full, 2½ pp., 13 May 1718.
" Nephew William Court and his sisters Gillaway."
My brother-in-law Thomas Alcock. My aunt Mrs. Grissell Echlin.
Kinsman Wm. Alcock [? of Waterford].   Kinsmen: Mr. Michael
Moore of Drogheda and his wife ; Richard Leigh of Cullenmore and
his wife Mary ; Robert Haly, Esq., (his late wife Mary) ; Mr. Patrick
Lattin and his wife Jane ; Mr. Simon Alcock and his wife. (Legacies to
such children of these kinsmen as should be living at testator's death).
Niece Ann Robinson, wife of George Robinson of London, coachmaker.
Rev. Alexander Alcock, Waterford. Mary Alcock, daughter of
Robert Alcock late of Tower Royal in Bridge Row, London, deceased.
Mr. Robert Rowan, his wife and daughters. Mrs. Grace Wilson, her
daughter Martha Wilson, and her son Thomas Wilson of the Treasury.
Mr. John Alcock, Kells, Co. Meath, and his wife and children. Charles
Maul, Esq. Mrs. Elizabeth Richards, widow, and her sister Mrs. Aimy
Massy, widow, and her daughter Mrs Alice Benson, wife of George
Benson, and her kinswoman Mrs: Alice Crosse. Mrs. Katherine Lisle.
Mrs. Jane Mitchell, widow of Joseph Mitchell, (tenant in Capel Street).
Mrs Elizabeth Rice, wife of Capt. William Rice of Lt. Gen. Gorges
Regt., Robert Wallis their brother. Major John Dallway, his wife
Jane, and son Lieut. Col. Robt. Dallway, and daughters Jane, Mary
and Katherine Dallway. John Philip Eller and family, his daughter
Anna Maria Eller. Codicil leaves William Leigh, eldest son of Richard
Leigh, Esq., 5/- only, he having married without his parents' consent.

£300 to my poor relations. £100 to Blue Coat Hospital, Dublin.
£10 to poor of every parish in city and suburbs of Dublin, £20 to
St. Mary's Parish. Rev. Dean Frances, Thom. Bourk, Esq., and Charles
Campbell, Esq., to lay out £500 " in erecting a comodious free scoule
for parish of St. Mary's." John Hackett, my coachman. Nicholas
Bryan and Bryan Smith, servants.

Fainstown, B. Talbottstown, Co. Wicklow. Caple Street [Dublin].
The Strand [Dublin] (by death of Joseph Moland, gent., deceased).

Witnesses : Hugh Batho, Phillip Craven and Robert Norman, all
of Dublin, gents. Witnesses to codicil : Elizabeth Morley, spinster,
then living with said Mrs Elizabeth Richards, Alice Cross in above
Will named, Jane Brown, spinster, living with said Mrs. Richards.

Memorial witnessed by : John Gregson, clerk to Bruen Worthington,
Dublin, notary public, Mau. Eustace.

20, 414, 11074   Will. Alcock (seal)

156 CUSACK, ADAM, Rathgar, Co. Dublin, Esq.
31 Dec. 1711. Proved 6 Jan. 1717. Narrate, ½ p., 17 May 1718.

His children not to be left in care of their mother. Brother-in-law Terence Geoghegan, gent. Debts due to Peter Worrall and James Martin. William, Archbishop of Dublin, guardian to children.

Witnesses : Robert Blackall, clerk, James Horan, gent., and William Batter, victualler, all of Dublin.

Memorial witnessed by : William Batter, Ja. Rogers, John Barnwell.
21, 172, 11118   Ter. Geoghegan (seal)

157 DALTON, RICHARD, of Dublin, gent., now residing in parish of St. Andrew, Holborn, in the Co. of Middlesex. 14 Feb. 1717. Narrate, ¾ p., 14 June 1718.

Brother-in-law Bryan Kavanagh. Sister Rose Purcell. Brother-in-law John Burke and Margaret his wife.

Francis North, Dublin, gent., friend and a trustee. Edward and Henry North. A debt due to John Croker, gent. Wm. Swiny Esq., exor. and trustee. Thos. Wise, Esq. John Bourne, London, merchant. Caesar Colclough, Rosegarland, Esq., his son Anthony Colclough. Peter Sexton, Esq.

Brownswood, Brownscastle, Cresoge and Aghnagally, Co. Wexford. Adamstown [? Co. Wexford].

Witnesses : Bryan Stapleton, Dublin, gent., David Duane, London, gent., Joseph Johnson, servant to said Thos. Wise.

Memorial witnessed by : Robert Carew, Shapland Swiney, Bryan Stapleton.
22, 40, 11322   Will. Swiny (seal)

158 HOLMES, MARY, Dublin, spinster.
22 March 1717. Narrate, ½ p., 30 July, 1718.

Father Peter Holmes. Mother Mrs. Bridget Holmes, deceased. Sister Jane Maginis, widow. Nephew Peter Holmes. Sister-in-law Mrs. Lucy Talbott. Dr. Jeremiah Marsh, Dean of Kilmore, her very good friend, exor.

St. Mary's Lane, Oxmantown. Fisher Lane, Bull Lane als. Wolfe Lane, Proper Lane [Dublin].

Witnesses : Eliz. Dowell, Haytor Nugent, and Thomas Thornton,. all of Dublin.

Memorial witnessed by : James Wilde, clerk to Bruen Wothington,. Dublin, notary public, Rich. Burgh.

22, 137, 11621   Jer. Marsh (seal)

159 STOWELL, JOHN, Dublin, gent.

30 June 1718. Narrate, part in full, 1 p. 30 Sept. 1718.

Daughter Mary Stowell. Daughter Alice Stowell als. Cane. Grandsons John Cane and Richard Read.

Mathew Brown, St. Thomas Street, Samuel Taylor, Capell Street, Con. Mathews, New Roe, Hugh Roberts, carpenter, tenants. Edward Rodes, James Briggs, Marcus Lynch, Widow Butler, Mathew Elsmore,. tenants of Galway houses.

Houses and malthouse in St. Thomas Street, Dublin. Capell Street, Strand Street, New Roe, and Ormond Gate, Dublin. The Globe, " Ffahy's House," " The Reddshedd " and other houses in town of Galway.

Witnesses : Hannah Reade, Stonybatter, Co. Dublin, widow, Ellinor Ellwis of same, widow, and Laughlin Dolan, servant to testator.

Memorial witnessed by : Laughlin Dolan, Ed. Challoner.

21, 397, 11935   Mary Stowell (seal)

160 ROGERS, ROBERT, Licotna, County of the city of Cork, Esq.

7 March 1717. Narrate, 3 pp., 6 Nov. 1718.

Sons George, exor., and Christopher Rogers. Cousin Robert Rogers lately of North East Marsh of Cork. Grandsons : Noblet Rogers junr. and George Rogers, junr., sons of Alderman Noblet Rogers ; Robert Rogers, eldest son of Francis Rogers deceased, Corsley Rogers the second son, Francis Rogers the third son, and Richard Rogers the fourth son of Francis Rogers deceased. Nephews Robert and William Rogers, both of Ashgrove, Co. Cork, gents., trustees.

Richard Nason, tenant. Mr. Herbert Love, lessee. Peter Sargent, John Pomfrey, Ald. Edward Brown, Ald. Edward Hoare, Mary Maliburne als. Lumley, Denis Fling, Thomas Baker, Patrick Magh, Denis Morphey, boatman, tenants in parish of St. Mary Shandon, Cork. John Ralph and Thos. Mitchell, tenants in St. Peter's parish, Cork.

Mellefontstowne and Kippane (purchased from late trustees of Forfeitures) and Ballybracke in B. Barrymore, Co. Cork. Rathduff and Glauncaum in B. Barretts, Co. Cork. Houses in parishes of St. Mary Shandon and St. Peter, Cork city. Luotaghmore and Luotuaghbegg [situation not mentioned, ? Lota More, Lota Beg, Co. Cork].

Witnesses : Rev. Cornelius Hignet, Rathconey, County of the city of Cork, clerk, Edmond Barry and Thomas Barry, both of Cork city, scriveners.

Memorial witnessed by : Thomas Barry, Wm. Masters.

21, 438, 12068   George Rogers (seal)

161 MARSH, DR. NARCISSUS, LORD ARCHBISHOP OF ARMAGH PRIMATE AND METROPOLITAN OF ALL IRELAND. 22 Feb. 1711. Codicil, 28 April 1713. Précis, ¾ p., 6 Nov. 1718.

Marmaduke Coghill, Dublin, Esq., Doctor of Law, and Rev. John Stearn, D.D., Dean of St. Patrick's, trustees.

Little Finlaghtown als. Little Finglastown, Creroge, Grangeboyn, B. Deece, Co. Meath. Newtown and Clunbrun als. Clonbrun als. Clonbun, B. Navan, Co. Meath. A garden near St. Peter's Church in Drogheda. Stormonstown, Tulloghkeele, Cloyhanmoyle and Rathcannary, B. Atherdee, Co. Louth.

Witnesses : Rev. Benjamin Huson, Rev. Robert Howard, clerks, John Moland, Dublin, Esq. Witnesses to codicil : Said Benjamin Huson and Robert Howard, and Tristam Filby, Dublin, gent.

Memorial witnessed by : Rev. John Borough, Dublin, clerk, Hugh Smith.

21, 441, 12072.   Marm. Coghill (seal)

162 CUMBY, WILLIAM, Donmoone, Co. Waterford, gent. 18 April 1716. Full, 1 p., 12 Nov. 1718.

To be buried in the church of Killwatermoy. Wife Catherine Cumby. Son Thomas Cumby, exor. Nephew John Russell, Tallow, Co. Waterford.

Donmoone and Templevally [Co. Waterford].

Witnesses : Francis Ffoulke, clerk, Vicar of Parish of Tallow and Killwatermoy, Joseph Huddy of Tallow, gent., John Herdum of Castlemarter, Co. Cork, chandler, and Richard Andrews, Tallow, Esq.

Memorial witnessed by : Joseph Huddy, Robt. Hussey, Edwd. Hayes.

22, 324, 12147   John Russell (seal)

163 McCARTNEY, JOHN, Dromsavage, parish of Mullaghbrack,
Co. Armagh. 21 May 1716. Précis, ½ p., 18 Nov. 1718.
Wife Marrion. Sons James and Hugh McCartney. Lands of
Dromsavage, Co. Armagh.
Witnesses : Thomas Johnston, Armagh town, Daniel Madowell,
Derrynaught, parish of Mullabrack, and Arthur Graham, Bally-
herriland, Co. Armagh.
Memorial witnessed by : Arthur Graham, Jn. Brennand.
21, 483, 12207   James McCartney (seal)

164 SMITH, JOHN, Tullogh, Co. Catherlogh, Esq.
30 July 1716. Précis, ½ p., 22 Nov. 1718.
" His dear mother Rebecca Jones." Wife Elizabeth Smith.
Brother Luke Smith. His real and personal estate.
Witnesses : Wm. McCormuck, drawer at the Walsh's Head, John
Common, perrywigmaker on Cork Hill, Thos. Warren, notary public.
Memorial witnessed by : Thos. Warren, John Wilkinson.
22, 352, 12251   Elizabeth Smith (seal)

165 WITHRINGTON, JOHN, Dublin, Esq.
23 Sept. 1718. Précis, ½ p., 3 Dec. 1718.
His wife. Sister Bennett. Brother-in-law Thos. Gledstanes, Dublin,
merchant, exor. Rt. Hon. Sir Ralph Gore, Chancellor of the Exchequer
in Ireland, and Sir Gustavus Hume, Castlehume, Bart., trustees.
His real estate.
Witnesses : Alexander Nesbitt, Dublin, gent., Andrew Nesbitt his
clerk, John Jolly, servant to the said Thos. Gledstanes.
Memorial witnessed by : Henry Buckley, Dublin, Bruen Worthington, notary public.
22, 382, 12330   Thos. Gledstanes (seal)

166 McCUTCHION, ADAM, Belfast, Co. Antrim, merchant.
3 May 1712. Narrate, ¾ p., 3 Jan. 1718.
His two eldest children Thomas and Jane. Daughters Isabell and
Margaret. Brother James. Brother Robert's children. His sister
Craig, her son Archibald. His brother-in-law Archibald Craig. His
brother-in-law Robert Allen. Joseph Innis and William Stevenson,
two of the trustees.
Bellygrass and Bellytruston, Co. Down.

Witnesses : Rev. Samuel Ross, Londonderry, James White, Belfast, cooper, and John Hamilton, then apprentice to said William Stevenson. Memorial witnessed by : James White, Robert Armstrong.

John Johnston (seal)
his wife Jane Johnston (seal)
als. McCutchion, a legatee
21, 554, 12485   Joseph Innis (seal)

167 ELLIS, THOMAS, Monaghan, Co. Monaghan, gent.
21 Aug. 1717. Full, 1¼ p., 5 Jan. 1718.
To be buried in church of Monaghan. Wife Elizabeth, an exor. 5/- each to sons Robert and Francis Ellis and daughter Elizabeth Spear als. Ellis, having given them their portions. Sons Richard, William, John, Thomas, Henry, Usher, Edward and Samuel, daughter Rebecca, and a child to be born. Mary White deceased, [? wife's daughter].

Henry Richardson, Esq., John Gilmor, Monaghan, merchant and Richard Robinson of same, gent., overseers. Mr. Hector Graham. Mr. Richard Allen, Monaghan, an exor. ·

Lands of Corlea, Pilleady, Killikennagan [situation not mentioned]. Witnesses : Jas. Stennous, John Gilmor, Jo. Wright, Richd. Robinson.

Memorial witnessed by : Norris Thompson, John Gil(l)mor.

Richard Allen (seal)
23, 37, 12495   Eliz. Thompson als. Ellis (seal)

168 BRIDGES, EDWARD, Kinsale, Co. Cork, architect.
2 March 1713. Narrate, ¾ p., 26 Jan. 1718. Died 4 April, 1718. Wife Margt. Bridges. Son Edward Bridges of Cork. merchant, exor. Son Richard Bridges. Daughter-in-law Martha, wife of Richard Harris of Cork, carpenter. Nephew Wm. Bridges, Bandonbridge.

George Bodwin, Kinsale, lessee. 40/- per annum for ever to poor of Kinsale, a sermon to be preached each year in parish church of Kinsale on day of his death. His houses and malt house etc. in Kinsale.

Witnesses : William Bullen, gent., Samuel Irwine, shopkeeper, Henry Hamett, ale seller, all of Kinsale.

Memorial witnessed by : William Bullen, Joseph Bullen.
22, 459, 12579   Edward Bridges (seal)

169 BUTLER, ANTHONY, Ballihalowick, Co. Cork, gent.
21 May 1718. Died June. Précis ½ p., 3 Feb. 1718/19.
Richard Tonson, Munnans, Co. Cork, trustee. James Kingston,
holder of a mortgage. Mr. William Bondler's heirs. Lyly Donovan
my now servant. Rev. Mr. John Hungerford. Samuel FitzJames
Kingston.
Ballihalowick als. Bearnahallo [Co. Cork].
Witnesses : George Wood, Parish of Cahara, Co. Cork, gent., John
Taylor, Kilskughinugh, Co. Cork, farmer, and Timothy Donovan,
Carrigbawn, Co. Cork, farmer.
Memorial witnessed by : Thos. Walton, junr., Kineery, Co. Cork,
gent., E. St. George.
22, 478, 12624   Richd. Tonson (seal)

170 ROE, CHARLES, Ballantaget, parish of Kilmore, Co. Armagh.
23 Feb. 1716. Narrate, ½ p., 17 Feb. 1718.
His wife. His two sons William and Thomas Roe. Daughter Anne,
widow, late wife of Wm. Marcer, deceased. Daughter Mary, wife of
John Workman.
ClonMcKate [Clonmakate], Canonease, Tinilkiney, Aghanelan and
Richmond [? Co. Armagh], Carvily and Rossnaglogh, B. Dartroe,
Co. Monaghan. Faultagh, Aughillagh and Ballantaget [Co. Armagh].
Witnesses : Thomas Lawson, Killmarearty, Co. Meath, gent.,
Thos. Cusins, Clare, gent., Chas. Atkison, Bellanagown, Thomas
Dobson, Mannor of Richmond, weaver and Edwd. Ceany, Ballantagert,
farmer, all in Co. Armagh.
Memorial witnessed by : John Atkinson, Drumeree, Co. Armagh,
gent., Bruen Worthington.
22, 524, 12734   Thos. Roe (seal)

171 COLLEY, SARAH, wife of Henry Colley, Castle Carbery,
Co. Kildare. 7 May 1715. Narrate, ¾ p., 3 March 1718.
Her husband Henry Colley, his son Richard Colley. " Her brothers
John Boswell and Chas. Baldwin," overseers. Her sister Cradock's
children—niece Mary Cradock, niece Jane Cradock, nieces Sarah and
Elinor Cradock and nephew John Cradock. Nephews John Baldwin,
Robert and Alexr. Boswell. Nieces Eliz. Boswell and Mary Carey.
Mr. Gunning and Mr.Weldin, tenants. Mrs. Jane Williams, annuitant.

"The Pyde Horse" and other houses in Winetavern Street. Cook Street [Dublin].

Witnesses: William Ford, founder, George Jeffers, pewterer, both of Dublin, and Thos. Wallace and Charles Tharp, apprentices to said Wm. Ford.

Memorial witnessed by : William Ford, Roger Long.

23, 91, 12803   Jane Cradock als. Russell (seal)

172 MIDLETON, RICHARD, Dublin, tallow chandler.

19 Jan. 1718. Codicil 24 March 1718. Narrate, 1¼ p., 17 April 1719.

Wife Mary Midleton, extx. and son Thomas, exor. Daughter Elizabeth Braddock. Son-in-law Charles Braddock. Brother Joseph Midleton. Brother's daughter Ann Lear.

Christopher Ince, Dublin, tallow chandler, exor. His dwelling house and holding in St. Patrick Street, Dublin, held under the Vicars Chorall of Patricks. Ormonde Street, Dublin.

Witnesses : John Underwood, merchant, Wm. Clacass, carpenter, and John Smith, notary public, all of Dublin. Witnesses to codicil : Thos. Rose, Dublin, tallow-chandler, and said John Smith.

Memorial witnessed by : John Smith, Thos. Rose.

24, 58, 13028   Mary Midleton (seal)

173 BATEMAN, JOHN, Killeen, Co. Kerry, Esq.

25 Aug. 1717. Narrate, 1¾ p., 23 April 1719.

His wife. Eldest son Rowland, second son George, third son Thomas, fourth son John Bateman. Eldest daughter Mary Bateman. Daughter Frances Bateman. "His true and well beloved Bror. Eyre Evans of the Inner Temple, London, Esq.," exor. His wife or Eyre Evans to be guardian of said children during their minority. Father-in-law Col. George Evans, Carassy, Co. Limerick.

Derreen, Ardrivall, Mulleen and Commons of Mulleen and Derreen, [? parish of] O'Brenan, Knockanadine Tyleagh, Farrangalees, Fine-fieragh and Cluontarraffe, all in B. Troughenackny [Trughanacmy], Co. Kerry. Delis in B. Corkaguiny, Co. Kerry. Inchincanner, Kill-sarean, Ballykintawra, Glawnleagh, Knockbegg, Coungillagh, Mills of Cugrigh, Scartaghleny als. Carmaghleeny, Knockhily and Gortacopple, all in B. Troughenackny [Trughanacmy], Co. Kerry.

Witnesses : Nathaniel Evans, Castleroberts, Co. Limerick, gent.,
John Evans, Faningstown, Co. Limerick, gent., Patrick Furnell,
Castleroberts, and Freelove Martin, Killeen.

Memorial witnessed by : John Evans, Nicho. Spierin.

25, 9, 13081   Anne Bateman (seal)
                                    widow of testator

174 EVANS, RALPH, the elder, Dublin, bricklayer.

10 Dec. 1717. Narrate, ¾ p., 2 May 1719.

Wife Joan Evans. Daughters Elizabeth Taylor and Mary Dodd.
Sons John and Ralph Evans. Son Peter Evans . . . "if alive and
come to this Kingdom."

Widow Rhodes, Mr. Berry, Capt. Nevill, Mr. Anjeu, tenants. Mr.
Donnellan. Mr. Claute.

Details his silver etc. in his house in Grafton Street, Dublin. Gt.
Ship Street, King Street, Stephens Street, St. Stephen's Green and a
house called the Black Birds at St. Stephen's Green, William Street,
Dawson Street, Duke Street, a holding at Rathmines, yards in I.H.
Alley near Hawkins Key, the Lime Kiln and all its tackle, holdings in
Baggotrath and Merrion Street [Dublin].

Witnesses : George Wheeler, joiner, Richd. Carroll, Walter Fling,
bricklayer, all of Dublin.

Memorial witnessed by : James Bowden, clke. to Bruen Worthington,
public notary, Hen. Buckley, notary public.

23, 213, 13152   John Evans (seal)

175 MILLS, RICHARD, Dublin, gent.

9 April 1719. Narrate, ½ p., 2 May 1719.

Wife Mrs Bridgett Mills. Grandson Richard Nuttall, son of my
daughter Mary Nuttall als. Mills and her husband Joseph Nuttall.

Simon Anyon, Dublin, gent. and said Joseph Nuttall, exors.
Benjamin Parry, Esq., lessor.

My dwelling house and garden in Turnstile Ally near College Green,
Dublin.

Witnessed : Edwd. Richardson, Esq., Samuel Richardson, gent.,
and Edwd. Challoner, gent., all of Dublin.

Memorial witnessed by : Edwd. Challoner, Sam. Richardson.

23, 214, 13156   Jos. Nuttall (seal)

176 WATKINS, ABRAHAM, Cork, Esq.

12 July 1715. Narrate, 1 p., 4 May 1719.

His married wife Mary Watkins, extx. Daughter Mary Watkins, extx. Daughter Mary Watkins (not to have one penny "if she married with Darby Cartie the fidler "). "Her three sisters." Daughters Ann, Saragh and Amy Watkins. Sons Richard and Abraham Watkins.

KilmcSymon. The Potter's Field near the North Gate of Bandonbridge. The George house within the North Gate.

Witnesses : Daniel Gibbs, gent., Jno. Allin, alderman and Wm. Alwin, gent., all of Cork, who, with the extx. made oath at Cork 22 April 1719 in presence of Jno. Morley (Mayor) and Simon Dring.

Memorial witnessed by : Thos. Barry.

24, 92, 13174   Mary Watkins (seal)

177 FITZGERALD, ROBERT, Lisquinlane, Co. Cork, Esq.

Will not dated. Précis, ½ p., 20 June 1719.

Confirms a settlement dated 29 and 30 April 1715. Nephew Robert, second son of Thomas Uniacke, Esq., of Corkbegge, Maurice, third son of said Thomas.

Lisquinlane and Corkebegg, Co. Cork.

Witnesses : Norman Uniacke, Curraheen, Co. Cork, Doctor of Phisick, David Connell, same, yeoman, Katherine Greehy, Youghall, Co. Cork, spinster.

Memorial witnessed by : Joseph Chearley, Dublin, gent., J. Croker.

23, 296, 13445   Thomas Uniacke (seal)
(as guardian to his said
son   Robt.   Uniacke
being a minor under
the age of 8 years)

178 McDOWELL, JOHN, parish of Mullaghbrack, Co. Armagh.

12 Feb. 1712. Précis ¼ p., 22 June 1719.

Son Daniel McDowell. Son John. Grandson William McDowell. Hugh Grier's children. John Scott, son of Quinsen [Quintin] Scott.

Witnesses : Alex. Ferguson, John Woods and George Williamson (their marks) all of Derrynaght, Co. Armagh.

Memorial witnessed by : John Brennand, Armagh, Co. Armagh, Deb. Brennand.

23, 299, 13458   Daniel McDowell (seal)

179 HUTCHINSON, JAMES, Knockballymeagher, Co. Tipperary.
13 May 1718. Full, 1¾ p., 30 June 1719.

Wife Sarah. Sons James and John Hutchinson, exors. To "my brother David's three daughters viz. Mary Abigall and Martha " £10, £15 to his daughter Rebecka. Cousin Jonathan Hutchinson.

Geashon Boate and Joshua Strangman [Mountmellick] overseers. Will. Fehan, Loughlin Larkan, neighbours. Richard Comins, Connor Breen, Jonnies Herd. George Russell, former lessee. Thos. Borton, lessee. James Hodins, tenant. £10 to Mountmellick Monthly Meeting for poor Friends.

Knockballymeagher, Timoney, Baunmadrom, Ballikelly, turf from Ballikelly Bog, Knockro, Fadarna, Collan and Copolabeg, Co. Tipperary.

Witnesses : John Parr, Killishmeesty, Queen's Co., George Russell, Ballymullin, Queen's Co., Edward Shortell, Knockballymaher, Co. Tipperary, yeoman.

Memorial witnessed by : James Wilde, clerk to Bruen Worthington, Dublin, notary public, Hen. Buckley, notary public.

25, 66, 13532   James Hutchinson (seal)

180 RICHARDS, JOHN, Parke, Co. Wexford, gent.
7 Oct. 1712. Précis, ½ p., 2 Oct. 1719.

Nephew Thos., son of his brother Thos. Richards. Nicholas and Edward, brothers of said Thos. Richards junr. Lands of Sommerstown and Ballyboggan.

Witnesses : Thos. Lonargan, surgeon, James Murray, sadler, and Henry Hatton, gent., all of Wexford.

Memorial witnessed by : George Mosse, Dublin, gent., Tho. Ward.

23, 443, 13993   Thos. Richards (seal)
                                        (junr.)

181 WILLIAMS, JOHN, Drumgare, parish of Se[a]go[e], Co. Armagh,
freeholder. 25 June 1718. Précis, ½ p., 21 Oct. 1719.

Wife Ann. Son William. Land left to testator by his mother, then in possession of Edmd. McKonwell and Thos. Dillworth, in Drumgare. Robt. Cozns and James Toulerton [? Foulerton], exors.

Witnesses : John Toulerton [? Foulerton], Mounraverdy, Co.

Armagh, tanner, John Meckemson, Lagacory, Co. Armagh, weaver
and James Dobson, Drumlee, Co. Tyrone, weaver.
Memorial witnessed by John Toulerton.
24, 385, 14103 Ann Williams (seal)

182 INGOLDSBY, HENRY, Dublin, gent.
12 Oct. 1719. Full. ¾ p., 24 Oct. 1719.
Wife Elizabeth Ingoldsby, extx.
Cloundiralaw, Kilmurry, Clounearkir, Ballyharney, Ballygehir,
Chionrosse, Derrmadaine, Derrinahiky, Dorrigechy in Drounidignis,
Brinvorane, Cross, Ballydumacene als. Corrurage (two thousand acres
in all) in parishes of Kilofeine, Killmurry, Killsidaine, Killmekill, in
B. Cloundirala [Clonderalaw], Co. Clare, and all other real estate.
Witnessed : Jas. Shereby, junr., Dublin, gent., Abraham Pannill,
Dublin, apothecary, Robert Ellis, Terrinure, Co. Dublin, gent.
Memorial witnessed by : John Downing, Dublin, gent., David
Willson (Wilson).
24, 392, 14127 Eliz. Ingoldsby (seal)

183 PERCIVALL, DAVID, Dublin, merchant.
9 May 1718. Précis, ½ p., 26 Oct. 1719.
Wife Elizabeth Percivall. Son Samuel Percivall. Daughters
Martha and Grace.
John Onion and Mrs. Forrest, tenants. Bryan Magleiglan.
Kevin Street, Cappell Street and Cross Lane, near Cappell Street,
Dublin.
Witnesses : Rev. Ralph Darling, Dublin, clke., Thomas Hales,
Marrabone Lane, Liberty of Thomas Court and Donore, Co. Dublin,
hatter, John Smith, public notary.
Memorial witnessed by : John Smith, Thomas Bulkeley.
23, 481, 14130 Eliz. Percivall (seal)

184 SMITH, MATHIAS, Cork city, gent.
10 July 1718. Full, 2 pp., 13 Nov. 1719.
My six grandchildren sons and daughters of my son Mathias Smith
deceased, viz. Mathias Smith, John Smith, Baptist Smith, Jane Smith,
Catherine Smith, Elizabeth Smith. My three grandchildren, son and.

daughters of Nathaniel Harvey deceased, viz. John Harvey, Katherine Harvey, Mary Harvey. Daughter Anne Goss, Anthony Goss her now husband. Granddaughter Elizabeth Goss. Daughter Mary Harvey, extx. Grandson Mathias Smith, son of Baptist Smith, deceased. Sister Elizabeth Patch. Sister Susana Mather.

John Allin, Cork, alderman (a friend), cousin John Sullivan, Cork, gent., and Wm. Oliffe, Cork, shopkeeper, trustees. Mrs. Mary Pennington. Servant Stephen Trustrum, (an apprentice), all brewing utensills etc. My old servant John Morris.

Premises near the South Gate of Cork, Cloverfield, fields at end of Fryer's Walke (being part of the lands of Killeens, South Liberties of Cork), and fee and leasehold lands.

Witnesses : Wm. Chartres, junr., Cornelius Lyne, Thos. Barry.

Memorial witnessed by : Wm. Chartres, junr., Wm. Evans.

23, 515, 14264   Mary Harvey (seal)

185 BAYLY, JOHN, Castlemore, B. Muskery, Co. Cork, Esq.

16 Dec. 1718. Narrate, 2¼ p., 17 Nov. 1719.

To be buried at Movidy. Wife Ann Bayly. Daughter Anne Rye, wife of George Rye, Esq., her eldest son George Rye and her second son Bayly Christopher Rye. His daughters Jane Travers, Mary Shears, Elizabeth Bayly and Margaret Bayly. His sister-in-law Mrs. Jane Walton. His brothers-in-law Thos. Tuckey and Christr. Tuckey. His son-in-law Henry Shears.

" A settlement formerly made by his father payable unto his sister Jane Walton " (rent charge on Castlemore etc. lands). Francis Rogers, Esq., a lessee. John Hawke, servant. Morrice Kennelly.

Castlemore, Cloghduffe, Scart, impropriate tythes and glebe of Kilbonane als. Killbonny, all in B. Muskery, Co. Cork. West Watergate Lane, city of Cork. Knocknanirke East and West, Garrancreagh, Lackereagh and Kilglass, B. Muskery, Co. Cork.

Witnesses : George McCormick, Castlemore, clerk, Henry Sweet, Aharlabegg, Co. Cork, gent., Dennis Donovane, Castlemore, steward to said testator.

Memorial witnessed by : Thos. Barry, Wm. Chartres, and Wm. Chartres, junr.

23, 523, 14296   George Rye (seal)

                           Anne Rye (seal)

186 MAEODAX (MAEODOX), ANNE, city of Cork, spinster.
9 Dec. 1719. Narrate, ¾ D., 21 Nov. 1719.

Brother Joseph Madox. Francis Harrison, Bealgooley, clothier, grandson of Laurence Harrison, late of city of Cork, tanner, deceased. Catherine and Mabel Barber, daughters of Mabel Barber, of Cork, widow. Rev. Henry Maul, clerk, rector of parish of Shandon, Cork, and Richard Daunt of parish of Christ Church, merchant, exors. Legacy to poor of Bandon.

Knocknahowly als. Knockicaulea, and Bealgooley, B. Kinalea, Co. Cork.

Witnesses : James Lamon, Cork, chirurgeon, Richard Dalton of same, " cordwinner " and Andrew Rock of same, gent.

Memorial witnessed by : John Bastard, Thos. Barry, Daniel Crone, Jno. Whiting.

23, 536, 14351. Richd. Daunt (seal)

187 FITZGERALD, ROBERT, Lisquinlane, Co. Cork.
10 June 1718. Précis, ½ p., 10 Dec. 1719.

Nephew Robert, second son of Thos. Uniacke of Corkebegg, Esq., Maurice, third son of said Thomas.

Lisquinlane and Corkebegg, Co. Cork.

Witnesses : Norman Uniacke, Currakeene, Co. Cork, Doctor of Physic, David Connell of same, yeoman, Catherine Greehy, Youghall, Co. Cork, spinster.

Memorial witnessed by : Nathaniel Taylor, New Ross, Co. Wexford, gent., Geo. Sutton.

26, 22, 14518. Thos. Uniacke (seal)
(guardian of said Robert Uniacke being
a minor under age of 8 years)

188 MITCHELBURNE, RICHARD, Dublin, gent.
31 Jan. 1715. Narrate, ½ p., 24 Dec. 1719.

Wife Mary als. Jackson, extx. Sister Mrs. Rachell Sandham. Niece Mrs. Elizabeth Syms. Niece Mrs. Mary Syms. Law. Crow, eldest son of his cozen Jane Crow. Richard Lamb, second son of his cozen William and Anne Lamb. His brother Mitchelburn.

Michael and John Syms, William Crow, Jane Kirby and her

children, Alice Charles, Richard Dickinson, Cornett John Russell, John Osborn (friend) and Sarah his wife, legatees.

Ballyarthur, the two Ballanas [? Ballanagh, Co. Wicklow], Knock-duffe, Ballycullen [? Co. Wicklow], Ballynesragh, Killkashell and Rutland [situation not mentioned ? all in Co. Wicklow].

Witnesses : Richard Vincent, Francis Anderson, Dublin, gents., Francis Armitstead, clerk to said Francis Anderson.

Memorial witnessed by : Francis Anderson, Chris. Inch, Will. Crow.

25, 172, 14626.   Mary Mitchelburne (seal)

189 RILEY, EDWARD, Dublin, Esq.

18 July 1718.   Narrate, 3½ p., 18 Jan. 1719.

Wife Mary Riley. Son James Riley. A former settlement of £20 per annum for maintenance of the then wife of said James the son " whilst she continued his wife and resided in England." Daughter Martha Towers, Anthony Towers her only son. Daughter Anne Vincent. Her eldest son Edward Vincent, her second son Thomas, her third son Spencer and her fourth son Richard Vincent. His brother James. His grandson Richard Nuttall son of his daughter Lucy Nuttall deceased.

Walter Rily [? Riley], Castletown, Co. Meath, gent. Richard Mitchellburne, Ballyarthur, Co. Wicklow, Esq., and John Ormsby, Esq., trustees.

Lands of inheritance in counties Meath, Westmeath and Tipperary : Killeen, Rathmore, Flaghbegg, Fiermore, Killenmoda, Sheashaghinore, Burroskeane and fairs and marketts, Liscantane and bog and commons, and Gatross [? Gaulross] all in Co. Tipperary. Orestown, Killmain-hambegg, Leastowne, Felltown, St. John's Land, Kell, Gardenrath, Syddenrath, Rectorys of Gorly [Girley], and Martry, Tankardstown and tythes, Harlestown, Milltown als. Milestown, Boolish, Donog-patrick, Archerstowne, impropriate tythes etc., all in Co. Meath. Williamstown, Simonstown and Mayne, Co. Westmeath. Ormond Key and High Street, Dublin. Ballymurroghroe, Co. Wicklow.

Witnesses : Rev. James Cunningham, Armagh, clerk, Richard Cunningham, Dublin, merchant, Francis Anderson, Dublin, gent.

Memorial witnessed by : Francis Anderson, J. Stothard.

                                      Ann Vincent (seal)

25, 190, 14709.   Rich. Vincent (seal)

190 WHITEFIELD, ROBERT, Dublin, girdler.
23 Oct. 1718. Précis, ¼ p., 28 Jan. 1719.
Daughter Sarah Billing als. Whitefield, wife of Thomas Billing.
Robert Billing, their eldest son. Grandson Whitefield Billing (since
deceased). His four grandchildren Susanna, Sarah, Whitefield and
William Billing. Brother-in-law John Russell. Cousins Wm.·Westland
and Gabriel Jordan, Dublin, merchants (exors.). Edward Surdeville,
Dublin, alderman and his wife Susanna Surdeville, overseers.
Land in Co. Kerry which he had by his wife [situation not men-
tioned]. St. Mary's Lane, Castle Street and Skinner Roe, Dublin.
Witnesses : Jane Daniel, wife of Henry Daniel, Dublin, goldsmith,
Thomas Ogle, Dublin, merchant, and Samuel Cotton, Dublin, notary
public.
Memorial witnessed by : Samuel Cotton, Will. Devall.
26, 100, 14769. Tho. Billing (seal)

191 BALDWIN, MARY, wife of Charles Baldwin of Dublin, Esq.
25 April 1712. Précis, ¼ p., 11 Feb. 1719.
Her real and personal estate to said Charles Baldwin, exor. Niece
Mary Warren. Her estate in Co. Cork.
Witnesses : Robert Mason, Dublin, alderman, St. George Jackman,
Dublin, gent., an attorney of H.M. Court of King's Bench, and John
Odlum, gent., now an attorney of H.M. Court of Exchequer.
Memorial witnessed by : John Odlum, Wm. Longfield.
27, 11, 14915. Cha. Baldwin (seal)

192 CONNOR, CORNELIUS, Burrow of Brandon [? borough of
Bandon], Co. Cork, gent. 1 Sept. 1719. Narrate, 1¾ p., 27 Feb.
1719/20.
Son Daniel Connor. Grandson William Connor. Grandson Daniel
Connor, exor. Grandson George Connor. Good friend Henry Lumley,
Cork, gent.
Rathcullen, Curraghenebryan, Goganshill, Ballyholine, Coolytooder,
B. Muskery, Co. Cork. Coolfadoe [situation not mentioned].
Witnesses : Daniel Connor, senr., of the Burrough of Bandon,
Esq., James Daniel, Bandon, merchant, and Jervis Dawson, Bandon,
clothier.
Memorial witnessed by : James Daniel, Ed. Barry.
Hen. Lumley (seal)
27, 39, 15069. Dan. Connor, senr. (seal)
G

193 OGLE, SAMUEL, Dublin, Esq.

4 March 1718. Full, ½ p., 4 March 1719.

Wife Ursula Lady Baroness Dowager of Altham. "Having made provision for all my children. . . ."

Lands purchased near estate of his wife. "Lands which I have purchased in Kingdom of Ireland."

Witnesses : Richd. Nutley, Dublin, Esq., Richard Stone, Doctor of Laws and Wm. Bowles, gent., both of Dublin.

Memorial witnessed by : Wm. Bowles, Rowld. Bradstock.

26, 185, 15115.   Ursula Altham (seal)

194 WILDER, MATTHEW, Castlewilder, Co. Longford, Esq.

22 Sept. 1719. Narrate, part in full, 1½ p., 8 March 1719/20.

Sons Stewart, James, Charles, John, and Theaker. Daughters Catherine and Sarah. His real and personal estate.

Witnesses : Francis Isdell, Abbyshroul, Co. Longford, gent., William Moxham, Rasallagh, Co. Longford, gent., and Wm. Moxham of same his son.

Memorial witnessed by : Samuel Ahmuty, Robt. Savage.

27, 59, 15143.   Stewart Wilder (seal)

195 NESBITT, ALBERT, Toberdally, King's Co., Esq.

5 Jan. 1709. Codicil 16 Jan. 1709. Narrate, 2 pp., 29 Mar. 1720.

His kind mother-in-law. His late wife Thomasin deceased. His eldest son James, second son Gifford, third son Duke, his eldest daughter Frances, and daughters Lettice, Hellen, Abigail, Thomasin and Margerett. To sister Ann £16 per annum for life provided she lived with and took care of his said children. His sisters Margarett, Elizabeth, Jane, and Catherine. His brother George. His two brothers William Nesbitt, Esq., Alexr. Nesbitt, gent. and cousin Thomas Nesbitt, gent., trustees. Overseers : Rt. Rev. Simon [? Digby], Lord Bishop of Elphin, Rt. Hon. Lord Chief Baron Rochfort, Wm. Conolly, John Wakely, John Moore, Esq., his brother George Nesbitt, Rev. Mr. Joseph Graves, Mrs. Lettice Loftus, his said sister Ann, Edward Bermingham and Colley Lyons, Esqrs., his brother-in-law John Nesbitt and James Collins. James Mills, tenant. John Eaton, debtor.

Largysallaghe, Ardera, Drumberin, Carrick and Ballydownane [situation not mentioned]. Toberdally, King's Co.

Witnesses : Andrew Calderwood, Dublin, gent., and Anna Calderwood his wife. Alice Nesbitt, Dublin, widow. Witnesses to codicil : Anna Calderwood, Alice Nesbitt and James Collins of King's Co., gent. Memorial witnessed by : Henry Buckley, James Mills.
25, 356, 15293. Alexr. Nesbitt (seal)

196 COOPER, JOHN, Catherlough, merchant.
2 Feb. 1717. Précis, a few lines, 1 June 1720.
Margaret Scooley, daughter to his late wife. His daughter Elizabeth. Rev. Hugh Young, exor. His real and personal estate.
Witnesses : Rev. Hugh Young (since deceased), Edward Purdon, clerk, and Richard Scooley, gent., all of town of Catherlogh.
Memorial witnessed by : James Wilde, clerk to Mr. Bruen Worthington, Dublin, notary public, Jas. Bowden.
29, 16, 15832. Margaret Scooley (seal)

197 POCKRICH, RICHARD, Aughnamallatt, parish of Drumsnatt B. and Co. Monaghan. 22 Dec. 1718. Part in full, ½ p., June 1720.
Eldest son Richard Pockrich. Son Newburgh Pockrich. Daughter Lettice Green. Trustees Brockhill Newburgh, Esq., John Barlow, Esq., and Mr. Henry Green.
Witnesses : Rev. John Gill, clerk, Rector of Killmore, Ralph Barlow, Aughnamallatt and Edward Dancy.
Memorial witnessed by : John Gill, Henry Barlow.
Newburgh Pockrich (seal)
John Barlow (seal)
29, 43, 15917. Henry Green (seal)

198 CORKER, ESTHER, Dublin, widow.
Last day of April 1719. Précis, ½ p., 30 June 1720.
Daughter Ann Corker, exor. Her brother Sir Richard Bellingham deceased. Rev. Dr. John Bolton, Dean of Derry, exor. Mrs. Alice Nelmes [sister].
Dubber, Co. Dublin. Mellifore als. Merrifield, Co. Dublin.
Witnesses : Elinor Taaffe, servant to testator, John Mulys, Dublin, merchant, Bruen Worthington, Dublin, notary public.
Memorial witnessed by : Bruen Worthington, John Mulys.
28, 33, 16095. Ann Corker (seal)

199 ROCHE, EDWARD, Ballynard, Co. Tipperary, gent.
8 May 1712. Narrate, 1 p., 13 Jan. 1720.
Wife Elizabeth Roche als. Butler. Daughter Hanagh McDaniel.
Great granddaughter Margt. Daniel. Daughter Ann Roche. Niece
Ellis Tobin. Granddaughter Bridget Roche . . . "her grandfather
John Tobin." Son David Roche. Brother Morish Roche deceased.
Debts due to Richard Daniel and Michael Tobin. Mathew Jacob,
St. Johnstone, Esq., John Pyke, Woodingstowne, Esq., Doctor James
Roche of Carrigeen and testator's wife, exors.
Ballynard, Ballyvadlea and part of Ballyvadin, Co. Tipperary.
Tallychussane [situation not mentioned].
Witnesses : Wm. Bacon, Garrett Goss, James Daniel, Richard
Daniel of Co. Tipperary, gent.
Memorial witnessed by : James Daniel, Pierce Commen, P. Mackett.
30, 31, 16222.   David Roche (seal)

200 EDGEWORTH, HENRY, Lizard, Co. Longford.
20 Nov. 1718. A codicil not dated. Narrate, 1 p., 3 Sept. 1720.
Wife Elizabeth, guardian of children and extx. Eldest son Henry
Edgeworth (married). "His two younger sons and daughter." His
second son Essex Edgeworth. His third son Robert Edgeworth.
Rt. Rev. Timothy Goodwin, Lord Bishop of Killmore and Ardagh,
and Rev. Essex Edgeworth, trustees and exors. John Smyth,
Esq., exor.
Estate in Co. Cavan and Leitrim. Drumcroe, Drumtanragh, Drum-
gore and Kiltifazy [? Killyfassy], Co. Cavan. Mulligan, Pallismore.
Witnesses : Joseph Logan, gent., Elizabeth Marsh, spinster and
Ellinor Dames, spinster, servants to testator, both of Lizard, Co.
Longford. Witnesses to codicil : said Joseph Logan, Catherine
Jenkins, servant to testator, and said Ellinor Dames.
Memorial witnessed by : Joseph Logan, William Cormick.
30, 97, 16596.   Elizabeth Edgeworth (seal)

201 FORSTER, JOHN, Chief Justice of the Common Pleas in
Ireland. 3 April 1720. Narrate, 1 p., I Oct. 1720.
Mentions settlements made on his first and second marriage. His
wife (then enceinte) guardian of his daughter Mary Forster. His son
Richard Forster. His daughters Ann and Sarah Forster. His daughter

Elizabeth. . . . "if he has no issue male by his present wife." Exors. " his brother the Bishop of Raphoe [Nicholas Forster], his wife and his sister Ann Forster."

Cloghran, Great and Little Forrest, Ballgriffin, Stackole, Dunny-carny [? Co. Dublin]. Kilmore. Lands in the County of Dublin.

Witnesses : John Ker, Dublin, gent., Jas. Walker, servant to testator, Richard Anyon, Swords, Co. Dublin, carpenter.

Memorial witnessed by : Jas. Walker, Cloghran, Co. Dublin, farmer, Jas. Leacock.

27, 233, 16755.   Ann Forster (seal)

202 HUDSON, WILLIAM, city of Dublin, brewer.

15 Dec. 1713. Précis, ½ p., 4 Oct. 1720.

Wife Elizabeth, extx. Brew House, malt house, etc. on Propper Lane, county of the city of Dublin.

Witnesses : James Tobin, Dublin, gent., Thomas Glass, late of same, tailor, John Owens, servant to said Elizabeth Hudson.

Memorial witnessed by : James ᴵ Wilde, clerk to Bruen Worthington, Dublin, notary public, John Brady.

28, 110, 16774.   Eliz. Hudson (seal)

203 KEARNS, REV. JOHN, Dublin, clerk.

30 Nov. 1719. Narrate, ¾ p., 3 Nov. 1720.

Wife Catherine Kearns. Son William Kearns.

Richd. Nuttley, Dublin, Esq., Rev. Nathaniel Hewetson and Rev. Nathaniel Whaley, trustees.

Leixlip, Co. Kildare.

Witnesses : Nicholas Quaytrod, curate of parish of St. Peter's, Dublin, Daniel Byrne, sexton of said parish, John Evans, Dublin, gent.

Memorial witnessed by : John Evans, John Castleton.

27, 277, 16953.   Catherine Kearns (seal)

204 DUFF, GEORGE, city of Dublin, linendraper.

22 Aug. 1720. Précis, ½ p., 3 Nov. 1720.

Wife Dorothy Duff. Brothers-in-law Wm. Boyes and Richard Boyes.

Pill Lane, Mountrath Street, Strand, Dublin.

Witnesses : James Boyes, son of said William Boyes, Thomas Smith, servant to said Dorothy Duff, John Smith, Dublin, notary public.

Memorial witnessed by : James Wilde, clerk to Bruen Worthington, Dublin, notary public, James Bowden.

30, 144, 16954.   Dor. Duff (seal)

205 JEFFCOTT, MATHEW, Tonriegh, parish BallymcElligott, Co.
Kerry, gent. 14 Sept. 1720. Narrate, ¾ p., 26 Nov. 1720.

Wife Mary (then enceinte). Son Thomas. Daughters Mary and Sarah. Exors. his father Robert Jeffcott, Wm. Gennis, Traly, merchant and his brother Thomas Jeffcott.

Tullygarran, a freehold estate.

Witnesses : Edmond Bastable, Co. Kerry, Lucretia Strech, Cork, Thomas Chute, Ballybegg, Co. Kerry, Mary White, Lissoolin, Co. Kerry.

Memorial witnessed by : Lucretia Strch als. Strech, Tho. Church.

29, 281, 17252.   Thomas Jeffcott (seal)

206 BEXTON, WILLIAM, Dublin, victualler.
21 May 1719. Narrate, ½ p., 26 Nov. 1720.

Wife Mary Bexton, exor. "Sister Jane Lewis and her brother Thos. Burne als. Young." His friend Arthur French, Clonequin, Co. Roscommon, Esq., exor.

His dwellinghouse in Grafton Street, Dublin.

Witnesses : Benjamin Slater, tallow chandler, Arthur Bostock, victualler, John Farrell, grocer, all of Dublin.

Memorial witnessed by : John Farrell, John Smith, notary public.

29, 284, 17270.   Mary Bexton (seal)

207 FREND, BENJAMIN, Ballyrehy, King's Co.
23 Jan. 1718. Narrate, 1¼ p., 1 Dec. 1720.

Wife Bridget Frend als. Kynaston. Son John Frend. Son Benjamin Daughter Ann Frend. Daughters Catherine, Hannah and Mary.
" His son and daughter Ogilvie." Granddaughter Bridget Ogilvie.

Uncles Peter Padfield, Thomas Padfield and Edward Padfield. Testator's Aunt Scott. Testator's brother and sister Cuff. "Brother Jonathan Darby and Jonathan his son."

Thos. Tydd, Knockarly, King's Co., gent., and Jon. Scott, Emell, said Co., gent., trustees. Mary, wife of said Thomas Tydd. Ralph Newman, Dennis and Frances Carroll, Godfrey Boate, Esq., Richard Scott, Angell Scott, Jonas Percy, Jon. Baldwin and his wife, Thos. Franck, William Minchin, Esq., Benjamin Talbot and William Talbot his son, Jon. Kent. Esq.

Ballyrehy, King's Co. Rathurd, Donaghmore, Rulagh in the county of the city of Limerick. Boskill, Knockanegh and Temple Michael, Co. Limerick. Gorteenshingane, Clonakenny, Ballynamoe and Lisduff [situation not mentioned]. Woods in King's Co. and Co. Tipperary. £10 to churchwardens of Dunkerrin parish for repair of church, £5 to poor.

Witnesses : Nichol. Morres, Lattragh, Co. Tipperary, gent., Wm. Gabbett, Cahirline, Co. Limerick, Esq., John Dobbs, Ballyrehy, King's Co., yeoman.

Memorial witnessed by Richard Gason, Ballycommon, Co. Tipperary, gent., John Cowley.

31, 11, 17308.   John Scott (seal)

208 SMITH, ROBERT, Dublin, goldsmith.

26 Oct. 1720. Précis, ¼ p., 15 Dec. 1720.

Wife Ann Smith als. Barrett. His three children William, Ann and Mary Smith. Late brother John Smith, his widow Mary Smith (overseer). Thomas Billing, Dublin, jeweller and Thomas Walker of same, goldsmith, exors.

His real and personal estate. Lands in Stackole, Co. Dublin. Cranes on Usher's Key, and one crane in Wine Tavern Street, Dublin.

Witnesses : Patk. Smith, Dublin, watchmaker, Wm. Sumner, Dublin, public notary.

Memorial witnessed by : Will. Sumner, notary public, Wm. Souch.

28, 228, 17412.   William Smith (seal)

209 WHITE, JOHN, Cappagh, Co. Tipperary.

20 Sept. 1718. Narrate, ¾ p., 16 Dec. 1720.

Daughter Rebecca White, extx. Daughter Catherine White. Son

Newport White. Son Richard White. " His brother Deane."
House etc. at Cappagh. Longford, Co. Limerick. His real and
personal estate.

Witnesses : Thomas Deane, late of city of Dublin and now of
Dromore, Co. Cork, Esq., Morgan Hickey late of Toom and now of
Ballintemple, clerk, Thomas Barnes, city of Kilkenny, alderman.

Memorial witnessed by : Thomas Barnes, Richd. Terry.

31, 30, 17419.   Reb. White (seal)

210 PURDON, SIMON, Tenneranna, Co. Clare, Esq.

28 Sept. 1720. Narrate, 2½ pp., 28 Jan. 1720/21.

Wife Helena Purdon. Eldest son George Purdon, settlement 1717
on marriage of said George with Jane Eyre, daughter of Edward
Eyre, Esq. Second son Simon, third son Edward, fourth son William
and fifth son John Purdon. Daughter Margaret Finch. Grandsons
Simon Finch, William Finch and Edward Finch. Daughter Barbara.
Daughter Helena Marie. Daughter Elizabeth.

Tenneranna. Woods of Bielkelly, Carhueny and Cahirballymulrony.

Witnesses : Redmond Barry, Ballyclogh, Co. Cork, Esq., John
Roan, Backfield, Co. Clare, gent., Richard Roan, Backfield, Joseph
Vosar, Tenneranna, Co. Clare, yeoman.

Memorial witnessed by : Joseph Vosar, John Phillips.

28, 283, 17623.   Edwd. Purdon (seal)

211 DELANE, GEORGE, Dublin, glazier.

26 Sept. 1720. Précis, ½ p., 28 Jan. 1720.

Eldest son Denis Delane. Owen Loyd, Croghan, Co. Roscommon,
Esq., Rev. Patrick Delany, senr. Fellow of Trinity College, Dublin,
and William Burne, Dublin, gent., trustees and exors.

His real estate in countries of Roscommon and Galway and elsewhere.

Witnesses : John Rowlatt, servant to testator, William Souch,
clerk to William Sumner, notary public, and said William Sumner.

Memorial witnessed by : William Sumner, Richd. Berkeley.

28, 287, 17632.   Wm. Burne (seal)

212 HODGKINSON, RICHARD, Belfast, Co. Antrim, gent.
24 Jan. 1720. Narrate, ¾ p., 3 Feb. 1720.
Wife Sarah Hodgkinson. Daughter Jean Hodgkinson. Son Richard Hodgkinson. His sister's son Thomas Banks of Belfast.
A holding in Mill Street, Belfast.
Witnesses : Archibald McNeile, Belfast, apothecary, Francis Davenport, Belfast, merchant, Thomas Wilson, apprentice, servant to Mr. McNeile.
Memorial witnessed by : Archibald McNeile, Thos. Wilson.
Thos. Banks (seal)
28, 309, 17713.
Jean Hodgkinson (seal)
daur. of said testator

213 TAYLOR, CHRISTOPHER, Dublin, gent.
29 Dec. 1717. Narrate, 1 p., 17 Feb. 1720.
His wife Anne (then enceinte) an exor. Eldest son Warneford Taylor. His younger children. Samuel Adams, Esq., exor.
Lands in Kilgobbin, Co. Dublin.
Witnesses : Patrick Mitchell, Doctor of Physic, Edward Croker, apothecary, Samuel Cotton, public notary, all of Dublin.
Memorial witnessed by : Capt. Robert Parry, Will Hamilton.
29, 324, 17829.   Anne Taylor (seal)

214 READ, JAMES, Newry, Co. Down, merchant.
17 Feb. 1710. Narrate, 1 p., 25 Feb. 1720.
Son James and said son's wife Isabell Heron. Daughter Jane. Daughter Mary, her husband Thomas Assop, her children. His young daughter Sarah. His sister Margaret. "If his son William come back" a legacy to him. 5/- to son John if he return home.
Nicholas Bagnall, Esq. Robert Murdock and John McMachon, tenants.
Meadow in Co. Armagh belonging to his tenement in town of Newry. Lisdrumliscagh, Dromore, Loughorn, Shin, Corcrickee [situation not mentioned].
Witnesses : Robert Murdock, Robert Gordon, both of Newry, merchants, James McCullan, city of Dublin, schoolmaster.
Memorial witnessed by : James McCullan, John Camak.
27, 481, 17874.   Mary Assop (seal)

215 MAXWELL, ARTHUR, Drumbeg, Co. Down, Esq.
2 Nov. 1720. Codicil 19 Jan. 1720/21. Narrate, 7 pp., 25 Feb. 1720/21.

Wife Anne Maxwell. Sister Margaret Hamilton als. Maxwell, her husband Archbald Hamilton, her sons James Hamilton, Belfast, merchant, Arthur Hamilton, Liverpool, merchant, Archbald Hamilton, then of Rotterdam, and her daughters Mary Hamilton and Ann Hamilton. Grand-nephew Maxwell Hamilton, son of Arthur Hamilton of Liverpool. Niece Katherine Mankin als. Hamilton, James Hamilton her brother, her husband Michael and her son Arthur Mankin.

Sister-in-law Mrs. Elinor Stewart and her daughter Anne Stewart. Niece Anne Stewart of Newry, widow, her son Arthur, her second son Alexander, her third son James, her daughter Katherine Stewart.

Niece Katherine Rainey. Nephew William Rainey, junr., Belfast, merchant (sole exor. and trustee), his sons Arthur, second son John, third son William.

Sister Elizabeth Shaw als. Maxwell. Niece Mary Shaw. Sister Mrs. Helena Dalway als. Shaw. Brother Henry Dalway. Nephew Robert Dalway and his wife and three sisters Betty, Elinor and Leny Dalway. Niece Jane Kenedy als. Maxwell of Londonderry, widow. to " Brother Oliver McCausland of Strabane, Esq., £20 for use of his niece Jane Kennedy of Londonderry."

Person obtaining possession of testator's estate to take name and arms of Maxwell. Hugh Henry, Dublin, Esq., William Rainey, junr., Belfast, trustees. Joseph Marriott, Thomas Street, Dublin. Arthur Maxwell, son to John Maxwell late of Strabane, Patrick Maxwell of Belfast. John Dalway, Dublin, Esq., and his wife.

Other legatees : Isaac McCartney, Esq., Rev. James Killpatrick of Belfast (friend), James Cobham, Broad Island (friend), Robert Rainey, Newry. George Long, Loughbrickland, Michael Bruce, Hollywood (friend). Arthur Maxwell, son to George Maxwell, Laird of Dalswinton near Dumfries in Scotland. Andrew Craford. James Stewart of Kirkdonnald. Alexander Tomkins, Prehenne, Esq., his wife and his mother. Richard Maxwell, Strabane, Esq., and his wife. John Brown, Killileagh. Archibald Edmonstone, Duntreath, Esq., and his lady. Edward Bruce, Esq., Mr. Patrick Bruce and his wife. Rev. James Bruce. £3 per annum stipend to Mr. Patrick Bruce for his two seats in the meeting house of Drumboe so long as he is preacher to that congregation. John Malcom and elders to distribute legacy to poor of Dunmurry congregation.

His leases "in and about Newry." His house called Gray Steele. Drumbegg, Tulligowan and B(a)llicowan.

Witnesses: William McCullogh, Ballydrain, Co. Antrim, gent., Gaven Barr, Tulligowan, Co. Down, farmer; James Stevenson, Drumbeg, farmer, John Gowdy, servant to testator.

Witnesses to codicil: David Donnaldson, Drumbeg, farmer, said Gaven Barr and James Stevenson.

Memorial witnessed by: Gaven Barr, John Ker.

| | H. Henry (seal) |
| 27, 484, 17879. | Jos. Marriott (seal) |

216 RUCKMAN, RICHARD, Corke Street alias Dolphinsbarne Lane in the Manor and Liberty of Thomas Court and Donore and County of Dublin. 1 Nov. 1716. Narrate, ¾ p., 3 May 1721.

Wife Jane Ruckman. Son Richard Ruckman. Daughter Elizabeth Draper. Granddaughter Jane Draper. Daughter Jane Bulkely als. Ruckman. Daughter Anne Adcock, her son Richard.

Richard Pue, Dublin, coffeeman. Mary Price, Philip Walker. James Draper. Jonathan Smithers, tenant.

His house etc. in Cork Street. Maribone Lane and Thomas Court, Roper's Rest Lane [Dublin].

Witnesses: William Dick, William Lyon, then clerks to Samuel Cotton, Dublin, notary public, and said Samuel Cotton.

Memorial witnessed by: Philip Gibson, clerk to Samuel Cotton, Dublin, notary public, Bar. Gordon.

31, 72, 18233. Elizabeth Draper (seal)

217 BELL, EDWARD, Ballyboy, King's Co., tanner.

20 March 1720. Full, 1 p., 6 May 1721.

Son William Bell. Daughter Elizabeth Crafford. Trustees: Rev. Peter Laplacette, Vicar of Fireall, and Mr John Drought of Ballyboy: Katherine Mahan [? Mahon], a faithful servant of mine. "My freeholds." Leather and goods in my tanyard. Garryduffe.

Witnesses: Philip Beranger, Ballyboy, gent., Cornelius Mahon, same, shoemaker, John Hall, Ballycanty, King's Co.

Memorial witnessed by: John Hall, Will. Barry.

28, 440, 18259. John Drought (seal)

218 CATHCART, ALLAN, Enniskillen, Co. Fermanagh, Esq.
  25 Dec. 1705.   Full, ¾ p., 8 May 1721.
  Wife Anna Cathcart. " I also leave with her [testator's wife] what money may be got by the brief relating the burning of Eniskilling in June last."
  Capt. Charles Hamilton (partner).   William Hamilton, attorney. My friend John Fulton.
  Ballychoolrey.[1]   My tan house.
  Witnesses : William Roscrow and Thomas Roscrow, both of Eniskillen, Co. Fermanagh, Charles Hamilton, Belcoo, Co. Fermanagh, gent.
  Memorial witnessed by : Thomas Roscrow, John Cathcart.
  29, 443, 18261.   Anna Cathcart (seal)

219 PEYTON, SIR JOHN, Gt. Britain Street, Dublin, Bart.
  27 Feb. 1719.   Narrate, 1 p., 9 May 1721.
  Wife Rebecca Lady Peyton, extx. Catherine Williams, widow of his late nephew Edward Williams deceased. Said nephews three children. Cousin Hannah Murray, widow, extx.   John Todd, exor.
  Rt. Hon. the Lord Ferrard, tenant, Rt. Hon. Benjamin Parry, tenant, both in Gt. Britain Street. Mr. O'Connor the mathematician, tenant, Caple Street.   Mr. Nevill, tenant.
  His house in Gt. Britain Street, Dublin. Cooke Street, Back Lane, Caple Street and Island Bridge, Dublin. His real and personal estate.
  Witnesses : Robt. Sisson and Samuel McCall, Dublin, Nicholas Daily, Dublin, clerk to said testator.
  Memorial witnessed by : Robt. Sisson, John Todd.
  29, 453, 18303.   Reb. Peyton (seal)

220 BERNARD, THOMAS, Clonmulsk, Co. Catherlogh, Esq.
  25 Feb. 1720.   Narrate, 1¼ p., 19 May 1721.
  Wife Deborah Bernard.   Eldest son Charles Bernard.   Second son Franks Bernard.   Third son Joseph Bernard.   Daughter Ann Bernard.
  " His brothers Joseph Bunbury and Phillip Bernard, Esqrs.". .
  Harry Dungan, Redmond and Daniel Phelan, tenants.

---

[1] An abstract of this will at the *Genealogical Office* gives this place as Ballywhorey and mentions a few legatees not to be found in the will as recorded at the Registry of Deeds.

Ballypic[k]as, Clarbarracum, Bolybegg, Queen's Co. Drumselig, Balliglishine [Ballyglishen, Queen's Co.], Derrifore Bog. Bellclogh. Queen's Co. Ballybar and Clonmulsk, Co. Catherlogh.

Witnesses : William Nesbitt, Catherlogh, clerk, Thomas Doyle, Garryhunden, Co. Catherlogh, mason, Bartholomew Newton, Bushellstowne, Co. Catherlogh, gent.

Memorial witnessed by : Robert Wallis, Dublin, notary public, Isaac Walsh.

Franks Bernard (seal)

31, 128, 18402. Joseph Bernard (seal)

221 KNOX, THOMAS, Lougheaske, Co. Donegal.

15 Sept. 1717. Full, 1¼ p., 1 July 1721.

Cousin Lettice Knox. Sister Lettice Knox als. Short. Sister Elizabeth Knox als. Parke. Thomas Young, son of my sister Katherine Knox. (exor.), . . . her other children. Cousin [? Mrs.] Richard Mansfield . . . her sons Ralph and Francis and her daughters. Uncle Patt. Hamilton, his son George. Charles Knox, natural son of my brother Charles. The reputed child of mine now with sister Parke, £20 to put him to some trade. Cousins Ralph, Francis and Charles Mansfield. Cousin William Hamilton of Killetter. Cousin Ja. Hamilton of Lough McHall and his nephew Archie Hamilton. Cousin Jenny Dixon and her sister Lettice.

Thomas Knox, son of George Knox. George Knox and his brother Andrew. Capt. James Hamilton of Brownhall and his brother Abraham. Mr. Hamilton of Ballinfatter. Major Guy Carleton, his lady, his brother Christopher [Carleton] and sister Irwin [Carleton]. Alex. Murray, Broughton, Esq., " I leave the seneschall's place or office of Broughton's estate to Mr. Wm. Conyngham and his heirs for ever." Creighton Young. The daughter of Mr. Gowan [? McGowan]. The daughter of Mr. Cooper. Alexander Nesbitt, attorney, and Mr. Wybrants (debtors). My good friend Doctor Hamilton. Capt. John McCausland. Oliver Nugent. The son of Mr. Macky. The daughter of Mr Ferguson. The son of Moses Thompson. McGowan and Mrs. McGowan. Tho. Brown and his sister Jenny. Rebecca Knox and Ja. Brown and his son. My servant James Willson. My setting dogs to Mr. Ralph Gore. John Young, Esq., exor. Rev. Dr. And. Hamilton, Oliver McCausland, Esq., and Alexander Nesbitt, attorney, supervisors of will.

Lougheaske, Mannellan [? Co. Donegal]. To be buried at Killimard or elsewhere. Legacy to poor of parishes of Donaghmore and Killimard. Witnesses : Robert Bustard, gent., Henry Gorell and John Woodward, yeoman, all of Lougheask, Co. Donegal.

Memorial witnessed by : Isaac Walsh, Robert Wallis, notary public.

31, 183, 18697. Alexr. Nesbitt (seal)

222 PALMER, FRANCIS, Farron, Co. Mayo, Esq.

3 June 1721. Narrate, 1 p., 4 July 1721.

" Father Roger Palmer, gent. decd." Legacy to Roger Palmer senr. Roger Palmer junr., son of Roger Palmer senr. Testator's wife Charity Palmer als. Annesley. Son Thomas Palmer.

Rt. Hon. Thomas Lord Nugent of Riverstowne, William Nugent, Esq., Egnas Nugent, Esq., and their mother the Lady Nugent, mortgagors. Francis Knox and Arthur Knox, Esqrs.

His estate in counties of Mayo, Sligo, Roscommon, Leitrim and Westmeath, viz. : Castlelackan, Killadvioge [Kildavaroge], Castleduny, Beltra, Knockbogh, Carrow McCullin, Palmerstown, Crossmolina and Mullinmore with the iron works thereon, Iniscoe and other lands, Kellcoulogh, Cloghbrack and Dernine, Gorteneadin, Killderrick, Carrigbarrett, Ballyenelty, Rathmoreenay, Cloonaloghan, Ballynalecka, Killcoe, Runmore, Kellgarruffe, Knockba, Beltrassna, Ummune, rectorial tythes of B. of Gallen, Killdermot and tythes thereof, Stockcela, town and lands of Knox's and Dunamonua, all in Co. Mayo. Ragebb, Knockban, Ardgelly, Co. Sligo. Dungarbey, Co. Leitrim. Rossmore, Donnellane, Co. Roscommon, purchased by him from James Donellan, Esq., and his trustees upon an Irish Act of Parliament. Moyduffe [situation not mentioned].

Witnesses : James Hughes, Richard Wills, Charles [? Cobbe] Lord Bishop of Killalla, Patrick Fargus, Fargus Fargus, James Hughes junr., all of the Co. Mayo, gents.

Memorial witnessed by : James Hughes, senr., James Hughes, junr.

29, 546, 18721 Roger Palmer (seal)

223 STOPFORD, JAMES, Courtown, Co. Wexford, Esq.

23 Feb. 1719. Full, 2 pp., 14 July 1721.

My wife Frances Stopford als. Jones. My eldest son James. My son-in-law Phillip Doyne, Esq., my daughter Elizabeth Stopford

Doyne his present wife. My daughters Anne Stopford and Katherine Stopford. My three younger sons—William, 2nd, Thomas, 3rd, and Joseph Stopford, youngest.

The real estate decended to me from my ancestors. A further estate decended to me.

Witnessed : William White, Ballynatra, Co. Wexford, gent., John McConnell, servant to testator, John Savage, Dublin, gent.

Memorial witnessed by : James Wilde, clerk to Bruen Worthington, Dublin, notary public, Roger Reily.

32, 25, 18788   Phillip Doyne (seal)

224 CLARK, ANDREW, Dublin, gent.

14 Feb. 1720. Full, ¾ p., 18 July 1721.

Sister Catherine Clark, sole extx. Lands of Atherdee, Co. Louth and elsewhere in the kingdom of Ireland.

Witnesses : Eliz. Wilson, Joseph Rous, merchant, Nicholas Anderson, gent., all of Dublin.

Memorial witnessed by : Nichs. Anderson, Isaac Walsh.

31, 217, 18817   Catherine Clark (seal)

225 HUGHES, PETER, Dublin, Esq.

13 March 1718/19. Full, a few lines. 28 July 1721.

Sister Hannah Hughes, extx.

Witnesses : Thomas Clayton, servant to testator, Elizabeth Otwell, servant to Mrs. Sumner, John Thorvin, Dublin, perukemaker.

Memorial witnessed by : Maurice Magrath, Dublin, gent., Letitia Hendren.

32, 41, 18888   Hannagh Hughes (seal)

226 BOYD, JOHN, Rathmore, gent.

25 April 1720. Narrate, ½ p., 11 Aug. 1721.

His wife. Son James Boyd. Daughter Jane. Son-in-law John McDowell. Last daughter Elizabeth Boyd. James Crawford, John McDowell, Alexander Adair, exors.

Freehold estate in the townland of Ballymacklehoile, in B. Massereen. Part lease of Ballyrobert, B. Belfast. Rathmore, Hurkleton [? Hurtletoot in parish of Antrim], Cravery in Dunsilly [situation not mentioned].

Witnesses: Alexander Brown, Moyedom, clke., Josias Ennis, Rathbeg, yeoman, James Craig, Ballynoe, linendraper, all in Co. Antrim.

Memorial witnessed by: Alexr. Brown, Alexr. Hutcheson.

James Crawford (seal)
John McDowell (seal)
32, 56, 18944   Alexander Adair (seal)

227 MORONY, JAMES, Clonmel, merchant.

24 April 1721. Narrate, ¾ p., 11 Aug. 1721.

His father Francis Morony. His mother. His wife Mable Morony, her marriage articles 8 Nov. 1711. His holdings in Clonmel.

Witnesses: James Unacke, Esq., council-at-law, Cappa, Co. Tipperary, John Mandevil, Clonmel, gent., James Morony, junr., Clonmel, merchant.

Memorial witnessed by: John Gough, Youghall, Co. Cork, gent., James White.

32, 56, 18947   Mable Morony (seal)

228 DALY, JOHN, Ballydaly, Co. Kerry, gent.

11 Oct. [? 1721]. Narrate, ½ p., 25 Oct. 1721.

His mother Margaret Leasy. His brother Florence McCarthy, Killquane, Co. Kerry, gent., exor. His nephew James Purcell. His brother Andrew Shehane, Joan his wife and sister of testator. Brother Owen Daly, his wife Margaret Daly. His sister Barbara Daly. Bryan Daly.

Witnesses: Denis Sullivan, Barduff, Owen Moriarty, Lougherbegg, Cornelius Cahill, Killquane, all in Co. Kerry.

Memorial witnessed by: Owen Moriarty, Denis Sullivan.

31, 329, 19327   Florence McCarthy (seal)

229 McDONNELL, JAMES, Kilkee, Co. Clare.

9 May 1714. Narrate, 1 p., 22 Nov. 1721.

Wife Elizabeth. Eldest son Randall, exor. Second son Charles McDonnell, exor. James McDonnell, youngest son. Daughter Mary McDonnell als. Forster.

Nicholas Westby, Esq., exor. Wm. Morgan, Nathaniel Dea, Robert Cahan and John Morony, tenants.

Kilkee, Killmurry, Ballyonane, Corbally, Killdeema, Lisgireen, Lismuse, Forrowermore, Lissheen, Killeroan all in Bs. Moyarta, Clonderalaw and Ibrican, Co. Clare.

Affick, Clonnecullin, Gurrane, Moyasta, Derrybrick and Crossbegg, all in B. of Moyarta and Islands, Co. Clare.

Witnesses : Robert Weeks, Co. Cork, gent., John Dane, Cork, gent., Felix Gallagher, Ennistimon, Co. Clare, gent.

Memorial witnessed by : Felix Gallagher, Will. Devall.

33, 33, 19545   Ch. McDonnell (seal)

230 BARKER, RICHARD, Meath Street, near the city of Dublin,
       gent. 10 Nov. 1721. Narrate, 1 p., 25 Nov. 1721.

His mother Mary Barker, widow, (£10 to buy mourning and defray charge of her journey to her friends in England). Nephew Richard Field. Nephews and nieces, Boyle Field, James Field, Margt. Field, Mary Field. £10 to James Field and his wife.

William Desborough and his wife. Margaret White, Meath Street, daughter to William White lately decd. Charles Viscount Blessinton. Thomas Dwyer, servant. Thomas How, Earl Street, Dublin, merchant, and Joseph Fade of the Glibb in Thomas Street, Dublin, banker, exors.

His dwelling house in Meath Street. Mountkennedy, Co. Wicklow. His real and personal estate. Lands called Three Castles, Co. Wicklow, taken in trust by lease for testator from Charles Viscount Blessinton by George Morgan of Blessington, Co. Wicklow, innkeeper.

Witnesses : Vincent Roe, dyer, Paul Halpin, surgeon, Thos. Merefield, notary public, all of Dublin.

Memorial witnessed by : Thos. Merefield, Si. Weldon.

31, 397, 19577   James Field (seal)

231 STANLEY, MICHAEL, Comminstown, Co. Tipperary, Esq.
       11 March 1719. Narrate, 2 pp., 19 Dec. 1721.

Wife Frances Reade als. Stanley, extx. Eldest son Michael Stanley, being still a minor, had married Margarett Butler, a Papist, without testator's consent. Second son Phillips Stanley. Daughter Ann Stanley, second daughter Elizabeth, third daughter Rose. Uncle

H

Thomas Stanley. Kinsman Henry Prettie, senr. Kingswell Pene-father, Newpark, Co. Tipperary, Esq., and David Low, junr., Fethard, trustees. Col. Richard Buckworth, exor.

Comminstowne, Curraghnody, Killeene and Ballyvanrane, Ballen-cura, Gortnegoona, Monedossane and Killbeg, all in B. Upper Ormond, Co. Tipperary.

Witnesses : Timothy Thomas, Cooper Crafford and Thomas Oldfield, all of Fiermoyle, Co. Tipperary, gents.

Memorial witnessed by : John Scott, Jno. Harrison.

33, 98, 19780　　　　　　　　　　　Hen. Prittie (seal)

232 NUGENT, SARAH, wife of Ridgly Nugent, gent.

26 March 1721. Full ½ p., 17 Jan. 1721/22.

Estate divided into four parts to "Mrs. Anne Graham my daughter-in-law that married to my son Winwood Graham decd. and to my three daughters Anne, Margaret and Sarah Graham." William Smyth, Esq., exor.

Kinafadd and Tycross, being part of Lenamacagh, King's Co.

Witnesses : Philip Reyly, gent., Francis Betagh, perrywiggmaker, Philip Reilly, gent., all of Dublin.

Memorial witnessed by : Philip Reilly, Magdelen Griffith.

33, 126, 19866　　　　　　　　　　Anne Graham (seal)

233 NUGENT, RIDGLY, Dublin, Esq.,

16 Feb. 1720. Narrate, ½ p., 18 Jan. 1721.

Wife Sarah Nugent. Daughter-in-law Anne Graham als. Paddon. His eldest daughter Anne Graham, his second daughter Margaret Graham, his third daughter Sarah Graham. His cousin William Smyth, Lyssen Hall, Co. Dublin, Esq., exor. To his servant Philip Reilly £150 in lieu of all his faithful services for several years past. His real and personal estate.

Witnesses : Andrew Caldwell, Michael Teeling, Philip Reilly, all of Dublin, gents.

Memorial witnessed by : Walter Bullin, servant to said William Smyth, John Canhan.

33, 129, 19873　　　　　　　　　　Wm. Smyth (seal)

234 SCOTT, WILLIAM, Annahagh, in barony and County Monaghan, gent. Not dated. Précis, ½ p., 26 Jan. 1721.

Eldest son John Scott. Aghavoill, Co. Leitrim, settled on testator at the intermarriage of his mother Mary Scott with Cornet Edward Forster.

Witnesses : Jos. Greer, Annahagh, weaver, John Own [? Owen], Killmore, gent., Henry Owen, Killmore, Co. Meath, gent.

Memorial witnessed by : Bruen Worthington, Dublin, notary public, Francis Forster, Quigillagh, Co. Monaghan, gent.

32, 337, 19893   John Scott (seal)

235 PALMER, ENOCH, Dublin, founder.

2 Jan. 1721. Narrate, 1 p., 29 Jan. 1721.

His father William Palmer. Brother Samuel Palmer. His three nieces Sarah Boyton, Mary Jackson and Elizabeth Makings. Michael Jackson husband of said Mary Jackson, and her four children. Nephew Enoch Makings. Cousin Josias Jones and his wife, two sons and daughter. Exors. said Michael Jackson and Michaell Boyton of Dublin, feltmaker.

Mr. Meredith and Peter Cillard, tenants. Ambrose Bruff. Premises in Mary's Abby and Mary's Lane, Dublin.

Witnesses : James Clark, innkeeper, Samuel Oates, grocer, John Smith, public notary, all of Dublin.

Memorial witnessed by : John Smith, and Alexr. McPherson, clerk to said John Smith.

                                                    Michael Jackson (seal)

32, 347, 19927   Michaell Boyton (seal)

236 PRATT, DR. BENJAMIN, Dean of Down.

In Dec. 1721. Narrate, ¾ p., 3 Feb. 1721/22.

His late father Joseph Pratt, Esq., deceased. His wife Lady Phillippa Hamilton als. Pratt, and his brother John Pratt, Esq., exors. Cousin Benjamin Pratt, Augher Pallice, Co. Meath, Esq., Nephew Thomas Pratt.

His estate in Co. Tyrone and Co. Cavan. Killmurry, Bellewstown, Davidstown and Ballintogher, Co. Meath.

Witnesses : James Bowden, Thomas Fitzgerald, James Wilde, all clerks to Bruen Worthington, public notary in Dublin.

Memorial witnessed by : Daniel Reading, Dublin, Esq., Henry Waters, servant to the Lady Phillippa Pratt.
31, 465, 19976   Philippa Pratt (seal)

237 WORTH, WILLIAM, Dublin, Esq.

20 Oct. 1719. Codicil 24 March 1719. Full, 3 pp., 26 Feb. 1721[1]

My late wife Lucy Lady Bulkley, Sir Richard Bulkley her former husband. Eldest son and heir Edward Worth, Esq. Second son James Tynte als. Worth, (estates given to said James by his uncle Henry Tynte, Esq.). To sons' wives £50 apiece. £20 to each of my grandchildren. Daughter Dorothy Worth. Edward Worth my eldest son, Doctor Edward Worth and Silvester Cross, Esq., my nephews, trustees.

Lawrence Sweet, tenant. Henry Parren. Mortgage on Dunbell due to John Smith. Samuel Barry. Dr. Christopher Loyd. Roger Anderson, my trusty servant. Cash notes I shall have at the time of my decease from Sir Alexander Cairnes, Hugh Henry, Esq., Alderman Burton and Francis Harrison, Esq. The hospital built by my father near the Dock of Kinsale.

Dunbell, Co. Kilkenny. My house in Au[n]gier Street, Dublin. Old Bawn [? Dublin]. My son Tynte's house in Dawson Street, Dublin. [House at] Rathfarnham, lands in Co. Cork, real and personal estate in principality of Wales or Kingdom of England.

Witnesses to will and codicil : John Ussher, Esq., John Moffitt, gent. both of Dublin, Garet English, servant to testator.

Memorial witnessed by : John Evans, Dublin, gent., John Moffitt.
33, 214, 20133   E. Worth (seal)

238 ROGERS, GEORGE, Lota, Co. Cork, Esq.

22 Jan. 1721. Narrate, 1¼ p., 3 March, 1721.

Wife Hannah Rogers, extx., to be guardian of daughters. His father Robert Rogers (will dated 7 March 1717). Daughters Elizabeth and Jane. Brother Christopher Rogers and John Hawkins to be guardians of daughters if testator's wife should die before daughters of age.

Widow Eliott, Mary Osburne, Mary Wilson. £30 to Trustees of the Green Coat Hospital for the use of the scholars.

---

[1]. See abstract 648.

Lotamore. Lands settled on him by marriage. Farrenverdownig als. Verdons Land, and Lackentubbermurry.

Witnesses: Hannah Hawkins, Mary Daviceau, Quint. Osborne, city of Cork, chirurgeon.

Memorial witnessed by: Quintin Osburne, James Weekes.

33, 228, 20162.   Hannah Rogers (seal)

239 TILSON, THOMAS, the elder, Dublin, Esq.

8 Nov. 1718. Narrate, ½ p., 15 March 1721.

Son Thomas Tilson, exor.

Island Bridge, Co. Dublin. Kilcock, Ernhill als. Fronhills, Borotlea als. Newtown, in B. Ophalia, Sherlockstown and Downings, Co. Kildare. Piercetown, Burresleigh als. Garrans, Rathmanagh in B. Eliogarty, Co. Tipperary.

Witnesses: Richd. Fenner, William Westbury, John Dunbar Bate, gent. and Samuel Cotton, notary public, Dublin.

Memorial witnessed by: Wm. Devall, James Bowden and Thomas Fitzgerald, all clerks to Bruen Worthington, notary public in Dublin.

31, 518, 20254   Thos. Tilson (seal)

240 THOMPSON, JOHN, Dublin, carpenter.

6 June 1721. Précis, ½ p., 16 March 1721/22.

Granddaughter Jane Orde, her present husband. Thomasin Mossop als. Thompson. My sister's son John Griffin. Simon Anyon, Dublin, gent., and Richard Whitmore, of same, merchant, trustees. Houses in Fleet Street, suburbs of city of Dublin.

Witnesses: John Broadhurst, Dublin, tailor, Miles Hosty, merchant, Samuel Cotton, Dublin, notary public.

Memorial witnessed by: John Broadhurst, Edward Challoner, Dublin, gent.

34, 20, 20257   Si. Anyon (seal)

241 TYRRELL, MAURICE, Kildangan, Co. Meath, gent.

17 Feb. 1721. Narrate, 1 p., 6 April 1722.

Brother Edmond Tyrrell, Comminstown, Co. Westmeath, gent. The children of his brother William Tyrrell and their mother Elizabeth Tyrrell. His brother Duke Tyrrell. Cousin George Tyrrell. His servant Elizabeth Gemon.

Knockanegowly, Garugh, Clonduff, Oldtowne, Cardinstown als. Ballycare in Knockabrow, Kildangan, and Ballydonnell. His farm of Stonehouse, Thomas Giffard, Esq., [? lessee].

Witnesses : John Tyrrell and William Tyrrell, Dublin, gents. and Garrett Tyrrell, Mullingar, Co. Westmeath, gent.

Memorial witnessed by : John Tyrrell, Richard Nelson, Dublin, gent.

34, 34, 20346   Ed. Tyrrell (seal)

242 MONTGOMERY, ALEXANDER, Ballileek, Co. Monaghan. 29 Aug. 1721. Codicil 24 March 1721. Full, 7½ pp., 18 April 1722.

My eldest son Thomas, undutiful and disobedient. Sons John, Alexander, Robert, Mathew and Hugh. Daughters Dorcas Irvine, Elizabeth and Sarah. My sons-in-law Christopher Irvine and John Montray [? Moutray]. My nephew Alexander Montgomery, son of my brother Robert Montgomery.

James Montgomery, a child now living at Mrs. James Grant's. Ann Montgomery, a child now living with Margaret Dunbar. To my servant Margaret Mulluys [? Mullins] £24 per annum. The wife of Alexander Nesbitt. My godson Alexander Nesbitt, junr., son of said Alexander. My loving friends John Corry, Castlecoale, Co. Fermanagh, Esq., Casper Wills, Clunagh, Co. Roscommon, Esq., my nephew Col. Alexander Montgomery, Robert Montgomery, Annarea, Esq., George Lesslie, Clownish, Co. Monaghan, clerk, Alexander Nesbitt, Dublin, gent., exors., trustees and guardians of said children. £10 to poor of parish of Kilmore.

Lisillie, Camlogh, Lisnisk, Brandrim, Feermaidnan, Drumquill, Clunaveran, Drumaclun, Kilnacleigh, Crumlin, Cornaglare, Killibritt, Tullenarny, Tullygillan, Crosses, Teerfeenoge, Aghantavin, Rae, Aghaboy als. Taghaboy, Lisserilly, Tatnegall, Drumquilly, Edegeish, Drumleick, Aghadrumerclim, Drumbarrow, Drumullin, Tonary, Rediry, Billis, Mulladuffe, Mullabane, Aghalogans, Cavan, Chinicky, Tonnygarcy, Skinagin, Balldarug, Drumdaghin, Gartackeechan, Killcosher, Killeleen, Lissnagonery, Glasslough, tenement and park in Monaghan, the six church land tates of Killmore, Killivan, Kelvy and Kellibegg (held by lease from Rev. Dean Lesslie), Leck als. Leek, all in Co. Monaghan.   Kileran, Ballyirk, Lisseene, Cooleeny, Lissdonnally,

Gorthana and Anfield, Co. Tipperary. Drinidaly, Co. Meath. Tenement in Cavan, Co. Cavan. Tenement near Liffer, called John Irwin's tenement and Park, Co. Donegal. Shanco, Cleenbeynagh, Malick, Cloodeharrow, Fearbecky als. Feerbrecky, Lecarrow als. Gartlachan, Arnemullagh. Clausabane, Coylemore als. Keilmore, Cloonehelty, Taghnarrow, Cloo[n]fower, Durow, Arneskin, Ballynefinegan, Gortnemaddin in Ballyfinigan, Cloonagh, Mungagh, Corganasse, Ballywollaghan, Carballas, Cleenherrin, all in Co. Roscommon.

Witnesses to will : John Gill, clerk, rector of parish of Kilmore, Co. Monaghan, Baptist Johnston, Tully, said county, gent., Archibald Moore, town of Monaghan, apothecary, Edward Maine, Kilmore, gent.

Witnesses to codicil : James Irvin, Iniskilling, Co. Fermanagh, doctor of physic, said Archibald Moore, Thomas Cole, servant to testator.

Memorial witnessed by : Will. Devall, James Bowden, clerks to Bruen Worthington, Dublin, notary public.

33, 324, 20464   Alexr. Nesbitt (seal)

243 WILEMAN, THOMAS, Skeagh, parish Drumsnatt, barony and county Monaghan, Esq. 6 March 1721, Narrate, part in full, 1 p., 26 April 1722.

Nephew Ralph Wileman, John Wileman his eldest son, Parnwell Wileman his eldest daughter, Lettice Wileman second daughter and Thomas Wileman second son of said Ralph. £2 per annum for life to " Jane McCamis " wife to the said Ralph Wileman " if she leav's [? outlives] the said Ralph after my decease."

Thomas Wileman, son of Catrine Bradey of Coolsallagh, Co. Monaghan. Henry Clarke, his two youngest sisters and his son Wm. Clarke, Anysavry, Co. Armagh. Elizabeth Leeland, wife to William Leeland, Co. Fermanagh. Margt. Scoals als. Wileman, wife to John Scoales, Killderagh, Co. Monaghan, 20/- apiece to each of her sons. Elizabeth Noble, wife to Arthur Noble of Smithsborough, Co. Monaghan. Samuel Swancy, his wife and children, of Bellagh, Co. Monaghan. Richard Pockrich of Aughnamallagh, Co. Monaghan, Francis Aldrige of Co. Cavan, John James of Druminkin, Co. Monaghan, Edward Smith of Clounlough, Co. Monaghan, Thomas Dawson of Belenacanty, John Forster of Tullaghan, and James Fluker of Skeagh, debtors. Robert Montgomery, Annyrea, Co. Monaghan and John Forster of Tullaghan, said county, exors.

Dundrumon's, Derrilidigan, Callaragh, Drummock, Carrifinlagh, Skeagh, Druminkin, Carrowbarrow, lease of the Church land and 4 acres of Cohin, all in Co. Monaghan. Drumrád, Drumcarr and Drumcarbin, in Co. Cavan.

Witnesses: James Fluker, Skeagh, Thomas Hall, Carrowbarrow, Henry Allford, Skeagh, all in Co. Monaghan.

Memorial witnessed by: James Fluker, Henry Allford.

34, 66, 20518   Ralph Wileman (seal)

244 FREEMAN, RICHARD, Roundwood, Co. Wicklow, farmer.
    11 April 1722. Narrate, ¾ p., 2 May 1722.

Wife Ann Freeman. Daughter Margaret Freeman. Sons Ralph, Richard and James Freeman. Sons-in-law John Jones, John Fox. Part of portion due to Robert Freeman, Newrathbridge, Co. Wicklow, farmer, (exor.).

His farm of Roundwood.

Witnesses: Wm. Ball, Ballynecorr, Arthur Hoey, Feglin, William Rose, Newrybridge, all in Co. Wicklow, gents.

Memorial witnessed by: Wm. Ball, John Smith, public notary.

33, 359, 20559   Robt. Freeman (seal)

245 FORREST, DANIEL, Dublin, gent.
    22 April 1720. Codicil 19 June 1721. Narrate, 1¼ p., 26 April
    1722.

Wife Mrs. Ann Forrest, extx. His sister Elizabeth Dixon. "All the children of his late brother Charles Forrest late of the city of Dublin, alderman, decd. which he had by his sister-in-law Mrs. Barbara Forrest als. Ransford his late wife."

Charles Street, Dublin. Ballydowd, B. Newcastle and Uppercross, Co. Dublin.

Witnesses: Edmond Curtis, Dublin, gent., Barnabas Connor and Richard Pageitt, of the same, hatters.

Codicil witnessed by: Henry Rowley, Maberath, Co. Meath, gent., William Reed, Dublin, yeoman, John Ker, same, gent.

Memorial witnessed by: John Ker, Wm. Devall, clerk to Bruen Worthington, Dublin, notary public.

32, 472, 20576   Ann Forrest (seal)

246 BROWNE, REV. RICHARD, Coolecour, parish Macromp, B. Muskery, Co. Cork. 12 July 1710. Précis, ¼ p., 19 May 1722.

Wife Mary Browne (since deceased) extx. His children. Coolecour, Maglass, Dundarrick, Brahane, Moychosker and Lackmaloe, B. Muskery, Co. Cork, and all other his real estate.

Witnesses : George McCarmick, Evillary, Co. Cork, clerk, James Ryan, Macroom, Co. Cork, innkeeper, Daniel Grice, Deshue, Co. Cork, yeoman.

Memorial witnessed by : Ambrose Cramer, Cork, merchant, exor. of will of Mary Browne, deceased, James Hurt, his clerk, Benjamin Johnston, Cork, public notary.

33, 404, 20703   Ambrose Cramer (seal)

247 BROWNE, MARY, widow of Rev. Richard Browne, deceased. 20 June 1721. Précis ¼ p., 19 May 1722.

Sons Richard, Thomas, Charles, Allin, and Valentine Browne. Her two daughters Frances Woodstock and Susanna Cramer. Her son-in-law Ambrose Cramer, sole exor.

Coolcour, Maglass, Dunderrick, Monehusker, and Lackmaloe, all in B. Muskery, Co. Cork. Brahane, B. Muskerry, Co. Cork. Lease of Slaveen [situation not mentioned].

Witnesses : Rev. William Tenison, Macroom, Co. Cork, clerk, Humphrey Massy, Millstreet, near Macroom, Robt. Ash, Coolcour, gent.

Memorial witnessed by : James Hurt, clerk to said Ambrose Cramer, Benjamin Johnston, Cork, notary public.

                                  Ambrose Cramer (seal)
35, 46, 20704   Susanna Cramer (seal)

248 CONSTABLE, THOMAS, Loggan, Co. Wexford, farmer. 10 Feb. 1709/10. Narrate, ¾ p., 30 May 1722.

His wife Alice Constable als. Brownrigg. Son Thomas Constable. Second son Henry Constable. " His other children and grandchildren." Brother William Constable. Overseers " his brother Henry Brownrigg and his son Joshua Nixon." Exors. said wife, and Abraham Nixon of Coolattin, Co. Wicklow, Esq.

" His right to the farm of Cumerduffe, farm of Loggan after the death of his mother " and rest of real and personal estate.

Witnesses : Wentworth Hodgkinson, Ballard, gent., John ffred, Coolattin, cooper, both of the Lopp of Shelelagh, Co. Wicklow, and John Savage, parish of St. Peter, Dublin, gent.

Memorial witnessed by : Joshua Nixon, Killenure, parish Ahould, in the half B. of Shelelah, John Coates of the same, gent.

33, 427, 20786   Alice Constable her mark
                                               (seal)

249 STORY, GEORGE WARTER, D.D., Dean of the Cathedrall Church and Diocese of Limerick. 15 Sept. 1721. Précis, ¾ p., 2 June 1722.

His wife Catherin, sole extx. His brother Thos. Story. His sister Mrs. Anne Elliott. Legatees : His friend Francis Linley near Bradford, Co. York, the children of Rev. Mr. Ward formerly Dean of Connor, Anne Lawson als. Graham.

Lands etc. in several parishes of Kirklinton, Ronelisse and Arthuret, County of Cumberland. Lands in Counties Limerick and Tipperary and elsewhere.

Witnesses : Rev. Talbot Keene, of Cassell [Cashel], Co. Tipperary clerk, John Pyke, Woodenstown, Co. Tipperary, Esq., William Fitz-Gerald, Sixmilebridge, Co. Clare, Esq., Richard Butler, Stephen Baker and Charles Wells all of city of Bristol, Great Britain, gents.

Memorial witnessed by : Henry Prittie, Silvermines, John Dawson, Greenane, Co. Tipperary, Esq., John Blennerhassett, Dublin, gent.

34, 121, 20841   Catha. Warter Story (seal)

250 HASSETT, JOHN, Crooked Staff, Co. Dublin, beer brewer. 8 June 1722. Narrate, part in full, ¾ p., 27 June 1722.

Son John Hassett. My daughter Mary Bray. My daughter Deborah Hassett. Daughter Ann Hassett. Son Thos. Hassett. Son-in-law Morris Bray and Thos. Leake of Elbow Lane, linen weavers, exors.

Wm. Hunter, tenant, Mr. Carroll, Mr. Welsh, Mr. Gunnett, tenants, Mutton Lane. Widow Shaw, Mr. Cope, tenants, Crooked Staff.

His dwellinghouse, brew house and malt house. Crooked Staff. Truck Street als. Brabston Street. Mutton Lane.

Witnesses : Pierce Roussell, Crooked Staff, Co. Dublin, merchant, Simon Anyon, Dublin, gent., Thomas Davenport, Dublin, gent.

Memorial witnessed by : Thos. Davenport, Edward Challoner, Dublin, gent.

36, 35, 21100   Deb. Hassett (seal)

251 EDGEWORTH, FRANCIS, Edgeworthstown, Co. Longford,
       Esq. 21 July 1708. Narrate, ½ p., 17 July 1722.

Wife Mary Edgeworth, extx. Son Richd. Edgeworth (heir). " His own brothers." Rev. Benjamin Span guardian of son.

Real and personal estate in Co. of Longford, or elsewhere, house in Dublin and " all his pretentions in the world."

Witnesses : James Darby, John Forester, Dorothy Bradston.

Memorial witnessed by : John Forester, James Nugent lives at Carpenterstown, Co. Westmeath.

35 111, 21251   Richd. Edgeworth (seal)

252 BROWNE, STEPHEN, Dublin, gent.
       8 July 1722. Précis, ¾ p., 24 July 1722.

Charles Aylmer, Ballycannon, Co. Kildare, Esq., and Oliver Weston, Dublin, gent., trustees. Edmond Tobin, Dublin, brewer, tenant. Wm. Quin, farmer.

St. Thomas Street, Dublin. Clondalkin als. Clondacon, Co. Dublin.

Witnesses : Andrew Nugent, Doctor of Physick, Myles Reily, merchant, Pa. Dease, merchant, James Duffy, merchant, all of Dublin.

Memorial witnessed by : James Duffy, Simon Cleere, Dublin, gent.

36, 72, 21296   Ol. Weston (seal)

253 DOVER, MARY, Dublin, widow.
       1 Dec. 1721. Précis, ½ p., 5 Oct. 1722.

Her late husband Wm. Dover, gent., deceased. Her son Thomas Clark Dover. Her daughter Elizabeth. Her daughter Anna Maria Nelson. Her daughter Hester. Her sister Ann Clark. A debt due to Mr. John Faulkner. All her estate, lands, etc.

Witnesses : Gideon de Laune, James Spike, both of Dublin, gents., Benjamin Lyons, Castlelyons, King's Co., gent.

Memorial witnessed by : Thomas Mullock, James Wilde, both of Dublin, gents.

37, 166, 21700   Thos. Clark Dover (seal)

254 GRIFFITH, DAVID, Dublin, gabbert owner.
14 July 1721. Précis, ½ p., 2 Nov. 1722.

Son Thomas Griffith. Grandson Robt. Griffith. Grandson Michael Dickes. His three grandchildren David Griffith Neilson, Nells Neilson and Saunderson Neilson. His daughter Mary Coleman, wife of George Coleman, extx.

Witnesses : William Brown, Dublin, perukemaker, Wm. Sumner, public notary therein.

Memorial witnessed by : Wm. Souch, clerk to Mr. Wm. Sumner, Wm. Sumner.

36, 134, 21809   Mary Coleman (seal)

255 CAMPBELL, JOSIAS, Dublin, Esq.
17 March 1720. Codicil 13 Sept. 1722. Narrate, 2½ pp., 2 Nov. 1722.

His mother Margaret Campbell. His wife [Letitia]. His eldest son Samuel Campbell, his second son George Campbell. Testator's eldest daughter Margarett Campbell, Agnes Campbell second daughter, Letitia Campbell third daughter, Catherine Campbell fourth daughter, Jane Campbell fifth daughter, Alice Campbell sixth daughter.

Dr. George Martin, Dublin, doctor of physick, and Patrick Ore, Clough, Co. Antrim, gent., trustees and guardians. Money owed by Josias Cuningham and Daniel Cuningham his son. Lands in Co. Leitrim, Westmeath and Monaghan. Patrick Street, Dublin.

Witnesses : James Reily, Dublin, Esq., Council-at-law, Thos. Richardson, Dublin, gent. one of the attorneys of H.M. Court of King's Bench, James Anderson, Dublin, gent., son of Francis Anderson, one of the attorneys of H.M. Court of Exchequer.

Codicil witnessed by : Rev. James Teate of Crochan, Co. Cavan, Anna his wife, and Mary Mitchell of Crochan, school mistress.

Memorial witnessed by : John Ryan, Dublin, gent., Francis Mahon, Dublin, merchant.

36, 135, 21811   George Martin (seal)

256 LESLIE, VERY REV. JOHN, Dean of Dromore.
11 July 1716. Codicil 13 Sept. 1718. Full, 2½ pp., 6 Nov. 1722.

To be buried in the ancient burying place of my ancestors in the parish church of Donagh in the town of Castle Leslie.

Wife Elizabeth Leslie. My nephew Henry Leslie. My nephew Robert Leslie. My niece Jane Leslie. All my books and manuscripts to nephews Robert and Henry Leslie. Michael Ward and Charles Campbell, both of Dublin, Esqrs., and David Wilson, of same, gent., trustees.

My mansion house of Castle Leslie and the demesne lands thereunto belonging. Legacies to poor of Deanery of Dromore, parish of Drumully als. Newtown Butler, Co. Fermanagh, and of Donagh, Co. Monaghan.

Witnesses to will and codicil : Rev. William Hamilton, Archdeacon of Armagh, John Pringle of Callidon, Co. Tyrone, gent. and Samuel Black of Creegy, Co. Monaghan, gent.

Memorial witnessed by : Said William Hamilton, Robert Lowry junr., Aghenis, Co. Tyrone, gent.

34, 338, 21829 David Wilson (seal)

257 BENTLY, JOHN, Hurtstown, Co. Clare, Esq.

21 July 1722. Narrate, 1 p., 8 Nov. 1722.

His father Capt. Thomas Bently deceased. His deceased wife Deborah Bently als. Evans. His wife Elizabeth Bently als. Lady Elizabeth Deane. His son Henry Bently. His son Simon Bently. His son Thomas Bently. His daughter Margery Bently. His grandson John Massy. His brother William Bently. Henry Ivers, Esq., and his son-in-law Mr. Wm. Massy, exors.

Ballyneglea, B. Tulla, Co. Clare. Kilmallock, Co. Limerick. Farms of Coilagh and Ballyneglea, and Killseilly [situation not mentioned].

Witnesses : John Raymond, Limerick, gent. James Brien, Gortneclough, Co. Clare, farmer, Wm. Turner, Callurgh, said county, farmer, and John Hicky, Nenagh, Co. Tipperary, Doctor of Physic.

Memorial witnessed by : Wm. Turner, John Phillips, Cappananagh, Co. Limerick, gent.

36, 150, 21857. Henry Bently (seal)

258 RHODES, ALICE, Dublin, " widow and admx. of Lott Rhodes her beloved husband then lately decd." 11 Feb. 1720. Précis, ¼ p., 14 Nov. 1722.

Daughter Margery Rhodes, extx. Thomas Court [Dublin] and all her own lands, etc.

Witnesses : Patrick Getty, Dublin, clothier, John Enos, same, gent,
David Stanton, same, gent.

Memorial witnessed by : James Wilde and Wm. Devall, both
clerks to Bruen Worthington, public notary, Dublin.

36, 181, 21958.   Marg. Rhodes (seal)

259 BLOUNT, CHARLES, Killfeacle, Co. Tipperary, gent.

10 July 1722. Narrate, ¾ p., 20 Nov. 1722.

His sister Mary Medlicott, her husband. His sister Martha Delafee.
His aunt Valentine Magniac in London. His nephew George Bl[o]unt.
His nephew Samuel Bl[o]unt.

Mathew Bunbury of Kilfeacle, Esq., trustee and sole exor. A debt
due to John Damer, Esq. Robert Foulkes, Esq.

Ballybirane, Feorthugh, Ballyglass, Ballydavid, Pollough, Mone-
more, Lisnegraule, Dromomarkie and Ballyduffe.

Witnesses : James Uniacke, Cappagh, Co. Tipperary, Esq., Robert
Foulkes of Youghall, Esq., William Black, Tipperary, apothecary.

Memorial witnessed by : Ja. Uniacke, Cornelius Cahill of Longston,
Co. Limerick, gent.

34, 388, 22019.   Matt. Bunbury (seal)

260 BOLTON, CHARLES, Waterford, Esq.

2 May 1718. Narrate, 1¼ p., 3 Dec. 1722.

His wife. Brother Rev. Mr. Hugh Bolton. Cousin Wm. Bolton
(exor.) who lives at Faithlegg, son of Thomas Bolton. John Bolton,
son of said William. If no issue of said Rev. Hugh, Wm. Bolton or
John Bolton then property to Captain John Bolton who lives in
Dublin for life. John Bolton, second son of said Captain John Bolton.
Testator's brothers Daniel and Henry. Children of his brother Michael
deceased. Cousin Henry and Stephen Bolton and their children.

If Andrew May (third son of Edward May, Esq., of Mayfield) or his
sons succeed to estate they are to take surname of Bolton " or else
to go to James May eldest brother of said Andrew May who is the right
heir of said Charles Bolton who in such case is not obliged to change
his name." Thomas Christmas, Esq., of Waterford city, and Michael
Head, Inns of Court, London, gent., trustees.

Jonestown, Curduff, Rath, Crehanagh, Barebehie and Gurtardagh,
all in Co. Waterford. " Lands of the North and South of Ballylynch

in Co. Tipperary." Faithlegg, Killmacomb, Ballynammointragh, Killure, Ballyvelly and Garrugarruffe, Co. Waterford.

Witnesses : Arthur Gamble, John Thomson and Philip Mortimer, all of Carrick, gents.

Memorial witnessed by : John Kennedy and Wm. Devall, Dublin, gent.

34, 417, 22154. William Bolton (seal)

261 WEBB, WILLIAM, Garrane, Co. Limerick, Esq.

16 Nov. 1722. Précis, ½ p., 14 Dec. 1722.

Wife Ann Webb, extx. His father William Webb senr. His nephew Wm. Webb, son of James Webb. Cousin James Dickson.

Ballymartin, Kildonell, Lackengrenane als. Lackenegrenane in B. Pubblebrien, Co. Limerick.

Witnesses : John Van Lewen, Doctor of Physic, James Webb, gent. and George More, gent., all of city of Dublin.

Memorial witnessed by : James Webb, Robert Hoare, Dublin, gent.

34, 429, 22245. Ann Webb (seal)

262 COTTON, SAMUEL, Dublin, gent.

16 Sept. 1722. Narrate, 1¼ p., 24 Dec. 1722.

Wife Ruth Cotton, extx. and guardian of children. Son Whiteside Cotton. Son Henry Cotton. Youngest son Samuel Cotton. Daughter Mary Cotton. Trustees : John Ker, Dublin, gent., William Aston, same, merchant, Mark West, same, carpenter.

To wife his house in Cabbra Lane, Co. Dublin for herself and children. St. Patrick Street and White Cross Alley, suburbs of city of Dublin. House adjoining to the Tholsell in Skinner Roe, Dublin (held by Widow Darby and her undertenants). House in Skinner Roe where Mr. Robert Caddell then dwelt. Ram Alley, Dublin, tenants Mr. Hugh Reid and Mr. John Wilson. Stafford Street, tenants Joseph Bury and Mrs. Mary McCullogh, Jervis Street [Dublin]. Rathmoyle, B. Cullenagh, Queen's Co.

Witnesses : Mathew West, Dublin, merchant, Thomas Quin and Barry Gordon, then clerks to said testator.

Memorial witnessed by : Barry Gordon, John Carter late clerk to said Saml. Cotton.

34, 453, 22305. Ruth Cotton (seal)

263 LAMBLEY, WILLIAM, city of Cork, alderman.
12 July 1721. Précis, ½ p., 22 Jan. 1722.
Wife Sarah Lambley, extx. Mr. Swithin White, Mr. James Browne, Mr. Edward Fenn, trustees. All his real and personal estate.
Witnesses : James Crooke, junr., merchant, George Wood, merchant, John Sullivan, gent., all of Cork.
Memorial witnessed by : Moses Glover, Cork, gent., Arthur Keefe, Cork, Esq.
37, 205, 22423.   Sarah Lambley (seal)

264 WALKER, JOSEPH, Dublin, goldsmith.
19 Jan. 1722. Full in part, 1 p., 28 Jan. 1722.
Wife Elizabeth Walker.   Sons : Mathew Walker, John Walker, James Walker, Nathaniel Walker, Daniel Walker.
Holding in Harold's Cross called Hely's Garden. Skinner Alley. "My holding in Skinner Row which I now live in," cellar under the shop, etc. Caple Street. Lots on North Strand [Dublin].
Witnesses : Margaret, wife of John Greenwood, Harold's Cross, weaver, Ephraim Thwaites, Doctor of Physic, Nathaniel Kane, Dublin, merchant.
Memorial witnessed by : Nathaniel Kane, John Wardle, Dublin, gent., Simon Anyon, same, gent.
34, 481, 22468.   Eliz. Walker (seal)

265 McCARROLL, ROBERT, Ballycastle, B. Carey, Co. Antrim,
gent. 8 Aug. 1720. Narrate, ¾ p., 14 Feb. 1722.
His son Lessly McCarroll.   His daughter Christian McCarroll. Robert McCarroll, pretended son of Charles McCarroll deceased. Nephew William McCarroll, eldest son of his brother Simon McCarroll.
Mr. John Dunlop of Garteonny, Andrew Steward of Park and his nephew William McCarroll, guardians and overseers of will.
Rodon, Malnedivan and Cullkenny in parish Ramoan, B. Cary, Co. Antrim.
Witnesses : William Ettenby, Thos. Fitzpatrick, Simon McCarroll and Wm. McCarroll, all of Ballycastle, Co. Antrim.
Memorial witnessed by : Arthur Workman, Lisburn, Co. Antrim, Wm. McCarroll, Ballycastle.
37, 259, 22639.   Wm. McCarroll (seal)
                                   (Testator's nephew)

266 HARFORD, WILLIAM, Dublin, victualler.

21 Dec. 1720. Narrate, ½ p., 16 Feb. 1722.

Wife Elizabeth Harford, exor. His sister Mary Ewing als. Harford. Rev. Mr. Edward Sampson, exor.

" The house wherein he then dwelled " [? in Dublin]. Aghaderry Itra, Co. Monaghan, and his real and personal estate.

Witnesses : Thomas Bibby and Daniel Dunovan, Dublin, victuallers, Charles McCarthy, drawer to testator.

Memorial witnessed by : Thos. Berriff (or Berriss), Dublin, gent., Wm. Barry, Dublin, scrivener.

37, 265, 22672. Eliz. Harford her mark (seal)

267 BLESINGTON, RT. HON. MOROGH [MURROUGH], LORD VISCOUNT. 25 Feb. 1711. Codicil 12 May 1714. Précis, ½ p., 28 Feb. 1722.

Wife Rt. Hon. Ann Lady Viscountess Blesington. A settlement of 6 June 1709.

Newtown, Co. Kildare. Blackhall, Co. Kildare. Manors of Glandelogh and Skawgheen, Co. Wicklow, and Fortrey, Co. Wicklow. A house in the town of Blessin[g]ton, Co. Wicklow wherein Mr. Welsh the present Minister of Blessin[g]ton then lived, and all real and personal estate.

Witnesses : Benjamin Parry, Dublin, Esq., Ralph Vaughan, servant to testator, Bruen Worthington, Dublin, notary public.

Codicil witnessed by : Charles, then Earl of Mountrath since deceased, Rt. Hon. Wm., Viscount Mountjoy, Richard Turner, London, Esq., Counsellor-at-Law.

Memorial witnessed by : John Young, clerk to Bruen Worthington, public notary, Dublin, and said Bruen Worthington.

36, 337, 22752. A. Blesington (seal)

268 MONTGOMERY, HUGH, Derrygonely, Co. Fermanagh, Esq.

10 Feb. 1720. Full, 2 pp., 8 March 1722.

My wife, exor. My eldest son Nicholas, second son Hugh, third son Richard. Daughter Jane, daughter Margarett, daughter Sidney. Daughter Sarah, her husband Brockill Green. Brother Robert Montgomery of Derrybrusk and my friend John Corry of Castle Cole,

I

Co. Fermanagh, exors. £5 to poor of parishes of Inishmacsaint and Devenish.

Drumero als. Dunbarr als. the estate of Derrygonelly. Lands in manor of Diranafogher als. the estate of Monea. Rosailton and church land.

Witnesses : Robt. Weir, Monaghan, John Trotter, Robinstown, and Alexr. Atchison, Corryard, all in Co. Fermanagh, gents.

Memorial witnessed by : Alexr. Nesbitt, Dublin, gent. and his servant Daniel Byrne.

34, 525, 22803.   Nich. Montgomery (seal)

269 VIGORS, URBAN, Old Leighlin, Co. of Catherlogh, Esq.
2 Sept. 1710. Narrate, ½ p., 17 April 1723.

Urban and Bartholomew Vigors, the two eldest sons of Thomas Vigors son of the devisor. Margarett, wife of testator's son Thomas. Appoints "his two sons Richard [and Thomas] Vigors his sole executors."

Lands of Seskin and Ballyneboly [? Co. Carlow].

Witnesses : William Egan, late of Rathgarvan, Co. Kilkenny, gent., Dudly Reddy, gent. and William Thomas, clerk, both of Old Leighlin.

Memorial witnessed by : John Washington, gent., and William Crow, yeoman, both of Ballybar, Co. Catherlogh.

37, 355, 23026.   Bartholomew Vigors (seal)

270 GRIFFIN, WILLIAM, Garden Lane, city of Dublin, malster.
20 Feb. 1722. Narrate, ½ p., 24 April 1723.

Wife Margaret Griffin. Daughter Margarett Bennett als. Griffin. Son-in-law John Bennett. Brother John Griffin. Friends John Bennett and Thomas Algane, exors.

Leonard's Alley, Catherine's Street [Dublin].

Witnesses : Laughlin Kelly, comber, Thomas Halgan, weaver, Derby Dermott, yeoman, all of Dublin.

Memorial witnessed by : Laughlin Kelly, Thos. Halgan.

37, 364, 23064   Margaret Griffin her mark (seal)

271 WILLIAMS, CHRISTOPHER, Dublin, gent.
19 Nov. 1722. Précis, ½ p., 29 April 1723.
His father John Williams. His brother Thomas Williams, exor.
His brother John Williams.
His servant John Gascoigne. All his worldly substance, etc.
Witnesses : John Dugon, tailor, Richard Higgins, gent., both of
Dublin.
Memorial witnessed by : John Dugon, John Young.
37, 371, 23088   Thos. Williams (seal)

272 VERDON, EDWARD, Dublin, joiner.
9 April 1723. Full, 2¼ p., 29 April 1723.
Wife Alice Verdon, exor. Son John Verdon. Daughter Elinor
Ottey, her late husband Wm. Ottey, deceased. Granddaughter
Elizabeth Ottey. My sister Jane McMullan. £10 to John Verdon
son of my brother Will. Verdon, and all my working tools. My wife's
two nephews Lawrence Pain and Thos. Pain, exors.
Mr. Frasier, Mr. Gunning, Mrs. Brown, Rev. Edward Mottley,
tenants, Usshers Street. 40/- to poor parish boys of St. Michan's,
Dublin.
The house I now live in on Usher's Key, Dublin, except the shop
and room behind the same wherein my daughter Elinor Ottey lodges.
Hamond Lane, Dublin, Loghboy, Dublin.
Witnesses : James Wilde, William Devall, clerks to Bruen
Worthington, public notary, Dublin.
Memorial witnessed by : James Wilde, Bruen Worthington.
                                             Alice Verdon (seal)
35, 424, 23089   Ellin Ottey (seal)

272 B CRYMBLE, CORNELIUS, " of Knocker in the county of
Antrim or Carrickfergus, Esq." 23 March 1717. Précis, ½ p.,
4 May 1723.
Wife Ann Crymble, exor. Son William Crymble. Grandson Cornelius
Crymble, son of Charles Crymble of Ballyclare.
Wm. Murray, tenant in Liberty of town of Carrickfergus. David
Crafford, Belfast, gent., exor. All his estate lands and tenements.
Witnesses : Patrick Adair, Liberty of Carrickfergus, gent., Alex-
ander McDowell of same, farmer, Gerald Byrne, Dublin, gent.

Memorial witnessed by: Alexander McDowell, Alexander Hutchinson, clerk to Robert Donnaldson of Dublin.

Gideon Jacques (seal)
Ann Jacques (seal)
als. Crymble, wife of
said Gideon

35, 433, 23131

273 MATHEW, JOHN, Dunmurry, Co. Antrim, farmer.

23 Jan 1717. Précis, part in full, ¾ p., 7 May 1723.

To be buried in the churchyard of Drumbegg. His wife. His son Gilbert Mathew, exor. Legacy to son George Mathew if he return home exor. Legacy to son Arthur at his return home. My firearms to be divided among my three sons.

Rebecca Robinson, daughter of Joseph Robinson and Ann Mathew his wife. Wm. Legg of Malone.

The Black Mountain. The seven acres whereon Mr. Malcom dwells. Glanhead. 14 acres whereon his son Gilbert then lived [situation not mentioned].

Witnesses: James Harrison, John McCormick.

Memorial witnessed by: Robert Smith, Lisburn, Co. Antrim, gent., David Gillespie, Downpatrick, Co. Down, gent.

38, 44, 23197   Gilbert Mathew (seal)

274 BENNETT, ROBERT, Rasillagh, Co. Wexford, gent.

30 March 1720. Narrate, ½ p., 18 May 1723.

Brother William Bennett of Cullenstowne, exor. Niece Hannah Bennett. Niece Mary Lett, wife to William Lett. His sister Ann Chambers. His nephew Henry Chambers. Lands of Ballyclemock, Co. Wexford.

Witnesses: Charles Tottenham, Tottenhamgreen, Co. Wexford, Esq., John Tench, Bryanstown, Co. Wexford, gent., Gerald FitzGerald, Ballyclemock, Co. Wexford, gent.

Memorial witnessed by: Charles Tottenham, John Cliffe, New Ross, Co. Wexford, Esq.

35, 472, 23353   Wm. Bennett (seal)

275 MALOWNY, CHARLES, Ballyhagin, B. Carbury, Co. Kildare, farmer. 7 July 1713. Narrate, ¾ p., 21 May 1723.

Wife Catherine Malowny als. Walsh. His brother Walter Malowny and his brother-in-law Nicholas Walsh, exors. His brother Edmd. Malowny, his son (testator's nephew) John Malowny.

Ballyhagin, Co. Kildare. Lullymore and Lullybegg, B. Offaly.

Witnesses: Philip Craven, Carbury, merchant, Christopher Walsh, Ellistown, farmer, Garrett Keating, Carbury, gent., all in Co. Kildare.

Memorial witnessed by: Christopher Walsh, James Wilde, Dublin.

36, 429, 23380   Nicholas Walsh (seal)

276 KEMPSTON, GRACE, Dublin, widow.
9 May 1723. Narrate, ¼ p., 24 May 1723.

Her grandson Henry Kempston, his sister Grace Kempstone als. Pearson. Her grandson John Kempston, his sister Ellinor Kempston, his father John Kempston, Esq. (son of testator). Her grandson Thomas Kempston. Her granddaughters Grace Cuffe and Grace Acton. Her son-in-law Thomas Acton, Esq., and her good friend Rev. Mr. John Wynne clerk, exors. and guardians of grandson Thomas during his minority.

Killnavarra, Co. Cavan. Lands and fairs in Co. Cavan, viz. The two Derrys, Drumeliss, Derrygarahan and the customs of Trinity fair usually held at Ballyhillion. Crobally and Derrylatta, Co. Kilkenny. Killkerryhill and Barrettstown, Co. Kilkenny. Three houses in Cook Street, Dublin, held under St. Ann's Guild.

Witnesses: Jacob Charleton, gent., John Banfill, ale draper, Wm. Sandys, gent., all of Dublin.

Memorial witnessed by: Wm. Shiell, James Maule.

                        Tho. Acton (seal)
35, 481, 23398   John Wynne (seal)

277 ECCLES, JOSEPH, Rathmoran, Co. Fermanagh, gent.
2 Aug. 1709. Codicil 9 Nov. 1710. Narrate, ¾ p., 24 May 1723.

His only brother Charles Eccles of Fintonagh, Co. Tyrone, Esq. A debt due to Hugh Raney.

Rathmoran als. Ardmagh, B. Clankelly, Co. Fermanagh. Agha-drumsee, Killygorman, Tatenageeragh, Tatenegolan, Tateneaoinine

[? Tattintonegan], Dromesow, Aghanequill, Drumswords, Derryna-
wilke, Creaghmacnees, Mullyloghog, Curaghees, Curlaghaloone,
Bossalagh, in B. Clankelly, Co. Fermanagh. Shanock, Co. Fermanagh.
Lamey als. Lurganboy, and Lisnamallagh, B. Clankelly, Co. Fermanagh.

Witnesses : Luke Stanford, Belturbet, Co. Cavan, gent., Moses
Richards, gent., Thomas Ashe, Magherafelt, Co. Londonderry, Esq.

Witnesses to codicil : Wm. Balfour, Esq., Joseph Caldwell, John
Kerr, gent., all of Lisnaskee, Co. Fermanagh.

Memorial witnessed by : John Buchanan, John Creery, James
Wachup, all of Fintonagh, Co. Tyrone, gents.

37, 441, 23399   Cha. Eccles (seal)

278 WILSON, RICHARD, Belfast, Co. Antrim, gent.
  2 Dec. 1711. Full, 1¼ p., 30 May 1723.

Wife, sole extx. Son Richard Wilson. Son William. Son John.
Daughters Elizabeth, Barbara, Mildred.

Estate or lands of inheritance in the Co. of Tyrone. Liskittle, Tully-
legg, Tierglassogitrah, and Tierglassogoutragh.

Witnesses : Matt. French, then of town of Belfast, clerk, Nathaniel
Byrtt, Belfast, gent., David Wilson, Dublin, gent.

Memorial witnessed by : David Wilson, John Downing, Dublin,
gent.

36, 437, 23453   Richd. Wilson (seal)

279 VAN HOMRIGH, ESTHER " one of the daughters of Bartholomew Van Homrigh late of the city of Dublin, Esq."
  1 May 1723. Précis, ½ p., 18 June 1723.

All her worldly substances and real and personal estate to Revd.
Doctor George Berkeley one of the Fellows of Trinity College in
Dublin and Robert Marshall of Clonmell, Esq., subject to payment of
her debts and legacies.

Witnesses : James Doyle, Edward Thrush and Darby Gaffney, all
of the city of Dublin.

Memorial witnessed by : Thomas Prior, John Young, both of Dublin,
gents.

36, 452, 23570[1]   Geor. Berkeley (seal)

---
[1] See appendix for copy of this memorial.

280 BATHO, HUGH, Dublin, Esq.

10 May 1723. Narrate, 1¼ p., 21 June 1723.

Wife Mary Batho (formerly Mrs Mary Downing, widow). Recites a marriage settlement 3 Dec. 1706. Daughter Alice Batho, sole extx. Killykeeghanmore, Killvkeeganbegg, Killvaniell als. Killmaniell, Knockabehony als. Killecreene, Tatenamona, in B. Clenawley, Co. Fermanagh. A house in Sciccamore Alley, Dublin, called the Sciccamore Tree. His dwelling house in Glasnevin [Dublin]. Jervis Street, Dublin. Houses etc. in town of Ballyboy [situation not mentioned]. Malpas, Co. of Chester, Great Britain.

Witnesses : Edmond Sturgys, Dublin, watchmaker, Richard Prest, clerk to Henry Buckley, notary public, and Henry Buckley.

Memorial witnessed by : John Todd, Dublin, gent., Henry Buckley.

36, 458, 23601.   Alse Batho (seal)

281 KYLE, HUGH, Dublin, merchant.

3 May 1723. Précis, ½ p., 4 July 1723.

Wife Margery Kyle (then enceinte). His children Samuel and Hannah Kyle. His real and personal estate.

Witnesses : John Warren, servant to testator, Wm. Souch, clerk to Wm. Barry, Dublin, scrivener, and said Wm. Barry.

Memorial witnessed by : Wm. Souch, Wm. Barry.

36, 478, 23725.   Mara Kyle (seal)

282 DROGHEDA, HENRY EARL OF.

25 May 1713. Précis, ¾ p., 17 July 1723.

His agent Charles Campbell. Tully, Co. Kildare with the mills, fairs and markets thereof. Two houses in Dublin he then dwelt in one of which he bought from Mr. Phelps the carpenter. Rents of Lordship of St. Mary's Abby and Grange of Clonliffe and all other lands settled upon his wife for her jointure. King Street near Smithfield and Channell Row, Dublin. Lands in County of Monaghan, Carrickeen, Killevoyleerum, Tatereagh [? Tattyreagh] and Brackagh. Ballurgan, Ballyboymore and Ballyboybegg, Co. Louth. Milltown als. Kingsmilltown and Adamstown als. Fedanstown, B. Newcastle, Co. Dublin. Dromcarr, Hickockmore, Rulestown als. Cappockrulestown als. Litterulestown, B. Atherdee [Ardee], Co. Louth. Houses etc. in and about town of Drogheda, formerly belonging to Ignatius and Christopher Peppard. Alderman Norman of Drogheda, lessee.

Witnesses : Anthony Sheppard, Newcastle, Co. Longford, Esq., Henry Westenra, late of Dublin, Esq., deceased. William Colvill, James Turner and William Willock, all of Dublin, gents.

Memorial witnessed by : Wm. Colvill, William Fawcett, Dublin, gent.

39, 35, 23841.   Will. Moore (seal)
one of the sons and devisee of above
named Henry Earl of Drogheda deceased

283 WHITESIDE, Capt. JOSHUA, Malone, Co. Antrim.
11 March 1721. Précis, ½ p., 3 Sept. 1723.

Wife Esther Whiteside. His leasehold lands under, Earl of Donegall and all other real and personal estate.

Witnesses : Michael Taylor, Malone, farmer, and Adam Taylor his son, and Moses Cherry of Belfast.

Memorial witnessed by : Moses Cherry, Joseph Hewitt, Ballymony, Co. Armagh, gent.

39, 82, 24126.   Esther Whiteside (seal)

284 PUTLAND, THOMAS, late city of Dublin, merchant, after of Chelsea, Middlesex. 16 Nov. 1722. Narrate, 3½ pp., 14 Sept. 1723.

His wife Meriel Putland. Eldest son Thos. Putland junr. (deceased). Jane Rotton, dau. of Jno. Rotton, Dublin, gent., wife of said Thos. junr. His son Sisson Putland. His son George Putland. His daughters Martha Putland and Hester Putland. His grandson Thomas Putland, son of testator's son Thos. deceased.

Thos. Curtis, Dublin, alderman and John Ellis, Dublin, cutler, trustees. A mortgage due from Sir Kildare Borrowes on lands in Co. Kildare. Thady Fitzpatrick. Gregory Byrne, Francis Delarne, Sir John Dillon, Arthur Dillon, Murrough Viscount Blessington (mortgagors and mortgagees.

Knocknamohill (Knockmohill) als. Knocknamore als. Knockanemota, Ballynefinshoge and Ballymenagh als. Ballymona als. Ballymoneene, Carrinegollin, Carraghnolan, all in Co. Wicklow. Two houses on Ormond Quay, city of Dublin, houses in Castle Street, Dublin. Lands etc. in Co. Kildare and Kingdom of Ireland purchased from the Earl of Limerick.

Witnesses : Thos. Kernan and Thos. Woulfe, Dublin, merchants, Nathaniel Cole and Edwd. Bradwell, London, gents.
Memorial witnessed by : Wm. Devall and Thos. Mullock, clerks to Bruen Worthington, public notary, Dublin.
38, 268, 24193.   Sisson Putland (seal)
                                     of Chelsea, Middlesex, Esq.

285 LEY [Mrs] ANN als. BABE, Dublin, "spinster."
30 March 1723. Précis, ½ p., 17 Sept. 1723.
My son-in-law Wm. Savage and Ann his wife. My granddaughter Mary Savage, her sister Dorothy Savage.
House in West Street, Drogheda, set to Alderman John Leigh. House on Bull Ring, Drogheda.
Witnesses : Wm. Edwards, Dublin, apothecary, John Miller, perukemaker, Charles Reilly, Dublin, gent.
Memorial witnessed by : John Miller, Henry Ludlow, Dublin, gent.
39, 92, 24208.   William Savage (seal)

286 BARTON, WILLIAM, Thomastown, Co. Louth, Esq.
22 Sept. 1721. Précis, ½ p., 23 Sept. 1723.
Benjamin Burton and Francis Harrison, Dublin, Esqrs., trustees. His real and personal estate.
Witnesses : Thos. Fortescue, Dromiskin, Co. Louth, Esq., Jno. Foster, Dunleer, Co. Louth, Esq., Rev. Boyle Travers, Strabanon, Co. Louth, clerk, Rev. Peter Jackson, Killincoole, Co. Louth, clerk.
Memorial witnessed by : Andrew Caldwell, Dublin, gent., Wm. Devall, clerk to Bruen Worthington, public notary, Dublin.
38, 281, 24239.   Fran. Harrison (seal)

287 FENTON, JOHN, Urney, Co. Tyrone, farmer.
8 Aug. 1721. Narrate, ¾ p., 24 Sept. 1723.
His wife. His eldest son James Fenton, son William and youngest son John Fenton. His daughter Elenor Fenton. His daughter Jennett Fenton. Rev. Mr. William Holmes (or Homes) and Mr. John Love exors.
Lyslap [Lislap, Co. Tyrone], Lurgan, Buey [Lurganboy, Co. Tyrone], Glencory and Gortgranathan [? Gortgranagh], in Manor of Newtownstewart.

Witnesses : William Holmes, John Holmes and William Holmes, all of Peacock Bank, B. Strabane, Co. Tyrone.
Memorial witnessed by : John Holmes, Peacock Bank, Co. Tyrone, gent., James Hood, Dublin, gent.
41, 22, 24270.   John Fenton (seal)

288 KING, GEORGE, Kilpeacan, Co. Limerick, Esq.
27 June 1719. Précis, ¾ p., 20 Sept. 1723.
His wife Margaret King.   Estate in B. Conagh, Co. Limerick. Kilpecan, Killmorris, Rathmoile, Skeanea, Ballyshane, Carnemeerlevane, Knocknebolighshy and Ballyinroghue, all in Bs. of Publebryen and Smallcounty, Co. Limerick.
Witnesses : Richd. Pomeroy, Ballysimon, Esq., Thomas Gooduck, Graige, gent., and John Hicky, Killpecan, yeoman, all in Co. Limerick.
Memorial witnessed by : Francis Cripps, Dublin, gent., John Hicky.
38, 280, 24336.   Margaret King (seal)

289 BETAGH, RICHARD, Dublin, chirurgeon.
16 Oct. 1723. Précis, ½ p., 22 Oct. 1723.
Nicholas Lincoln, Dublin, merchant, Raymond FitzSimons, Dublin, merchant, Richard Mallory and Farrough McDaniel, both of Dublin, gents., and Mathew Read, Dublin, periwiggmaker, trustees. Cappock als. Cappoge, parish and B. of Castleknock, Co. Dublin.
Witnesses : George Martin, Doctor of Physic, Rose Reilly, wife of Philip Reilly, gent., and Abraham Sheriff, gent. all of the city of Dublin.
Memorial witnessed by : James Wilde and Wm. Devall, Dublin.
38, 335, 24475   Matt. Read (seal)

290 PLEADWELL, TOBIAS, Mountmellick, Queen's Co.
19 March 1718. Narrate, ¾ p., 11 Nov. 1723.
Kinsman William Pim, son of his nephew Moses Pim, late of Lackah, Queen's Co., deceased, not to sell or alien the premises bequeathed to him to any person " except to the name and family of the Pims of the posterity of his decd. Brother-in-law John Pim late of Mountrath."
John Barcroft of Arkill, Co. Kildare, Henry Ridgeway and Joshua

Strangman, both of Mountmellick and Gershon Boat, late of Mount-rath, lessees of part of his holding on which the Meeting House of his friends the People called Quakers is built. His dwelling house etc. in Mountmellick.

Witnesses: Henry Sumner, apothecary, Lougharne Harris, merchant, John Mosse, sadler and John Biglands, gent., all of Mountmellick.

Memorial witnessed by: Wm. Devall, Thos. Mullock.

40, 129, 24619   Wm. Pim (seal)

291 KERR, ELIZABETH, widow of John Kerr, Dean of Diocese of Ardagh. 18 July 1719. Précis, ½ p., 16 Nov. 1723.

Grand-nephew Charles Dowdall, son of John Dowdall and Teenny Smothergill als. Kerr. Lease of Ballycloghan [situation not mentioned].

Witnesses: Thos. Featherston, Ardagh, Co. Longford, gent., Wm. Bleur, of same, gent., Thos. Newcomen, Doverl, Co. Longford, Esq.

Memorial witnessed by: Thos. Featherston, and John Young, Dublin, gent.

40, 143, 24684   Chas. Dowdall (seal)

292 ARMSTRONG, ANDREW, Mauristown, Co. Kildare. 19 Jan. 1721. Précis, ½ p., 22 Nov. 1723.

" His dearly beloved wife commonly known by the name of Lady Westport and then residing in Linlithgow in North Britain." His uncle Archibald Armstrong, trustee. His brothers Hugh and Charles Armstrong, trustees. His nephew Edmond Armstrong, son to his brother William Armstrong deceased. His brother-in-law Milo Bagot.

His real estate in Co. Kildare. Lands of Mauristown.

Witnesses: John Claxton, Togginstown, Co. Kildare, gent., Thos. Pender, Newbridge, said county, yeoman, Patrick Carrell, servant to Robert Parkinson, Dublin, Esq.

Memorial witnessed by: Thos. Mullock, James Wilde, both of Dublin, gents.

41, 105, 24775   Chas. Armstrong (seal)

293 LYNCH, MARY, Keiltycurra, King's Co., widow of Nicholas Lynch decd. 30 . . . 1721. Narrate, ½ p., 2 Dec. 1723.

Her son Wm. Lynch. Her son Jonathan Lynch.

Seven small houses or tenements in Pimlico and Elbo Lane, Manor of St. Thomas Court, suburbs of city of Dublin, six small houses in St. Thomas Court. Lease of the farm Keiltycurra, King's Co.

Witnesses : Mary Smith, wife of Robt. Smith late of the city of Dublin, grocer, Joseph Harrison, Brown Street, liberties of Thomas Court and Donore, Co. Dublin, weaver, Deborah Gilbart, Dublin, spinster, and Joshua Gilbart, Dublin, gent.

Memorial witnessed by : Joseph Harrison, Jno. Smith, public notary, Dublin.

38, 430, 24881   Wm. Lynch (seal)

294 CHARTRES, WILLIAM, senr., Cork, Esq.

28 Nov. 1723. Narrate, 1 p., 31 Jan. 1723/24.

His wife Mary Chartres. His eldest son William Chartres Esq. His grandson William Chartres Fitzwilliam. His son John Chartres. His son Thomas Chartres. Philip French and John Morley, both of Cork, aldermen, overseers of will.

Wm. Allen, John Connor, William Martin, tenants of houses in South West quarter of city of Cork. His dwelling house and two tenements adjoining on Tuckey's Key [Cork]. Killmichael in the Dursey Islands. Ballygenane, Coolsalagh and Peardstown, B. Kinnalea and Kirricurrihy, Co. Cork. Lands adjoining the Lough of Cork (Mr. Swithin White, lesee). Lands of Coppingerstang (leasehold).

Witnesses : John Maurnan, Cork, pewterer, William Rose, Rathkeal, Co. Limerick, gent., William Evans, Cork, gent.

Memorial witnessed by : Robt. Wallis, notary public, Wm. Simmins, gent., both of Cork.

39, 271, 25238   John Chartres (seal)

295 BOLTON, Dr. JOHN, Dean of Derry.

29 May 1721. Narrate, 1½ p., 15 Feb. 1723.

Son Thos. Bolton. Son Richard Bolton. Son Joseph Bolton. Daughter Elizabeth. Grandson Thomas Norman. His daughter Norman's other children.

Estate in Aughton near Ormskirk in England. Freehold estate in B. of Dunboyne, Co. Meath purchased from Nichs. Plunkett of Dunsoghly, Esq., deceased, viz. Upper Gunnoges [Gunnocks], Old Braceton, Maginnisses Farm, Stroakstown, Greenspark, Lower Gunnoges [Gunnocks]. His right of advowson and presentation or and into the Vicarage of Ratoath, Crackanstown, Thornhills in Ratoath, Little Lagore, Co. Meath, Ballymore and mill, Elgarstown, Moortown, Creekstown, Co. Meath. St. Margaretts [situation not mentioned]. Blind Key, Dublin. Ship Key Street, Londonderry and land in liberties of Londonderry. Thirty-six acres at Brookhall [? Londonderry] purchased from Sir Mathew Bridges. Money testator "paid out in building a new Dean's House with outhouses in Bishop's Gate Street adjoining the churchyard of Londonderry."

Witnesses : Revd. James Sotheby, Londonderry, clerk, Edward Houston, of same, gent., Christopher Raines, servant to testator.

Memorial witnessed by : Thomas Mullock, James Wilde, both clerks to Bruen Worthington, public notary, Dublin.

42, 1, 25397   Jo. Bolton (seal)

296   NEWTOWN-BUTLER, Rt. Hon. THEOPHILUS LORD [BARON]. 20 Feb. 1721. Codicil 30 Jan. 1722. Full, 3 pp., 16 March 1723.

Body to be deposited " with that of my dearest wife lately deceased in my vault in St. Ann's Church in Dawson Street, Dublin." Corpse of wife to be brought from Bath. My brother Col. Brinsley Butler, sole exor. My brother Lieut. Col. James Butler and his wife (" my sister Mrs. Ann Butler"). My sister the Countess of Meath. My sister Glover als. Butler. My sister Judith Marsh als. Butler. My nephew Francis Marsh her son. My niece Judith Butler. £10 to each of my nephews. Picture of my grandfather Sir Theophilus Jones.

Trustees : Rt. Hon. Allen Broderick Viscount Middleton, Rt. Hon. Wm. Whitshed, Lord Chief Justice of the King's Bench, Ireland, the Hon. Thomas Marlay, H.M.'s Solicitor General, and Robert Percival of Knightsbrooke, Esq. Annuity to Mrs. Ann Brent.

My real estate in counties of Cavan and Fermanagh. £13 per annum for ever to minister and churchwardens of parish of St. Ann's, Dublin, in trust " to buy five shillings worth of bread to be had in good loaves and distribute the same amongst the poor every Sabbath Day at the parish church of St. Ann's aforesaid." Codicil says that John Jones of Belturbet, Co. Cavan, who formerly managed testator's affairs, was not to be again employed.

Witnesses : Richard Hopkins, Dublin, upholsterer, Patrick McGlin, Dublin, yeoman, J. Thompson, Killybandrick, Co. Cavan, gent.

Codicil witnessed by : John Maddison, Dublin, gent., said J. Thompson, said Patrick McGlin.

Memorial witnessed by : John Thompson, David Wilson.

41, 245, 25645   J. Butler (seal)

297 ALLEN, PATRICK, St. Wolstan or Allenscourt, Co. Kildare, Esq. 5 July 1720. Précis, ½ p., 31 March 1723.

His wife Ann Allen als. Dowdall. His real and personal estate.

Witnesses : Simon Clarke, Dublin, gent., Ullick Wall, Pollardstown, Co. Carlow, gent., James Dowdall, Dublin, gent.

Memorial witnessed by : Anthy. Doyle, Dublin, Thomas Carr, Fleet Street, Dublin, gent.

42, 78, 25722   Ann Allen (seal)

298 RAWDON, SIR JOHN, Moyragh, Co. Down, Bart. 4 Oct. 1723. Précis, ½ p., 9 April 1724.

" Rt. Hon. Marmaduke Coghill, Dublin, Esq., and his brother Richd. Levinge of Monyleath, Co. Westmeath, Esq." trustees. His real estate etc. in Co. Meath.

Witnesses : John Dunbarr Bate, attorney in the Court of Common Pleas, Dublin, Francis Lee, Dublin, gent., Richd. Gunne, Dublin, stationer.

Memorial witnessed by : " Chas. Levinge, Esq., second son to the Rt. Hon. Richd. Levinge Knt. and Bart. Lord Chief Justice of the Common Pleas," John Dunbar Bate.

40, 286, 25765   Dorothy Rawdon (seal)

299 SHEIDOW, WILLIAM, Dublin, merchant. 7 April 1724. Précis, ½ p., 15 April 1724.

His mother Mary Rooe als. Sheidow. His wife (then enceinte). His son William Sheidow. Thom. Rooe and Stephen Rooe, his brothers of the half blood.

Freehold of Little Ballintruer, Co. Wicklow and his other freeholds in Liberty of Donore and Co. Dublin.

Witnesses : Christopher Russell, Dublin, surgeon, Francis Browne, Dublin, stationer, Denis Lynch, same, victualler.

Memorial witnessed by : Denis Lynch, Patrick Hamilton, clerk to Edward Dalton, Dublin, public notary.

42, 94, 25793 Thos. Rooe (seal)

300 BURKE, EDMUND, Meelick, Co. Galway, Esq.
23 Oct. 1722. Précis, ¾ p., 27 April 1724.

Wife Mary Burke. Son Rickard Burke. Son Thomas Burke. Daughter Elizabeth. Daughter Katherine.

Meelick and Clunrush, in Half B. of Leitrim, Co. Galway. Sarah Hogan als. Burke to have " graising of four collops " on said lands for life. Woods of Clunrush.

Witnesses : Wm. Burke, Dublin, gent., Michael Tohy and John Cammane, servants to testator.

Memorial witnessed by : Wm. Burke, Thos. Burke his clerk, and Andrew Hearn, Hearnesbrooke, Co. Galway, gent.

42, 126, 25890 Rick. Burke (seal)

301 STAFFORD, EDMOND FRANCIS, Brownstown, Co. Meath,
Esq. 4 Sept. 1722. Full, 1 p., 4 May 1724.

My mother and my wife guardians of my daughter Ann during her minority. Cousin Bartholomew McNaghten. £12 per ann. to "my coz. Rowen for her life . . . without her husband's intermeddling therewith." Cousin Alexander McNaghten. Cousin Edmd. McNaghten.

Sir Compton Domvile and Archibald Stewart of Ballintoy, clerk, trustees. Kenedy Stafford, eldest son of Henry Stafford. Recites settlement of Co. Antrim lands made 1722 between "myself and Isabella my wife of the first part, the Hon. Brigad. David Creighton and Wm. Sampson of Inch, Co. Donegal, Esq., of the second part, and Sir Compton Domvile, Bt. and Alexr. McNaghten of Dublin, Doctor of Physick, of the third part."

Ballybeg, Ballykenedys, Ballyrevan, Chreighnakeragh, Limneherty, Lisroddan, Curnary, Ballintullagh and Glenon and other lands in Co. Antrim.

Witnesses : William Forward, Castleforward, Co. Donegal, Esq., Thos. Jackson, Dublin, Esq., David Wilson, Dublin, gent.

Memorial witnessed by : David Wilson, Thos. Downam Clarke, Dublin, gent.

40, 309, 25982 Alexr. McNaghten (seal)

302 BATES, JOHN, city of Dublin, gent.

   9 April 1724.   Narrate, ¾ p., 6 May 1724.

His eldest brother Mr. Thomas Bates clerk.   His younger brother Mr. Michael Bates.   Niece Elizabeth Barlow als. Peppard.   Robert Higgins, Dublin merchant, trustee.

Estate of inheritance near town of Lymm, Co. of Chester or elsewhere in Kingdom of Great Britain.   His houses etc. opposite to the Castle Gate in city of Dublin.

Witnesses : Edwd. Lord, Dublin, apothecary, Thos. Cooke, senr., Thos. Cooke, junr., Dublin, public notaries.

Memorial witnessed by : Frances Johnston, Dublin, spinster, Thos. Cooke, junr.

40, 313, 26003   Robt. Higgins (seal)

303 ANDREWS, RICHARD, Tallow, Co. Waterford, Esq.

   11 March 1716.   Précis, ½ p., 9 May 1724.

Wife Margt. Andrews.   Nephew Richard Andrews, son of his brother Boyle Andrews.   Mr. John Andrews, son to his said nephew Lieut. Richd. Andrews, exor.   His real and personal estate.

Witnesses : Moses Christian, Dublin, victualler, Maurice Magrath, Dublin, gent., Nicholas White near Mitchelstown, Co. Cork, gent.

Memorial witnessed by : Maurice Magrath, Wm. Devall, Dublin, gent.

41, 307, 26039   Richd. Andrews (seal)

304 YOUNG, JOHN, senr., Belfast, merchant.

   29 Aug. 1722.   Narrate, 1 p., 4 June 1724.

His wife Mary Young.   Eldest son Alexr. Young, exor.   Second son Hugh Young.   His four youngest children.   £100 " to the children of Gilbert McTeer by his daughter Jane Young."   Son Charles Young. Son Robert Young.   Third son James Young.   Wm. Millikin, son to his daughter Abigail Young by Robt. Millikin.

Daniel Mussenden, Belfast, Wm. Stevenson, Ballymacarrett, exors.

Ballydian, Co. Down.   Listender, Co. Down.   Ballynickole, Co. Down. The townland commonly called the Fish Quarter [situation not mentioned ? Co. Down].

Witnesses : James Park and Thomas Stevenson, Belfast, merchant, James McTeer, Belfast, merchant.

Memorial witnessed by : James Park, Thomas Sturgeon, both of Belfast.

Alexr. Young (seal)

39, 433, 26213   Hugh Young (seal)

305 BOYSE, JACOB, Dublin, Esq.

23 May 1724. Narrate, ½ p., 9 June 1724.

Sister Patience Vicary. Nephew Samuel Boyse, exor. Nephew Jacob Boyse, exor. Nephew Nathaniel Boyse.

Ballydusker, Polrain, Talbotstown, Ballyraine, Graige, Grange, Ballyhaly, Ballyclury, Little Assaly and Ballough Island, all in Co. Wexford.

Witnesses : Cusack Baldwin and James Nixon, Dublin, gents., James Lindsay, Dublin, perukemaker.

Memorial witnessed by : Thos. Cooke, junr., notary public, George More, his clerk.

41, 351, 26263   Jacob Boyse (seal)

306 BOYSE, MARY als. PAPE als. GEE, widow of Joseph Boyse of Dublin. 10 Feb. 1723. Full, 1 p., 2 July 1724.

Recites articles 1706 between Thos. Gee, Leap, King's Co., gent., Joseph Boyse, Dublin, clerk, and testatrix by name of Mary Pape als. Gee, widow, the daughter of said Thomas Gee, previous to marriage of testatrix and said Joseph Boyse.

My daughter Hannah Loftus and her husband Simon Loftus, exors. My son Thomas Pape. My daughter Ann Johnston. My grandson James Pape.

Walking Street, city of Kilkenny, Mr. Ryan, Mr. John Sargent, Mr. Meagh, Mr. Silvester, Mr. Martin Stapleton, Mr. Lawrence St. Lawrence and Mr. Denis Gormond, tenants of same.

Witnesses : Robert French, Dublin, Esq., Michael McManus, late of Dublin, attorney, deceased, Wm. Tyrrell, Dublin, attorney.

Memorial witnessed by : Robert French, John Digby of Landenstown, Co. Kildare, Esq.

40, 397, 26480   Hannah Loftus (seal)

K

307 CHAIGNEAU, LEWIS, Dublin, merchant.

16 July 1723. Full, 1¾ pp., 13 July 1724.

To be buried near my wife in St. Patrick's Churchyard. My only son David Chaigneau, Esq., exor. My daughter Eliz. Renouard. My brother Isaac Chaigneau, Dublin, merchant and John Porter, Dublin, alderman, trustees. Legacy to Abraham Sanvaget, Dublin, glover, and his wife.

Eustace Street, Dublin. The George and London Tavern in Fishamble Street. Houses in Kennedy's Lane. Benjamin Dawson, tenant, Eustace Street. Robert Bentley, Widow Johnston, John Cuthbert, Michael Teeling, John Smith, Esq., tenants on north side of Kennedy's Lane.

Witnesses : Wm. Devall and Adam de Glatigny, both of Dublin, gents., Wm. Parry, Dublin, public notary.

Memorial witnessed by : Thos. Mullock, Dublin, gent., Wm. Devall.

42, 336, 26560   Dav. Chaigneau (seal)

308 GROVE, THOMAS, Grovehall, Co. Donegal, Esq.

15 April 1724. Narrate, ¾ pl, 28 July 1724.

Brother James Grove, exor. Brother William Grove.

Rev. Mathew Leslie and Ezekiel Cuningham, exors. Thomas Lea. Winifred White. Grania Lewis. His servant Michael McAvahan.

Mulloghippe, Leater, Aughawinie and Grovehall [situation not mentioned].

Witnesses, signing at Dromolla, Co. Cavan : Alexr. Brooke, Cavan, apothecary, Thomas Lea, Tullamore, gent., and Richard Weaver, Tully, notary public, all in Co. Cavan.

Memorial witnessed by : Rich. Weaver, Ben. Johnston, notary public.

39, 497, 26690   James Grove (seal)

309 SILVER, JOHN, Fountain, Co. Waterford, Esq.

28 May 1724. Codicil 29 May 1724. Narrate, ¾ p., 19 Sept. 1724.

Wife Joan Silver, extx. Sister Ann Silver. His daughter Elizabeth Silver. His children. His youngest daughter Joan Silver.

Daniel Redding, Dublin, Esq., Richard Richardson of same, Esq., trustees.

Ballycroning, Ballycottm, Ballyrobbin, B. Imockelly, Co. Cork. His real estate in Co. Tipperary. His estate in Co. Leitrim.

Witnesses to will and codicil : Edward Warren, Thomas Sandford, both of Kilkenny, aldermen, Joseph Deane, Dublin, gent.

Memorial witnessed by : Wm. Shiell, Dublin, gent., Owen Morrison, Ballycroning, Co. Cork, gent.

42, 436, 26959   J. Silver (seal)

310 PEIRSON, RICHARD, Selby, Yorkshire.
      7 June 1724. Précis, ½ p., 5 Oct. 1724.

His mother Ruth Lamb. His sister Ann Warring. His brother Thos. Firman, exor.

Real estate in Great Britain and Ireland. Real estate at Horristown in said Kingdom of Ireland, about 5 years of his lease then to come.

Witnesses : Thos. Rawdon, ropemaker, John Jewett, malster, Edmond Woodsworth, gent., all of Selby.

Memorial witnessed by : Jas. Wilde, Wm. Devall, clerks to Bruen Worthington, public notary in Dublin.

42, 465, 27051   Tho. Firman (seal)

311 SOUTHWELL, SIR THOMAS, Castlemartyr, Co. Limerick,
      Bart. 22 Aug. 1713. Narrate, ¾ p., 9 Oct. 1724.

Wife Dame Meliora Southwell. His son Thomas. His other sons Henry, Robert, William and Richard. His brother Hon. Col. Wm. Southwell, Robert Taylor, Esq., of Ballynort, Co. Limerick, Joseph Deane, Esq., of Crumlin and Robert Oliver of Cloghnotfoy, exors.

Mr. John Bellaquer his son Thomas's "governor." Mrs. Frances Rogers.

His house etc. in Clontarf, Co. Dublin, held by lease from Mrs. Mary Vernon and Mr. Edward Vernon her heir at law. Kilcooleen, Singland, Clounagh, Loghill, Lisskilleen, Gortavelly, Knockbrack, all in B. Connelloe, Co. Limerick. Cartine, Pollogh, B. Coshma, Co. Limerick. Portrynand and Great Knockneskennagh, Gortnebouly, Rathgrogane, Fahebane, Latterrugh "and Garrybane in Ardagh," Acrenruddery als. Knight's Acre, and Scartnenacre, in B. Connelloe, Co. Limerick.

Witnesses : Hanniball Hall, surgeon, Daniel Hintze, Bartholomew Clossy, gent., Thos. Cooke, notary public, all of Dublin.

Memorial witnessed by : Rev. Mr. Frederick Usher, Clontarf, Co. Dublin, clerk, John Sparkes, Dublin.

42, 469, 27072   Mel. Southwell (seal)

312 TAAFE, ELINOR, Dublin, widow of Edward Taafe, Dublin. gent. 26 June 1718. Full, 1 p., 17 Oct. 1724.

My son Richard Taafe. My daughter Elinor Taafe. My daughter Sarah Gregge. My daughter Ann Parker. My grand-daughter Hoult Hugas. " Four of my grandchildren . . . Hoult Taafe, Mathias Taafe, Martha Taafe, Sarah Gregge " [? *if these are the four grandchildren*]. Grandsons Mathias Taafe and Edwd. Gregge. Grandson Hoult Taafe, son of Richard Taafe. A sum owing to Bartholomew Rivers.

My land in England and Ireland. My two houses in High Street known by the name of the Ship and Black Swan. My lands of Drumcarr, and Little Ruellstown, and Hickockmore, B. Atherdee, Co. Louth.

Witnesses : Patrick Sinclare, High Street, Dublin, merchant, Edward Wall, Dublin, woollen draper, Thomas Wills, Dublin, woollen draper.

Memorial witnessed by : Richard Field, Dublin, merchant, Patrick Sinclare. James Powell, Kevin Street, Dublin, gent.

42, 478, 27112   Richard Taafe (seal)

313 BOWYER, CATHERINE als. GOULDING, Grangemore, B. Tireragh, Co. Sligo, widow. 1 April 1724. Précis, ½ p., 27 Oct. 1724.

Her eldest son Wm. Bowyer. Her second son John Bowyer. Mathew Ormsby, Rathlee, Co. Sligo, Esq., exor.

Faleanaclarin, Grangemore and Faleavany, Co. Sligo.

Witnesses : Thomas Ormsby, Ballymoony, gent., Mathew Ormsby, junr. of Rathlee aforesaid, son of said Mathew Ormsby, and Richard Scott, Frankford, said county, gent.

Memorial witnessed by : Mathew Ormsby, junr., Robert Buntin, Sligo, gent.

43, 30, 27149   Math. Ormsby (seal)

314 MARTIN, ROBERT, Rackeragh, Co. Tyrone.

24 March 1715. Précis, ½ p., 16 Nov. 1724.

Wife Margaret Martin als. Charleton then enceinte. Brother John Martin. His sister Mary. His father John Martin of Grange, and Wm. Martin of Aghnadollow, exors.

The sessiough of Rackeragh, B. Omagh, Co. Tyrone. Sessiaghnabrockagh, said B. and County.

Witnesses : Andrew Duncan, Glennan, B. Omagh, Co. Tyrone, Robert White of Sessighnabrockagh, Co. Tyrone.

Memorial witnessed by : Andrew Duncan, James Brattan of Newbridge, Co. Monaghan, gent.

43, 64, 27383   John Martin (seal)

315 HANLON, ALEXANDER, city of Dublin, innkeeper.

13 Feb. 1713. Narrate, ¾ p., 10 Dec. 1724.

His wife Hanna Hanlon. His daughter Catherine Hanlon. His daughter Isabela Hanlon. His son Alexr. Hanlon. His mother Catherine Hanlon.

Redmd. Hanlon of Letterkenny, Co. Donegal, merchant and John Boyd of same, merchant, and Alexr. Johnstone, Dublin, pewterer, exors.

His dwelling house in Caple Street. House etc. in Ballybough Lane, Dublin.

Witnesses : James Kormagh, Patrick Caldwell then of the city of Dublin, merchant, and John Caldwell, of same, gent.

Memorial witnessed by : John Paddon and Joseph Rose, clerks to William Barry of city of Dublin, scrivener.

44, 76, 27618   Alexr. Hanlon (seal)

316 DUNCANNON, WILLIAM VISCOUNT.

11 Aug. 1724. Narrate, ¾ p., 18 May 1724.

His eldest son and heir Brabazon Ponsonby, exor. His daughter Dorothy Ponsonby. His son-in-law Col. Thomas Newcomen. His second son Henry Ponsonby, Lady Frances wife of said Henry. His youngest son Folliott Ponsonby.

His friend John Langrish, overseer. Rev. Mr. Robt Watts, minister of the parish of Fidown.

Town and lands of Delgany, held by lease from Earl of Meath.

Lands of White Church and New Graige [situation not mentioned] "His acquired real estate."

Witnesses : Philip Bernard, Kill, Co. Catherlogh, Esq., John Dent, Bessborough, Co. Kilkenny, servant to said testator, Bartholomew Newton, Castledermot, Co. Kildare, notary public.

Memorial witnessed by : William Colvill and Wm. Shaw, Dublin, gent.

44, 87, 27684   Duncannon (seal)

317 WHARTON, LUCY MARCHIONESS OF, and MAR-CHIONESS OF MALMESBURY[1]. 9 Dec. 1715. Précis, ½ p., 19 Feb. 1724.

Her daughter Lady Jane Wharton (under 17 years). Alexr. Denton, then of Hillesdon, Bucks., Esq., and now one of the Justices of H.M. Court of Common Pleas in Westminster, exor. Her real and personal estate.

Witnesses: Charles Bayliffe, of the Six Clerks office, gent., Wm. Dixon and Richd. Wolfe, both of Lincoln's Inn, gents., and Oxinbridge Harwood, Lothbury, London, gent.

Memorial witnessed by : Wm. Dixon of Lincoln's Inn, gent., Oxinbridge Harwood, Lothbury, London.

45, 104, 28146   Alexr. Denton (seal)

318 HOARE, RICHARD, Dublin, Esq.

    25 July 1724. Précis, ½ p., 10 March 1724.

His wife. His son Edward Hoare. His daughter Mary Hoare. His brother Robert Hoare.

Inchilea, Dromiscanlane and Carrigagulla, B. Muskerry, Co. Cork, purchased from Mr. Edwards.

Witnesses : Hercules Rowley, Her. Upton, both of Dublin, Esqrs. Elizabeth Whiteside, servant to said testator.

Memorial witnessed by : Thomas Best, Dublin, servant, Elizabeth Whiteside.

46, 193, 28288   Elizabeth Hoare, widow

                                  (seal)

---

[1] Her husband was created Marquess of Wharton and Marquess of Malmesbury 15 Feb. 1714/15. She died at Aylesbury, buried 14 Feb. 1715/16. *The Complete Peerage* by G. E. C.

319 SAVAGE, PATRICK, Portaferry, Co. Down.

21 April 1724. Précis, ½ p., 27 March 1725.

His wife. His eldest son Rowland Savage. His son Edwd. Savage.

Ballyfuneragh with the fresh Water Lough thereunto belonging [situation not mentioned], and real and personal estate.

Witnesses : Hugh Savage, Drumaroud, Rowland Savage, Currook, and Henry Savage, Portaferry, all in Co. Down, gents.

Memorial witnessed by : Mark Savage, Portaferry, Henry Savage, Portaferry, bailiff.

46, 219, 28397   Edwd. Savage (seal)

320 PALMER, ROGER, senior, Palmerstown, Co. Mayo, Esq.

12 Oct. 1724. Précis, ½ p., 16 April 1725.

Son Thomas Palmer. Glanhurst [situation not mentioned] and lands etc. in Counties of Mayo, Sligo, Leitrim, Roscommon or elsewhere.

Witnesses : Arthur Knox, Forebegg, Co. Mayo, Esq., John Hughes, senr., and James Hughes, junr., both of Lecarrowinfolle, Co. Mayo.

Memorial witnessed by : James Hughes, senr., James Hughes, junr.

43, 343, 28482   Thos. Palmer (seal)

321 COLE, JOHN, Castlelough, Co. Tipperary, gent.

5 March 1724. Full, ¾ p., 17 April, 1725.

My father Michael Cole, of Castlelough, exor. My uncle Col. Richard Cole, exor. My uncle Arthur Lord Baron of Ranelagh.

Ballyvoir, Sheshumry, Knocknesnaly als. Cragatimore, Druminakelly, Clonecoole, Knockonterush, "Ballyvoirgin and Ballyvurneen equivalent to Knocktereen." Killinenagh, Gorteenrishlough and Cappontrusheen, Killclaran, Derrynagittah als. Gurtrinane, Arlevane, Ligurt, Derryvinane, Knocktoreen als. Tironea, in B. Tullagh, Co. Clare. My other real estate.

Witnesses : Rev. Benjamin Lloyd, Killalee, Co. Clare, clerk, Stephen Allen, Killownne, Co. Tipperary, Esq., Peter Brian, Pallice, Co. Tipperary, chirurgeon.

Memorial witnessed by : John Scott, Limerick, gent., Thos. Studdert, Kilkylin, Co. Clare, Esq.

45, 153, 28557   Mich. Cole (seal)

322 MITCHELL, JOHN, Machregorach, Co. Antrim, gent.

26 May 1724. Narrate, ¾ p., 19 April 1725.

His wife, exor. His son William, exor. His son John Mitchell. His brother Hugh Mitchell. His son Hugh Mitchell. His daughter Elizabeth. His daughter Rose. His brother-in-law Henry McCulloch and his brother James Mitchell, overseers.

His freehold of Machregorach and Mynis, tenements in Glenarme, lease of Craigantanwilly, [? Co. Antrim]. £1 to poor of parish of Glenarm.

Witnesses : John Brice and John McCamrick, servants to testator, and Hugh Mitchell, Glenarme, Co. Antrim.

Memorial witnessed by : Said Hugh Mitchell, Alexr. Hutcheson. Dublin, gent.

44, 208, 28562   Will. Mitchell (seal)

323 GOOLD, ROBERT, Drominey, Co. Cork, gent.

20 Feb. 1719. Précis, ½ p., 21 April 1725.

His son Pierce Goold. His son Robt. Goold. Exors. said Pierce Goold and Patrick Goold.

His farm of Ballynekilly [situation not mentioned] and all his leases farms etc.

Witnesses : Pierce Goold, Michl. Goold, Wm. Fling and Jno. McDermond, all of and near Charleville, Co. Cork.

Memorial witnessed by : Michael Goold, Michael Quin of Charleville, Co. Cork.

43, 365, 28583   Pierce Goold (seal)

324 PARKINSON, RICHARD, Tullyanaghan, parish of Magheralin, Co. Down, draper. 16 June 1722. Narrate, 1¼ pp., 25 April 1725.

Wife Elinor Parkinson. His goods etc. " to be divided into ten shares and his wife and children each to have a just share except his son Jno. whose proportion he left to his three eldest daughters to be equally divided amongst them." Son John Parkinson (under 21 years). Son Joseph Parkinson. Exors. his wife Elinor, and Thos. Usher and John Usher.

" His freehold farm and dwelling-house with the appurts. and the turff moss that belong to it which he then lived upon." " His freehold farm that John Usher then lived upon which he purchased from his brother John." " His freehold farm purchased from Edward Usher."

Witnesses : Edward Usher, Edenballycoggen, Nathaniel West, Ballymaconan and James Perry, Perrymount, all in Co. Down, gents.

Memorial witnessed by : James Perry, John Usher, Ballymcmean and Gawen Martin, Tullyanaghan, parish of Magheralyn, Co. Down, gent.

43, 384, 29651   Ellinor Parkinson, her mark
                                          (seal)

325 CRAMER, JOHN, Kilkenny, baker.

18 Jan. 1724. Narrate, 2 pp., 7 May 1725.

To " his brother Francis and his son John Cramer " one English crown each. His niece Elizth. Sanders. Margarett Leake his wife's sister.

His servant maid Mary Robbins als. Hindes, her unnatural husband. His godson John Jackson, son of Peter Jackson of Kilkenny, baker, a legacy " provided he prove a good boy." Frances Jackson. Ed. Smith, son to Joseph Smith in the Irishtowne, weaver. Sons of deceased Will Freerson. George Robinson's family. Sarah Bancroft. Rev. Doctor Wm. Andrews, Archdeacon and Vicar Genll. of the Diocese of Ossory, overseer of will. His Worshipfull Edwd. Warren, Esq., Mayor of the city of Kilkenny, Derby Egan, Esq., Recorder of said city, Rev. Thomas Martin, curate or minister of parish of St. Mary's and Wm. Spratt and John Sergent, churchwardens of said Parish, and their successors, trustees. The trustees to make a fee farm of his concerns for special uses, including fees for Protestant apprentices and " every Friday in the year the Protestant poor of St. Mary's Parish in the city of Kilkenny as Mary Parris, Mary Poor, Widow Collins etc. and their successors successively for every [ever] poor of said Parish being Protestants should have given them . . . . a loaf of wholesome bread to the value of four pence and two pence sterling."

His house in North Ward in city of Kilkenny thereafter for ever made over to Green Coat Hospital in the parish of St. Mary Shandon in the city of Cork and " he wills that a skillfull baker be tenant in the house to make the bread for the poor." His will to be fairly engrossed in vestry book of parish of St. Mary, Kilkenny.

Witnesses : Wm. Spratt, Kilkenny, perywiggmaker, John Sergent,

Kilkenny, joyner, John Rath, Kilkenny, merchant, Edwd. Dowling, Kilkenny, yeoman, Benjamin Meares, Kilkenny, alderman.

Memorial witnessed by : Thomas Cantwell, Kilkenny, gent., John Carler, Kilkenny, coachman.

Edward Warren (seal)
Mayor of Kilkenny and a trustee
46, 321, 28803   Mary Poor (her mark and seal) widow
one of the poor of the Parish
of St. Mary, Kilkenny.

326 JONES, ROTH, Dublin, Esq.

12 May 1725. Narrate, 2¼ pp., 22 May 1725.

His nephew William Morris son of his late sister Lettice by Thomas Morris late of Mountjoy, Co. Tyrone, Esq., deceased. His sister Ann Morris. His nephew Roth Morris, son of Patk. Morris late of Silverwood, Co. Armagh, deceased by his sister Ann. His nephew Francis Courtney son of Francis Courtney late of Carrickbroad, Co. Armagh, deceased by his sister Mary likewise deceased. Ellinor the daughter of his late brother Arthur Jones, Walsh her supposed husband. Mathew Ford and Phillemon Brownlow, Esqrs., trustees. William Brownlow, Lurgan, Co. Armagh, Esq., Edward. Lyndon, Esq., one of the Masters of H.M. High Court of Chancery in Ireland, and Richd. Malone, Esq., Counsellor-at-law, exors.

Lands etc., in Counties of Down and Armagh and Louth or elsewhere in Kingdom of Ireland. Lands in Silverwood and Teignavan, Co. Armagh.

Witnesses : John McGawly, Tully, Co. Westmeath, Esq., Bryan Connor, Dublin, perukemaker, ffagh Farrell, Dublin, gent.

Memorial witnessed by : Jas. Wilde, Thomas Mullock, both clerks to Mr. Bruen Worthington, Public notary, Dublin.

46, 359, 28915   Wm. Jones als. Morris (seal)

327 PERCY, HENRY, Esq.

Codicil 8 Aug. 1722. Narrate 1 p., 5 June 1725.

His will in hands of Rev. Claudius Gilbert. His daughter Hannah Percy als. Hoey. His father-[in-law] William Paul. His son-[in-law] Richard Warren [husband of testator's daughter Mary]. His grandfather Emerson.

Witnesses : George Warren, Grangebegg, Co. Kildare, gent., Rev. Alex. Bradford, Ballyadams, Queen's Co., clerk, and Henry Essington, Dublin, gent.

Memorial witnessed by : Henry Essington, Terence Gorman, Dublin, gent.

45, 209, 29052　　　　　　　　　　　　Wm. Paul (seal)

328 PERCY, HENRY, Seskin, Co. Wicklow, Esq.
　　　10 Dec. 1720. Narrate, 1 p., 5 June 1725.

His late wife Elizth. Paul als. Percy. His son Emerson Percy. His daughters Mary Warren, Elizth. Montgomery, Ann Percy, Harriott Percy and Jane Percy. His daughter Hannah. His brother Robt. Percy.

Richard Warren, Ballydarton, Co. Catherlogh, Esq. To Mary Wells, £200 per annum. Wm. Paul, Moyhill, Co. Catherlogh, Esq., Rev. Claudius Gilbert, D.D., Vice Provost of Trinity College, Dublin, Richard Warburton, Dublin, Esq., Counsellor-at-law, exors.

　His real and personal estate. His house in Abby Street.

Witnesses : Wm. Westberry and Terence Gorman, both of Dublin, gents., Thomas Merefield, Dublin, public notary.

Memorial witnessed by : Terence Gorman, Henry Essington, Dublin, gent. ·

43, 481, 29053　　　　　　　　　　　　Wm. Paul (seal)

329 HODDER, BARBARA, wife of Thomas Hodder, Ballinterry,
　　　Co. Cork, Esq. 20 Feb. 1724. Full, ¾ p., 13 Sept. 1725.

My niece Mrs. Elizabeth Campion. My niece Mrs. Mary Jenkins and her sister. My niece Mrs. Barbara Jenkins. My niece Mrs. Anne Gray. My niece Mrs. Barbra Forward. My niece Mrs. Jane Forward. My sister Gray. My nephew Joseph Jenkins. My nephew Ralph Jenkins, £40, " not to be paid till he has served out his full seven years apprenticeship." My nephew Abel Jenkins, £40, (ditto). My nephew John Gray. My nephew Mr. William Gray. My nephew Mr. Wm. Forward (under age) " my heir to the reversion to lands and spiritualities of Fermoy and houses."

Mr. John Campion and Mr. Francis Gray, exors. Widow Vowell,

tenant. £5 to poor of parish of Shandon, same to parish of Fermoy. My plowland of Ballinterry after Mr. Thos. Hodder's death.

Witnesses : Richard Nason, Malfettstown, Co. Cork, gent., Henry Thomas, Rathcormock, Co. Cork, tanner, Wm. Nason, one of the sons of said Richard Nason.

Memorial witnessed by : Robert Blakely, Cork, sword cutler, Wm. Simmins, Cork, gent.

44, 352, 29738   Eliz. Campion (seal)

330 STRONG, JAMES, Tawlagh, parish of Ballymahon, Co. Cavan, gent. 24 Aug. 1725. Précis, ½ p., 14 Sept. 1725.

Wife Jane Strong als. Coverdell. His son William Strong, exor. His son Thomas. His two daughters.

His right etc. in town and lands of Taulaugh.

Witnesses : John Chevers, Aghacreevy, Co. Cavan, gent., Alexr. Walker, Williamstown, Co. Westmeath, hatter, Wm. Wood, Aghakillmore, Co. Cavan, gent.

Memorial witnessed by : James Heany, St. Michael's Lane, Co. Dublin, gent., James Wilde, clerk to Mr. Bruen Worthington, Dublin, public notary.

47, 117, 29743   Wm. Strong (seal)

331 McDONNELL, HENRY, Drumcondra Lane, suburbs of city of Dublin, gardiner. 26 July 1725. Narrate, ¾ p., 23 Sept. 1725.

Wife Susanna McDonnell, exor. His daughter Sarah McDonnell. His daughter Elizabeth Reed. His son-in-law Mr. Shannon. His grandson Henry McDonnell son to his son Henry McDonnell.

Widow Lawrence, tenant. Mr. David Howell, exor. His land houses and leasehold interests in and about Drumcondra Lane. Land in McDonnell's Lane leading from Drumcondra Lane to his then dwellinghouse.

Witnesses : Rev. Wm. Sibbald, Dublin, Wm. Sumner, Dublin, public notary.

Memorial witnesses by : Wm. Sumner and Samuel Boyd his clerk.

47, 127, 29792   Susanna McDonnell, her mark
                                              (seal)

332 ALLEN, RICHARD, Monaghan, Esq.

14 Oct. 1724. Narrate, ¾ p., 6 Nov. 1725.

Wife Jane. His nephew Anthony Coltman and Elizabeth Coltman als. Richardson his wife, Richard Coltman, son of said nephew, and Henry Coltman, second son of said Anthony Coltman.

Lands of Knaghill, leased to John James, B. and Co. Monaghan. Lands of Dromrootagh, commonly known by names of Lissearny, Lissanore, Dromacruttin and Dromrootagh, all in said B. and county. His real and personal estate. His dwelling-house in town of Monaghan, with garden, malt house and kiln, etc. Meadows and Parks in Rouskey.

Witnesses : Rev. John Dennis, Monaghan, D.D., Oliver Douglass, clerk, Rector of Tehallan, Co. Monaghan, James Grean of Tehallan, gent.

Memorial witnessed by : James Grean, Edward Mathews, Dublin, gent.

44, 455, 30093   Anthony Coltman (seal)

333 NEWBOLD, THOMAS, Ballyfennan, Queen's Co., gent.

6 March 1723. Full, ½ p., 13 Nov. 1725.

My wife Hanna Newbold. My son Anthony Newbold. Daughter Mary Newbold. My sister Ann Newbold. My sister Mary Russell. My brother Robert Newbold. Twenty moidors to my brother Frank Newbold. My sister Catherine Fitzgerald als. Newbold. My sister-in-law Dorothy Russell.

Henry Bambrick of Garrans and Joseph Russell of Coolerain, exors.

Ballyfennan, sister Ann Newbold having a part interest left by my mother Mary Newbold deceased.

Witnesses : Jno. Russell, Cullinagh, Denis Murphy, Castletownomy, Charles Ryan of same, Derby Lennan, Ballyfennan, all in Queen's Co., farmers.

Memorial witnessed by : Derby Lennan, Anthony Gale, Skinner's Alley, Co. Dublin, gent.

47, 197, 30174   Ann Newbold (seal)

334 WILSON, THOMAS, Thornwell in Lenamarra[n], King's Co., farmer. 30 Jan. 1724. Full, 3 pp., 15 Nov. 1725.

My wife Mary Wilson. My eldest son Thomas Wilson. My younger son Benjamin Wilson. My two sons Thomas and Benjamin Wilson.

My brother-in-law Thomas Bewley. My brother-in-law Mungo Bewley. My brother-in-law George Bewley. My sister Margaret Winter of Rogerstown. My brother Winter.

Joseph Inman, senr. My servant maid Sarah Widdoes. " My friends and relations viz : my brothers Joshua Clibborn, Thomas and Mungo Bewley and Joseph Inman " exors. Joseph Knott, son to William Knott. Legacy to poor Friends called Quakers belonging to Edenderry Meeting of which I am a member.

" My farm of land . . . in King's Co. . . . on south side of the lane begining at Monistiroris ford and so along to the Watering Pool near my dwelling-house and thence along by the mearing which was formerly the bounds between George Bewley and me leading to Ballybrittan bounds " (held by lease from Alderman Francis Stoyte). My lands about 800 acres at or near the head of Misshumeny River, in the county of Philadelphia in America. My lands at Skullkill, about 5 miles from Philadelphia, about 236 acres, and about 20 acres near city of Philadelphia, and two lots in said city.

Witnesses : William Heslep, Ballymorane, King's Co., farmer, Thomas Bennett, Monasteroris, King's Co., blacksmith, John Greenhow, Rogerstown, King's Co., farmer.

Memorial witnessed by : John Paddon, clerk to Wm. Barry, Dublin, scrivener, and said Wm. Barry.

45, 503, 30220　　　　　　　　　　Benjamin Wilson (seal)

335 CROSSLY, AARON, Dublin, herald painter.

Last day of Feb. 1723. Partly in full, 1 p., 26 Nov. 1725.

Wife Abigail Crossly. My two daughters Frances and Susanna Crossly. Rev. Pascade Ducas, Dublin, clerk, Thomas Carleton and Edward Exshaw, Dublin, painters, trustees. Thomas Corker, merchant. William Dawson.

My dwelling-house in Dame Street. My two houses in Eustace Street on plots of lands held by leases from Benjamin Chetwood, Dublin, gent. and Ann Eustace als. Chetwood his wife. A lot of ground with the large smith's forge thereon, in Great Britain Street als. Ballybough Lane near Dublin. A house etc. in Grafton Street, Thomas Browne, coachman, tenant.

Witnesses : Barnaby Middleton, grocer in Dame Street, Law McManus, victualler at the sign of the Punch Bowl in Eustace Street, Dublin, Sam. Tyrrel, Dublin, notary public.

Memorial witnessed by : Samuel Tyrrel, Daniel Falkiner, Dublin, merchant.

46, 483, 30351   Abigail Crossly (seal)

336 WORTH, WILLIAM, Rathfarnham, Co. Dublin, Esq.

5 Nov. 1725. Narrate, ¾ p., 29 Nov. 1725.

His wife then enceinte. To his father Edward Worth. Esq., all his Latin books. To his mother Mrs. Worth all his English books. To his sister Jane Worth all his French books. His sister Dorothy Worth. His sister Alicia Worth. His sister Sarah Worth. His father-in-law Richd. Saunders. Rev. Christ. Lloyd, D.D. His real and personal estate.

Witnesses : Jane Backley, Dublin, widow. Wm. Howard, Esq., and Wm. Westbery, gent., both of Dublin.

Memorial witnessed by : Wm. Westbery, James Duncan, servant to said Edward Worth.

47, 235, 30371   E. Worth (seal)

337 HARMAN, Capt. CHRISTOPHER, Kilmacnoran, [Co. Cavan].

11 Oct. 1722. Précis, ¼ p., 8 Dec. 1725.

Wife Ann Harman. His only daughter Elizabeth Harman. Mr. Wm. Harman, exor. Sister Mrs. Jane Ebzery, extx. His sons Mr. Christopher Harman and Mr. John Harman.

Lands of Kilmacnoran [situation not mentioned] and real and personal estate.

Witnesses : Will Lathum, then of Kilmacnoran, gent., Wm. Ebzery, of same, gent., John Farrell, servant to said William Lathum.

Memorial witnessed by : Wm. Ebzery, John Thompson, Killibandrick, Wm. Little, Redhills.

                         Jean Ebzery (seal)

49, 10, 30466   William Harman (seal)

338 NOWLAN, MARK, Dublin, gent.

27 Jan. 1723. Narrate, 1 p., 8 June 1725.

Sister Mrs. Mary Smith. Brother-in-law Mr. Benjamin Smith, husband of said Mary. His nephew Bankes Crooke only son living of his deceased sister Katherine Crooke als. Nowlan. His nephew

Thomas Cooke, junr., only son living of his deceased sister Elizabeth
Cooke als. Nowlan. Quayle Somervell, eldest son of his niece Eliz.
Somervell als. Quayle. Mr. Thomas Thorp, tenant. Joseph Bury,
Dublin, Esq., trustee.

St. Patrick Street and Plunkett Street, Dublin. Ground and holding
at Naas, Co. Kildare. A house at corner of High Street and Christ
Church Lane, Dublin.

Witnesses : Thos. Quin, Dublin, apothecary, George Moore and
James Standish, clerks to said Thos. Cooke, junr.

Memorial witnessed by : Said James Standish, and Wm. Jorden
also clerk to said Thos. Cooke, junr.

49, 54, 30668   Thos. Cooke, junr. (seal)

339 BOLTON, WILLIAM, Waterford, baker.
        13 May 1725. Narrate, ½ p., 17 Jan. 1725/26.
Wife Lucy. His daughter Mary McDaniel. His daughter Hanah
Scroder. His daughter Rebeca Tylar. His son Wm. Bolton.

His dwelling-house, yard, shed, etc. in Waterford. His dwelling-
house, shop, yard, etc. held from Richard Hoare, Esq.

Witnesses : Wm. Eccles, Waterford, innholder, Wm. Hagherin,
Waterford, yeoman, Maurice Rogers, Waterford, gent.

Memorial witnessed by : Maurice Rogers, Thos. Cotton, Waterford,
printer.

47, 300, 30698   Hanah Scroder (seal)

340 HUTCHESON, ALEXR., Drumalig, parish of Tonaghneeve,
        Co. Down. 25 Sept. 1711. Narrate, ¾ p., 26 Jan. 1725.
His only son John Hutcheson, exor. His grandson Frans. Hutcheson.
His grandson Robt. Hutcheson. His grandson John Hutcheson. His
two grandsons Wm. Wallace and Jno. Young, the two second sons then
living of his two daughters Beatrix Wallace and Mary Young.

" Half of the townland of Drumalig aforesaid whereof he was then
seized in inheritance."

Witnesses : Hugh Fisher then of Edenderry parish, Co. Ardmagh
and now of South Carolina, in America, gent., Thos. McCounchy,
Ballybrawley and Thos. Dobbin, late of Trinascobe, deceased, both in
the parish and county of Armagh.

Memorial witnessed by : Wm. Bruce, Thos. Drennan (or Drenan).

47, 311, 30761   Francis Hutcheson (seal)

341 NEWENHAM, THOMAS, Cork, Esq.

12 Nov. 1721. Codicil 16 June 1722. Narrate, 2 pp., 3 Feb. 1725.

Wife Elizabeth. His eldest son William Newenham, exor. His second son Robert Newenham. His third and youngest son Francis Newenham.

Ballyphehane, Kaghabegg, Parkenecrussy, in South Libertys of city of Cork. Lehanamore als. Lehanemore, in South Libertys, city of Cork. Ballycranigg, Gortagowlane and Garrendaragh als. Garrandaragh, in South Libertys, city of Cork. All real and personal estate.

Witnesses : William Hawkins, then Mayor of Cork, now of the same, alderman, Daniel Crone, Cork, Esq., George Blackall, Dublin, gent.

Witnesses to codicil : Daniel Crone, Esq., Daniel Crone, junr., of Cork, merchant, and George Hodder, Cork, gent.

Memorial witnessed by : Robert Hoare, Cork, gent., William Simmins, of same city, gent.

48, 114, 30847   Wm. Newenham (seal)

342 BARLOW, LEWIS, Ballynafearagh, Co. Westmeath, gent.

25 Nov. 1723. Partly in full, ½ p., 7 Feb. 1725.

My wife and younger chilren. My eldest son Theodorus Barlow, exor. My good friend Jno. Smith of Cathernstown, Co. Westmeath, exor.

Ballyfearagh and part of Nicholstown, Glaskenagh als. Glaskenemore and Ballykerin, B. Ratheondagh, Co. Westmeath. Brogtonstown in B. of Moyeshill and Magherghadernan, Co. Westmeath.

Witnesses : John Minchin, Dublin, gent., Humphry Blair, Dublin, upholder, Henry Buckley, Dublin, notary public.

Memorial witnessed by : Henry Buckley, Will French his clerk.

47, 344, 30910   Theodorus Barlow (seal)

343 SPENCER, RICHARD, Dublin, sword cutler.

5 April 1726. Précis, ⅞ p., 29 April 1726.

His wife Mary Spencer. His daughter Anne Mountgomery. His son-in-law Alexander Mountgomery.

His house in Montrath Street, Dublin.

Witnesses : Samuel Lewin, Dublin, gent., James Barry, Dublin, drawer, John Carter, Dublin, notary public.

L

Memorial witnessed by : John Carter, Thomas Bowcock and George Roe, servants to said testator.

48, 280, 31582   Mary Spencer, her mark (seal)

                          Alex. Mountgomery (seal)

344 LYSAGHT, NICHOLAS, Brickfield, Co. Limerick, Esq.
     24 Sept. 1724.   Codicil 25 Aug. 1725. Full, 3 pp., 7 May 1726.
   " My body to be decently interred by my dear wife and children in in the church of Ballyclogh if I happen to dye in Co. of Limerick or Co. of Cork." Son and heir John Lysaght. My second son Nicholas Lysaght, my son Arthur Lysaght (both under age). My daughter Ann. My daughter Mary. My sister Magdalen Cuningham.
   Berkeley Taylor of Ballynort, Esq., John Croker of Ballynegard, Esq., and testator's son John, exors. and guardians. Friends Robert Oliver of Clonadfry and Bartholomew Purdon, Esq., additional guardians. To poor of parish of Ballyclogh £4 yearly for ever, same to poor of Kilmallock, to be paid out of tythes of parish of Drumtarriffe, B. Duhallow, Co. Cork.
   Ballinvelly als. Brickfield, Co. Limerick. Ardehoig als. Mountnorth, Curraghlehane (Curoghlehone), Clareen, Garriduff, Ballynalta and Ballycussin, in B. Orrery and Kilmore, Co. Cork, " my copyholds in Mallow all the aforementioned lands being my paternal estate." Lands impropriate tythes etc. of parish of Drumtarriffe, " Fayers and marketts of Shandrum which I purchased from Lyonell late Earl of Orrey viz. the lands of Lisrobin, Foybreagh, Glassihinlin, Minetena, Meenskeaghy, Collogh, Tureer, Caghill [? Tureen Caghill], Knockscorane, Knockskegh, Knockspunane, Knockane, Gereaghmeenin, Manus, two Meenclees, Minehaha, Glenekeil, Knockaclarigg, Turreenfinine, Reineboulemeen, Gorman, Tureenemeer, Knocknenanagh, Tureen Dermot, Tureen Jon. O'Loghlin, Minliny, Tureen Donnell, the said tythes of Drumtarriffe and fayres and markets of Shandrum with the several plotts of ground in Shandrum " also Wallingstowne, Courtstown, Inishera Island commonly called the Little Island, Co. Cork (purchased from Randall Chaytor, Esq.), Fish Weyers of Tullegull. Moorstown and Rossnetstowne, Co. Limerick (purchased from Richard Earl of Bellomont, Mr. James Godsell now lessee). Dorenstowne and Martinstowne etc. (Mr. John Swayne, lessee) and lands of Coshe (Mr. Samuel Bennett lessee) in B. Coslea, Co. Limerick, purchased by testator from Earl of Bellomont.

Witnesses : Edward Napp, Cork, alderman, John Harper, Cork, banker, James Harnett, Cork, banker, John Armstead, cashier to said John Harper and James Harnett.

Witnesses to codicil : John Mead, Cork, Esq., Darby Fusiny and Lawrence Poyse, servants to said testator.

Memorial witnessed by : William Devall, Thomas Mullock, Dublin, gents.

48, 309, 31690 Jon. Lysaght (seal)

345 MAY, JOHN, Clothworkers Square, liberty of Thomas Court and Donore, "Dutch spiner." 11 Aug. 1718. Précis, part in full, ½ p., 2 Aug. 1726.

Wife Cicilia May, extx. My sons Peter and John May. My goods and chattles real and personal.

Witnesses : John Lowton, Chambers Street, clothier, John Johnson, Meath Street, Marshall of the Liberty of Thomas Court and Donore, John Thompson, Coles Alley, gent., all near the city of Dublin.

Memorial witnessed by : Simon Anyon, Dublin, gent., John Johnson.

48, 523, 32456 Cicilia May, her mark
(seal)

346 AUCHMUTY, JOHN, Newtown, Co. Longford, Esq.
19 May 1726. Précis, ½ p., 13 Aug. 1726.

Son Richard Auchmuty. Rev. Luke Sterling, Mount Dutton, Co. Meath, clerk, and Francis Featherston, Greenrock, Co. Longford, gent., trustees.

Newtown, Sonna[g]h, Ballinruy als. Kingstown, Aghnamaddy, all in Co. Longford.

Witnesses : John Boyle, one of the students of Trinity College, Dublin, William French, clerk to Henry Buckley, Dublin, public notary, and said Henry Buckley.

Memorial witnessed by : Wm. French, Henry Buckley.

51, 6, 32572 Rich. Auchmuty (seal)

347 COOKE, SIR SAMUEL, Dublin, Knight.
8 July 1726. Précis, ¼ p., 15 Sept. 1726.

To his son Thomas Cooke, merchant " the lease that he had from

Charles Campbell, Esq., deceased." [situation not mentioned].

Witnesses : Edmond FitzGerald, servant to Rev. John Ellis, Dublin, clerk, Ann Allen, wife of George Allen of same, brewer, and said George Allen.

Memorial witnessed by : George Allen, John Smith, public notary, Dublin.

49, 439, 32780   Tho. Cooke (seal)

348 CURTIS, ROBERT, Island Bridge, Co. Dublin, Esq.
25 July 1726. Précis, ½ p., 19 Sept. 1726.

His eldest son Wm. Curtis, exor. His son Robert Curtis, clerk. His son Chambre Curtis.

His real and personal estate.

Witnesses : Edward Curtis, Dublin, apothecary, Nathaniel Smith, Dublin, merchant, Robert Curtis, Dublin, barber.

Memorial witnessed by : Mary Wright, Dublin, spinster, Dennis Delany, Dublin, gent.

50, 230, 32789   Will. Curtis (seal)

349 GILBERT, JOSHUA, Bow Street als. Loughbuoy, in suburbs of
city of Dublin, gent. 26 June 1724. Narrate, 1¼ p., 27 Sept. 1726.

Wife Cordelia Gilbert, extx. His son Ezekiel Gilbert. His daughter Mary Smith als. Gilbert. His other daughter Deborah. Nephew Wm. Lynch, Kiltycorragh, King's Co., gent., exor.

His dwelling house in Bow Street als. Loughbuoy, Dublin, and a house adjoining, Mr. Mathew Chambers tenant. A ground rent payable to Rev. Dean Jeremiah Marsh, another to Mr. Moland. His holdings or premises now in the tenure or possession of Capt. St. George, Mr. Patrick Miller and Mrs. Eliz. Hodginson [situation not mentioned]. Houses in Smithfield, suburbs of city of Dublin, Mr. Luke Reily, perukemaker, Mr. Thomas Hewletts and Mr. Jno. Reily, tenants. White's Alley, suburbs of city of Dublin (Mr. Wm. Jenkinson, tenant). Premises in St. Thomas Court, Dublin.

Witnesses : John Reily, Dublin, innkeeper, Luke Reily, Dublin, perukemaker, Thos. Reily, Dublin, gent.

Memorial witnessed by : John Moland, junr., Dublin, gent., Eliz. Hodgkinson, Dublin, spinster.

50, 240, 32845   Cordelia Gilbert (seal)

350 WEST, JAMES, Cranlamore, Co. Longford.

[15 Jan. 1725]. Précis, ½ p., 8 Nov. 1726.

His wife. Thomas West, son to his late brother Francis West. Cornet John West, brother to said Thomas. His brother George West, exor. His brother John West. His brother Hodson [husband of testator's sister Anne West].

Drumnacrear, Milltown and Coreloon [? Corlona, Co. Leitrim]. Mollanstown, Knockering and Derrydreenagh [situation not mentioned].

Witnesses : James Flinn, Cranlamore, yeoman, Catherine Maculagh, servant to testator, Benjamin Span, Dublin, merchant.

Memorial witnessed by : James Flinn, Wm. Devall.

51, 140, 33119   Geo. West (seal)

351 HODDER, WILLIAM, [Hoddersfield], Co. Cork, gent.

20 Oct. 1725. Précis, ¾ p., 28 Nov. 1726.

Wife Ann Hodder, exor., (marriage settlement of 31 Dec. 1713). His son William Hodder. His two daughters Hannah and Ann. John Hodder, George Hodder, Danl. Webb and Samuel Hodder, overseers. To wife jewels etc. " the plate which was her father Webbs and brother Webbs " . . and goods at Hoddersfield.

Witnesses : Thomas Hodder, junr., and Fras. Hodder, both of Fountainstown, Co. Cork, gents., Thos. Weston, Ballinrea, said County, gent.

Memorial witnessed by : said Thos. Hodder, junr., of Fountainstown, John Hodder of Dunbogy, Co. Cork, gent.

50, 366, 33386   Ann Hodder (seal)

352 TOBIN, ELIZABETH als. O'BRIEN, Dublin, widow.

25 April 1726. Précis, ½ p., 8 Dec. 1726.

Her godson Joseph Robinson. Her servant maid Elizth. Brown. Her dear friend Mrs. Mary Haay, Joseph Haay, eldest son of said Mary exors. Legacy to Parish Boys of St. Michan's and St. Mary's Parish, suburbs of city of Dublin. A house in Drumcondra Lane, Dublin.

Witnesses : Jon. Bell, Dublin, surgeon, Jon. Hackett, Dublin, hair merchant, Thos. Hewlett, junr., Dublin, gent.

Memorial witnessed by : Thos. Hewlett, junr., Francis Mullowny, Dublin, writing clerk.

52, 57, 33515   Mary Hay (seal)

353 SMITH, BENJAMIN, Keenoge, Co. Monaghan.

31 Aug. 1713. Précis, ½ p., 28 Jan. 1726.

In consideration of the friendly [acts] done to him bequeathes his property to "Mr. John Barlow (of Aghnemallagh, Co. Monaghan) and his uncle Benjamin Rose," exors.

Keenoge, Aghneclough, Anyelkan,[1] Shirwin and Anyeldran,[1] Co. Monaghan.

Witnesses : Rev. John Gill, Francis Foster and James Robinson, all of Co. Monaghan, gents.

Memorial witnessed by : John Gill, Robert Scott, Dublin, gent.

50, 456, 33799   Jo. Barlow (seal)

354 VERNON, JOHN, Dublin, merchant.

24 Dec. 1718. Précis, ½ p., 7 March 1726.

Francis Huysh, Rector of Clysthydon, Co. of Devon, devissee. His real and personal estate.

Witnesses : Henry Hunter, yeoman, Cornelius Halliwell, gent., Faithfull Farrant, woolcomber, all of parish of St. Michl. Wo[o]d-street.

Memorial witnessed by : Thomas Barsham, and William Annesley, both of Inner Temple, London, gents.

53, 8, 34186   Francis Huysh (seal)

355 FORD, ROBERT, Dublin, merchant.

20 Aug. 1726. Narrate, ¾ p., 11 March 1726/27.

Eldest son Robert Ford. His younger son Roger Ford. Premises bequeathed to son Robert " settled by him on his said son Robert on the inter-marriage of his present wife Mary."[2]

Mrs. Kilpatrick, Mr. Dawson and Mr. Chapelow, tenants, St. George's Lane. " The trade carried on between him [the testator] and Charles Thrap." North Strand, Dublin. (St.) George's Lane and Dames Street, Dublin. Upper and Lower Comb, Dublin. Skinner's Alley near the Coomb. Barrack Street and St. James Street, Cook Street and York Street, Dublin. Lands and mill in Milltown, Co. Dublin. . " and

---

[1]. One or other of these is probably the townland of Anny, B. Farney, Co. Monaghan.

[2]. Robert Ford the testator had nine children. His wife's name was Mary. His eldest son Robert married Mary Ellis in 1724.—*Betham Will Pedigrees*, Genealogical Office.

Bagtroth near Dublin city [Baggotrath] (by lease from Viscount
FitzWilliam) bequeathed by William Ford of Drogheda, alderman, to
his brother " the testator.

Witnesses : William Munkittrick, Robt. Boyton, Dublin, gent.,
John Smith, same, notary public.

Memorial witnessed by : Den. Delany and Henry Hanlon, Dublin,
gents.

53, 13, 34207   Robt. Ford junr. (seal)

356 SMITH, ANTHONY, Carlow, carpenter.
   11 Jan. 1726. Précis, ½ p., 17 Aug. 1727.

His grandson Anthony Smith, son of Abraham Smith. Col.
Walter Weldon and George Jackson, both of Carlow, exors. " Lease
of Maryland at Blessington."

Witnesses : Will Byrne, Darby Ryan, yeoman, and John Carthone,
woolcomber, all of Carlow.

Memorial witnessed by : Henry Hanlon and Dennis Delany, Dublin,
gent.

51, 478, 34410   Geo. Jackson (seal)

357 GOODLAT, WILLIAM, Derrygally, parish of Killiman, Co.
   Tyrone. 5 Dec. 1726. Narrate, 1¼ p., 24 May 1727.

Nephew William Richardson of Mulloghatinhy, Co. Armagh, exor.
Niece Jane Richardson. His grand-nephew Thomas Richardson.

Derrygally, Gortrea and Glentevey, in parishes of Killiman and
Clonfecle, Co. Tyrone. " His chattle lease of the two Drommads "
[situation not mentioned, ? Drumad, Co. Tyrone], held of the See of
Armagh.

Will proved 24 Mar. 1726/27, in Consistorial Court of Armagh by
oaths of Symon Haselton of Bovean, said parish of Killaman, gent.,
and John Bovell of parish of Clonfeckle, weaver, witnesses with
Wm. Haselton of Bovean, Co. Tyrone, gent.

Memorial witnessed by : Andrew Carmichael, Dungannon, Co.
Tyrone, commissioner for taking affidavits in said county, John Bovell.

53, 152, 34838   W. Richardson (seal)

358 HARRIS, JOSEPH, city of Cork.

26 Oct. 1722. Précis, ½ p., 31 May 1727.

His wife Judith Harris. His father Daniel. His mother Mary Harris. His sister Jane Harris. After death of these four persons the yearly issues and profits of his estate bequeathed unto the Bishop and Mayor of Cork and their successors for ever " to be for the foundation and support of a mathmatical lecture."[1]

Witnesses : Thos. Wallis and Richard Good, Cork, Barry Love of said city, mathematical instrument maker.

Memorial witnessed by : John Peirce, clerk to Robert. Wallis, Cork, public notary, and Wm. Simmins, Cork, gent.

52, 367, 34883   Daniel Harris (seal)

359 DROGHEDA, HENRY EARL OF

26 May 1727, codicil 27 May. Narrate, ¾ p., 7 June, 1727.

His wife the Rt. Hon. Charlot Countess of Drogheda. His brother the Hon. Edward Moore. Hon. Richard Stewart, George Rochfort, Peter Ludlow, Thos. Carter and Richard Ash, Esq., to whom, as trustees, his real estate had heretofore been conveyed. Rt. Hon. Trevor, Lord Viscount Hillsborough, and John Johnston, Dublin, Esq., trustees. Gold watch to John Healy of city of Dublin. Anthony Walsh, the testator's steward.

His lands etc., the real estate of the Family. Ballyanscanlan, Co. Louth.

Will and codicil witnessed by : Richard Bettsworth, Dublin, Esq., Douglass Baker and Charles Caldwell, Dublin, gents.

Memorial witnessed by : Theobald Bourke, drawer at the Lyon in Warbough's Street, Dublin, and Dennis (Denn) Delany of same, gent.

54, 77, 34941   Hillsborough (seal)

360 LEIGH, FRANCIS ROBERT, Dublin, Esq.

8 May 1727. Narrate, ¾ p., 13 June 1727.

His eldest son John Leigh. His deceased brother Robert Leigh. His uncle Robert Leigh. £200 to his son Robert Leigh when thirty five years. His son Andrew Leigh.

Frayarstown, and Graigs, Co. Kildare. Salmonstown, Co. Dublin. Holds a mortgage on the late Caesar Colclough's estate. His house at

---

[1] See " The Will of Joseph Harris, Cork, 1722 " by W. H. Welply. *Cork Historical and Archaeological Society.* Vol LI, No. 173.

Longrange, Co. Wexford.   Dwelling on Aran Key, Dublin, and rest of his real estate.

Witnesses : Andrew Nugent, Doctor in Physic, Edwd. Scott, merchant, Andrew Geoghegan, gent., all of Dublin.

Memorial witnessed by : Andrew Geoghegan, Judith Leigh, daughter of said Francis Robert Leigh.

52, 403, 35048   John Leigh (seal)

361 BURDETT, SIR THOMAS, Garryhill, in the county of Catherlogh, Bart. 15 April 1724.   Narrate, 1 p., 16 June 1727.

His son William Vigors Burdett.   His niece Catherine Savile (Savill). His sister Anne Weldon als. Burdett wife of Thomas Weldon, Esq., their sons John and George Weldon.   His good friends and relations George Burdett of Lissmallin, Co. Tipperary,   the Rev. Archdeacon [Benjamin] Neale and John Beauchamp, Esq., exors. Hon. Robert Doyne, late Lord Chief Justice of the Common Pleas, the Rt. Hon. the Lord Duncannon, and the Hon. Francis Barnard, Esq., overseers of will.

His real and personal estate. His woods etc. on lands of Garryhill. The marriage portion of his mother Catherine Burdett als. Kennedy chargeable on the estate of Mount Kennedy.

Witnesses : Henry Ware, Hugh McFarran, Dublin, gents., John Dillon, one of the Attorneys of the Court of Exchequer in Ireland. Memorial witnessed by : Charles Dillon and Francis Lodge, Dublin, gents.

54, 112, 35080   Benj. Neale (seal)

362 DROGHEDA, MARY DOWAGER COUNTESS OF

27 June 1716. Codicil 19 Jan. 1722. Narrate, 2¾ pp., 20 June 1727.

Her husband Henry, late Earl of Drogheda, deceased (his will dated 25 May 1713).   Reciting a demise of 1704 and a settlement made by the said Earl by lease and release August 1699 of his estate upon the intermarriage of his eldest son and heir apparent Charles Lord Moore since deceased. Her son Robert Moore. Her son Capell Moore. Her brother Michael Cole, Esq. The children of her sister Margt. Burdett. Her brother Arthur Lord Ranelagh. Wm. Willock, Dublin, gent., trustee. Charles Campbell, Esq.

Lordship of St. Mary's Abby and lands of Grange of Clonliff and tythes thereof.

Witnesses : George Forrest, London, gent., the said Countess of Drogheda's late servant, and Wm. Colvill and James Turner, Dublin, gents.

Codicil witnessed by : Israell Woolston, London, gent., George Forrest.

Memorial witnessed by : Wm. Colvill, David Loyd, servant to said Robert Moore.

53, 212, 35132   Robert Moore (seal)

363 BLYKE, DUDLEY, [Kilcurley], Co. Louth, Esq.

23 March 1725. Narrate, ¾ p., 20 June 1727.

His wife Mary Blyke. His brother Peter Blyke. His nephew John Trueman. Sarah Wedston [? Waston] sister to said John Trueman. Nathaniel Trueman of Kilwarly, Co. Down and Henry Smith of Drumiskin, clerk, trustees.

His estate of freehold and inheritance, all his leases, etc. [situation not mentioned].

Witnesses : Phillip Reily, Dundalk, apothecary, Edward Macartan and John Banber, both of Killcurley, Co. Louth, farmers.

Memorial witnessed by : Brabazon Noble and Denis Delany, Dublin, gents.

54, 131, 35144   Mary Blyke (seal)

364 ORMSBY, JOHN, Athlacca, Co. Limerick, Esq.

18 June 1717. Codicil 27 June 1724. Narrate, 1 p., 21 June 1727.

Wife Mary Ormsby (a settlement made 4 March last past on his intermarriage then intended). Doctor Duncan Comyng, his said wife's father, and Mary Comyng his wife. Lawrence Steele, Rathbride, Co. Kildare, Esq., and James Howison, Dublin, gent., trustees.

Athlacca. " His uncle Postume's [Postume Ormsby] estate " [situation not mentioned] and rest of his real estate.

Witnesses : John Disney, county of the town of Galway, Esq., Thos., Cooke, junr., late of city of Dublin, notary public, deceased, Thos. Cooke, senr.. Dublin, notary public.

Codicil witnessed by : Hanniball Hall, Dublin, chirurgeon, said Thos. Cooke junr., and Thos. Cooke senr.

Memorial witnessed by : Michael Jones, Dublin, gent., Will French, clerk to Henry Buckley, Dublin, notary public.

53, 219, 35161 Mary Ormsby (seal)

365 BELL, JOHN, Aughnacreevy, Co. Cavan, gent.

10 Jan. 1721. Narrate, ½ p., 1 June 1727.

Son Andrew Bell. Grandson John Bell. His brother Ralph Hines. Lands etc. in Aughnacreevy [Aghnacreevy], Co. Cavan.

Witnesses : Thomas Clarke, Corlismore, Co. Cavan, Eliz. Monnypenny, Woodtowne, Co. Meath, John Cunningham, Loughcrew, Co. Meath.

Memorial witnessed by : John Cunningham, James Hamilton, Dublin, gent.

53, 240, 35260 Andrew Bell (seal)

366 ROSSELL, SAMUEL, Curragh, Queen's Co., gent.

15 April 1727. Full, ½ p., 1 July 1727.

Wife Mary Rossell, extx. My nephew George Rossell of Olderigg. My nephew Simon Rossell of Catherlogh, in the County of Catherlogh. Mathew Humphrey of Catherlogh, an exor.

Clone and all other my personal estate [situation not mentioned]. The town and lands of Curragh, Queen's Co. All my real estate and freehold which I hold by fee farm deed or deeds from the Rt. Hon. the Earl of Thomond or otherwise [situation not mentioned].

Witnesses : James Fitzpatrick, Catherlogh, Co. Catherlogh, gent., Thos. Brown of same, gent., Henry Kelly, Olderrigg, Queen's Co., gent.

Memorial witnessed by : Thomas Brown, and Cornelius Cox of city of Dublin, gent.

54, 160, 35266 Mary Rossell (seal)

367 CASTELL, ALEXANDER, Ballyhack, Co. Wexford, gent.

2 Sept. 1727. Narrate, 1 p., 8 Nov. 1727.

Eldest son Silvester Castell and Elizabeth his wife. Son Edward Castell. Youngest daughter Sarah Castell. Son John Castell and his wife. Grandsons Alexander Castell (son of John Castell), Alexr.

Graves, Alexr. Hobbs and Alexr. Anderson. Sons-in-law William Hobbs and Ann his wife, Anthony Graves and Elizabeth his wife, George Anderson and Mary his wife. His brother James Castell and Ann his wife. His brother James Castell, Esq., and Rev. James Borrows and Anthony Cliffe of Dungulph, exors. and guardians of younger children Edward and Sarah.

Mainstowne, B. Iffa and Offa, Co. Tipperary "settled on testator and his heirs by deed of settlement made by his father-in-law William Nicholson and his mother Eliza his wife" dated 25 April 1695. Richardstowne, said B. and county, purshased from his brother James Castell.

Witnesses : Philip Jones, Waterford, cutler, John Lacombe, Waterford, taylor, Joseph Cooke, Waterford, notary public.

Memorial witnessed by : Joseph Cooke, Richard Kinselagh of Dungulfe, Co. Waterford, yeoman.

55, 92, 36025   Ant. Cliffe (seal)

368 KENT, JOHN, Polroane, Co. Kilkenny, gent.

5 Feb. 1725. Full, ¾ p., 8 Nov. 1727.

My wife Catherine Drew als. Kent. My brother Robert Kent. My nephew Samuel Mathews. My nephew John Mathews. My two brothers-in-law Daniel Gates and Charles Bucknall. My niece Frances Bucknall (under twelve years). Exors. Daniel Osborne, Affady, Co. Kilkenny, Esq., and Charles Bucknall, Esq.

Polroan, and real and personal estate. £50 to poor of Union of Rathkerane.

Witnesses : Edmd. Jackson, Curluddy, Co. Kilkenny, gent., William Smith, Waterford, Doctor of Physick, Joseph Ivie, Waterford, notary public.

Memorial witnessed by : Said Joseph Ivie, aged about twenty seven years, Thomas McCragh, Waterford, gent.

55, 94, 36037   C. Bucknall (seal)

369 GREEN, ABRAHAM, Ballymacross, Co. Limerick, Esq.

7 April 1724. Narrate, 1¾ p., 26 Nov. 1727

His wife Annabell Blenerhassett, articles of intermarriage 5 Nov. 1694. His nephew Henry Green of Co. Fermanagh, exor. His grand-nephew Abraham Green aged about five years, son of said Henry.

His nephew Brockhill Green, brother of said Henry. His nephew Nicholas Green, son of his brother Francis Green. His niece [Hester] Martin. His estate of inheritance and personal estate. His servant Thos. Bourke. His servant Jane Kinkade. Honnor Backram. Brian McThomas McGuier. Slany, widow of John Borane. Elizabeth Lillis, wife of Edmond McMahon. Patrick Behane. Richard Bourke of Dromsalla, gent. Legacy to poor of parish of Cahircon.

Witnesses : John Vincent, Limerick, alderman, Benjamin Barington, Limerick, pewterer, William Keating, Pallisgreny, Terence Magrath, Garrydolish, Richd. Bourke, Dromsallagh, Richard Moore, Limerick, innholder, all in Co. Limerick.

Memorial witnessed by : Terence Magrath, Roger Moore of Bohurnegragy, Co. Limerick, gent.

55, 120, 36178   Hen. Green (seal)

370 GORE, HENRY, Sligo, Co. Sligo, Esq.

13 Feb. 1725. Précis, part in full, ½ p., 2 Dec. 1727.

Brother Richard Gore of Sligo.

Lands in Co. Monaghan. Real estate in Great Britain, house in Chinkporthatch in Essex, my house in Marreen Square in London.

Witnesses : Thos. Osborne, Sligo, gent., Thomas Corcoran, Sligo, merchant, David Boyd, servant to testator, Henry Gore, Shannon, Co. Sligo, gent., Henry Mara, Sligo, schoolmaster.

Memorial witnessed by : David Boyd, Denn. Delany, Dublin, gent.

55, 152, 36313   Richd. Gore (seal)

371 DONERAILE, ARTHUR VISCOUNT.

7 April 1726. Narrate, ½ p., 18 Dec. 1727.

His son Hayes St. Leger and son's wife Eliz. Dean. His brother Sir John St. Leger. Arthur St. Leger, son of his eldest son Arthur St. Leger. His daughter Eliz. Aldworth. His granddaughter Mary Aldworth. His sister Mary Gethins. Gertrude Armstead granddaughter of his said sister Gethins.

Money due by mortgage etc. from Redmond Barry of Rathcormack, Robert Ryves of Ballycaddane, Richard Keating and James Levallin. Mr. S. Lake. Bartholomew Purdon.

Lands in Co. Waterford. Lands in Queen's Co., purchased from

Hugh Dixon, Esq., [situation not mentioned]. £600 to be laid out, £15 per annum to a schoolmaster to instruct poor children of parish of Doneraile, residue for clothing thirteen poor children. £500 to purchase lands, income thereof to be applied to poor of said parish.

Witnesses : Eaton Stannard, Esq., one of H.M. Council-at-law, Brettridge Badham, Esq., and Robert Wallis, notary public, both of city of Cork.

Memorial witnessed by : James Webb, Dublin, one of the attorneys of the Exchequer, Humphrey Butler his clerk.

53, 470, 36463   Hayes St. Leger (seal)

372 LEATHES, WILLIAM, parish of St. George in the Liberty of Westminster, Middlesex. Signed at Brocket Hall, parish of Hatfield, Herts. 4 March 13 George I, 1726. Précis, part in full, ½ p., 13 Jan. 1727.

My nephew Hill Mussenden. My leasehold estates in the Kingdom of Ireland, in Manor of Belfast and Co. of Antrim.

Witnesses : Samuel Grice, Sandridge, Co. of Hertford, clerk, Joseph Andrews, Brockett Hall, yeoman, William Barker and Charles Noy, both of Hitchin, Co. of Hertford, gents.

Memorial witnessed by : Ambrose Newton, parish of St. Mary's, Alderman Bury, London, gent., Moses Leathes of parish of St. Margaret's, Westminster, Esq., John Gordon, Inner Temple, London, Esq.

54, 508, 36610   Hill Mussenden (seal)
                                       now residing in London

373 MILDMAY, DANIEL, Antrim, Co. Antrim, merchant. 11 March 1726. Narrate, ½ p., 15 Jan. 1727.

His wife Mary Mildmay, extx. His daughter Elizabeth Mildmay. His daughter Mary Mildmay. His brother Henry Mildmay. John Allen, Drumnadarragh, parish of Dunnagar, Co. Antrim, tanner and George McMaster of town of Antrim, merchant, exors.

Edentrillick (Edintrillick) in parish of Dromore, B. Lower Iveagh, Co. Down.

Witnesses : William Whiteside, James Neilson and William Curry, all of town and County of Antrim.

Memorial witnessed by : William Curry, Joseph Willson of Antrim.

54, 511, 36617   Mary Mildmay (seal)

374 DOUGHERTY, CHARLES, Drogheda, cordwainer.
19 Feb. 1723. Died 11 March following. Narrate, ¾ p., 27 Jan.
1727.
Son Michael Dougherty. His eldest daughter Catherine Dougherty.
His daughter Eliz. Dougherty. His brother's son Paul Dougherty.
His brother John Dougherty. Exors. his brother Owen Dougherty
(since deceased) and daughter Catherine.
Laragh and Carrowreagh in B. Clenkey [Clankee], Co. Cavan.
The lease of his dwelling-house wherein he lived [? in Drogheda].
Witnesses : Patrick Delahoide, merchant, John Hamlin, gent.,
Francis Evans, taylor, and Patrick Devlin, all of Drogheda.
Memorial witnessed by : Michael Teeling, Dublin, gent., one of the
Attorneys of H.M. Court of Exchequer, John Banks, Dublin, perry-
wigmaker.
53, 509, 36701   Catherine Dougherty (seal)

375 GRACE, OLIVER, Brittas, Co. Tipperary, Esq.
12 Jan 1719. Narrate, ½ p., 29 Jan. 1727.
His wife Elizabeth, then enceinte. His eldest daughter Elizabeth
Grace. His second son Patrick Grace. His four children Richard,
James, Anne and Mary Grace. His eldest son John Grace. His wife
Elizabeth Grace, Edward Mandevile, Ballydine, Esq., Lovelace Taylor
of Noan, Esq., Richard Butler of Ballynetrinch, gent., and Justin
McCarthy of Springhouse, exors. His real and personal estate.
Witnesses : John Purcell, Clonmacoge, Co. Tipperary, gent.,
Daniel Collins, Springhouse, yeoman, John Birrane, Springhouse.
yeoman.
Memorial witnessed by : John Birrane, and Edward Landas,
Clonmell, Co. Tipperary, gent.
54, 537, 36731   Eliz. Grace (seal)

376 LEWIS, THOMAS, Aughmacart, Queen's Co., gent.
28 Aug. 1727. Narrate, ¾ p., 27 Feb. 1727/28.
His wife, extx. His son Henry Lewis. Son Thomas Lewis. His
granddaughter Elizabeth.
Garivoan and Coolruaghbegg [situation not mentioned]. Money due
by mortgage on two houses in Clonmell made by Mr. Cranwell. Money

owed to Thomas Christmas, Esq. Lands of Canvistown [? Canvars-
town] and Lisneleah, Co. Kilkenny (leased from Ambrose Lane, Esq.).
Raplah and part of Aughmacart, Queen's Co.

Witnesses : Thos. Palmer, Ballygarry, Queen's Co., Esq., Cornelius
Lyons, Shraugh, Queen's Co., schoolmaster, William Moore, servant
to said Henry Lewis.

Memorial witnessed by : William Moore, Robt. Boyton, clerk to
John Smith, public notary in Dublin.

55, 301, 37038   Henry Lewis (seal)

377 NEWBURGH, HENRY, Rahick, Co. Cavan, Esq.
19 Dec. 1727. Narrate, ½ p., 1 April 1727/28.

His mother Letitia Berry. His brother Obadiah Newburgh. Nephew
Henry, son of said Obadiah Newburgh. His niece Letitia Newburgh.

His real estate in Co. Cavan and personal estate.

Witnesses : James Hartley, Dublin, apothecary, James O'Brien,
late servant to said Henry Newburgh, now servant to Wm. Berry,
Dublin, Esq., Elizabeth Oriell, Dublin.

Memorial witnessed by : George Moore, public notary, Dublin, and
said James O'Brien.

56, 131, 37278   Letitia Berry (seal)

378 BROWNLOW, JAMES, Arbor Hill, Dublin, gent.
17 Feb. 1727, codicil 20 March 1727. Narrate, 1 p., 17 April
1728.

His daughter Hannah Brownlow, guardian of his daughter Mary.
Arthur Reynell, guardian to his son Richard Brownlow. John Richard-
son, guardian to his son Thomas Brownlow. His worthy friends
Arthur Reynell, Esq., John Richardson, Mr. Walter Stephens and his
daughter Hannah Brownlow, trustees. Codicil mentions his daughter
Hannah then the wife of Mr. Walter Stephens.

His lands tenements and hereditaments in Great Britain and Ireland.
Mentions rent due by the tenants of his estate in Great Britain to
which he was entitled in right of his cousin Ann Furnell. His dwelling
house on Arbor Hill with the garden and field behind the same. Forty
shillings to poor of parish of St. Paul's.

Witnesses : William Stear, Co. Meath, Esq., John Mullen, Dublin,
perukemaker, Henry Buckley, Dublin, notary public.

Codicil witnessed by : Rev. James Walsh, Dublin, clerk, William Stephens, Dublin, Esq., said Henry Buckley.

Memorial witnessed by : Hen. Buckley, Joseph Landers his clerk.

56, 156, 37389 Walter Stephens (seal)

379 WARING, JOHN, parish of St. Clement Danes, Middlesex, woollen draper. 24 Dec. 1727. Précis, ½ p., 18 April 1728.

His daughter Mary Waring. His granddaughter Mary Waring. His son Jon. Waring. His son Richard Waring. His nephew William Waring son of his brother Richard Waring. Said brother Richard Waring exor.

Lands commonly known by the name of Anna Carnew in the parish of Garvaghy near Dromore, Co. Down, and Fieday [? Fedany] in said parish.

Witnesses : Glisson Maydwell (Maidwell) in parish of St. Clement Danes, glassman, Fotherly Baker in parish of All Hallows, London, gent., and Mary Wood, of parish of St. Clement Danes, spinster.

Memorial witnessed by : Glisson Maydwell, Robert Griffith in parish of St. James, Westminster.

57, 92, 37397 Richd. Waring (seal)

380 PAYNE, JOHN, Bow Street, Dublin, gent.

23 Dec. 1723. Narrate, ½ p., 27 April 1728.

His wife Elizabeth Payne. " His daughter-in-law [? step-daughter] Elizabeth Barnes," [1] wife of Marcus Barnes of Cookstown, Co. Meath, gent." His son [? stepson] Andrew Kelly. An annuity payable to said Kelly's mother.

Three houses in Bow Street als. Loughboy in suburbs of city of Dublin. Hon. Gustavus Hamilton, and Hon. Anne Lambert, widow, tenants, Bow Street.

Witnesses : Edward Croker of Capell Street, suburbs of city of Dublin, apothecary, Sarah Croker, wife of John Croker of Dublin, gent., and Charles Hobson, Dublin, gent.

Memorial witnessed by : Charles Hobson, Morgan Donovan, Dublin, brewer.

56, 168, 37441 Andw. Kelly (seal)

---

[1] She is described as the step-daughter and Andrew Kelly as the testator's stepson in *Betham's Will Pedigrees*, Genealogical Office.

M

381 HAMILTON, JAMES, Ballinegarvie, Co. Antrim, Esq.
    8 Dec. 1727. Narrate, 2 pp., 7 May 1728.
    His wife, extx. His eldest son John Hamilton. His daughter
Rachel Hamilton. His son William Hamilton. His cousin William
Hamilton of Mount Hamilton. Legacy to heirs of testator's sister
Euphemia Cunningham by Robert Cunningham of Strabane. His
brother John Hamilton of Ballyholly, Co. Londonderry. Henry
O'Hara of Crebilly, Esq., Wm. Hamilton of Mount Hamilton, Robert
Cunningham of Strabane, merchant, Patrick Orr of Carnbeg, gent.,
and Capt. Wm. Hamilton of Coshandun, trustees.
    The old and new farms of Ballynegarvie. Lands of Glenwhirry, and
Ballynekillskean and the corn mill thereon, in Co. Antrim, and rest of
real estate.
    Witnesses : Henry Shaw, Ballygelly, Thomas Weir of Hamilton's
Grove and Wm. McGee.
    Memorial witnessed by : Thomas Weir, David Cochran of Maddykill,
Co. Antrim.

Rose Hamilton (seal)

57, 107, 37499   Pat. Orr (seal)

382 SMITH, THOMAS, Waterford, alderman.
    24 June 1727. Narrate, 1 p., 9 May 1728.
    His wife. His son-in-law Robt. West, exor. and trustee. His son
William Smith. His son John Smith. His daughter Anne West. His
son-in-law Mr Daniel Taylor and his wife Jane Taylor. His daughter
Jane Taylor. His daughter Ellinor Cavanagh. His granddaughter
Anne West. His grandson Wm. West. His grandson Robert West.
    His real and personal estate. Lease of St. Catherine's Abby
[situation not mentioned]. A house in Patrick Street, a little house
in Cook Lane [? in Waterford].
    Witnesses : Alexr. Boyd, Waterford, Esq., William Barker, Water-
ford, alderman, Thomas Burton, Waterford, gent.
    Memorial witnessed by : Thomas Burton, Joseph Cooke, Dublin,
notary public.
56, 187, 37536   R. West (seal)

383 BOWEN, HOWELL, of parish of Kilcoleman, Co. Cork, Esq.
    5 March 1727. Full, ¾ p., 11 May 1728.
    My brother John Bowen. My nephew Francis Lee, junr., exor.
My sister Ann Cuttle. My sister Elizabeth Holloway. My brother

Thomas Bowen. My sister Mary Knaven. My sister Elizabeth Bowen relict of Wm. Bowen.

John Rice, son of Christopher Rice, Fishamble Street, Dublin. Francis Lee, senr. Elizabeth Lewis, relict of Joseph Lewis. £20 to Thomas Lewis " and grasing his cattle free until November next upon Old Castle if it continues so long unset or sold." £50 to Henry Vallis for his maintenance. Ann Collens, daughter of Mary Collens. My right and title of the ship Saragh, etc. to my godson Robert Massy son of Humphry Massy, Esq.

Knight Street in Ballingarry [situation not mentioned]. Old Castle, Co. Cork. Carriga Taw [situation not mentioned. ? Carrigathou or Carrigatogher, Co. Cork].

Witnesses : Dennis Mahony, Cork, gent., Thomas Lewis, Old Castle, Co. Cork, gent., John Healihy of same, yeoman.

Memorial witnessed by : Dennis Mahony, Thos. Alleyn, Cork, gent.
56, 194, 37571   Francis Lee, junr. (seal)

384 ISAAC, SIMON, Ballywalter, Co. Down, Esq.

18 July 1727. Narrate, ¾ p., 8 June 1728.

Wife Ann. Son John Isaac, and his wife Jane, exor. Son Robert Isaac.

House etc. in Ballywalter, Co. Down, wherein he lived, with the four parks opening to the road by the Windmill. Lis(s)owin and Chintineglar.[1] Hollywood with the priory house, garden and parks thereunto belonging [situation not mentioned]. Legigoane, Ballyhalbert and Ballyesbro and Ballywalter, mills and mill lands [situation not mentioned, ? Co. Down].

Witnesses : Elizabeth Tullekens, wife of Capt. Arnaldus Tullekens of Col. Montegue's Regt., David Lennox of Hollywood, Co. Down, farmer, Brien Mackerty, servant to testator.

Memorial witnessed by : David Lennox, Robert Donnaldson, Belfast, Co. Antrim, gent.
55, 484, 37927   Jon. Isaac (seal)

---

[1] I have not been able to trace the modern form of this name. Perhaps the suggestion that it derives from the Gaelic *Sean-tigh na gcliar* is not too far-fetched.

385 McDOWELL, BENJAMIN, Rathmore, parish of Dunegar, Co.
Antrim, linendraper. 22 Dec. 1725. Narrate, ¾ p., 26 June,
1728.

His two daughters Elizabeth McDowell and Anne McDowell. His
son John McDowell. Son Benjamin. Thos. Banks, Belfast, gent.,
John Allen, Drumnadarragh, linendraper, George McMaster, Antrim,
Co. Antrim, gent., exors.

Rathmore, profits of Dunegar Mill and of the Fair Bogg, lands of
Still [? Stiles], parish of Antrim, Ballyrobert, parish of Templepatrick,
all in Co. Antrim.

Witnesses :   William Rodger and Robert Carswell, both of
Rathmore, aforesaid, linendrapers, William Boyd, Dunegar, farmer.

Memorial witnessed by : William Rodger, William Boyd.

55, 512, 38065   Anne McDowell (seal)

386 HAWKINS, WILLIAM, Rossellstowne, Co. Kilkenny, gent.
6 Nov. 1726. Précis, ¼ p., 8 July 1728.

Daughter Elinor Hawkins (sole heiress), exor. " All my lands and
estate."

Witnesses : William Sunderland and Patrick Mills, Rossellstowne,
Co. Kilkenny, yeoman, Wm. Hogan, Thomastown, Co. Kilkenny,
yeoman.

Memorial witnessed by : Wm. Sunderland, Daniel Murphy, Dublin,
gent.

55, 531, 38185   Elinor Murphy als. Hawkins (seal)

387 KNOX, THOMAS, Dungannon, Esq.
2 April 1727. Précis, 1 p., 25 July 1728.

Col. Edward Brice of Belfast, Co. Antrim, his brother-in-law, and
Arthur Knox of Tweebeg, Co. Mayo, Esq., trustees. His son-in-law
Charles Echlin, Esq., and Ann Echlin als. Knox his wife. His nephew
Thomas Knox, Esq.

Ballymeaghan, Strandtown als. Bellymeser [Ballymisert], Knox
als. Knockcolumkill, Bellydoologhan, mills etc. of Ballyknockan,
Munlogh, Crayloghgarrcroby, in B. Castlereagh, Co. Down. Magher-
anly, Ednegone, Drumneth, Tullyheinen, Tullyreine, Corbud, Kill-
macrew, Ballyeany, " the Deary lands " and part of Quilly, Co. Down
(held from See of Dromore).

Witnesses : John Brown, George Lamie and John Jorden, all of Dungannon, gents.

Memorial witnessed by : John Brown, Edward Jones, clerk to Edward Mathews, Dublin, gent.

55, 536, 38383   Cha. Echlin (seal)

388 CLIBBORNE, JOSHUA, Mote of Greenoge, Co. Westmeath.
   gent. 21 Feb. 1727. Narrate, 1 p., 13 Aug. 1728.

His wife Sarah Clibborne, exor. His eldest son John Clibborne. Son Robert Clibborne. Son George Clibborne. Son James Clibborne. His sons George, Abraham and Joshua. His brother-in-law Henry Pemberton, Dublin, merchant, and Robert Leckey, Kilnock, Co. Catherlogh, exors. Trustees : John Leckey, Killmeney, Co. Catherlogh, John Gee, Moveaghty, Co. Westmeath, gent., Jonathan Robinson, Lysomyney, said county, feltmaker, John Leckey, junr., of Bally-lahane, Queen's Co., farmer.

Mote of Greenoge, Co. Westmeath. Lands of Newtown and Lurgan, King's Co., whereof he was seized of an estate of inheritance. Boylart, King's Co. Houses and lands held by lease from Wm. Hanlock, Esq. [situation not mentioned]. Clonbnakhalo [? Clonbrock hollow], Upper Clonlonan wood and Clonaltrera wood, Co. Westmeath.

Witnesses : Edmond Braithwaite, Dunegan, Co. Westmeath, gent., Richd. Homan, of same, gent., Daniel Tailford of Mote aforesaid, merchant, and Samuel Castleton, Ballynegarvey, said county, gent.

Memorial witnessed by : Thomas Ringwood and Anthony Cope, Dublin, gents.

56, 400, 38476   George Clibborne (seal)

389 IREDELL, BENJAMIN, Great Bray, Co. Wicklow, clke.
   18 May 1728. Narrate, ¾ p., 19 Aug. 1728.

His six children viz. his eldest daughter Elizabeth, his eldest son Richd., his second daughter Frances, his third daughter Anne, his fourth daughter Jane and his youngest Benjamin.

Debt due to Thomas Towers, Esq. Wm. Butler and Mark White, both of Dublin, gents., exors.

" His freehold estate in Smithfield Lough and Duck Lane." White Fryer Street, White Fryer Lane and Aungier Street [? all in Dublin].

Witnesses : Will. Caldwell, Delganny, Co. Wicklow, clerk, Jos. Butler, Dublin, chirurgeon, Richard Butler, Dublin, gent., Thos. Strong, Bray, gent.

Memorial witnessed by : Denn. Delany, Dublin, Henry Hanlon, Dublin, gent.

58, 51, 38519   Will. Butler (seal)

390 LOVETT, EDWARD, Dublin, Esq.

25 March 1725. Précis, ½ p., 23 Aug. 1728.

His son John Lovett. His daughter Clotilda Lovett (who will be 19 years in 1728). His sister-in-law Clotilda Lady Eustace. His sister-in-law Euphemia Haughton, her second son Richard Haughton. His brother-in-law George Haughton, Esq.,and Henry Coddington, Dublin, Esq., and Rev. James Harvey of Killeane, Co. Wexford, exors. and guardians.

Farm of Drina [situation not mentioned], and his real estate.

Witnesses : Val. Needham, Dublin, clerk, Ralph Blundell and Lewis Jones, Dublin, Esqrs.

Memorial witnessed by : Henry Hanlon, Denn. Delany, Dublin, gent.

57, 298, 38552   Hen. Coddington (seal)

391 WHITSITT, JOSEPH, Grange, parish of Clonfecle, Co. Tyrone.

26 April 1728. Narrate, ½ p., 2 Nov. 1728.

His only son Wm. Whitsitt, exor. His daughter Elizabeth and her husband. His brother John Whitsitt. Jos. son of his brother John. Jos. Graves, son to his sister Mary. Brother John Graves and Michael Cross exors.

Lands of Grange and Sheloran and his houses etc. (left by his father) in and about Dungannon, all in Co. Tyrone. Freehold of Mullnacash, Co. Monaghan. Dungorman [? Co. Tyrone], now in possession of his daughter Elizabeth and her husband.

Witnesses : William Dunbarr, Lewis Walsh, Donnell McDonnell, all of Dungannon, Co. Tyrone.

Memorial witnessed by : Wm. Dunbarr, Andrew Charleton, Dublin, gent.

57, 379, 38960   William Whitsitt (seal)

392 VAUTEAU, MARY MAGDALEN, city of Dublin, widow.
  15 Dec. 1726. Précis, ½ p., 7 Nov. 1728.
Her eldest son John Jacob Vauteau. Her second son Isaac Vauteau.
Her youngest son Peter Vauteau exor. Her goods, chattles and estate.
£5 to poor of French Church in St. Patrick's, Dublin.
  Witnesses : Samuel Boyd, clerk to Wm. Sumner, public notary,
Dublin, William Drury, same, and said Wm. Sumner.
  Memorial witnessed by : Wm. Drury, Will. Sumner.
56, 519, 39018   Pet. Vauteau (seal)

393 WESLEY, GARRET, Dangan, Co. Meath, Esq.
  13 March 1727. Narrate, 1 p., 21 Nov. 1728.
To be buried in chancel of the church of Laracor, Co. Meath. His
wife. William Westbery, Dublin, gent., trustee. Residue of estate to
Richard Colley, Dublin, Esq., sole exor. Joseph Ash, Ashfield, Co.
Meath, Esq., trustee.
His real estate in Ireland. £500 to Blue Coat Hospital in Dublin.
£600 for a charity school for boys to be set up in Trim, Co. Meath.
  Witnesses : Richard Fenner, John Dunbar Bate and William
Fenner of Dublin, gent., and said Richard Colley by the name of
Richard Wesley (which surname of Wesley he has taken upon him
pursuant to a provisoe in said will).
  Memorial witnessed by : William Fenner and John Tracy of Dublin.
58, 206, 39194   Rich. Wesley (seal)
                                    (Richard Wesley als. Colley)

394 MIDLETON, ALAN VISCOUNT.
  19 April 1726. Full, part narrate, 5½ pp., 29 Nov. 1728.
My wife Ann Viscountess Midleton. My eldest son St. John Brodrick
and his present wife Anne. My younger son Alan Brodrick is only of
the half blood to my eldest son they being born of different mothers.[1]
Lucy and Ann Courthope, sisters of Col. John Courthope, said Lucy
mother of said Alan Brodrick. Articles made before the marriage of

---

[1] Alan Brodrick, Viscount Midleton, had three wives. His first, Catherine,
daughter of Redmond Barry, was mother of St. John Brodrick. He married
secondly in 1693 Lucy Courthope, and thirdly, in 1716, Anne, widow of
Michael Hill. *The Complete Peerage*, by G.E.C.

Alan Lord Brodrick [the testator] with Mrs Ann Hill, widow, dated 30 Nov. 1716. My friend Sir Edward Crofton, Mote, Co. Roscommon, Bart., and my brother the Rt. Hon. Thomas Brodrick of Wansworth, Co. Surrey, Esq., (" he being the head of my family and a great honour to it ") both members of H.M. most Hon. Privy Council of the Kingdom of Ireland, trustees. Charles Campbell, trustee.

Ardleagh, South Glanure, North Glanure, Ballynokilly park, Teannagh, part of Boherash (now or late in Michael Robert's possession), Knockanecorbally (Martin Mullshenoge, tenant), North Crogh Ikerry als. North Curragh Ikerry als. Glynn, in B. Fermoy, Co. Cork. Ballyneruine in B. Barrymore, Co. Cork. Glanworth als. Glanure [situation not mentioned. ? Co. Cork]. Peperhard, parish of Peperhard, and lands of Oxenford, parish of Whitley, Co. Surrey. Reversion of lands in Co. Waterford, purchased from Stephen Stanley, Esq., deceased, and Sir John Stanley, Knight. Ballyvodick and Killmaclenny [situation not mentioned]. Rathcannon and lands in Glanehyry, Co. Waterford. Ballytowlase, and other lands in B. Imokelly, Co. Cork, formerly the estate of James Levallin and purchased from him. The estate which belonged to St. John Brodrick [testator's father] late of Wansworth in the Co. of Surrey, Knight, and by him devised to Thomas Brodrick, Esq., son of said St. John Brodrick, deceased, for life, partly in Kingdom of England and partly in Kingdom of Ireland.

Witnesses : Edward [Synge] Lord Archbishop of Tuam, William Allen, Dublin, gent., Henry Buckley, Dublin, public notary.

Memorial witnessed by : Henry Buckley, William Cane, Dublin, gent.

57, 465, 39282   Edw. Crofton (seal)

395 SLOANE, WILLIAM, parish of St. James, Westminster, Middlesex, Esq. 11 May 1726. Précis, ¼ p., 12 Dec. 1728.

His real and personal estate.

Witnesses : John Jackson, apothecary in Pall Mall, Westminster, William Harrison his journeyman, and Thomas Bonsham, Inner Temple, London, gent.

Memorial witnessed by : Roger Flemyng, Dublin, gent., said Thomas Bonsham.

59, 68, 39430   Wm. Sloane (seal)
                                   son of testator and a devisee.

396 MOLYNEAUX (MOLYNEUX), SAMUEL, parish of St. George, Hanover Sq., Middlesex, secretary to H.R.H. the Prince of Wales. 15 Jan. 1717. Narrate, part in full, 1 p., 23 Dec. 1728.

My wife the Lady Elizabeth Diana Capel(l) als. Molyneux, extx. My marriage settlement 2 April 1717.

Real estate in Counties Armagh, Kildare and Roscommon. Lands etc. in Oxmantown, Dublin, Mr Butler, lessee.

Witnesses: George Saville, Gray's Inn, Middlesex, Esq., John Eckersall, St. James's House, Westminster, Esq., secretary to Her Majesty, Jeremiah Prat and Thos. Brady, then clerk to testator.

Memorial witnessed by: John Eckersall, Mathew Lamb, Lincoln's Inn, Co. Middlesex, gent.

58, 278, 39498   E. D. Molyneux (seal)

397 SLATER, LUTHER, Clarendon Street, Dublin, painter. 27 May 1725. Précis, ¾ p., 13 Jan. 1728.

His grandson Slater Allin, son of Robert Allin and the late Elizabeth Allin als. Slater.

Lawrence Benson, sawyer, exor., his two children Samuel and Sarah Benson. Samuel Morgan, Great Sheep Street, Dublin, joiner, exor., and said Robert Allin.

A dwelling house in Clarendon Street, and real and personal estate.

Witnesses: Thomas Evans, Dublin, gent., Jane Benson, wife of said Lawrence Benson, Robert Simons, Dublin, harnessmaker.

Memorial witnessed by: Thomas Evans, Robt., Boyton, clerk to John Smith, public notary, Dublin.

58, 305, 39601   Lawrence Benson (seal)

398 TAYLOR, JOHN, Belfast, Co. Antrim, merchant. 10 Sept. 1728. Précis, ½ p., 21 Jan. 1728/29.

His wife. His two sons John and Arthur, exors. His leaseholds and interests in Counties Antrim and Down.

Witnesses: George Johnston and Thomas Martin, both of Belfast, Co. Antrim, merchants, and Robert Henderson of same, glover.

Memorial witnessed by: Thos. Martin, Robert Legg, Dublin, attorney.

                     John Taylor (seal)

58, 320, 39657   Arthur Taylor (seal)

399 GIBSON, ELIZABETH, city of Limerick, widow.

4 Feb. 1727. Précis, ½ p., 4 Feb. 1728.

Her son Henry Gibson, exor.

The front house and lonny behind the same wherein Paul Faryes deceased and John Boucherye lived . . . which she held by lease from said Faryes [situation not mentioned]. To said son Henry baker's trough and all other materials belonging to the baking trade.

Witnesses : Charles Copley, Limerick, alderman, Richard Morgan, Limerick, cordwainer, Thomas Stoakes, Limerick, yeoman.

Memorial witnessed by : Charles Copley, William Holland, Limerick, clothier.

59, 135, 39767   Henry Gibson (seal)

400 LEESON, HUGH, Dublin, gent.

2 Feb. 1720. Narrate, 1¼ p., 12 March 1728.

His mother Alice Leeson. His wife Elizabeth Leeson. His son Hugh Leeson. " His said son Ralph " [? second son]. His daughter Katherine Leeson. His brother William Leeson. If his sister [Rebecca][1] Antrobus should die without issue a legacy to St. Ann's Church, Dublin, for poor widows and orphans. His sister Ann Jeffors. His brother[-in-law] John Antrobus, Dublin, clerk, testator's wife, and his brother George Mosse, Dublin, gent., exors. £10 to Incumbent and churchwardens of St. Kavans Church, suburbs of city of Dublin.

The house he then dwelt in in Duke Street, Dublin, and real and personal estate.

Witnesses : Katherine Flemyng, Dublin, widow, Hellina Flemyng, her daughter, and Rev. John Madden, Dublin, clerk.

Memorial witnessed by : Mathew Paggeitt, clerk to Benjamin Johnston, Dublin, public notary, Zack. Nolan, clerk to George Mosse, gent., attorney in H.M. Court of Common Pleas, Ireland.

60, 103, 40084   Eliz. Leeson (seal)

401 SHAW, JOHN, Ballytweedy, Co. Antrim, gent.

11 Jan. 1728. Narrate, ½ p., 22 April 1729.

Trustees : His brother Thomas Shaw of Ballyministragh, his kinsman James Crawford of Ballysavage and William McCulloch of Piedmont, all in Co. Antrim. His daughter Helen Shaw. His son Henry Shaw. His real and personal estate.

---

[1] The will of John Antrobus, proved 1761, mentions his wife Rebecca, sister of Hugh Leeson. *Betham Will Pedigrees.* Genealogical Office.

Witnesses : William Agnew, Kilwaughter, gent., William Cuningham, Ballyrobbin, surgeon, John McNeily, Carngrany, farmer, Josh. Wilson, Antrim, gent., all in Co. Antrim.

Memorial witnessed by : Will. Agnew, Daniel Kelly, clerk to Robert Donnaldson, Dublin, gent.

Henry Shaw (seal)

60, 160, 40331   Will. McCulloch (seal)

402 HULL, WILLIAM, Lemcon, Co. Cork, Esq.

7 Dec. 1726. Full, 1¼ p., 26 April 1729.

My wife Elizabeth Hull. My son Richard Edward Hull. My nephew Richard Tonson of Tonsonstown, in parish of Drowmaleage [Dromdaleague], Co. Cork, Esq. Exors. my friends Sir Emmanuel Moore of Dunnemore, Bart., Emmanuel Moore of Maryborough, Esq., Henry Becher of Creagh and Edward Herbert, senr., of Kilhow, Co. Kerry, Esq. All my real estate and lands of inheritance.

Witnesses : Daniel Donovane, Dunmanus, Co. Cork, gent., Owen Lander, Lemcon, Co. Cork, gent., seneschal of the manor of Lemcon, and Dennis Donovane, Dunmanus, farmer.

Memorial witnessed by : Daniel Donovane, Nicholas Genge, Tonsonstowne, gent.

60, 168, 40368   Rich. Tonson (seal)

403 WEST, JOHN, Clogher, parish of Downe, clerk.

9 Sept. 1726. Narrate, ¾ p., 29 April 1729.

A legacy to his brother Gadson to be paid out of a bond due to testator by his mother Hanah and brother Francis West. His sister Mary Teate. His brother Richard West. His sister Jane Gadson. Edward Benson and George Gregory of Downe, clerks, exors.

Houses and tenements in Killough [situation not mentioned]. The quarter of land of Clogher called Chambers quarter.

Witnesses : James Teate, gent., James Patterson, yeoman and Renald Lynchy, yeoman, all of Clogher.

Memorial witnessed by : James Teate, John Caddell of Downpatrick, Co. Down, gent.

Edwd. Benson (seal)
Geo. Gregory (seal)

60, 174, 40396   Mary Teate (seal)

404 LUMLEY, HENRY, Cork city, gent.
  23 Jan. 1728. Narrate, 1¾ p., 30 April 1729.
  Nephew John Key. Nephew William Raincock of Penrith, Co. of
Cumberland, merchant. George Raincock of London, merchant and
John Raincock of London, merchant, said nephew's sons and brothers
of testator's grand-nephew Hugh Raincock. Grand-nephew and exor.
Hugh Raincock, of Cork, gent., to take name of Lumley instead of
Raincock. Dorothy Raincock, Margaret Raincock and Grace Rain-
cock, daughters of said William Raincock.
  Capt. Daniel Connor of Bandon, and Mary Connor his wife. Sarah
Wade, Jane Lapp, Mary Connor, Hannah Connor and Elizabeth
Connor, daughters of said Daniel Connor. William Connor, George
Connor and Henry Connor, sons of said Daniel Connor. His servant
Sarah Packer. His servant John Williams. Ellinor Murphy. £50
each to Minister and churchwardens of St. Paul's, Cork, St. Mary
Shandon, Cork, and St. Peter's, Cork, for the poor.
  Lands at Skelton, Cumberland. Estate in Ireland. His estate on
the Marsh of Cork.
  Witnesses : William Chartres, Esq., Wm. Kirkpatrick, merchant,
Richard Harrison, gent., all of Cork.
  Memorial witnessed by : Wm. Chartres, Richard Harrison.
58, 536, 40416   Hugh Lumley (seal)

405 MEADE, DAVID, Tisaxon, in the Liberties of Kinsale, Co. Cork,
  gent. 5 Dec. 1724. Narrate, 1¼ p., 20 June 1724.
  His wife Mary Meade. His father-in-law Thomas Owgan of Monteene,
Co. Cork, gent., trustee and exor. His aunt Mary Meade. His three
sisters-in-law Martha Owgan, Barbara Owgan and Rebecca Ware.
His cousin Martin Meade of Commons, Co. Cork, gent. David Meade
his father [? father of testator]. His friends and relations John Hurley,
Dennis Keefe, Jane Meade, widow, Elen Sweeny, widow, and Roger
Heas (Dennis Keefe and Roger Heas are left legacies in trust for their
wives). Debts due to James O'Hea. Arthur Barnard, Esq., holder of
a mortgage. Jeremiah Browne of Kinsale, gent., exor. Catherine, wife
of John Macraith of Kinsale.
  Lands of Kippagh (or Cipagh) in Libertys of Kinsale, Michael Dawly,
tenant. "Barry Tisaxon sit. between White Castleford and the
bounds of Ballywilliam." Lands of Killany in Liberty of Kinsale,
Co. Cork, (held by lease by William Meade, clerk).

Witnesses : John Macraith, Kinsale, gent., John Owgan, Killyobin, Co. Cork, gent., James Ware, late of Lisrowick, Co. Cork, deceased.

Memorial witnessed by : John Owgan, John Pierce, clerk to Robert Wallis, Cork, public notary.

61, 145, 40912   Thos. Owgan (seal)

406 ROE, RICHARD, Clontilew, Co. Armagh, gent.

   2 Aug. 1715. Narrate, ½ p., 28 June 1729.

His only sister Mary Roe, exor. His half brother Arthur Powell. His mother Elinor Powell deceased.

His friend Walter Bond of Aghnacloy, Co. Armagh, gent., exor. Wm. Richardson, Esq., overseer.

Tullimikoll, parish and county of Armagh. Lands and tenements in the mannors of Killevy and Clontilew, Co. Armagh, and all other real and personal estate.

Witnesses : Robert McConchy, Armagh, innkeeper, George Gough, Armagh, merchant, Edwd. Bond, Bondville, Co. Armagh, Esq., Wm. Pooler, Ballycromy, Co. Armagh, gent.

Memorial witnessed by : Wm. Devall, Dublin, public notary, Thos. Mullock, Dublin, gent.

60, 307, 41002   Ed. Bond (seal)

407 VIGIER, JACOB, Ransford Street, in Libertie of Thomas Court and Donore [Dublin], silk weaver. 8 Nov. 1726. Narrate, ½ p., 1 July 1729.

Wife Mary Vigier. " His three sisters Mary Vigier als. Butler, wife of Isaac Butler, Ann Vigier, senr. als. Duran, wife of Peter Duran, Ann Vigier, junr., als. Travers [wife of or daughter of] Isaiah Travers."

Mr Thos. Dods, Dublin, upholder and Mr John Studders, exors. His dwelling house in Ransford Street.

Witnesses : Richd. March, St. James Street, Dublin, wigmaker, Andrew Dixon, Ransford Street, victualler, Samuel Suffolk, parish of St. Catherine, schoolmaster.

Memorial witnessed by : Andrew Dixon, Thomas Ringwood, Dublin, gent.

60, 311, 41020   Mary Butler als. Vigier

            (seal) her mark.

408 RELLICK, WILLIAM, Dublin, gent.

9 Jan. 1728. Narrate, ¾ p., 10 July 1729.

Wife Sarah Rellick als. Hanlan, extx. Marriage articles dated 1 July 1682 previous to their marriage made by the testator and his father James Rellick, and Hugh Hanlan, father of said Sarah. His sister Barbara Ford, widow. His niece Elenor Ford. His nephew William Ford. His nephew Michael Ford. To Patrick Ford £5.

Patrick Hanlan and Mary his wife. Debts due to Oliver Weston, gent., Margt. Blake, widow, and Mary Haly, widow.

His estate of freehold and inheritance in two front houses on North side of St. James Street, Dublin, with a malt house backwards and appurtenances thereunto belonging formerly in possession of Joseph Marriot, gent., and then in possession of Philip Maloney and Richard Fitzgerald, and all other his real estate.

Witnesses : John Cooper, Carlingford, Co. Louth, clerk, Patrick Connor and Thomas Connor, both of Dublin, gents.

Memorial witnessed by : James Goddard and Thomas Ringwood, both of Dublin.

60, 329, 41099　　　　　　　　　　　　Sarah Rellick (seal)

409 BURGIN, THOMAS, city of Dublin, carpenter.

20 June 1729. Narrate, 1½ p., 14 July 1729.

Son William Burgin. Ratifies a settlement made on the marriage of his daughter Mary with Gabriel Lloyd. His daughter Susanna Mathews. His son-in-law William Mathews. His grandchildren Elizabeth Mathews, Thomas Mathews and Alice Mathews. Daughter Elizabeth Burgin. Trustees, his son-in-law Gabriel Lloyd and his good friend Mr Alexr. Bagnall.

Mr Atkinson, tenant, Garden Lane, Dublin. Bridgefoot Street, Dublin, Mr Campbell a tenant. Holding in Bridgefoot Street set to Mr Woods. His dwelling house, holding adjoining set to Mr Leadbeater, and a backhouse adjoining set to Patrick Langan, cooper, all in St. Francis Street, Dublin.

Witnesses : Wm. Lunell, Dublin, clothier, Isaac Wilkinson, Dublin, gent., Simon Anyon, Dublin, gent.

Memorial witnessed by : Simon Anyon, Edward Clancy of Dublin.

59, 410. 41120　　　　　　　　　　　　Elizabeth Burgin (seal)

410 WILLS, RANDOLPH, city of Cork, gent., but now in the city of Dublin. 28 June 1729. Narrate, ¾ p., 28 July 1729.

His brother Thomas Wills. His brother John Wills. John Mansfield, Cork, linen draper, exor. Luke Wills, son of Sherly Wills, cooper, Cork. Margaret Lutherberry of Cork. Gile Francis, Cork, chandler, exor. His landlady Mary Green of the city of Dublin.

His farm of land adjoining Crossbarry between Cork and Bandon. His real and personal estate.

Witnesses : John Green, taylor, Ambrose Green, attorney of the Exchequer, and Thomas Morrett, apprentice to said John Green, who live in Patrick Street, Dublin.

Memorial witnessed by : Thomas Morrett, John Callaghan, Dublin, gent.

John Maunsell (seal)

61, 227, 41206   Giles Francis (seal)

exors. and devisees.

411 HUTCHESON, JOHN, Ballyrea, Co. Ardmagh.

6 March 1728. Narrate, ¾ p., 9 Aug. 1729.

His wife Rachel Hutcheson, extx. To his son Francis Hutcheson, exor. all his books and MSS. Son Robert Hutcheson, exor. His daughter Rhoda Hutcheson. His son Alexander Hutcheson. His son John. His brother-in-law James Johnston. Son Hans Hutcheson.

Drumaligg, Co. Down, then settled on said Francis Hutcheson by testator's father's will dated 25 Dec. 1711. Carradown (Corradown), B. Trugh, Co. Monaghan. Tilledan and Drumnolan, Co. Monaghan. Anaghbeg [? B. Trugh, Co. Monaghan].

Witnesses : Alexander Johnston, James Johnston.

Memorial witnessed by : Thomas Drennan, James Meares, Dublin.

61, 248, 41278   Francis Hutcheson (seal)

412 WILKINSON, ZACHARIAH, Antrim, Co. Antrim, chandler.

13 July 1728. Full, ½ p., 7 Oct. 1729.

My father . . . shall have a right to the dwelling house he now lives in. My wife Elizabeth, exor. My daughters Elizabeth and Catherine. Rev. William Hartson, clerk, exor. House lands etc. in town and parish of Antrim.

Witnesses : Henry Weir, apothecary, Mathew King, merchant, and Joseph Wilson, gent., all of town and county of Antrim.

Memorial witnessed by : Alexander Hanna, Antrim, merchant, James Wilde, public notary.

61, 344, 41565   Elizabeth Wilkinson (seal)

413 SMITH, JAMES, Belfast, Co. Antrim, brewer.

29 Nov. 1726. Narrate, 1 p., 10 Nov. 1729.

Trustees : his wife Hanna Smith, his brother Nathan Smith and William Stevenson of Ballymacart, Co. Down. His four children James, Sarah, Elizabeth and Mary. Overseers : said trustees and Mr Daniel Mussenden, Mr James Park of Belfast, Co. Antrim, merchants, and Mr John Gregg of Glanavey, Co. Antrim.

North Street, Belfast (freehold etc. purchased from George Bigger of Dublin, merchant, 1719) " upon which freehold his present dwelling house, office, houses, malthouses and brew house do now stand."

Witnesses : Mathew Davison, John Wilson, Edwd. Logan, all of Belfast, Co. Antrim, yeomen.

Memorial witnessed by : Mathew Davison, Edwd. Logan.

60, 428, 41789   Hannah Smith (seal)

414 VANDELEUR, JAMES, Cragg, Co. Clare, clerk.

9 Sept. 1729. Narrate, ¾ p., 27 Jan. 1729/30.

Eldest son Henry Vandeleur. Third son Francis Vandeleur. Rev. Mr Andrew Barclay of Newmarket and John Hickey of Sixmilebridge, Co. Clare, gent., exors.

Ballyvokan, Dromunduff, Gortnagaul, Blane, Shanagowl and Coultinegown [Coolteengowan], B. Clonderala, Co. Clare. Corkanagnochane, B. Bunratty, Co. Clare.

Witnesses : John Stephens, Ballysheen, Co. Clare, clerk, James Maghlin, Dromunekelly, Co. Clare, gent., Francis Mulguiny, Snaty, said County, yeoman.

Memorial witnessed by : John Stephens, John Bentley, Sixmilebridge, Co. Clare, apothecary.

64, 12, 42403   Hen. Vandeleur (seal)

415 NAPER, JAMES, Loghcrew, Co. Meath.

28 March 1717. Narrate, 1¾ p., 6 Feb. 1729.

A settlement made on marriage to his then wife Ann Naper als. Dutton. His eldest son Lenox Naper. His second son William Naper. His daughter Dorothy Ormsby als. Naper, her present husband, (if estate should come to her sons they are to take surname of Naper). His daughter Sarah White als. Naper, her husband, (ditto). His daughter Anna Maria.[1] His son [-in-law] Thomas White of Redhills, Co. Cavan, Esq. His brother Robert Naper, Esq.

John Wood of Rasmeed, Esq., and William Westbury, Dublin, gent., (exor.), [trustees]. John Tandy of Drewstown, Esq., (exor.), and Ambrose Jones of Loughcrew to collect rents etc. £8 per annum to Mr Ambrose Jones to keep the houses, gardens, park walls, etc. at Loghcrew and Drewstown in order. £100 for a monument in his pew, and £20 for repair of Loghcrew Church. James Tucker, a legatee.

Lands in province of Connaught purchased from trustees of Col. John Browne [situation not mentioned] and in the county of Kerry. Lands in Co. Westmeath called Ranamuddah and part of Brackereagh and the lands of Ballyfarell and Cullymore in the King's Co. (purchased from James Barry, Esq.,). His house in Queen Street, Dublin. Estate of John Wade of Clonobraney, Esq. [? held under mortgage].

Witnesses : David Charleton, Loghcrew, Co. Meath, clerk, Edwd. Fitzgerald, Moat, Co. Meath, gent., John Lord, Loghcrew, Co. Meath, weaver.

Memorial witnessed by : David Charleton, Chas. Reilly of Drewstown, servant to said John Tandy.

64, 38, 42508   John Tandy (seal)

416 MASON, ROBERT, Dublin, alderman.

1 April 1727. Narrate, 1 p., 9 Feb. 1729.

His real estate bequeathed among his five daughters : Rebecca Mason, then wife of Rev. Dean Mason, Mary Gerrard, then wife of Jonathan Gerrard, Dublin, brewer, Sarah Young, widow, Elizabeth Jenkin, wife of Thos. Jenkin, Esq., and Barbara Usher, wife of Henry Usher, Esq. Edward Keane, Clontarf, Co. Dublin, gent. and Jonathan Gerrard, trustees.

---

[1] Wife of Dillon Pollard, Esq.

N

Witnesses : Theobald Burke, Ballyfarnham, Co. Dublin, Esq.,
James Hoye, Dublin, vintner, Charles Phipes, Dublin, gent.

Memorial witnessed by : Thos. Ringwood and John Carmack,
Dublin, gents.

Jonat. Gerrard (seal)

62, 207, 42553 Edw. Keane (seal)

417 DAVENPORT, EDWARD, Edwardstown, Co. Cavan, Esq.

30 Aug. 1724. Codicil 20 Aug. 1728. Précis, ½ p., 12 Feb. 1729.
Wife Ann Davenport. His son Thomas Davenport. His real and
personal estate.

Witnesses : Rev. John Welsh, clerk, William Buxton, Atherdee, Co.
Louth, Esq., John Waddington, Lisboduff, Co. Cavan, gent.

Codicil witnessed by : Thomas Whyte, Redhills, Co. Cavan, Rev.
James Cottingham, Ardmagh, Co. Cavan, clerk, David Lindsey
(Linesly), Edwardstown, yeoman.

Memorial witnessed by : David Linesly, Thomas Ringwood, Dublin,
gent.

62, 213, 42576 T. Davenport (seal)

418 SOUTHWELL, RICHARD, Enniscouch, Co. Limerick, Esq.

9 Sept. 1729. Précis, ½ p., 20 Feb. 1729/30.

" His wife Agnes Southwell, Sir Maurice Crosby, Knt. and his brother
Henry Rose, Esq.," trustees. Eldest son John Southwell. John
Fitzgerald and George Rose, trustees.

Lands of Enniscouch (Enniscoush), Ballyhines, Ardbohill, Lissaddeen
and Ballivinterrourk, Co. Limerick, and all his lands, tenements and
hereditaments etc.

Witnesses : Donat O'Brien, city of Limerick, Doctor of Physick,
Henry Peacock of Enniscouch, gent., Jonas Leake, Rathkeil, Co.
Limerick, gent.

Memorial witnessed by : Hen. Peacock, Matt. Slatery and George
Studdert, all of the city of Limerick, gents.

62, 226, 42638 Hen. Rose (seal)

419 HALL, JOHN, Dolphin's Barn, Co. Dublin, gent.
  21 Dec. 1729. Précis, ¾ p., 21 Feb. 1729/30.
His brother Joseph Hall. His brother Thomas Hall. His brother
Samuel Hall. His brother Robert Hall. Trustees : his cousin Joseph
Hall of Cappagh, Co. Galway, gent., his brother-in-law John Hilliard
of Dolphin's Barn, Co. Dublin, gent., the Rev. Claudius Gilbert.,
D.D., Vice Provost of Trinity College near Dublin, Thomas Willington,
Ballymooney, King's Co., Esq.
  John Hilliard, junr., son to his brother-in-law John Hilliard. William
Thompson, son to his brother-in-law Thomas Thompson. John Davis,
junr., son to his brother-in-law John Davis. His real and personal
estate.
  Witnesses : Edmond Barry, Dublin, Doctor of Physick, Samuel
Jones, Dolphin's Barn, Co. Dublin, farmer, Miles Barrot [? Barrett],
Dolphin's Barn, miller.
  Memorial witnessed by : Samuel Jones, William Hale, Dublin,
attorney.
  62, 230, 42656 John Hilliard (seal)

420 LEDBEATER, JONATHAN, East Roddum, Norfolk, and
  Dublin, skinner and glover. 18 Feb. 1729. Précis, ½ p., 13
  March 1729.
His brother Joseph Ledbeater then of Cambride [? Cambridge] in the
kingdom of England. My brother Wm. Ledbeater.
  Robert Haughey and Robt. Flyng of Cornmarkett, merchants,
trustees. Legatees : Sarah Ormsby, wife of Simon Ormsby, Michael
Collins, Dublin, gent., Benjamin Bowen, Cornmarket, merchant.
  Houses on north side of Cornmarkett [Dublin].
  Witnesses : Elizabeth Pickering, Patt. Callan, brewer, George
Watson, Dublin, butcher.
  Memorial witnessed by : George Watson, Patt. Callan.
  63, 108, 42866 Mich. Collins (seal)

421 HOLROYD, JOHN, Dublin, Esq.
  30 Dec. 1729. Narrate, ¾ p., 28 March 1730.
His wife Sarah Holroyd. His eldest son Isaac Holroyd, exor. His
youngest son William Holroyd. His daughter Mary Holroyd. His
cousin Mary, wife of Gilbert Sheppard.

£500 to Blue Coat Hospital, Dublin, for the use of the boys therein. Mrs Mary Bryan.

Lands of Oldtown, Ferrans and Little Ardrum, Co. Meath. Lands near Clondalkin, Co. Dublin, and all his real and personal estate.

Witnesses : John Katherens and Joseph Landers, clerks to Henry Buckley, Dublin, public notary, and said Henry Buckley.

Memorial witnessed by : Joseph Landers, Henry Buckley.

62, 297, 42941   Isaac Holyroyd (seal)

422 LOWRY, ROBERT, Aghenis, Co. Tyrone, Esq.

1 Nov. 1728. Narrate, 1 p., 20 April 1730.

Robert Lowry, eldest son. Second son Galbraith Lowry. James Lowry third son. Daniel Eccles, Fintonagh, Co. Tyrone, Esq. and Alexr. McClintock, Dublin, gent., trustees.

Aghenis, Ballyboy, Loghmarrag, Killigivan, Tattymacolpan, Killadroy, Legacory [? Legacurry], Beaghs, Leattfearne [Letfern], Arvallees [Arvalee], Edenderry Tuckmill and corn mill, Garvaghys, Aghagallon, Mullagh, Crany [Cranny] and Drumgane, Tatymullmoney [Tattymulmona], Edenfogra [Edenfogry], Fallaghe[a]rn, Killymo[o]nan, Cornamucklagh, Lisneadin, Rakerinbegg (Rakeeranbeg), Tullyclenagh [Tullyclunagh], and Cornbrackan, Co. Tyrone. Drumin als. Drummterogan, Co. Armagh. Altydisart als. Chicester, B. Dungannon, Co. Tyrone.

Witnesses : William Hamilton, Callidon, Co. Tyrone, clerk, Archdeacon of Armagh, deceased, Moses Campbell, Callidon, clerk, John Pringle, Callidon, merchant, and John Sinclare, Callidon, innkeeper.

Memorial witnessed by : Alex. McClintock, Dublin, gent., and Patrick Darby his servant.

63, 180, 43134   Galbraith Lowry (seal)

423 MOLESWORTH, ROBERT, LORD BARON OF PHILLIPS-TOWN AND VISCOUNT MOLESWORTH OF SWORDS.

30 April 1725. Narrate, 1½ p., 27 April 1730.

His dear wife.[1] " A great part of his antient estate of inheritance in Ireland and his Lordship of Edlington in England " formerly settled on son John's marriage. Trustees : eldest son John Molesworth

---

[1] Laetitia, 3rd dau. of Richard (Coote) Baron Coote of Coloony. *The Complete Peerage*, G.E.C.

(exor.), his well beloved brother [in-law] Thomas Coote, Esq., Arthur
Newcomen of Dublin, councill-at-law, and Joseph Banks, Esq. Son
Richard Molesworth.   His five younger sons William Molesworth,
Edwd. Molesworth, Walter Molesworth, Coote Molesworth and Bysse
Molesworth.

"Lease of the Aulnage duty in Ireland from the King for 31 years
taken in his son William's name." Houses and lands in Dublin and
elsewhere in Ireland. Lands and tenements called Mensens Fields als.
St. Patrick's Well lands by St. Stephen's Green and a piece of ground
on east side of Dawson's Street near the churchyard of St. Ann's
Church, which testator purchased from Rt. Hon. James Tynte in the
name of Robert Adair, Esq., and ground in St. Stephen's Green, Dublin.

Witnesses : Arthur Davys, Knocksedan, Co. Dublin, Esq., John
Raymond, junr., then student in Trinity College, Dublin, Alexr.
Carroll, Dublin, gent.

Memorial witnessed by : James Goddard and Thomas Ashton,
Dublin, gents.

63, 197, 43190   Willm. Molesworth (seal)

424 WARREN, MARY, Dublin, spinster.

29 April 1730. Précis, part in full, ½ p., 14 May 1730.

Margaret Warren, widow and relict of Thomas Warren late of
Dublin, Esq., deceased, her [testator's] brother, extx. and devisee.
Charles Baldwin, Dublin, debtor.

"I am intitled to a moyety of all the lands, houses . . . whereof
Oliver Tallant late of the city of Dublin, Esq., deceased dyed seized of or
intitled unto situate in the city and suburbs of Dublin, County of
Dublin, County of Meath and elsewhere in this Kingdom."

Witnesses : Joseph Brogden, Dublin, draper, Joseph Turner,
Dublin, silkweaver, James Hamill, Dublin, gent.

Memorial witnessed by : James Hamill, Christopher Dalton, son of
Edward Dalton of Dublin, notary public.

64, 183, 43374   Margat. Warren (seal)

425 SCOTT, QUINTEN, Ballyrath, Co. Armagh, gent.

9 Aug. 1729. Narrate, ¾ p., 15 May 1730.

His wife Martha. His son William Scott. His daughter Martha.
His son John Scott. His son Robert Scott. His daughter Elizabeth

Kid. His daughter Mary Paul. His son William Scott and Daniel McDowel exors. Joshua McGeough and James Stephenson overseers. His freehold in Cornecrew [? Cornacrew, Co. Armagh], in possession of Luke McClinshey. Townland of Ballyrath.

Witnesses : Thomas Golphin, Tullymore, William Jenkins and Joseph Jenkins of Tullylast, all in Co. Armagh, gent.

Memorial witnessed by : John Perry of Ballyrath, Thos. Golphin.

64, 185, 43384   William Scott (seal)

426 NICHOLSON, CHARLES, Lieut. and adjutant in Col. Wm. Cosby's Regiment. 25 Jan. 1724-5. Précis, ½ p., 30 May 1730.

His cousins and sisters Frances [wife of] Farrell and Margery [wife of] Ormsby, daughters of Capt. Wm. Nicholson of Castle Baldwin [testator's uncle]. Arthur Knox of Castle Rea, Co. Mayo, mortagee.

All his estate in the counties of Leitrim and Mayo, his effects in the Island of Minorca and Dublin.

Witnesses : Owen Young, Castlereagh, John Bullingbrooke of same, James Magrah of same, all in Co. Roscommon.

Memorial witnessed by : James Magrah, Charles Rutlidge, Castlereagh.

                                    Frances Farrell als. Cary (seal)
62, 424, 43487   Margery Ormsby (seal)

427 EDGWORTH, ROBERT, Longwood, Co. Meath, Esq. 10 Sept. 1729. Précis, ½ p., 20 July 1730.

Recites tripartite deed of settlement 13 Aug. 1726. His son Packington Edgworth. Peter Ludlow, Thomas Loftus, Lewis Moore, Esqrs., and Edward Plunket, gent., [? exors.].

Real and personal estate in counties of Meath, Westmeath, Kildare, Longford and elsewhere in Kingdom of Ireland.

Witnesses : Ambrose Edgworth and Neale Geoghegan, both of Dublin, gents., Bartholomew Kelly and Miles Dunn, both of Longwood, yeomen.

Memorial witnessed by : Ambrose Edgworth, Neale Geoghegan.

64, 293, 43908   Packington Edgworth (seal)

428 JONES, DAVID, of the Liberty of Thomas Court and Donore [Dublin]. 10 July 1717. Précis, ½ p., 20 Aug. 1730.

His wife Mary Jones, extx. His daughter-in-law Eliz. Jones als. McCormack. " His nephew and niece John Doran and Sarah Doran his wife." His real and personal estate.

Witnesses : Edward Doran, Marrow Bone Lane, weaver, Wm. Drayton, Bride Street, Dublin, brazier, Dennis Moore, Bride Street, brazier.

Memorial witnessed by : Dennis Moore, Thomas Ashton, Dublin, gent.

John Doran (seal)

63, 388, 44047   Sarah Doran her mark (seal)

429 GOODWIN, RICHARD, Butlerstown, Co. Dublin, gent. 28 July 1730. Narrate, 1 p., 29 Aug. 1730.

His daughter Christiana Goodwin. Mr Robt. Goodwin officer of Commons and Mr Humphrey Denny of Ringsend, exors. John Goodwin, junr., butler of the Royal Hospital near Dublin. Andrew Goodwin, brother of said John Goodwin.

Two leases in Butlerstown and rest of real and personal estate.

Witnesses : James Cullen, Butlerstown, farmer, Dinnis Coffey, Butlerstown, farmer, Charles Meares, Dublin, public notary.

Memorial witnessed by : Charles Meares, Alex. Brodie, Dublin, gent.

64, 332, 44098   Robt. Goodwin (seal)

430 DOUGATT, ROBERT, Chanter of St. Patrick's, Dublin. 29 July 1730. Précis, ¾ p., 29 Aug. 1730.

Mary Dougatt, mother of testator, and his sisters Elizabeth Spence and Martha Strahan. Nephew Robert Spence. His sister Jane Bryan. His nephew Robert Bryan. John Wynne, Prebendary of St. Audeon, trustee.

Lambstown and other lands in Co. Wexford. Bolyart [Bolart], and other lands in King's Co. His advowson and right of patronage of the Rectory of Donaghmore, Diocese of Derry. Advowsons and right of patronage of the parishes of Crevagh, Newcastle and Ballintemple in the Diocese of Dublin, parish of Kilkenny West in the Diocese of Meath, and tythes of said parishes. Lands purchased by his uncle the late Lord Bishop of Dublin from the Commissioners of

H.M. Revenue and was part of the estate of Sir John Eccles, deceased, [situation not mentioned]. Impropriate tythes purchased by said uncle in counties Kildare, Dublin and elsewhere (to be applied to charitable uses), and real and personal estate.

Witnesses : James Jackson, public notary, Wm. Williams, gent., James Allam, surgeon, all of Dublin.

Memorial witnessed by : James Jackson, Bartholomew Delandre, clerk to Wm. Parry, Dublin, public notary.

63, 398, 44099   J. Wynne (seal)

431 GOODWIN, FRANCES, widow of Peter Goodwin late of the Royal Hospital near Dublin, Esq. 16 Dec. 1729. Narrate, part in full, 1 p., 5 Sept. 1730.

My son Richard Goodwin. Frances and Christiana Goodwin the two daughters of my said son Richard which he had by his late wife. My two daughters Ann Parker and Frances ffolliot. Rev. Sankey Winter, clerk, and Francis Tucker, Dublin, Esq., trustees.

A plot of ground formerly commonly known by the name of the Hartychoke in Kevans Port in suburbs of city of Dublin. The upper mills of Loaders part near Harold's Cross, B. Newcastle and Upper Cross, Co. Dublin. A house in High Street, Kilkenny (to be charged with £8 per annum to Mr James Goodwin for his life).

Witnesses : Henry Croker, Dublin, gent., Thomas Porse, Dublin, grocer, John Hart, Dublin, victualler.

Memorial witnessed by : Henry Price, a servant to Christopher Parker, Esq., in Henry Street, John Hart.

63, 405, 44142   Ann Parker (seal)

432 McCAVER, NICHOLAS, Antrim, Co. Antrim.

24 Feb. 1711. Précis, a few lines, 18 Sept. 1730.

" All his houses and lands to his son Henry."

Witnesses : Robert Welsh, Antrim, shoemaker, James McDonnell, late of the same, schoolmaster, John Bartly, Antrim, mason.

Memorial witnessed by : Mary Mildmay, widow, John Rainey, locksmith, James Wilde, public notary, all of Antrim.

64, 356, 44195   Henry McCaver (seal)

433 FAY, GEORGE, Castlepollard, Co. Westmeath, gent.
12 May 1730. Précis, ¼ p., 26 Oct. 1730.
Son Garrett Fay, exor. My brother Michael Fay. My estate of Tromrow [? Tromra], Co. Westmeath.
Witnesses : Morgan Ball, innkeeper, Peter Flanagan, chirurgeon, William Gragan, merchant, all of Castlepollard.
Memorial witnessed by : Morgan Ball, Bartholomew Delandre, clerk to Mr Wm. Parry, Dublin, notary public.
65, 66, 44388 Garrett Fay (seal)

434 PEYTON, REBECCA LADY, widow of Sir John Peyton, Dublin, Bart. 19 Feb. 1727. Narrate, ½ p., 28 Jan. 1730.
Her niece Mrs Jane Cooper. Her nephew Rev. Archdeacon William Williamson. Her niece Mrs Catherine Cayer.[1] Her cousin Mrs Dorothy Mortimer. Her son-in-law Mr Walter Bunbury. Her niece Hannah Murray, then of the city of Dublin, widow, extx.
Legacies to poor of St. Mary's and St. Audeon's parishes, Dublin. Her dwelling house in Great Britain Street, Dublin, and real and personal estate.
Witnesses : John Ford, John Curtis, grocer, William Crowe, gent., all of Dublin.
Memorial witnessed by : William Crowe, John Lyons, servant to John Maddison of Dublin, gent.
65, 202, 45097 Hannah Maddison (seal)

435 ANYON, ROBERT, Rathfarnham
2 Dec. 1730. Précis, ½ p., 17 March, 1730/31.
His niece Kensbarrow Challoner, his niece Elizabeth Challoner, his niece Mabell Challoner, his niece Margery Challoner (sisters). His sister Margery Challoner, widow.
House and lands in Clane [? Co. Kildare], his real and personal estate in the city of Dublin and town of Rathfarnham [Dublin].
Witnesses : Michael Brazell, papermaker, Christopher Jones, joyner, John Plunket, carman, all of Rathfarnham, Jeremy Wilson, clerk of the parish of Rathfarnham.
Memorial witnessed by : Christopher Jones, Michael Brazell.
65, 284, 45542 Kensbarrow Challoner (seal)

[1] *Betham's Will Pedigrees*, Genealogical Office, refer to niece Mrs Catherine *Carter* and to " niece Hannah Murray wife of John Maddison, gent."

436 SIMPSON, NICHOLAS, Cursed Stream, Co. Dublin, gent.

20 March 1726/7. Narrate, ½ p., 23 April 1731.

To Sarah Simpson als. Killingher [testator's wife] one shilling only. Half his property to her for Nicholas [? testator's eldest son] then apprentice with Mr Jonathan Maughan, and "the other half to be divided among the rest." Leases to his nephew John Simpson his brother's eldest son, then a clothier in Meath Street, for life, then to his eldest son [? testator's son] Nicholas Simpson and his heirs male, failing male issue to his brother [? testator's younger son] John Simpson, apprentice in Cork. Exors. his friends John Simpson and his son Nicholas Simpson both of Meath Street, clothiers.[1]

Patrick Darling, a papist foot soldier. Caleb Killinger, debtor.

Lease of Cursed Stream held from Lord Palmerston renewable for ever, lease of adjoining land held from Henry Brumer.

Witnesses : Robert Wousencraft, Meath Street, joiner, Richard Loyd, Upper Comb, sheerman, Edward Loyd, apprentice to said John Simpson.

Memorial witnessed by : Robt. Wousencraft, Thos. Ringwood, Dublin, gent.

65, 310, 45647   Nicholas Simpson (seal)

                         (of Meath Street)

437 HERBERT, DAME JANE.

22 Oct. 1728. Narrate, 1 p., 11 May 1731.

A marriage settlement 1720 made by testator by name of Dame Jane Herbert, wife of Richard Whitshed of the city of Dublin, Esq., of the house wherein they dwelt on east side of St. Stephen's Green, Dublin. Rt. Hon. Wm. Whitshed, Dublin, Lord Chief Justice of King's Bench, and Hon. John Pocklington to be trustees. Recites that said Wm. Whitshed is since deceased. Edward Knatchbull of the city of Dublin, Esq., second son of Sir Edward Knatchbull, Bart., a legatee.

Monasteroris als. Herbertstown, Coolian and other lands in King's County, Leitrim, and lands belonging to Sir George Herbert, Bart., deceased, Kilmainham, Co. Dublin. Coolenhanly, Thyhilly and Bally-henehanagh, all in B. Ballycowan, King's County.

---

[1] The Will of John Simpson of Meath Street, cloathier, proved 1730, mentions his two sons John and Nicholas, his grandson John son of said Nicholas, and testator's uncle Nicholas Simpson. *Betham's Will Pedigrees*, Genealogical Office.

Witnesses : Robert Jocelyn, Esq., Edward Dering and Mathew Goodfellow, gent., all of Dublin.

Memorial witnessed by Mathew Goodfellow and John Smith of Dublin, gent.

67, 178, 45783 Edw. Knatchbull (seal)

438 PROBY, THOMAS, Dublin, surgeon.

23 Sept. 1729. Narrate, ½ p., 12 May 1731.

Son Thomas Proby. His son John Nicholls and his daughter Elinor his wife. Trustees, Rev. Wm. Jackson, minister of St. John's in Dublin, Rev. John Gratton, minister of Clonmelthan, and Capt. Brent Smith.

The house he then lived in on Ormond Key.

Witnesses : William Aickin, Francis Aickin and Hugh Picknoll of Westpallstowne, Co. Dublin, farmers.

Memorial witnessed by : Thomas Ringwood and James Doddard, Dublin, gents.

66, 196, 45793 Elinor Nicholls (seal)

439 PARSONS, WILLIAM, Garradice, Co. Leitrim, Esq.

20 March 1730/31. Part in full, ¾ p., 19 May 1731.

My nephew William Percy. Alexander Percy, son of said nephew William, and all those inheriting my estate taking upon him or them the name of Parsons. Edward Ellis, overseer.

Witnesses : Lawrence Parsons, Garradice, natural son of said testator, John Whelan, of same, gardener, Thorlaugh Flin, Drumcullin, said county, farmer.

Memorial witnessed by : Samuel Turbutt, Dublin, hosier, John Scott, Limerick, gent.

67, 199, 45882 Will. Percy (seal)

440 ROBERTS, WILLIAM, Cullenwood, Co. Dublin, gent.

21 Feb. 1729. Narrate, 1 p., 20 May 1731.

His nephew William Jones. His nephew John Jones, exor. His nephew Joseph Jones. His niece Elizabeth Williams and her brother Samuel Boyd. His niece Dorothy Sybery. His cousin John Brock. Robert Roberts, Dublin, gent., exor.

Nicholas Lincoln and Mr John Marcarrell, then in possession of coach house and stables in Brock Lane, Dublin, held by leases by testator. Houses on Ormond Key, Dublin, wherein Mr John Cromie, Mr Wm. Cammock and Mr James Stevenson then dwelt. House on Ormond Key which Mr John Bailie then held under him. His holding in Abby Street, Dublin, demised to Mr Richd. Dawson. Dwelling houses, gardens, orchards, fields, etc. in Cullenwood (William Tuit, his nephew William Jones, Edward Hall, Edmund Sheil, tenants or in possession of parts of Cullenwood), in parish of St. Kevin's, Co. Dublin.

Witnesses : William Mankittrick and Robert Boyton, clerks to John Smith, public notary, Dublin, and said John Smith.

Memorial witnessed by : John Smith, notary public, Arthur Shepheard his clerk.

67, 201, 45891   John Jones (seal)

441 NEWMAN, CHARLES, Kilshanig, Co. Cork, gent.

24 Feb. 1729. Narrate, ½ p., 21 May 1731.

Adam Newman and Savage French, both of Cork, merchants, exors. Rev. Benezer Murdock, minister of parish of Kilshanig. John Dillon, Lower Quartertowne, Co. Cork, Esq. Anthony Callaghan of Dromore, Co. Cork. Daniel Callaghan, sixth son of the said Anthony Callaghan. Mr John Sullivan, attorney, city of Cork. Elizabeth Waglin, widow of Richard Waglin, senr., Thomas Bolster, John Witty, Robert Witty, John Farmer, William Farmer, John Bolster, George Bolster, John Carleton and Sarah Waglin, all of the parish of Kilshanig. His servants Edward Coorny, Daniel Barrett.

Witnesses : Richard Newman, Dromineen, Co. Cork, Esq.[1] Daniel Gibbs, Cork, gent., John Callaghan, Dromore, Co. Cork, gent.

Memorial witnessed by : Daniel Gibbs, William Evans, Cork, gent.

                                        Adam Newman (seal)
65, 363, 45907   Savage French (seal)

442 ABBOTT, WILLIAM, Bellaghlosky, Co. Tipperary, gent.

24 Dec. 1716. Full, ½ p., 22 May 1731.

Settlement made on son's marriage. My wife and five younger children. Wife's brother Thomas Smith of Ballingarry, exor.

---

[1] Richard and Adam Newman were the testator's brothers. *Betham's Will Pedigrees*, Genealogical Office.

Witnesses : James Smith, late of Bellaghlosky, Popish Priest, Hugh Hogan of same, labourer, Christopher Harwood, now of Dublin, glazier.

Memorial witnessed by : Ralph Smith, Lismackrory, Co. Tipperary, gent., John Scott, Limerick, gent.

65, 364, 45914   Thos. Smith (seal)

443 COLE, MICHAEL, Castlelogh, Co. Tipperary, Esq.

25 Aug. 1726. Part in full, ¾ p., 9 July 1731.

Exors. my wife Elizabeth Cole, my brother Richard Cole, Esq., his brother Lieut. Thomas Tenison.

Debts due to Mr Onge, Captain Dally, Mr Parker and Mr Lawrence Nihil. Mrs Rachel Cusack of Ballyna. A lease of 40 acres promised to Mr John Watson.

Lands of Castlelogh, Fahy, Coronode and Clonmony and other lands that I have in the parish of Castletown. My estate in Co. Clare [situation not mentioned].

Witnesses : Rt. Rev. Charles [? Carr], Lord Bishop of Killaloe, Howlett Parker, Newtown, Co. Tipperary, Esq., William Anderson, servant to testator.

Memorial witnessed by : Samuel Waller, Cully, Co Tipperary, gent., John Young, Limerick, gent.

Samuel Head (seal)
Limerick merchant.

67, 308, 46279   Elizabeth Head (seal)
wife of said Samuel and late
widow of testator.

444 TAYLOR, ELIZABETH, [Dublin], widow.

3 Dec. 1730. Précis, ½ p., 23 July 1731.

Her piece of ground of inheritance on the Merchant's Key in Dublin to be sold, Mr William Wes[t]by to have first profer, for benefit of Thomas Walker, son of Arthur Walker, pattinmaker.

Witnesses : Thomas Thresham, wigmaker, Thomas Walker, linen draper and George Walker, hosier, all of Cornmarkett, city of Dublin.

Memorial witnessed by : Michael Argent and James Goddard Dublin, gents.

67, 347, 46378   Arthur Walker (seal)

445 LANESBOROUGH, JAMES VISCOUNT.

15 Oct. 1722. [Proved in Prerogative Court 1724]. Narrate, part in full, 1¾ p., 2 Aug. 1731.

His wife [Mary] Viscountess Lanesborough. His sister Charlotte Lady Beaufoy eldest daughter of George then late Lord Viscount Lanesborough his father. John Bell Lane eldest and only grandson of his sister Mary Bingham afterwards called Mary Middleton deceased.[1] George Fox-Lane, eldest son of my half sister the Lady Galway.[2] James Fox-Lane, second son of his said (half sister) Lady Galway. Sackville Fox-Lane, third son of his half sister Lady Galway.[3] Persons claiming testator's lands and real estate to use surname of Lane and his arms in chief.

Trustees : George Hooper, Bishop of Bath and Wells, Hatton Compton of Grindon, Northampton, Lieut. General, [? Sir] Robert Dormer, Esq., a Judge in the Common Pleas, and James Middleton of Newtown Myddletown, Co. Longford, Esq.

Tulsk, Co. Roscommon and all other the lands in Co. Roscommon that belonged to his grandfather or great grandfather. Dromahaire, Co. Leitrim. Lanesborough, Rathline and Lisduff, Coolcroy and Carowle, B. of Rathline, Co. Longford. A house in Golden Square, parish St. James, Westminster. His house and grounds etc. near Knightsbridge, and near to the corners of St. James Park and Hyde Park [London].

Witnesses : Thos. Egerton, of St. James, Westminster, gent., Thos. Johnston of same place, gent., John Scrivener, of same, victualler.

Memorial witnessed by : Edward Emily, New Inn, Co. Middlesex, gent., Thos. Egerton, St. James, Westminster.

67, 366, 46443   Lanesborough (seal)

[Mary Viscountess Dowager Lanesborough extx.]

446 BUSHE, ARTHUR, Cork, Co. Dublin, Esq.

16 Nov. 1730. Narrate, 1 p., 25 Sept. 1731.

Brother-in-law James Forth, Esq., and John Staunton, Esq., trustees and exors. with son Wm. Bushe. Son Worsop Bushe. To daughter

---

[1] She married first John Bingham, secondly .... Middleton. *Betham's Will Pedigrees*, Genealogical Office.

[2] Frances, widow of Ulick Bourke, Viscount of Galway, married 1691 Henry Fox. *The Complete Peerage*, Vol. V., p. 612, by G.E.C.

[3] Sackville Fox, ancestor of family of Lane-Fox. *The Complete Peerage*, Vol. VII, p. 424, footnote, by G.E.C.

Letitia £1500 etc. on day of marriage. Sons William and John Bushe. Nieces Ann Berkeley, Mary and Barbara Hobson. Hannah Bushe als. Donnellan, then wife of testator's son Wm. Bushe.

Town and lands of Lower Grange, Co. Kilkenny (James Napper, Esq., an annuity out of the said lands). Lands of Cork als. Corkagh, part of which called Horse Park in lease to Carbury Byrne, Co. Dublin. Bramblestowne, Co. Kilkenny.

Witnesses : Samuel Hobson, Co. Kilkenny, gent., John Smalley, Co. Dublin, gent., John Barry, Brea, Co. Wicklow, innkeeper.

Memorial witnessed by : John Smalley, John Barry.

67, 434, 46698   Will. Bushe (seal)

447 ELLIS, HENRY, Cloonellan, parish of Cloongeesh, Co. Longford. 28 June 1728. Narrate, ½ p., 13 Oct. 1731.

His wife. His eldest son John. His son Thomas. His daughter Margaret Duke. Thos. Crofton, Mohill, Esq., Duke Crofton, Lurgan, gent., and Rev. Maurice Neligan of Longford, exors.

Lands of Cloonellan, part occupied by the Macans.

Witnesses : Rev. Michael Neligan, Carrick, Co. Leitrim, clerk, Elizabeth Neligan, wife of said Maurice Neligan of Longford, Co. Longford, clerk, Richard Dowler, Cloonellan, yeoman.

Memorial witnessed by : Richard Dowler, Thos. Hanly, Dublin, Esq.

65, 527, 46780   Thomas Ellis (seal)

448 HAMILTON, JAMES, Ballygraffan, clerk, Rector of Knock breda and Dundonnell, Co. Cown. 12 Jan. 1711. Narrate, 1 p., 27 Nov. 1731[1]

Wife Elenor Hamilton als. Wachob [Wauchope], exor. Son John Hamilton. His daughter Sophia Hamilton. His daughter Margaret Hamilton. Failing issue of testator's children lands etc. to " James Hamilton son to Thos. Hamilton of Currunshegoe, Co. Mayo " and his issue male failing them " to his brother David." His brother David Hamilton. His niece Ann Hamilton who is married to Collen Hamilton. His cousin Henry Maxwell of Finnabrouge, Esq., exor.

---

[1] Rev. James Hamilton was buried at Comber 11 April 1713. *Biog. Succession Lists, Dio. of Down.* Leslie and Swanzy.

His lands of inheritance. Cattogs and part of Ballygraffan. His dwelling house in Ballygraffan. Drumaghlish als. Drumalisk, B. Kineleartie [Kinelarty], Co. Down, which he bought from his brother-in-law William Wachob.

Witnesses : John Maxwell, Cattogs, Co. Down, farmer, William Steward, Newcumber, blacksmith, William Tayte, servant to said Elenor Hamilton, John Sloan, Ballygraffan, servant to testator.

Memorial witnessed by : William Tayte, Cornelius Rogers.

68, 86, 47116   Elenor Hamilton (seal)

449 MURPHY, JAMES, Dublin, miller.

22 Aug. 1727. Précis, ½ p., 24 Dec. 1731.

His wife Elizabeth Murphy. His daughter Mary Murphy (unmarried). His son-in-law John Bryn, and John Connolly exors.

His dwelling house in Caple Street in suburbs of city of Dublin.

Witnesses : John Connolly, Dublin, Cornelius Connell, Dublin, gent.

Memorial witnessed by : Cornelius Connell, Richard Bourke, Dublin, gent.

70, 49, 47313   John Connolly (seal)

450 ROCHFORT, GEORGE, Gallstown, Co. Westmeath.

5 April 1730. Narrate, 1½ p., 5 Jan. 1731.

Reciting indenture dated 1704 his father Robert Rochfort, Esq., the testator and his [testator's] then wife the Lady Elizabeth Moore, and others parties thereto. His eldest son and heir apparent Robt. Rochfort, exor. His son Arthur Rochfort. His son George Rochfort. His son William Rochfort. His three younger sons Arthur, George and William. His daughter Alice Rochfort. His daughter Thomazin Rochfort. His daughter Ann Rochfort. His wife, his mother Hannah Rochfort, widow, his brother John Rochfort, and Thomas Staunton, Esq., trustees.

Garryduffe and other lands in counties of Westmeath and Eastmeath. Mortgage on estate of Mr Silvester Devenish in Co. Westmeath and Roscommon. Ballynecloghy and other lands in Co. Westmeath, held by virtue of a fee farm lease made to testator's father by Sir Arthur Shaen, Bart., deceased. Greenmanagh, Killcoursey, Killnegeelaghan, Mahirmurry, Beggstowne, Lissnevarra and Templepatrick, Feamore, Rathcam and Fanu [? Farrow], Co. Westmeath. Houses etc. in High Street, Dublin, held by virtue of a fee farm lease from the Corporation called St. Scyth's Guild, and his lot near St. Nicholas Gate, Dublin.

Witnesses : Sir Henry Tuite, Sonnagh, Co. Westmeath, Bart.,
Rev. Michael McKinlie, Gallstown, Co. Westmeath, clerk, George
Rickeaby, servant to testator.

Memorial witnessed by : Edwin Sandys, Dublin, gent., John Saule,
clerk to said Edwin Sandys.

69, 75, 47343   Robt. Rochfort (seal)

451 HELSHAM, SAMUEL, Meath Street, Dublin.

    4 Dec. 1729. Part in full, ¾ p., 26 Jan. 1731.

My mother Elizabeth Berry. My cousin William Starling. " If
Daniel Berry late husband to said Eliz. Berry should be alive beyond
the sea."

Lease of my holding in Meath Street.

Witnesses : Arthur Wear, Meath Street, linen weaver, Joseph Lamb,
Crooked Staff, Co. Dublin, clothier, Ann Starling, Ann Street, Dublin,
widow.

Memorial witnessed by : Ann Starling, Robert Rooe, Crooked Staff,
Co. Dublin, clothier.

66, 447, 47439   Wm. Starling (seal)

452 BASHFORD, THOMAS, Carrickfergus, burgess.

    3 Jan. 1725. Précis, ½ p., 27 Jan. 1731.

His wife Mary. His daughter Mary. His brothers-in-law Henry
Magee and William Magee, exors.

His real estate in town of Carrickfergus devised to him by his father
Cornelius Bashford, burgess.

Witnesses : James Shankiland, tailor, William Milline, barber,
James Kirk, gent., all of Carrickfergus.

Memorial witnessed by : James Kirk, David Morrison, junr., of
said town, gent.

                           Henry Magee (seal)

69, 94, 47447   William Magee (seal)

453 MATHEWS, HUMPHREY, Tenny Park, Co. Wicklow.

    31 Jan. 1731. Full, ¾ p., 11 Feb. 1731.

My sister Elizabeth Thompson, my sister Mary Uniack, and my
niece Mary Lombard, exors. My real and personal estate.

o

Witnesses : Francis Bernard and James Uniacke, Dublin, Esquires, Patrick Hadsor, Dublin, perukemaker.

Memorial witnessed by : Patrick Hadsor, Richard Uniacke, Dublin, Esq.

66, 465, 47485   Eliza. Thompson (seal)

454 FRENCH, MATHEW, Ballyhubbock, Co. Wicklow, gent.

4 July 1731. Narrate, ½ p., 12 Feb. 1731/32.

Wife Betty French. His daughters Mary Catherine and Alice French. His daughter Harriott Elizabeth and his son William. His son Richard French. Richard Vincent, New Abbey, Esq. Alderman Humphrey French, Dublin.

Doohatt, Killerlahard, Derrycoiby, Killturk, Lehinch and Downady als. Derrygenedy with the woods growing thereon, Co. Fermanagh. Killduffekeeny, Shankhorne and Derryneglish, Co. Cavan. The farm rent out of lands of Dromgoole and Drumrean, Co. Fermanagh. His house in High Street [? Dublin]. His three lots in Oxmantown [? Dublin].

Witnesses : John Goodwin, Saunders Grove, gent., Malcolm McManus, Castlerudery, farmer, and Hanah Jackson, Gibbstowne, wife of William Jackson, farmer, all in Co. Wicklow.

Memorial witnessed by : John Goodwin, and Bartholomew Delandre clerk to William Parry, public notary in Dublin.

66, 467, 47602   Rich. Vincent (seal)

455 FERRARD [OF BEAULIEU], HENRY [TICHBORNE], LORD BARON.

18 March 1730. Full, 2½ pp., 3 March 1731.

Marriage settlement 1712 made by me on the marriage of my late son William Tichborne deceased. My son-in-law William Aston, Esq., Tichborne Aston his son my grandson. My granddaughters Arabella Tichborne and Wilhelmena Tichborne, daughters of my said son William. My granddaughter Sophia Aston, daughter of said Wm. Aston. Ralph (Lambert) Lord Bishop of Meath and my worthy brother-in-law Sir Thomas Taylor, Dublin, Bart., trustees, said Bishop of Meath to advise on education of grandson Tichborne Aston. My brother Colonel Tichborne. My godson Henry Hyat. My cousin

Riccard who now lives with me . . . her daughter. Henry Bellingham, Castlebellingham, Co. Lough, Esq., and Thomas Fortesque of Reynoldstown, Co. Louth, Esq., trustees. Sums owed to Master Cooke of Cookesborough, Master Wilson of Westmeath.

My mansion house of Beaulieu [Co. Louth] and the demesne thereunto belonging. My mannors, lands, tenements and hereditaments.

Witnesses : Jeremiah Smith, Drogheda, Esq., Ralph Hansard, Dundalk, Co. Louth, gent., Richard Lane, Dublin, servant to testator.

Memorial witnessed by : Richard Lane, William McCausland, Dublin.

69, 173, 47785   Wm. Aston (seal)

456 SMITH, HUGH, Dublin, hatter.

17 July 1730. Narrate 1 p., 6 April 1732.

His wife Elizabeth Smith, exor. His son Thomas Smith. His son Robert Smith. His daughter Margery Smith. His daughter Margret Smith. Nicholas Gibbon, Dublin, carrier and John Smith of same, carpenter, trustees. Thomas Gibson, Dublin, weaver and Francis O'Hara, Dublin, tailor, exors.

His houses, ground, lands etc. in and about the city and suburbs of the city of Dublin.

Witnesses : James Savage, Joseph Landers, clerks to Henry Buckley, Dublin, public notary, and said Henry Buckley.

Memorial witnessed by : James Savage, Henry Buckley.

68, 266, 47978   Elizabeth Smith (seal)

457 LENTHALL, WILLIAM, Dublin, Esq.

24 March 1729. Narrate, ½ p., 28 Oct. 1732.

His wife Dorothy Lenthall senr. His daughter Eliz. Lenthall then in London (under twenty one years). His daughter Dorothy Lenthall then in Dublin. His mother Mrs Alice Lenthall als. Burrows.

Joseph Rea, Waterford, Esq. holds monies. Mrs Elinor Mason. James Flack, John Conran, both of Dublin, gents., exors. His real and personal estate.

Witnesses : Nicholas Ricard, Samuel Graham and Adam Crump, all of Dublin, gents.

Memorial witnessed by : Nicholas Ricard, John Cormock, Dublin, yeoman.

66, 515, 48099   Ellen Mason als. Curry (seal)

458 BOLES, JOHN, Woodhouse als. Magorbane, Co. Tipperary.
14 Sept. 1730. Codicil 25 Nov. 1731. Narrate, 4 pp., 13 May 1732.
His wife Abigail Boles [als. Baker]. His daughter Anne Boles.
His daughter Jane Keating, a legacy left her by her grandfather
George Baker. His eldest son George Boles. His grandson John Boles,
eldest son of said George Boles. His grandson George Boles. His
grandson Richard Boles. His grandson Jonathan Boles, third son of
his son George Boles. His granddaughter Mary Boles. His grand-
daughter Margt. Boles. Legacy to his grandchildren by his daughter
Mary Chamberlaine, his grandson John Chamberlaine to have £50
more than any of his brothers and sisters. His grandchildren by his
daughter Elizabeth Hillary, (legacy left her by her grandfather
George Baker). His grandson Solomon Watson by his daughter
Abigail deceased. His grandson William Chamberlaine son of Jonas
Chamberlaine of little Killane, Co. Wexford. His grandson Samuel
Chamberlaine. His grandson Jonas Chamberlaine. His nephew
Thomas Boles of Kilbreedy, Co. Cork, Esq. " £300 to his grandson
John Watson . . . in case he should dye before the age of twenty one
years or day of marriage . . . the same to be divided between his
brother Solomon Watson and his sister Sarah Goodwin." His daughter
Anne Boles and his son-in-law Samuel Watson of Killconner, Co.
Catherlogh, trustees. To his son-in-law Solomon Watson of Clonbrogan the little piece of land which he had fenced in for a grave yard
[situation not mentioned]. £25 to his poor friends called Quakers
belonging to the Monthly Meeting of Cashell, Clonmell, Tipperary
and Killconnor.

Magorbane (Thomas Goodwin, lessee), Garrystockadoney, Foulks-
towne (Wm. Winsloe, lessee of part), Lancerstown, Clonbrogan
[situation not mentioned. ? all in Co. Tipperary]. Bosannagh, and
Curraghscarteen, B. Middle Third, Co. Tipperary, leased to Solomon
Watson, senr. His dwelling house called Woodhouse or Tenekelly
[Tinnakilly].

Witnesses : Mathew Jacob, St. Johnstown, Co. Tipperary, Esq.,
Henry Blackmore, near Cashell, gent., John Connor, Clonmell, gent.

Codicil witnessed by : Thomas Prince, near Cashell, Co. Tipperary,
gent., said Henry Blackmore, Piers Butler, near Clonbrogan, Co.
Tipperary, gent.

Memorial witnessed by : James Goddard, Bartholomew Delandre,
both of Dublin, gents.

70, 267, 48312   Samuel Watson (seal)

59 MEADE, Brigadier PATRICK.

9 April 1726. Full, 1 p., 5 Aug. 1732.

Declares himself member of Church of Ireland. To be buried either in Killmoon Church near my house or near my late wife in St. Paul's Church, Dublin. My wife Charlotte Meade, extx. My nephew Sir Richard Meade, Bart., and my brother-in-law John Bayly, overseers.

Curraghstown als. Meadesbrook, Co. Meath. My other lands in Co. Meath and elsewhere in Ireland.

Witnesses : Charles Hall, then apprentice to Joseph Dobson, Castle Street, Dublin, woollen draper, Christopher Dalton, son of Edward Dalton, Dublin, notary public, and said Edward Dalton.

Memorial witnessed by : Rev. John Madden, Killmoon, Co. Meath, John Bayly, Gowran, Co. Kilkenny, Esq.

70, 398, 48887   Charlotte Meade (seal)

460 TAYLOR, JOHN, Marrowbone Lane, Co. Dublin, brewer.

12 July 1731. Full, 2½ pp., 18 Aug. 1732.

My wife Martha Taylor. My eldest son Thomas (under twenty one years). My son Samuel. To my daughters Margaret and Martha £1,300 each, when twenty one years or on marriage. My three daughters Mary, Elizabeth and Ruth, £2,700 between them, (ditto). My brother Saml. Taylor. My sister Hannah Bignall, her husband Edward. My sister Elizabeth Clarke, my brother Thomas. My nephew James Taylor, son of said brother Thomas, (under twenty one years). Capt. Bignall, debtor. My wife, my father-in-law Mr. Nathaniel Dyer, John Falkner, Esq., and my brother Thomas, exors.

My lands of Moone and Garrionla [? Co. Kildare]. The concerns on or near Pimlicoe [Dublin] purchased from Mr Markham. Lands of Grange [? Co. Kildare] held from Mr Conolly. Concerns in Marrowbone Lane which I built and wherein I now live. Lands of Simonstowne [? Co. Kildare]. Field at Dolphin's Barn. Leases of ground on North Strand. My interest of the leases on the city Quay. Stubbins Mills [? Dublin] (— Smith, tenant). Lands at Harold's Cross. My house in St. Thomas Street, ditto in Mutton Lane, ditto in Skinners Alley. £4 to poor of Woodstreet Meeting. £4 to poor of St. Catherine's church.

Witnesses : Mathew Pageit, Thos. Rice, clerks to Benjamin Johnston, public notary, and said Benjamin Johnston.

Memorial witnessed by : Benjamin Johnston, Audley Evatt, clerk to said Martha Taylor.

69, 403, 48932   Martha Taylor (seal)

461 WILLIAMS, THOMAS, Rochestown, Co. Wicklow, farmer.

9 May 1732. Précis, ¼ p., 20 Oct. 1732.

My youngest son William Williams. My farm of Rochestown, leased from Rev. Thomas Whaley.

Witnesses : Jonathan Snell, Rochestown, farmer, Elizabeth Burroughs, wife to John Burroughs, of Ballycooge, said county, gent. and said John Burroughs.

Memorial witnessed by : Francis Wayne, Ballynehinch, said county, gent., Edward Sterling, Dublin, gent.

69, 469, 49225   William Williams (seal)

462 NEWCOMEN, CHARLES, Droming, Co. Longford, Esq.

2 July 1732. Narrate, 1½ p., 31 Oct. 1732.

His wife Edith Newcomen. His eldest son Thomas Newcomen, Esq., (married). His third son Charles Newcomen. His sons James and Charles, exors. His sister-in-law Jean Johnston als. Caldwell. His grandson Robert Newcomen. His grandson James Newcomen. His daughter Sarah. His second son James Newcomen. His daughter Frances. His wife, his son Thomas, and his cousin Arthur Newcomen, Esq., trustees.

Debts due by Sir John Caldwell, Bart., Mr Robt. Richardson, Mr John Dowdall. Town and lands of Oldtowne and Tully, Boghill and Myragh, Lisduff [Co. Longford] and Ballymakeegan [Co. Longford]. His lease of manor of Carrickglass [? Co. Longford] and his freehold lease of Kilterean. A mortgage on his estate of Cooleyshill [? Cooleeshil or Richfort], B. Ardagh, Co. Longford.

Witnesses : Rev. William Carmick, curate of the parish of Ardagh, John Davoale, Ballyloghan, Thos. Hanly, Lisgurnell, Co. Longford, gent.

Memorial witnesses by : Thos. Hanly, James Goddard, Dublin, gent.

                                 Jas. Newcomen (seal)

69,477, 49267   Chas. Newcomen (seal)

463 BYRNE, ELIZABETH, Dublin, spinster.

27 Oct. 1732. Narrate, 1½ p., 14 Nov. 1732.

Mentions a Chancery suit then proceeding, testator versus her cousin George Byrne. Rev. Wm. Jackson, D.D., Rev. Hugh Vaughan, M.A., William Hoey, Dunganstown, Co. Wicklow, Esq., and Thos. Acton, Dublin, Esq., trustees, to dispose of testator's rents etc. for benefit of Protestant charities.

Her lands etc. in Co. Wicklow. The twenty acres nearest to the parish church of Dunganstowne to the minister and his successors for ever as a glebe. Mr Constantine Cullen's lease of part of her Co. Wicklow lands to be renewed or £500 paid to him.

Witnesses : Joseph Sidebottom, Dublin, merchant, Joseph Landers, clerk to Henry Buckley, Dublin, public notary, and said Henry Buckley.

Memorial witnessed by : Joseph Landers, John Whyte, Dublin, gent.

72, 2, 49422   Will. Hoey (seal)

464 VIRGIN, MARY, Limerick, widow.

30 Aug. 1732. Full, 2¼ pp., 16 Nov. 1732.

My daughter-in-law Ann Virgin, (named in deed of lease of 1722 recited in Will). My cousin Thomas Ewer of Clonmell, Co. Tipperary, gent. His present wife Anne Ewer als. Virgin. My cousin Anne Ewer, sister of said Thos. Ewer. Desires to be buried in St. Mary's Church, Limerick " where my father is buried."

Mrs Elizabeth Dowdall, Mrs Anne Sandys, widow. Mrs Jane Knight. Mrs Martha Davis, widow. The Mayor, Bishop and Dean of Limerick. Alderman Foxrock. Susanna Mayne. The widow of Chancellor Keefe. Winifred McNemara and her sister. Anne Wilkinson, wife of Edwd. Wilkinson of Galway. The Rev. Mr John Tunnadine. Mr Simon White and Mr John Phillips (my friends).

Houses etc. on High Street, parish and ward of Blessed Virgin Mary, Limerick. My house etc. in Key Lane, Limerick, Mr Simon Holland lessee, to Dean of Limerick and his successors in trust to buy bread for Protestant poor in parish of Blessed Virgin Mary.

Witnesses : Richd. Maunsell, notary public, Benjamin Barrington, junr., pewterer, John Meade Richd., merchant, all of Limerick.

Memorial witnessed by : Benjamin Barrington, junr., John Meade Richd.

69, 512, 49459   Thos. Ewer (seal)

465　SAUNDERS, ROBERT, Dublin, Esq.
　　25 Oct. 1731.　Narrate, part full, ½ p., 17 Nov. 1732.
　His wife Mrs Ann Saunders.　My brother Morley Saunders, residuary legatee and exor.
　Lands of Cullenagh and Ballynegar, Queen's Co.　My estates in King's Co.　Eskareen, Co. Meath.　" All my lease lands in Co. Kildare and elsewhere . . . manor of Tonagh . . . and my estate . . . in Co. Cavan."
　Witnesses : Margt. West, Boolis, Co. Meath, spinster, John Hawkshaw, Dublin, Doctor of Laws, Wm. Main, Dublin, merchant.
　Memorial witnessed by : John Hawkshaw, Rowland Bradstock, Dublin, Esq.
71, 126, 49467　　　　　　　　　　Morley Saunders (seal)

466　COLLYER, THOMAS, Belfast, Esq.
　　1 Nov. 1732.　Narrate, ¾ p., 24 Nov. 1732.
　His then wife Barbara Collyer, sole extx.　Recites deed of settlement 20 Sept. 1721 made by testator by name of Thos. Collyer of Armagh, and Joshua Dawson of Castledawson, Abraham Bradley of Inner Temple, Esq., Barbara Duffe of Belfast, Co. Antrim, widow, and Barbara Duffe, the only daughter of said Barbara the widow.　Testator appoints John Duffe and John Arnold both of Belfast, gents., trustees.
　His estate of inheritance and freehold in the county of Down and Armagh, that is to say Dromskee, Edenterory, Killsarran als. Killsarell, all in parish of Dromore, Co. Down, Drumnamadder and Mororkan [Moyrourkan], called Banister's freehold in parish of Mullabrack, Co. Armagh, Corlust and Ballyargan, Tullyhugh, Lisra, his tenement in Tandragee, all in parish of Tandragee, Co. Armagh. Knocknamuckley, parish Sego, Co. Armagh.
　Witnesses : Margetson Saunders, John Eccles, John Burleigh, all of Belfast, Co. Antrim, gents.
　Memorial witnessed by : Henry Chritchley, James Goddard, Dublin, gent.
69, 527, 49548　　　　　　　　　　Jno. Arnold (seal)

467　BOND, JOHN, Grangemore, Co. Kildare.
　　23 Oct. 1731.　Narrate, ¾ p., 29 Nov. 1732.
　His son John Bond, junr., exor.　His daughter Elizabeth Poakesley, her two children John and Sophia.　His daughter Katherine Bond. His brother John Frazer.

His farm of Grangemore [Co. Kildare], his farm of Knockendarragh [Co. Wicklow], also Ballyneart, Co. Wicklow.

Witnesses : Sir W. Borrowes, Gilltown, Co. Kildare, Bart., Richard Vincent, Dublin, Esq., Darby Field, Donard, Co. Wicklow, farmer.

Memorial witnessed by : Richard Vincent, James Reilly, Dublin, gent.

73, 31, 49590   John Bond (seal)

468 STEARNE, ROBERT, Brigadier general.

    25 June 1729. Codicil 29 Oct. 1732. Narrate, ¾ p., 31 Jan. 1732.

His wife Elizabeth Stearne.

The towns, villages and lands of Ardeclugg, Garranenelonging etc. (John Herrick, tenant). Rent charge on lands of Iniskerane, Knocknetean, Coolmucky, Rathfelane, Ballyngully [? Ballynaguilla] and Knockshanavoy [? Knockshanawee] with the mills thereon (George Rye, Esq., lessee), all in Co. Cork. Two fee farm leases of houses in Castle Street, in St. Dominick's, Cork city, perfected in the name of his brother Mr Thomas Tuckey in trust for him (testator). The Spittle Lands in Sth. Liberties of Cork. Mortgages on estate of Wm. Gifford in Co. Cork. Part of Tuckey's Key, city of Cork, mortgaged to him by Wm. Chartres, Esq. Dunscomb's Marsh, city of Cork.

Witnesses : Timothy Hickey, city of Cork, Doctor in Physick, Hodder Rogers, Bridgetowne, Co. Cork, Esq., John Addis, Cork, merchant.

Codicil witnessed by : Thos. Baker, the Royal Hospital, Co. Dublin, apothecary, Ambrose Burrows, Major of the said hospital, William Gird of same, gent.

Memorial witnessed by : Rowland Eustace, Dublin, Esq., Joseph Leadbetter, Co. Cork, gent.

71, 188, 49989   Eliz. Stearne (seal)

469 DAWSON, ABRAHAM, Tamnaghmore, parish of Killaman, Co. Tyrone, gent. 26 Jan. 1732. Narrate, 1 p., 19 Feb. 1732.

His wife Sarah Dawson als. Hasleton. His son Lancelot Dawson. His son Ralph Dawson and his son John Dawson, exors. His son William Dawson. His daughter Elizabeth.

Dyan and Derranamoyle in parish of Galloon, Co. Monaghan (held by deeds of lease and release 1712 therein recited). Rehannon, Co. Tyrone.

Witnesses : Edward Dawson, junr., and Samuel Dawson, both of Tamnaghmore, gents., Andrew Carmichael, Dungannon, Co. Tyrone.

Memorial witnessed by: Edward Dawson, junr., Andrew Carmichael.

74, 98, 50179

Ralph Dawson (seal)
John Dawson (seal)

470 PAINTER, EDWARD, parish of St. Ann's, Dublin, dealer.
29 July 1727. Précis, ¼ p., 14 March 1732.

His wife Eliz. Painter, sole extx. His brothers Thomas and George.

His house in Ann's Street, parish of St. Ann's, in the suburbs of Dublin city, and rest of real and personal estate.

Witnesses : Thos. Jones, gent., and James Fotterall, both of Dublin.

Memorial witnessed by : James Goddard, Dublin, gent., Bartholomew Delandre, clerk to Wm. Parry, Dublin, notary public.

71, 233, 50345

Elizabeth Painter (seal)
her mark

471 WHITESITE, WILLIAM, Dreemore, Manor of Dungannon, Co. Tyrone. 9 March 1732. Narrate, 1 p., 24 March 1732.

His wife Mary Whitesite als. Calvert, exor. His daughter and only child Katherine Whiteside als. Richardson, exor. His son-in-law William Richardson, Esq. His nephew Thomas Greeves.

£25 to poor of the people called Quakers of Charlemount meeting, of which meeting testator was an elder, his friends and relations Thomas Greeves and James Piller to be trustees thereof. £10 to Joseph Calvert. His servant maid Sarah Gilmore. Hugh Donoghy, Mathias Calvert, debtors to testator. Isabel Hammersly, wife to Thos. Hammersley in the parish of Killaman, Co. Tyrone.

His real and personal estate. His freehold in Co. Monaghan in parish of Clounish, Adam Carser, tenant. His lease of part of Lord Charlemount's estate. Bernagh, Manor of Dungannon, Co. Tyrone.

Witnesses : John Cardell and Francis Cardell of Gortrea and True [? Truagh] in parish Killaman, Co. Tyrone, farmers, Andrew Carmichael Dungannon, Co. Tyrone, scrivener.

Memorial witnessed by : John Cardell, Andrew Carmichael.

Mary Whitesite (seal)

73, 181, 50407 Katherine Richardson (seal)

572 WORTH, EDWARD, Dublin, Doctor of Physick.

11 Nov. 1723. Précis, ½ p., 2 April 1733.

His kinsman and namesake Edward Worth, Esq., exor. His real and personal estate.

Witnesses: George Rochfort, late of Dublin, Esq., deceased, Mathew Ford, late of Seaford, Co. Down, Esq., deceased, Mathew Ford, junr., now of same, Esq.

Memorial witnessed by : Wm. Westberry, Dublin, gent., Joseph Landers, clerk to Henry Buckley, Dublin, public notary.

74, 145, 50436 E. Worth (seal)

473 TENNANT, DAVID, Galway, burgess.

20 Jan. 1717 Full, 1¼ p., 14 April 1733.

My wife Ann Tennant als. Fairservice. My son John Tennant. My daughter-in-law [? step-daughter] Ann Delamere als. Fairservice. Thomas Delamere, husband of said Ann Delamere, (now abroad).

My tanyard. My big boat. My small boat and nets. My real estate and parks in Galway. Rev. Thos. Wilkins, Shela Flaherty, widow, tenants of two houses. Thos. Staunton, Dublin, gent. and Monk Wall, Galway, alderman, exors.

Witnesses : John Tennant, Galway, shipwright, son of David Tennant, William Fisher, late of the same, deceased, Rev. Thos. Wilkins, Galway. clerk.

Memorial witnessed by : Thos. Wilkins, Ulick Lynot, Galway.

74, 160, 50517 Ann Delamere (seal)

574 ROSSELL, GEORGE, Olderrick, Queen's Co., gent.

29 Aug. 1732. Narrate, ½ p., 20 April 1733.

Reciting that his uncle Samuel Rossell, of Curragh, Queen's Co., deceased by his last will devised to his (Samuel's) wife Mary Rossell the town and lands of Curragh, Queen's Co. for life, with remainder to testator George Rossell. Testator's wife Ann Rossell, extx. His niece Mary Phillips, only daughter of his sister Jane Phillips. Patrick Loghlin. Rev. Mr Richard Grantham of Carlow and testator's wife to distribute £30 to the poor.

Witnesses : Robert Wolsely, town of Carlow, Esq., Samuel Lamok and John Bentley, of same, gents.

Memorial witnessed by : Phillip Bernard, town of Catherlogh, Ann Hall of same.

73, 217, 50577   Ann Rossell (seal)

475 HAMPSON, CHARLES POLLARD, Castlepollard, Co. Westmeath, Esq. 4 April 1719. Full, 1 p., 26 April 1733.

Then going to England. My wife [Letitia Pollard]. £2,000, when eighteen years, to my eldest daughter Elizabeth Hampson. Letitia Hampson my second daughter. My youngest son Charles Hampson. My second son Walter. My eldest son Dillon. Bulloyne [Boleyn] Whitney, Esq., Walter Burton, Esq., both of Dublin and Mr Lewis Roberts married to my cousin german Joynt, exors.[1]

My deceased father-in-law's real estate belonging to my wife. My real and personal estate. Several houses in Dublin, Aughnerewie, and Castle Pollard. Lands of Bratty [Co. Westmeath].

Witnesses : Samuel Turbutt, Dublin, hosier, Luke Cashell, Co. Westmeath, gent., John White, yeoman, servant to said Luke Cashell.

Memorial witnessed by : Samuel Turbutt, Wm. Cane, Dublin, gent.

72, 257, 50647   Cha. Hampson (seal)

476 MEDLICOTT, JAMES, Tully, Co. Kildare, Esq.
24 March 1728. Narrate, ½ p., 5 May 1733.

His wife Mary. His eldest son James Medlicott, exor. His son Talbot. His daughter Elizabeth. His daughters Katherine and Mary, twelve pence each. His brother Thomas Medlicott.

Town and lands of Lughill, King's Co. House in Peter Street, Dublin. Leases in Bride Street and Bigg Butter Lane, Dublin. Estate in Dunmurry, Co. Kildare. All other his real estate.

---

[1] The will of a Lewis Roberts of Dublin, Esq., proved 1726, mentions his wife Deborah. *Betham's Will Pedigrees*, Genealogical Office.

Witnesses : John Medlicott, Maddenstown, Co. Kildare, gent., John Creamer, servant to said John Medlicott, James Hearn, servant to testator.

Memorial witnessed by : James Goddard, Michael Argent, Dublin, gent.

72, 274, 50725   Tho. Medlicott (seal)

477 WILKINSON, Capt. WILLIAM, Dublin.
    13 April 1706. Full, 1 p., 21 May 1733.

My nephew Mr Michael Smith, eldest son of my sister Elizabeth Smith, said nephew's heirs to take name of Wilkinson. My niece Jane Smith, her father my brother-in-law Mr Joseph Smith of Ballentubber. My nephews William Smith the second son, Thomas Smith the third son, and Joseph Smith the youngest son of Elizabeth Smith. My nieces Ann Smith, Elizabeth Smith and Mary Smith. The eldest daughter of my cousin John Waring of Kilkenny. Children of cousin Daniel Berry of Athy. Children of Mr Joseph Higginson of Goldyduff. Mr Richard Wilding and Mr Peter Partington, both of Dublin. John Waring, Kilkenny, Daniel Berry, Athy and Joseph Higginson, Goldyduff, exors.

Fintire [? Finter] and Phillipstown, King's Co. Ballyogan, Co. Kilkenny and all other my real estate.

Witnesses : John Bennett, Athy, Co. Kildare, apothecary, John Gill, Dublin, stationer, Elizabeth Gill his wife.

Memorial witnessed by : Elizabeth Gill, James Cane, Dublin, gent.

72, 309, 50856   Mich. Wilkinson Smith (seal)

478 MURRAY, DAVID, Corkeeran, parish of Aughnamullen, Co.
    Monaghan, gent. 15 Jan. 1731. Narrate, ¼ p., 6 June 1733.

His sister Sarah Murray als. Culbreath. Cousin Sarah Culbreath als. Johnston. His cousin Mary Culbreath. His cousin James Johnston. The children of Andrew Campbell deceased. His cousin Joan Johnston. His cousin Nancy Johnston. His cousin Thomas Kea. His servant Joan Henry. His servant William Kerr. Geo. Kerr, John Kerr. His cousin John Culbreath (heir). Mr Robt. Wallace and John Culbreath, exors. His real and personal estate.

Witnesses : John Thompson, Cootehill, Co. Cavan, merchant, George Carr, Kirkiren, farmer, James Stannous, Aghnamullen, parish clerk, both of Co. Monaghan.

Memorial witnessed by : Michael Argent, Dublin, gent., Brabazon Noble, Dublin, gent.

71, 320, 50977   Robert Wallace junr. (seal)

479 PHILLIPS, GEORGE, Dublin, tallow chandler.
> 29 April 1729. Codicil 28 June following. Narrate, 1 p., 13 June 1733.

His wife Jane Phillips, exor., to maintain and educate his sons and daughters. William Empson, Esq., and Phillip Pearson, merchant, both of Dublin, exors.

Lands of Turrinure and Great Newtown, B. Newcastle, Co. Dublin. His holding fronting Mercer's Dock, Dublin, and his holding on the Coomb, Dublin, wherein he then dwelt.

Witnesses to will and codicil : Robert Boyton, clerk to John Smith, public notary, Dublin, Arthur Shepheard, also clerk to John Smith, and by said John Smith.

Memorial witnessed by : Henry McNall, Dublin, tallow chandler, and said John Smith.

73, 273, 51041   Jane Phillips (seal)

480 BORR, CHRISTIAN, Bigg Butter Lane, Dublin, Esq.
> 8 June 1733. Narrate, 1 p., 5 July 1733.

His wife Helena Maria Borr, sole extx., to be guardian of all his sons till 21 respectively. His son John Borr. His three younger sons Garret, Jacob and William. His brother-in-law Arthur Baldwin and his wife Editha Baldwin.

Lands of Ballynunry [? Ballynunnery, Co. Carlow], and Killcoole and all other his lands in the Co. Catherlogh. Pelletstowne with the mill thereon in Co. Dublin. Houses etc. in Michael's Lane, Schoolhouse Lane and Borr Court in city of Dublin. Houses etc. in Butter Lane and Kevan Street [Dublin].

Witnesses : Oliver Weston, Dublin, gent., Thos. Quinn, Dublin, apothecary, Edward Dalton, public notary, Dublin.

Memorial witnessed by : William Williams, Dublin, gent., George Wentworth, Dublin, gent.

73, 319, 51225   Helena Maria Borr (seal)

481 FOORD, WILLIAM, Pass, Co. Clare, Esq.

10 Oct. 1730. Précis, ¼ p., 3 Aug. 1733.

All his real and personal estate to his wife Mary Foord, sole extx.

Witnesses : John Bull, Limerick, clothier, William Adams, Pass, in the county of the city of Limerick, innkeeper, John Ingram, Limerick, gent.

Memorial witnessed by : John End, Cork, merchant, Dennis Hassey, Pass, Co. Clare, yeoman.

73, 349, 51373   Mary Foord (seal)

482 POWELL, GILES, Glinlary, Co. Limerick.

14 Aug. 1733. Narrate, ¾ p., 20 Sept. 1733.

His mother Eliz. Powell, exor. Hassard Powell, Esq., deceased [testator's father][1] and his wife Elizabeth. His brother Hassard Powell. His sisters Eliz. Ryves [als. Powell], Ann Powell and Mary Powell. Edwd. Moore Ryves, exor. and guardian of testator's brother till of age.

Glinlary, Reaske, Mitchellstowne, Hammon[d]stowne, Clocashy, Killgarruffee. Tully. Village and lands of Inchicome [? Inchacoomb, Co. Limerick]. Lands of Buellenlisheen, and Ballynamudough, Turneheen [situation not mentioned, ? Co. Limerick].

Witnesses : Ann Powell, John Dwyer, Wm. Linnane, Robt. Morgan.

Memorial witnessed by : Jon. Dwyer, Robt. Morgan.

Eliz. Powell (seal)

71, 385, 51581   Edwd. Moore Ryves (seal)

483 RALPHSON, JOHN, Dublin, formerly of Middle Temple, London, Esq. 20 Jan. 1731. Narrate, 1¼ p., 24 Sept. 1733.

His daughter Elinor Ralphson. His son William Ralphson, under fourteen years. Mary Ralphson, daughter of John Ralphson, late a lieutenant in Colonel Barrel's Regiment of Foot.

Rt. Hon. Sir Thos. Taylor, Bart., one of H.M.'s most Hon. Privy Council of the Kingdom of Ireland, Thomas Taylor, Kells, Co. Meath, Esq., Rev. Robt. Taylor, Dean of Clonfert and Robt. Waller, Allenstown, Co. Meath, Esq., trustees and exors. His servant Elizabeth Goodwin.

---

[1] Will of Eliz. Powell, proved 1751, and grant of Prerogative Administration Intestate of Hassard Powell dated 1 Oct. 1733. *Betham's Abstracts*, Genealogical Office.

Clongell and Fletcherstown als. Fletchellstown, B. Morgallon, Co.
Meath.

Witnesses : Phillip Reilly, Dublin, gent., Jas. Savage and Joseph
Landers, clerks to Henry Buckley, Dublin, public notary, and said
Henry Buckley. Memorial witnessed by : Joseph Landers, Henry
Buckley.

74, 363, 51607   [Sir] Thos. Taylor   (seal)

484 MINCHIN, JOHN, Inchmore, Co. Kilkenny, Esq.

26 July 1733,   Précis, ¼ p., 22 Oct. 1733.

All his interest etc. in lands of Inchmore, Inchbegg, Co. Kilkenny,
to his second son Humphrey Minchin.

Witnesses : Stephen Allen, Dublin, Doctor of Physick, Wm. Hoy,
Dublin, gent., Rev. Leonard Neill, Dublin, clerk, John Rice, Dublin,
notary public.

Memorial witnessed by : Edmond Eustace, clerk to Mr Francis
Lodge, one of the attornies of H.M. Court of Exchequer in Ireland,
Wm. Devall, public notary, Dublin.

72, 509, 51747   Hum. Minchin (seal)

485 COOKE, JOHN, Cooksborough, Co. Westmeath, Esq.

5 May 1730. Codicil 25 Oct. 1730. Full, 3 pp., 29 Oct. 1733.

My wife Elizabeth Cooke, exor. My daughter Dorcas[1] Reynell als.
Cooke, her husband Lieut. Richard Reynell. My eldest son Robert
Cooke. My third son John Cooke, exor. My daughter Martha Cooke,
my daughter Rebecca Cooke, my daughter Frances Cooke, my
daughter Elinor Cooke (all then unmarried, but in codicil a special
provision made for Elinor in case she should marry Samuel Lucas,
Esq., or any other person). My daughters Ann Rotton; Elizabeth
Reynell,[2] Cassandra Daniel, Jane Nugent and Mary Hudson already
provided for on their several marriages. Arthur Reynell, Tullynally,
Co. Westmeath, Esq., trustee. Rt. Hon. James Tynte (mortgages
on Old Bawn).

---

[1] The will of Richard Reynell of Killogh dated 30 April 1754 mentions his wife
Dorcas Cooke and James Nugent his brother-in-law.   *Betham's Will Pedigrees*,
Genealogical Office.

[2] Elizabeth, daughter of John Cooke of Cooksborough married 1720 Arthur
Reynell of Castle Reynell, Co. Westmeath.   *Betham's Will Pedigrees*, Genealogical Office.

My houses and tenements in Dames Street and Castle Lane, Dublin, Robert Adair, Esq., John Crampton, watchmaker, Geo. Riske, stationer and Mr Thomas Pooley, tenants. My estate in the Co. of Kilkenny settled on my son Richard Cooke. My house at Cooksborough.

Witnesses: Robt Adair, Dublin, Esq., Joseph Landers, clerk to Henry Buckley, Dublin, public notary, and said Henry Buckley.

Witnesses to codicil: said Robert Adair, Jane his wife, and Jane Sinnot, Dublin, widow.

Memorial witnessed by: Henry Critchley, Bartholomew Delandre, clerks to Wm. Parry, Dublin, public notary.

74, 400, 51786   Richd. Cooke (seal)

---

486 LETOURNELL [LATURNELL], ALLEN, Drum[a]lee, parish of Belturbett, Co. Cavan, gent. 25 April 1732. Narrate, part in full, 1 p., 6 Nov. 1733.

Testator to go beyond the sea into foreign parts. Well beloved sisters Mary Bullock als. Crow, Susanna Armstrong, Ann Hudson, Elizabeth Murtagh (one shilling each). All real and personal estate to Mr Moses Botham, Rosbran near Athy, Co. Kildare, yeoman. John Botham, eldest son of Moses Botham. Mary Botham, daughter of Moses Botham. Sarah Botham present wife of said Moses Botham. Said Moses and his heirs to take name of Latournell. Mr Luke Stanford, holds a mortgage.

Drum[a]lee and Kennahooebegg, in parish of Belturbett, Co. Cavan.

Witnesses: Joseph Higginson, Goulyduff, Co. Kildare, gent., Richard Higginson of same, gent., John Roper, servant to said Moses Botham.

Memorial witnessed by: John Roper, John Carmack, Dublin, gent.

71, 422, 51857   Moses Botham (seal)

---

487 HAYES, JEREMIAH, Cahirquillymore, Co. Limerick. 31 Aug. 1732. Narrate, 1½ p., 5 Nov. 1733.

His wife, her two daughters. His brother Daniel Hayes and his nephew John FitzGibbon, trustees. His eldest daughter Margaret Blen[n]erhassett. His grandson Hayes Blen[n]erhassett. His daughter Honoria Grady. His son[-in-law] [Standish] Grady. His brother William Hayes. His sister Mary Terry. His nephew Patrick Furnell. Desires to be buried in the old church of Tolobracky.

P

Lands of Cahirquillymore, Ballynanty, Knockstephen, Farantlaba and farm of Knockdromrooe in B. Connello [Co. Limerick]. His farm of Knockbrack and Rathbrassill, Co. Cork.

Witnesses : Patrick Terry, Limerick, Doctor in Physick, John Nihell, Glasscrione [? Glascloon], Co. Clare, gent., Ignatius Terry, Bohargeely, Co. Limerick, yeoman, Michael Hannan, Limerick, yeoman.

Memorial witnessed by : Ignatius Terry, Thomas Hopkins, Limerick, merchant.

75, 28, 52000   John FitzGibbon (seal)

488 HARBORNE, THOMAS, Dublin, formerly of Church Burrough, Co. Roscommon. 20 Nov. 1731. Narrate, ½ p., 23 Nov. 1733.

His son Bennett Harborne, exor. His cousin Hubbart Kelly, Co. Roscommon, gent. His friend Nathaniel Tomkins, Co. Lancaster, Great Britain. His old servant Thomas Gordon. Timothy Holmes, Esq., John Williamson, Esq., debtors. £50 to poor widows in and about Church Borough. His real and personal estate in Co. Roscommon and city of Dublin.

Witnesses : John Ware, James Dromagan, William Harborne, all of Dublin, gents.

Memorial witnessed by : William Harborne, Mary Murray, Dublin, spinster.

74, 465, 52084   Bennett Harborne (seal)

489 COPLEN, JOHN, Killcosgrave, Co. Limerick, gent.

2 June 1719. Narrate, ½ p., 30 April 1733.

Wife Susanna Coplen, extx. Richard Coplen Langford son of James Langford, brother of testator's said wife.

Lands, or part of lands of Killcosgrave, Ballycormuck, Knockane, Cloneykill, Ballycullinane, Farinfada, Gortmornburgasty, Lisneburgasty, Gortgarryneburgasty, Gortgarry, Gortmore, Garrymore, Garrymorebreckne, Garrynyste, Garrynycory, Craganecheckery als. Duronaghton, Gareinsty being part of the Mannor of Mount Trenchard, B. Connelloe, Co. Limerick.

Witnesses : Simon Warner, Callow, Co. Limerick, clerk, Silvester Lockwood, Shanagolden, Co. Limerick, chirurgeon, John Williams, Appletown, Co. Limerick, gent.

Memorial witnessed by : Robt. Langford, brother of said Richard Coplen Langford, Geo. Studdert, Dublin, gent.

76, 115, 52128   Richard Coplen Langford (seal)

490 BOOTH, JOHN, Sligo, Co. Sligo, gent.

9 May 1726. Narrate, ¾ p., 4 Dec. 1733.

His wife Catherine Booth. His brother Colonel Humphrey Booth, Elinor Booth wife of said Humphrey. Testator's nephew John Gore and his heirs to take name and arms of Booth. Testator's nephew Booth Gore and his heirs to take name and arms of Booth.

John Irwin, Tonergo, Co. Sligo, Esq., Wm. Smith, Knockshanner, Co. Sligo, Esq., and Wm. Knox, Dublin, gent., trustees.

His real estate, part in Co. Dublin. His real estates and leases for lives in Co. Sligo. His houses in Sligo.

Witnesses : Richard Evelyn, Christopher Chamberlain, both of Co. Dublin, Susanna Caddan now Susanna Irwin of Tonereogo, Co. Sligo.

Memorial witnessed by : Richard Evelyn, Henry Chritchly, of the city of Dublin, gents.

71, 464, 52168   John Irwin (seal)

491 VIZER, ROBERT, parish of St. Andrew, Dublin.

17 Feb. 1733. Précis, ½ p., 27 Nov. 1733.

A settlement made on marriage of Frances Powell with testator's kinsman Wm. Vizer. The four children of said Frances by said Wm. Vizer. His kinsman Ralph Vizer. Thos. Powell, Dublin, taylor, exor. Houses in George's Lane [Dublin].

Witnesses : Geo. Bable, Wm. Smith, stationer, Wm. Winnet his apprentice, all of Dublin.

Memorial witnessed by : Henry Chritchley and Bartholomew Delandre, clerks to Wm. Parry of Dublin, notary public.

71, 456, 52189   Thos. Powell (seal)

492 GREEN, NICHOLAS, Carker, Co. Cork, merchant.

9 Dec. 1725. Narrate, 1 p., 12 Jan. 1733.

His wife Bridget Green, sole extx. His daughter Bridget Evans wife of his son-in-law Nathaniel Evans. His daughter Susanna Green als. Nagle. His grandson James Nagle (under 20 years) and grand-daughter

Bridget Nagle (under sixteen years). His daughter Sarah Green. His daughter Ursula Green als. Giles. His grandsons Richard Giles, Nicholas Giles and George Giles, junr., (legacies when eighteen years respectively). His granddaughters Mary and Bridget Giles (legacies when sixteen years respectively). His sons-in-law Nathaniel Evans and George Giles and his nephew William Funesey, overseers.

Parkegortroe, lands of Ballyvodane [situation not mentioned]. His farm of Carkermore [? Co. Cork]. His farm of Knockleagh and Ballyngunnagh. His estate of the impropriate tythes of the parish of Doneraile and half plowland of Ballyduinine in parish of Cardogane.

Witnesses : David Funesey late of Doneraile, gent., brother-in-law to said testator, William Donoughee and David Walsh, both late of Carker, Co. Cork, farmers.

Memorial witnessed by : John Morrison, Cork, gent., Thos. Barry, Cork, gent.

73, 531, 52391   Bri. Evans (seal)

493 BUNTIN, THOMAS, Mellefont Street, parish of St. Mary,
Dublin, mason. 18 March 1731. Narrate, ½ p., 17 Jan. 1733.

His wife Margt. Buntin, exor. His sister Frances Handby als. Buntin, her daughter Jane. His nephew John Handby. Margaret Horribin, a legatee. John Sturges, exor.

Philip Peel to have the yearly sum out of Joseph Glaves holding [situation not mentioned]. Two houses in Mellefont Street (testator's dwelling house, and one in tenure of John Quin, mason). House known by the sign of The George, Mellefont Street, Allen McCally tenant.

Witnesses : Archbald Elliot, Edward Healy, Dublin, schoolmaster, Zenabya Sturges, wife to said John Sturges, Richard Hopkins, Dublin, clerk.

Memorial witnessed by : Michael Argent and Bartholomew Delandre, clerks to Wm. Parry, Dublin, public notary.

74, 532, 52418   Philip Peel (seal)

494 BLESSINGTON, CHARLES VISCOUNT
1 June 1729. Précis, ¼ p., 22 Feb. 1733.

William Bridgenden, John Williams, Dublin, gents., trustees. Francis Guybon, Hercules Davis, Esqrs., trustees. Mary Doyne, wife of Whitfield Doyne, Dublin, Esq. His real and personal estate.

Witnesses : Richard Dalton, Dublin, merchant, David Mullan and Edward Waller, both of Dublin, gents.

Memorial witnessed by : Edward Waller, Thomas Hall.

77, 64, 52732 John Williams (seal)

495 STOPFORD, ELIZABETH, Mustardsgarden, parish of Fartagh, Co. Kilkenny, spinster. 2 Feb. 1732. Précis, ½ p., 19 March 1733. Her niece Margaret Fielding. Her sister Charlotte Fielding. Her two leases of Mustards Garden.

Witnesses : William Welborne, Foulks Court, Co. Kilkenny, clerk, Thomas Ewers, Baunemore, said County, bricklayer, Ter. Creagone, Clonmell, Co. Tipperary, yeoman.

Memorial witnessed by : Joseph Stopford, Stopford Fielding, both of Dublin, gents.

77, 93, 52901 Margt. Fielding (seal)

496 KENDALL, CHARLES, Grove, parish of Newjerpoint als. Churchjerpoint, Co. Kilkenny, Esq. 18 June 1724. Narrate, 1¼ p., 24 April 1734.

His sister Mary Kendall. His cousin William Desborough of Clontarf Shades, Co. Dublin, victualler. His nephew Joseph Salmon, mariner.

Mary Coningham, eldest daughter of Daniel Coningham of city of Dublin, merchant. Capt. John Bolton, Dublin, and said Daniel Coningham, exors. and trustees. His servant Thomas Collits. His real and personal estate.

Witnesses : John Kelly, gent., Mathew Dutton, gent., Rev. Mathew Dutton, junr., clerk, all then of Dublin.

Memorial witnessed by : John Carmack, Dublin, gent., Bartholomew Delandre, clerk to Wm. Parry, Dublin, public notary.

77, 135, 53088 Dan. Coningham (seal)

497 PEIRS, SIR HENRY, Tristernagh, Co. Westmeath, Bart. 2 Oct. 1732. Précis, ½ p., 16 May 1734.

His wife the Rt. Hon. the Countess Dowager of Barrymore, extx. and guardian to all his children. His second son Henry Piers. Richard Warburton, Esq., trustee. His real and personal estate.

Witnesses : Elizabeth Howard, Bolton Street, Dublin, Edward Topham, Dublin, gent., John Bath, Dublin, gent.

Memorial witnessed by : Edward Topham, George Coates, Dublin, gent.

76, 146, 53310   Ka. Barrymore (seal)[1]

498 KENDALL, CHARLES, Walton's Grove, Co. Kilkenny.
28 May 1731. Narrate, ½ p., 20 May 1734.

His sister Mary Kendall. Thomas Bushe, second son of Arthur Bushe, Kilkenny, Esq. His nephew Joseph Salmon. Said Arthur Bushe and Rev. Richard Bambridge of Ballyhinch, Co. Kilkenny, clerk, exors.

Towns and lands of Walton's Grove and Oldtown, Co. Kilkenny.

Witnesses : John Birch, Kilkenny, gent., John Bayly, Enniscorthy, Co. Wexford, vintner, Thos. Collits, then servant to said testator and now servant to said Arthur Bushe.

Memorial witnessed by : Thos. Collits, Bartholomew Delandre, clerk to Wm. Parry, public notary.

77, 202, 53355   Arthur Bushe (seal)
                                    father and guardian of
                                    said Thomas Bushe.

499 DORAN, ELIZABETH orse. MERRITT, wife of Thomas
Doran of Finogh, Co. Tipperary, gent. 29 Jan. 1714. Narrate,
part in full, 1¼ p., 29 Oct. 1734.

Her eldest son and heir Captain Michael Merritt, Finoge, exor. My grandson William Merritt, the second son of my said son. Her daughter Margaret Merritt. Cassandra Head, wife of John Head, her other daughter.

James Harrison, Cloughjordan, Co. Tipperary, Esq., trustee and exor. Michael Rollston, second son of Arthur Rollston, Esq., Stephen Rollston, third son of Arthur Rollston.

Part of lands of Reninsly and Curraghviller, parish of Templekelly, B. Owny and Arra, Co. Tipperary. Farm of Finoge. Curraghmore, Ballyfinboy, Scanlane and Sheshragh, Killtomodan and Boherleagh, B. Lower Ormond, Co. Tipperary.

---

[1] Catherine, daughter of Richard Lord Santry, married 1729, as her third husband, Sir Henry Piers, Bart. *The Complete Peerage* by G.E.C.

Witnesses : Theophilus Legg, Rodeen, Co. Tipperary, chirurgeon, Robt. Newstead, Finagh, Co. Tipperary, gent., and Margt. Newstead his wife.

Memorial witnessed by : Robt. Newstead, Bartholomew Delandre, clerk to Wm. Parry, public notary, Dublin.

77, 459, 54347   William Merritt (seal)

500 MATHEWS, ARTHUR, Brittas, parish of Killead, Co. Antrim, gent. 7 March 1730. Narrate, part in full, ¾ p., 20 Nov. 1734.

My son Daniel His [testator's] daughter-in-law. His grandson Robt. Mathews, son of said Daniel. His grandson George Mathews. His granddaughter Mary Mathews. His grandson Arthur Mathews. His [grandson's] sister Eliz. Mathews (under twelve years).

His fee farm lease of Dungonnell [Co. Antrim], formerly his father's. Leases in Dungonnell. A lease in parish of Antrim being in the Five Towns of Dunsilly.

Witnesses : Samuel McCormick, Saml. Luke, both of Killead, Co. Antrim.

Memorial witnessed by : Joseph Wilson, George Frederick Boyd, Antrim.

77, 525, 54583   Robert Mathews (seal)

501 BREWSTER, WILLIAM, Hilltown, Co. Cork, Esq.

25 April 1731. Full, ⅓ p., 20 Nov. 1734.

" All my estate real and personal is chiefly owing and came to me by my beloved wife Ann Brewster." Same to said wife (extx.) and at her death she is " to dispose the same to any of my children as she thinks fit."

James Anderson and Jane Anderson his wife. Mrs. Susanna Ivie.

Witnesses : Thomas Hodder, Ballea, Co. Cork, Esq., Thomas Hodder, junr., Ballea, Co. Cork, gent., Edward Eves, Passage, Co. Cork, chirurgeon.

Memorial witnessed by : Thos. Hodder, junr., Francis Woodley, Dublin, gent.

79, 68, 54586   Ann Brewster (seal)

502 LAWDER, WILLIAM, Dublin, gent.
    15 Nov. 1734. Codicil 20 Nov. 1734. Narrate, ½ p., 14 Dec. 1734.

His father Frederick Lawder of Corr, Co. Cavan, Esq., exor. and guardian of testator's brother James Lawder (under twenty-one years).

Real and personal estate, freehold and leasehold.

Witnesses : John Connolly, Joseph Richey, ale seller, Wm. Crow, gent., all of Dublin.

Witnesses to codicil : Elizabeth Clarke, Dublin, widow, said Wm. Crow.

Memorial witnessed by : Wm. Crow, John Lawder, Dublin, gent.

79, 107, 54837   Fred. Lawder (seal)

503 GAFFNEY, JAMES, Milltowne, Co. Meath, innkeeper.
    3 Dec. 1734. Narrate, ½ p., 24 Jan. 1734/35.

To wife Ann Gaffney the messuage or tenement he then lived in [situation not mentioned]. His nephew James, son of his brother Francis Gaffney.

Witnesses: Patrick Hackett, Herbertstown, Co. Meath, gent. Patrick Boylan, Kilbride, Co. Meath, gent., Francis Gaffney, Archtowne, Co. Meath, farmer.

Memorial witnessed by : Francis Gaffney, Michael Argent, Dublin, gent.

79, 146, 55046   James Gaffney (seal)

504 THOMPSON, ELIZABETH, widow of Richard Thompson, Dublin, Esq. 14 June 1734. Full, 1½ p., 13 Feb. 1734/35.

My estate in Co. Wicklow to my grandson Mathew Reade and his heirs for ever provided he become a clergyman of the Church of Ireland before he attains the age of 30 years, otherwise to my daughter Elizabeth Reade, extx. My grandson Richard Reade. My grandson John Reade. My grandson William Reade. My granddaughter Elizabeth Reade. My granddaughter Martha Reade. " My sister Uniacke and her sons Richard (to my nephew Richard I leave all the plate that was his uncle Mathew's) John and Norman and her daughter Elizabeth."

Lease of lands of Ballysallagh, Co. Wicklow. Money owed by Mr Francis Palmer, Mr Ryan, to Rev. Thomas Cooke, Mr Ryan and testator's daughter Elizabeth Reade for charity. My house in Dublin Lands of Templelyon [? Co. Wicklow].

Witnesses: Patrick Ryan, Cashell, Esq., Rev. Arthur Webb, Webbsborrow, Co. Kilkenny, clerk, Richard Sandford, Rossonaragh, Co. Kilkenny, gent.

Memorial witnessed by: Arthur Webb, Richard Prest, Dublin, public notary.

76, 439, 55266

Richard Reade (seal) father of said Mathew and Richard Reade, being minors and husband of said Elizabeth Reade the extx.

505 TOPHAM, JAMES, Dublin, Esq.

20 Aug. 1722. Narrate, 1 p., 21 March 1734.

His sister Elizabeth Mitchell, Patrick Mitchell her eldest son. Topham Mitchell her second son. His sister's two daughters Katherine and Elizabeth Mitchell. Doctor Patrick Mitchell [? husband of said Elizabeth]. To Mr Wm. Hawkins, eldest son of Wm. Hawkins, Esq., £20 per annum for life. Same to Laetitia Hawkins, daughter to Wm. Hawkins, Esq. Rents, good and chattles etc. to Mrs Elizabeth Hawkins, wife of Wm· Hawkins, Esq. [Ulster] King of Arms. John Hawkins, son of Mr Hawkins aforesaid. Dr. Marmaduke Coghill and Thos. Marley, H.M. Solicitor general, trustees.

His estate in Co. Tipperary. His house in Church Street [? Dublin] wherein Daniel Gilmore then lived. His house in Patrick Street, therein Thomas Gibbons then lately dwelt. Ground and houses in Patrick Street and Lillies Lane. His houses in St. James Street in lease to Mr Bonham a brewer, Mr Ferueand, tanner, Mr Mercer and Mr Fenton. His real estate in Co. Dublin called the two Newtowns.

Witnesses: Martha Walsh, Dublin, widow, Henry Arkwright, Dublin, Esq., since deceased, Peter Blanchvill, then servant to testator.

Memorial witnessed by: Topham Mitchell, Dublin, gent., John Lindon, Dublin, servant to said Dr. Patrick Mitchell.

79, 225, 55521

E. Mitchell (seal)

506 HATTON, HENRY, Wexford, Esq.

2 Nov. 1734. Narrate, 2 pp., 5 April 1735.

His wife Edith Hatton. His eldest son Loftus Hatton, Wexford, gent., and his present wife. His three younger sons John Hatton (second son), Henry Hatton (third son) and George Hatton (fourth son), all of Wexford, gents.

Rev. Wm. Harvey, Wexford, clerk, George Lehunt, Ballymartin, Co. Wexford, Esq., Robert Colyer, Ballyneclash, Co. Wexford, Esq., trustees and exors.

His dwellinghouse in Wexford, with the stable yard, malt house, key and two gardens etc. adjoining. Little meadow and park in Liberties of the town of Wexford. Great Clonard and Knockhowlin in B. Forth, Co. Wexford. Tubberduffe, Ballinglonbog, Grove, Ballinclea, Raheencullen, Garryclough, Ballydermott, Cooltrundle, all in Co. Wexford. Courtilough, Killydrout als. Killduront, Garrymore, Ballybog, part of Garrymore, Oulartleighbeg, Ballybrogagh, and the Mill, all in Co. Wexford. Ballyneclash, Ballyna, Davidstown, all in Co. Wexford. Tythes great and small and glebes of parishes of Castle Ellis and Molonagh [Millenagh], Co. Wexford. Lease of Killconnib, Clonda, Ardcavan, Clones, Manor of Polerogan, Co. Wexford.

Witnesses : Thomas Richards, Rathaspick, Co. Wexford, Esq., Rev. Maurice Hughes, Wexford, clerk, John Goodall, Ferrybank, Co. Wexford, innholder.

Memorial witnessed by : Thomas Richards, Anthony Ryan, Wexford, gent.

John Hatton (seal)
76, 498, 55595   Henry Hatton (seal)
devisees in said will
George Lehunt (seal)

507 HATTON, HENRY, Wexford, Esq.

Codicil 9 Dec. 1734. Narrate, ½ p., 5 April 1735.

To his wife Edith Hatton town and lands of Knockhowlin, his interest in leases of Killconnib and Clonda, all situate in Co. Wexford.

Witnesses : James Heron, Wexford, tallow chandler, Anthony Ryan, Wexford, gent., John Marsh, Wexford, innkeeper.

Memorial witnessed by : Anthony Ryan, Thomas Richards, Rathaspick, Co. Wexford.

79, 238, 55596   Edith Hatton (seal)

508 FARRELL, JOHN, Waterford, merchant.

22 Jan. 1734. Précis, a few lines, 6 May 1735.

To his wife £20 per annum and use of his household goods.

Witnesses : John Hoy, junr., Waterford, chandler, Henry Tonnery, Waterford, apothecary, Joseph Power, Waterford, apothecary.

Memorial witnessed by : Henry Tonnery, John St. John, Waterford, writing clerk

81, 7, 55806   Christian Farrell (seal)

widow of testator.

509 MORTON, THOMAS, Mountrath, Queen's County, gent.

16 Nov. 1729. Narrate, ½ p., 8 June 1735.

His four daughters Elizabeth Morton, Mary Morton, Eliss Morton, Jane Morton. His sons James Morton and Francis Morton. His son John Morton, exor. His son George Morton. His son Thos. Morton, exor.

House and holding . . . the shop he then had [situation not mentioned]. Lease of the holding he then lived in in Mountrath. Clonbarrow and Knockaninagh [Queen's Co.]. A house he held from Wm. Trench, Esq., [situation not mentioned].

Witnesses : James Calcut, clothier, Wm. Delany, blacksmith, Henry Dugan, woolcomber, all of Mountrath.

Memorial witnessed by : Wm. Delany, Bartholomew Delandre, clerk to Wm. Parry, Dublin, public notary.

78, 316, 56048   James Morton (seal)

510 KENT, ROBERT, Pollroan, Co. Kilkenny, gent.

Signed 17 March 1734 in Waterford city. Précis ½ p., 6 June 1735.

His wife Mary Kent, extx. Rodolphus Green, Killmaline, Co. Waterford, Esq., and Daniel Taylor, Waterford, gent., trustees.

Town and lands of Pollroan, Dunanane, Ballygavin and Glingrant, Co. Kilkenny.

Witnesses : John Fell, Waterford, clerk to William Quife, Poulroan, Co. Kilkenny, yeoman, Joseph Cooke, Waterford, notary public.

Memorial witnessed by : William Quife, Thos. Green, Clonmell, merchant.

Rodol. Green (seal)

Danl. Taylor (seal)

Mary Kent (seal)

79, 320, 56062

511 FRENCH, PHILIP, Cork, alderman.
19 Nov. 1733. Narrate, 1 p., 14 June 1735.
His wife Penellope French, extx., and guardian of children during widowhood. His eldest daughter Elizabeth French, his daughters Penellope French, Frances French and Susanna French, unmarried and under twentyone years. His sons Phillip French, Michael French and Abraham French, (under twentyone years). His eldest son James French. His sister Frances French. His real and personal estate.
Witnesses : John Lane, dyer, Chr. Pillion, brewer, Davy Jervois, merchant, all of city of Cork.
Memorial witnessed by : John Welsh of Rath, Richard Baldwin, Crossmahon, gent., both in Co. Cork.

Penellope French, extx. (seal)

Elizabeth Baldwin (seal)

(Elizabeth French now Baldwin, who

since decease of said Philip French is

married to Wm. Baldwin, Esq.).

79, 336, 56139

512 ROE, VINCENT, Meath Street, Liberty of Thomas Court and Donore and county of city of Dublin, dyer. 17 March 1724. Narrate, 1 p., 17 Sept. 1735.
His wife Isabella Roe. His brother-in-law Robt. Rigmaiden, of Rathmaiden, Co. Meath, gent. George Garnett, Meath Street, tallow chandler, trustee.
Houses in Upper Comb and Meath Street, Dublin, one in Meath Street known by the sign of the Bear. One house on the Glibb. The house in Meath Street in which testator dwelt, the house adjoining in which Mr Marples, joiner, then lived.
Witnesses : Anthony Gibson, Dublin, grocer, Townley Thompson, late of Dublin, weaver, deceased, Thomas Pitt, Dublin, gent., deceased.
Memorial witnessed by : Charles Harding, Dublin, joiner, Arthur Shepheard, clerk to John Smith, public notary, Dublin.

78, 388, 56727   Robt. Rigmaiden (seal)

513 CROFTS, JAMES, Carcalla, Co. Clare, now of Dublin.

30 Aug. 1735. Full 2 pp., 22 Sept. 1735.

My wife Elizabeth Crofts als. King. My daughter Mary Ford als. Crofts, her present husband Edwd. Ford. My cousin Jno. Ayree.

Legacy to " my extx. Mrs Fredisweda Vale als. Davis " for her own use and not for benefit of any husband she now has or hereafter may have. My friend Edmond Hogan, gent., trustee. My friend Oliver Arthur.

Town and lands of Carcallamore, Carcallabegg [Cahircallowbegg, B. Islands, Co. Clare], and Kiltie, Shannano, Ballynaheda, Drimatchy, Cappanafenoge, Derrybegg and 44 acres of lands of Clonrone [situation not mentioned ? Co. Clare]. Moiety of rents for maintaining a charity school in Ennis, Co. Clare, ("a Protestant schoolmaster and as many Protestant children as my trustees . . . shall find the rents sufficient to support "), Bishop of Killaloe, Rector of Drumcliff parish for the time being, Fras. Burton of Burcregy, Esq., and said Edmond Hogan and their heirs for ever, trustees.

Witnesses : Rev. David Burches, minister of parish of St. Mark, Dublin, Richd. Steele, Dublin, gent., John Allin, clerk to said Richard Steele.

Memorial witnessed by : David Burches, Richd. Steele.

80, 509, 56741   Freds. Vaile (seal)

514 MASON, JOHN, Dublin, weaver.

31 July 1735. Narrate, ½ p., 24 Sept. 1735.

His wife Dorothy Mason, exor. His son John Mason (under twenty-one years), exor. His two daughters Elizabeth Powell als. Mason and his son-in-law William Powell, and Mary Ransford als. Mason and his son-in-law Henry Ransford, one shilling each.

His house wherein he lately dwelt and built by him in Braithwaite Street, Liberty of Thomas Court and Donore [Dublin]. House in Poole Street in the Liberty aforesaid.

Witnesses : Tully Conry, Pimlicoe, schoolmaster, James McBride, Poole Street, shoemaker, James Cluffe, same, sheerman, all in the Liberties aforesaid.

Memorial witnessed by : James Saunders and Bartholomew Delandre, clerks to Wm. Parry, public notary in Dublin.

80, 513, 56753   Dorothy Mason (seal)

                              her mark.

515 MORTON, JOHN, Mountrath, Queen's Co.

9 May 1735. Précis, ¼ p., 16 Oct. 1735.

To his brother Francis Morton, exor., all his right etc. in his leases in and near Mountrath left him by his father's will.

Witnesses : Wm. Delany, Mountrath, Queen's Co., blacksmith, James Calcutt, Mountrath, clothier, James Calcutt, junr., Mountrath, clothier.

Memorial witnessed by : James Calcutt, senior and James Calcutt, junior.

79, 451, 56855   Fras. Morton (seal)

516 NORCOTT, EDWARD, Ballyellis, Co. Cork, gent.

12 Sept. 1735. Narrate, 2 pp., 4 Nov. 1735.

His wife Mary. His daughter Alice Norcott (unmarried). His daughter Dorothy Knox. His son Charles Hyde Norcott and his daughter Frances Foulks already provided for on their marriages. His brother Wm. Norcott of Springfield, and Yelverton Foulks of Killgraham, exors.

Lands of Ballyellis and Knop[p]ogue, [Co. Cork]. His holdings in town of Mallow. His lease of Dromineen [? Co. Cork].

Witnesses : Daniel Riordan, Mallow, Co. Cork, apothecary, Henry Brereton, Mallow, brazier, Lawce. Maguire, Mallow, tanner.

Memorial witnesed by : Henry Brereton, Belcher Pedder, Castlebarry, Co. Cork, gent.

78, 421, 56957   Wm. Norcott (seal)

517 NASON, WILLIAM, Rahenity, B. Barrymore, Co. Cork, gent.

28 May 1735. Full, 1½ p., 21 Nov. 1735.

My wife Jane Nason. My daughter Ann Nason. £50 etc. to child to be born. My father Mr John Nason (holds part of lands of Rahenity). My cousin Wm. Nason, Cork, merchant, exor.

My dwelling house and lands of Rahenity, and my real and personal estate.

Witnesses : Joseph Deyos, Cork, merchant, Richd. Kinefick, Cork, merchant, Russell Wood, Cork, notary public.

Memorial witnessed by : Richd. Kinefick, Simon Long, Cork, clothier.

79, 515, 57162   William Nason (seal)

518 [BROWN], PETER, BISHOP OF CORK AND ROSS.[1]
22 July 1735. Narrate, 1 p., 21 Nov. 1735.

Left all his improvements at Bishop's Court, his buildings etc. at Ballinaspic or Bishopstown, (his intention being that the dwelling house built by him may be always a country retreat for all his successors Bishops of Cork), his real and personal estate, etc. to his cousin Rev. Peter Watherouse, Chantor of Cork. To his cousin Jerom Russell, brother to the Rev. Archdeacon of Cork [? Thomas Russell], his interest in ground on south side of St. Stephen's Green, Dublin.

Witnesses : Thos. Weeks, Cork, gent., Edward Litherland, virger of the Cathedral Church of St. Finbarry, Cork, Richd. Sampson, clerk to said Thos. Weeks.

Memorial witnessed by : Thomas Weeks, Philip Roche, clerk to Russell Wood, Dublin, gent.

78, 470, 57183   Peter Waterhouse (seal)

519 SUTTON, ELIZABETH, als. ELLWELL, wife of Captain David Sutton, New Ross, Co. Wexford. 15 Dec. 1731. Narrate, ¾ p., 11 Dec. 1735.

Her husband David Sutton. Her grandniece Elizabeth Kellett, daughter to Adjutant Richard Kellett of Lord Molesworth's Regiment. Deborah Haddock als. Kellett, wife of said Richard Kellett and mother of said Elizabeth. Her niece Catherine Haddock als. Chudleigh then wife to Mr Thos. Chudleigh of Kinsale.

Her real estate, viz : Lands called Mansfieldstown then in tenure of Daniel Coveny and Miles Hamline, in Liberties of Kinsale, Co. Cork, four closes or fields without Nicholas's Gate at Kinsale then in possession of Widow Newman, wife of the late John Newman of Kinsale apothecary, deceased, part of lands of Ballynecobby then in possession of Mr John Hales and Mr Denis Leary, both of Kinsale, all which lands etc. are adjacent to the town of Kinsale.

Witnesses : Nicholas Stafford, New Ross, Co. Wexford, apothecary, Edvanus Walsh, of same, schoolmaster, John Wallace of same, servant to said David Sutton, Richard Arsdekin, of same, Doctor of Physic.

Memorial witnessed by : John Wallace, Samuel Smith, New Ross, merchant.

83, 15, 57348   David Sutton (seal)

---

[1] See Brady's *Records of Cork and Ross*, Vol. I. p. 318, Vol. III, p. 71.

520 GREEN, GODFREY, Moorestown, Co. Tipperary, Esq.
19 Aug. 1735. Codicil 20 Aug. 1735, second codicil 21 Aug.
1735. Full, 2½ pp., 16 Dec. 1735.

My uncle John Green of Abby, Co. Limerick, Esq., exor. My kins-
man Godfrey Green of Ballinvohir, Co. Kilkenny, gent. My kinsman
John Green, eldest son and heir apparent of my kinsman Godfrey
Green of Greenville, Co. Kilkenny, Esq. My kinsman George Green
of Abby, Co. Limerick. My uncle Rodulphus Green of Killmanihan,
Co. Waterford, Esq. My uncle Samuel Green deceased. My uncle
Thomas Green of Low Grange, Co. Kilkenny, Esq. My uncle Benjamin
Green late of Dungarvan, Co. Waterford, Esq., deceased. My uncle
Gilbert Green. My uncle Richard Green. My nephew Godfrey Cooksey.
My sister Cooksey. £20 apiece to each of my nephews and nieces. My
kinswoman Mrs Chadwick and her husband. My god-daughter Mrs
Bunbury. £200 apiece to each of my natural children Samuel and
Valentine. My kinswoman Catherine Green, eldest daughter of
Godfrey Green of Greenville. Margarett Green, wife of said Godfrey
Green of Abby. My kinsman Lovelace Tayler, Esq., and his family.
My nephew Bacon.

Rev. Simon Fortune. My friend Mr Nathaniel Taylor. Doctor
Rickard Bourke, his sister the widow Carroll, deceased, and her
children. Margarett Dobbyn.

All my lands in Counties of city of Limerick, Tipperary and Waterford. Body to be interred in the church of Clonmell next my grandmother or sister. Bonds perfected by Mathew Pennefather and his
son to me.

Witnesses : Thomas Maunsell, Dublin, Robert Powell, Dublin, gent.,
John Lack[a]y, Clonmell, Doctor of Physic.

Witnesses to first codicil : Thomas Maunsell, Samuel Waller,
Dublin, Esq., John Lack[a]y.

Witnesses to second codicil : Samuel Waller, [John] Lack[a]y, James
Mansfield, servant man of said Samuel Waller.

Memorial witnessed by : Thomas Maunsell, William Odell, Dublin,
gent.

83, 20, 57376   John Green (seal)
                                  eldest son of Godfrey
                                  Green of Greenville, Co.
                                  Kilkenny.

521 BRISCOE, REBECCA, Aungier Street, Dublin, widow.

25 Aug. 1731. Codicil 17 Nov. 1735. Full, 1 p., 20 Dec. 1735.
To be buried in St. Bride's Church. My husband Temple Briscoe,
Esq., deceased. My daughter Dorothy Briscoe. My daughter Hester
Mayle, £5 to each of said daughter's children. My daughter Ann
Croker, £5 to each of said daughter's children. The children of my
daughter Sarah Whiteside deceased. My grandson Wm. Whiteside.
My daughter Henrietta Cole and my son-in-law Thomas Cole. Exors.
my friends Boylen Whitnas [? Boleyn Whitney], Esq., and John
Wynne clerk. Codicil mentions two houses assigned to testator by
Mr Edward Hind [situation not mentioned], and money lent by her to
Nathaniel Evans, Esq.

House in Aungier Street wherein I now dwell. House in Digg Street
wherein Charles Kemys, Doctor in Physic, now dwells.

Witnesses : Wm. Hoey, Dunganstown, Co. Wicklow, Esq., Thomas
Lehunte, Dublin, Esq., Blachford Whyne, qr. master in Lieut. Gen.
Pearce's Regiment of Horse.

Codicil witnessed by : Wm. Pearll, mariner, Edmd. Bomford,
vintner, both of Dublin.

Memorial witnessed by : Bartholomew Delandre, clerk to Wm.
Parry, public notary, Dublin, Edmd. Bomford.

78, 509, 57414   Dorothy Briscoe (seal)

522 QUINN, MARGARET, Ballygannon, Co. Wicklow, spinster.

16 June 1735. Full, ½ p., 30 Dec. 1735.
My kinsman Thomas Quinn of Dublin, apothecary, exor. My
friend Mary Potts. My friend Elizabeth Hammond. Rev. Mr John
Wynne, exor. My real and personal estate.

Witnesses : John Blackford, Wicklow, clerk, William Frost, Bally-
hiskin, Co. Wicklow, gent., Catherine Frost, Coolebegg, Co. Wicklow,
spinster.

Memorial witnessed by : William Frost, Joseph Landers, clerk to
Henry Buckley, Dublin, public notary.

81, 283, 57459   Thos. Quinn (seal)

523 LEEDS, MICHAEL, Fulham, Middlesex, gent.

27 March 1728. Précis ½ p., 3 Jan. 1735.
To his wife Elizabeth Leeds all his real estate.

Q

Witnesses : John Reilly, Middle Temple, Esq., Saml. Wiggins, late of Fulham, tobacco pipe maker, James Coppin [? Coppinger], Rochester, Kent, tobacco pipe maker.

Memorial witnessed by : James Coppin [? Coppinger], Edmd. Reilly, New Bond Street, parish of St. George, Co. Middlesex, gent.

82, 184, 57471   Elizth. Wiggins (seal)
                                        James Coppinger swears to
                                        execution of will, and that he
                                        saw Elizabeth Leeds als.
                                        Wiggins, wife of testator and
                                        since his death married to Mr
                                        Samuel Wiggins, sign the
                                        memorial.

524 LEONARD, EDWARD, Drumbroces, Co. Fermanagh.

12 Oct. 1734. Part in full, part narrate, ½ p., 16 Feb. 1735.

A marriage settlement made on my son Andrew. His brother [in-law] Arthur Foster of Carrickmckoster, and nephew James Foster of Drumgoon and nephew Andrew Johnstone of Corriny, exors.

Witnesses : Edward Leonard, Lisnegole, Bryan Reilly, Clancrunell, John McLaughlin, Drumbroces, Co. Fermanagh.

Memorial witnessed by : Bryan Reilly, James Armstrong, Drumee, Co. Longford.

78, 531, 57580   Andrew Leonard (seal)
                                        son of testator.

525 STAFFORD, JNO., Ross, Co. Wexford, gent.

5 June 1735. Précis, ½ p., 26 March 1735/36.

His wife Joan Stafford. His son Jon.

His lease of Maudlintown situate near Wexford, Co. Wexford "subject to some debts due to his brothers 4 and sister and to Mr Jack Hatton."

Witnesses : Jno. Cahill, junr., merchant, Anthy. Carny, tailor, Thos. Archer, schoolmaster, all of New Ross.

Memorial witnessed by : Anthy. Carny, Dennis Meagher, Monart, Co. Wexford, yeoman.

82, 336, 58042   Joan Stafford (seal)
                                        her mark

526 PARRY, Rt. Hon. BENJAMIN, [Dublin].

6 Sept. 1734. Narrate, 1 p., 29 March 1736.

All his lands in College Green and Turnstile Alley in the city of Dublin, and lands and tenements in Co. Armagh near Newry to his cousin Doctor John Hawkshaw for life and after his death to his brother Rev. Mr Benjamin Hawkshaw, then to his cousin Francis Price, son to Mrs Marcella Price and his heirs male, him or they to take name of Parry ; for want of such heirs male taking the name of Parry to his cousin Robert Bulkeley of Granaght, Isle of Anglesey for life, he taking the name of Parry, after his death to his first son successively and the heirs male, taking the name of Parry, and for want of such heirs to his cousin Francis Price (exor.) and his heirs for ever.

Leasehold lands in Bride Street, Stephen Street or elsewhere in city of Dublin, his South Sea Stock and rest of personal estate to Rev. Benjamin Lhoyd of Killalce and to his son Rev. Rice Lhoyd as trustees for said Francis Price.

Witnesses : Owen Lewis, Dublin, chirurgeon, Joseph Landers, clerk to Henry Buckley of said city, public notary, and said Henry Buckley.

Memorial witnessed by : Bartholomew Delandre and Henry Chritchley, both of Dublin, clerks to William Parry, public notary in Dublin.

83, 157, 58069   Fran. Price (seal)

527 REILLY, THOMAS, Pimlico, Dublin, dyer.

17 Feb. 1735. Narrate, 1½ p., 1 April 1736.

His daughter Frances Greenham, her present husband. His daughters Rebecca, Jane and Sarah (all under eighteen years and not married). His cousin John Reilly of Michael's Lane, Dublin, gent., and Wm. Ears of Coales Alley, Dublin, merchant, trustees of Pimlico property. His son-in-law John Greenham and Wm. Kells, weaver, trustees of other property.

His dwelling house on Pimlico, and two houses fronting Pimlico, also the dye house, back house ground and holding held by lease from Bernard Brown, Esq. Two houses etc. in Earl Street, Dublin, (Mary Kelly, dwelling in cellar under one of the houses to enjoy same for life). His house on the Co[o]mb[e] then in possession of Ephraim Litchfield and Robert Adams. His holding in Abby Street then in possession of Patrick Steuart, merchant.

Witnesses : Nathaniel Shelwell, Solomon Sampson, both of Pimlico, Dublin, weavers, Arthur Shepheard, Dublin, scrivener.

Memorial witnessed by : Saml. Fodger, Dublin, weaver, Arthur Shepheard.

84, 75, 58108   John Greenham (seal)

528 MANWARING, THOMAS, Dublin, cooper.

14 Feb. 1735. Narrate, ½ p., 6 April 1736.

His real and personal estate to his only daughter Mary Manwaring when twentyone years or on marriage. His granddaughter Ann Manwaring. The sons of John Manwaring of Newmarkett in Donore, Co. Dublin, weaver. Thos. Tresham, Dublin, hosier, and John Hall of same, shoemaker, exors.

Witnesses : Wm. Hardy, Dublin, hosier, Edwd. Challoner, Dublin, gent., John Thompson, Dublin, gent.

Memorial witnessed by : Edwd. Challoner, John Thompson.

83, 168, 58133   Jno. Hall (seal)

529 MALONE, DANIEL, Dublin.

1 Nov. 1735. Précis, ½ p., 8 May 1736.

His wife Elizabeth Malone and his son-in-law John Row, exors.

A dwelling house and two lease holdings of lands at Red Mills near Chapple Izod [Co. Dublin]. Part of the Glebe lands at Red Mills. House at Sicamore Ally [? Dublin], wherein John Vandermere lives.

Witnesses : Ja. Hewetson, late of Dublin, gent., deceased. Dorothy Malone, spinster, niece of testator.

Memorial witnessed by : Michael Argent and Bartholomew Delandre, clerks to William Parry, public notary in Dublin.

81, 453, 58308   Elizabeth Malone (seal)

530 LAWDER, EDWARD, Kilclare, Co. Leitrim, gent.

5 Sept. 1735. Narrate, ½ p., 15 May 1736.

His wife Isabella, exor. His brother James Lawder. His father James Lawder, Esq., exor.

His real estate known by the names of Kilclaremore, Kiltinashinagh and Mullaghboy, in parish of Killtubred [Kiltubbrid], B. and County of Leitrim.

Witnesses : Jerom O'Dugenan, Drumlakin, Co. Leitrim, doctor in physic, Chas. Conry, Killmore, Co. Roscommon, yeoman, Jno. Lawder, Dublin, gent.

Memorial witnessed by : Chas. Conry, Jno. Lawder.

82, 414, 58381 James Lawder (seal)
(father of testator)

531 BRETT, FLORENCE, Fordom's Alley, Donore, Dublin city, cloathier. 1 March 1734. Précis, a few lines. 25 May 1736.

Rest of his real and personal property devised to his son Peter Brett.

Witnesses : John Brett, Dublin, presser, Edwd. Challoner, Dublin, gent., John Allen, Dublin, gent.

Memorial witnessed by : Edwd. Challoner, John Thompson, Dublin, gent.

84, 116, 58529 Petter Brett (seal)

532 GABBETT, WILLIAM, Caherline, Co. Limerick, Esq.

25 July 1727. Narrate, ½ p., 27 May 1736.

His eldest son William Gabbett. His son Jno. Gabbett. William Freeman, Castlecurr, Co. Cork, Esq., and Thos. Walter, Baggotstown, Co. Limerick, gent., trustees.

His estate and interest in town and lands of Caherline, Ballyhobine, Tonetiry, Ballyvorheen, the Two Griernanes, Killeagh and Carrigerila, the farms of Clashbane, Baggotstown, Boherduff and Dunwillen [situation not mentioned. ? all in Co. Limerick].

Witnesses : Jas. Uniack, late of Cappagh, Co. Tipperary, Esq., deceased, Jas. Webb, late of Dublin, gent., deceased, Jno. Williams, Appletown, Co. Limerick, farmer.

Memorial witnessed by : Thos. Maunsell, Dublin, gent., Richard Maunsell, Limerick, Esq.

82, 456, 58566 Tho. Walter (seal)

533 REGNAUT, Capt. NOAH, [Glasnevin, Co. Dublin].[1]

18 March 1735/36. Narrate, ½ p., 28 June 1736.

To his wife Elenor (extx.), arrears of his half pay as cornet, also arrears due to him as Riding Master in the Castle, etc. His son Noah Regnaut, then in Portugal. His four grandchilden. £100

---

[1] The address given in " *Index to Prerogative Wills of Ireland*," Vicars.

in hands of his son-in-law Boyle Baggs to be divided among his said grandchildren.

Mortgage due to testator upon three houses in Great Brittain Street, [Dublin].

Witnesses : Ledvina FitzGerrald, spinster, John Mason, gent., both of Dublin, and Rev. Richard Parker, Glasnevin, Co. Dublin, clerk.

Memorial witnessed by : James Saunders and Bartholomew Delandre clerks to Wm. Parry, Dublin, public notary.

85, 19, 58861   Ellen Regnaut (seal)

534 PARNELL, THEOBALD, Dublin, Esq.

27 May 1736. Narrate, part in full, ¾ p., 30 June 1736.

Jno. Parnell, son of my uncle the Hon. John Parnell, late one of the Judges of H.M.'s Court of King's Bench in Ireland. All his real estate to Wm. Burgh, Dublin, Esq., and Jno. Burke, Palmerstown, Esq., trustees. My kinsman Thos. Burgh, Esq., Barrister-at-law, only son of said Wm. Burgh, exor. Ann Burgh, wife of said Thos. Burgh. Dorothea Burgh and Eliz. Burgh, sisters to said Thos. Burgh. £50 per annum to Bryen Robinson, Esq., Doctor of physic, " in trust for his sister Jane Broughton for her life " [? testator's sister].

Witnesses : Andrew Shepheard, Dublin, gent., Lewis Magrath, Clonmell, Jno. Magrath, Redmondstown, both in Co. Tipperary, gents.

Memorial witnessed by : Andrew Shepheard, John Corker, Dublin, servingman.

82, 525, 58871   Tho. Burgh (seal)

535 BUDDS, PETER, Garragh, Queen's County, gent.

7 Aug. 1734. Narrate, 1 p., 30 June 1736.

His wife Jane Budds. His son Benjamin Budds. His son-in-law William Bryon. His son-in-law Joseph Howise. His grandchildren Daniel Bryon and Mary Bryon. His three sons Rossell Budds, Samuel Budds and Benjamin Budds. His two grandchildren Peter Howise and Jane Howise. His daughter Elizabeth Harris. His daughter Christian Budds (unmarried).

Rev. George Crump, Richard Grantham, junr., council-at-law, both of Carlow, and George Rossell of Clonmore, Queen's Co., gent., exors.

House and lands of Garragh. The Spaw house and garden. Lands of Curraghbrice. House in Castle Street, Carlow.

Witnesses : Isaac Butler, Dublin, George Stanley, Coolenagh and Rich. Shortal, Grange, both Queen's Co., gents.

Memorial witnessed by : Patrick Laughlin, Clanmore, Queen's Co., gent., James Saunders, clerk to Wm. Parry, Dublin, public notary.

84, 150, 58878   Jane Budds (seal)

widow to testator.

536 MADDOCK, ISAAC, formerly of Dublin, now of Enniscorthy, Co. Wexford, gent. 18 Aug. 1735. Narrate, ¾ p., 27 Aug. 1736.

His wife Catherine Maddock. His brother James Maddock. A payment due by his said brother James Maddock to the widow Fleming. His sister Alice Maddock. The daughters of his brother Jacob Maddock deceased. His brother Abraham Maddock. His brother-in-law John Phillips. His sister Sarah Nunn. His sister Elizabeth Roberts, a legacy bequeathed to her by her mother Hanna Maddock, deceased. His wife Catherine Maddock, his uncle Isaac Dobson and his brother Jas. Maddock, exors. £3 per annum to Nurse Burgis for life. His real and personal estate to his brother James Maddock if testator's wife has no child.

Witnesses : Arthur Gore, Saunders Court, Co. Wexford, Esq., Wm. Sandwith and Henry Sandwith, Glasnecarrick, said county, farmers.

Memorial witnessed by : Susanna Barkey, Dublin, spinster, George More, public notary, Dublin.

86, 54, 59280   Jas. Maddock (seal)

537 ERWIN, ROGER, Capt. Lieut. in Major General Moyle's Regiment of Foot. 14 April 1736. Full, 1 p., 7 Sept. 1736.

My cousin Mervyn Pratt, Cabra, Co. Cavan, Esq. Charles Coote of Coote Hill, Co. Cavan, Esq., and William FitzHerbert of Shercock, said county, Esq., exors. My manservant James Walley. Mary Grace, wife of Robert Grace, soldier in said General Moyle's company.

Rassan, Listunis, Kiltochar, Kilderry, Derrylachan, Drumhalah and Killinure, all in B. Castleraghans, Co. Cavan. All other my lands in said Barony.

Witnesses : Ensign John Cuppaidge, Serjeant John Harvey, Corporal Peter Jack, all in aforesaid regiment.

Memorial witnessed by : John Cuppaidge, James Saunders, clerk to Wm. Parry, Dublin, public notary.

James Walley (seal)
Mary Grace (seal)
(her mark).

85, 121, 59320

---

538 BABINGTON, WILLIAM, Strabane, Co. Tyrone, Esq.
16 June 1735. Narrate, ¾ p., 22 Sept. 1736.

His wife Catherine Babington. Lands whereof he was then seized or to come to him in right of his late father, or as heir at law of his late brother Henry Babington in B. Kilmacrenan, Co. Donegal. His brother Ralph Babington. His brother Thomas Babington. His brother Richard Babington. Jno. Johnson, clerk, John St. Clare, Esq., and said Thomas Babington, exors.

Town and lands of Trenemullan, B. Raphoe, Co. Donegal. Corry, parish of Clandevadogg, Co. Donegal. Lands of Urney, Co. Tyrone (leasehold). His dwelling house, interest or freehold in town of Strabane.

Witnesses : Wm. Johnson, an attorney of Court of Exchequer in Ireland, dwells at Finglas Bridge, Co. Dublin, Henry Tegart, now at London listed in the First Troop of Horse Guards at Westminster, Hugh Carr, menial servant to the testator, now dwells at Clandevadoge, Co. Donegal.

Memorial witnessed by : said Wm. Johnson, Wm. Carter, clerk to Thos. Bradish, attorney of Court of Exchequer, dwells in Patrick Street, Dublin.

86, 84, 59392   Kath. Babington (seal)

---

539 COX, Lieut. WILLIAM, Island Bridge, near Dublin.
30 April 1736. Précis, ½ p., 30 Sept. 1736.

His nephew Robert Cox then belonging to Chelsea College in Great Britain. His niece Elizabeth Flood, her son Jonathan Flood. His niece Ann Williams.

Witnesses : Edward Griffitts, Island Bridge, gent., John Rice, public notary, Dublin.

Memorial witnessed by : John Warham, Dublin, gent., Arthur Shepheard, Dublin, scrivener.

83, 397, 59440   Elizabeth Flood (seal)

540 SHINSTONE, MARGRET, Dublin, widow of Jonathan Shinstone, late of city of Dublin, ironmonger. 13 Nov. 1735. Précis, ½ p., 13 Nov. 1736.

Her effects and worldly substance to be divided equally between her four daughters of the said Jonathan, Mary Shinstone, Ann Shinstone, Elizabeth Barber als. Shinstone wife of James Barber, and Margaret Bath als. Shinstone wife of Michael Bath. Said James Barber and Michael Bath excrs.

Witnesses : Margrett Farrell, wife to John Farrell, Dublin, yeoman, Wm. Beaghan, then of the same, turner, Daniel Dwyer, of the same, cooper.

Memorial witnessed by : Wm. Grey, Bartholomew Delandre, Dublin, gent.

83, 449, 59730   Jas. Barber (seal)

541 GREGORY, REV. GEORGE, clerk, curate of parish of Down. 24 June 1732. Full, ¾ p., 7 Feb. 1736.

My wife Ann Gregory. My eldest daughter Theodora Gregory. My second daughter Eliz. Arthur als. Gregory. A lease perfected to my son-in-law Alexander Arthur 19 April 1729. My youngest daughter Ann Gregory (my third daughter). My eldest son Roger Gregory. My eldest son's daughter Dorcas Gregory. My second son George Gregory (unmarried). My third and youngest son Ralph Gregory (unmarried). My niece Ann Gregory my brother's daughter. Rev. Dr. Edwd. Mathewes, Vicar General of the Diocese of Down, my friend, trustee and exor. My lands within the Liberties of the city of Limerick, and real estate.

Witnesses : Edward Benson, Down, clerk, Henry Humphrey Adams, Down, clerk, Chas. Brett, Ballynewport, Co. Down. gent.

Memorial witnessed by : Edwd. Mathewes, Newcastle, Co. Down, Esq., Chas. Brett.

86, 286, 60378   Edwd. Mathewes (seal)

552 FOX, CHARLES, Foxhall, Co. Longford, Esq. 7 Sept. 1722. Narrate, ½ p., 8 Feb. 1736.

His son Peyton Fox, exor. His son Robt. Fox.

His farm of Cloontemullan and Cloonbegg. Farm in parish of Piercetown known as the five acres. Part of Relick and Rath, Mr Wm. Salmon, lessee [situation not mentioned].

Witnesses : Jno. Kennedy, Co. Westmeath, Doctor of Physic, Patrick Cahill, Cloghageene, Co. Longford, farmer, Lewis Meares, Dublin, Esq.

Memorial witnessed by : Lewis Meares, Thos. Hanly, Dublin, gent.

86, 288, 60387   Pey Fox (seal)

543 BROWNE, ROBERT, Ballinvohir, Co. Cork.

11 June 1731. Narrate, 1¾ p., 18 Feb. 1736.

His wife Elizabeth, guardian of his children. His son Henry Browne. His second son Walter Browne. His third son Thomas Browne. His son Francis Browne. His son Robert Browne. His son George Browne. His son John Browne. His son Tynt Browne. To his daughter Jane Browne and to his daughter Elizabeth Browne £200 each on marriage. His friend Thos. Burgess, Labically, Co. Cork, gent., and his son Henry Browne, exors.

Real estate in Co. Cork. His dwelling house of Ballinvohir.

Witnesses : Gawen Lane, Ballymacallen, Co. Cork, gent., George Browne, Castletown, Co. Cork, gent., John Locker, Knockenannig, said county, gent.

Memorial witnessed by : John Locker, Philip Roch, clerk to Russell Wood, Cork, gent.

Eliz. Browne (seal)
widow of deceased

85, 366, 60533   Jane Browne (seal)

spinister

544 RYVES, CHARLES, Dublin, Esq.

18 Jan. 1736. Narrate, ¾ p., 2 March 1736.

His wife Mary Ryves. His eldest daughter Penelope Ryves als. Dean. His youngest daughter Ann. A settlement made on the marriage of his daughter Mary Ryves als. Candler and Rev. Dr. Wm. Candler. Richd. Helsham, Dublin, Doctor of Physic, and Joseph Harrison, Dublin, gent., exors.

Lands of Foyle and Coolecashel, in Co. Kilkenny. Ballyeene, Co. Kilkenny.

Witnesses : Joseph Landers, Edwd. Sterling and Jno. Kathrens, all of Dublin.

Memorial witnessed by : Jno. Kathrens, Bartholomew Delandre, clerk to Wm. Parry, Dublin, public notary.

86, 331, 60610   W. Candler (seal)

545 WALKINSHAW, JAMES, Dromart, Co. Armagh, gent.

23 Oct. 1736. Narrate, ½ p., 3 March 1736/37.

His wife Margaret Walkinshaw, exor. His only son James Walkinshaw, under twentyone years. His brother-in-law Joseph Boyd of Armagh, apothecary, exor. Testator's said wife, James Kirkpatrick and Joseph Boyd, guardians of his said son and six daughters. His then dwellinghouse, land etc. in Dromart.

Witnesses : William Pye, Armagh, gardener, James Hardy, Dromart, Co. Armagh, gent., Christian Montgomery now wife of John Elliott near Banbridge, Co. Down, farmer.

Memorial witnessed by : Hugh Provand, Dublin, druggist, John Moffitt, Dublin, gent.

87, 69, 60616   Joseph Boyd (seal)

546 WILSON, ROBERT, Augher, Co. Tyrone, merchant.

4 Jan. 1730. Précis, ½ p., 8 March 1736.

His wife Mary Wilson, extx. His dwelling house and two other houses etc. in town of Augher, Co. Tyrone.

Witnesses : James Thompson, Dublin, gent., William Amerson, Augher, innkeeper, John Shipeerd, Ballymagowan, yarn merchant.

Memorial witnessed by : John Shipeerd, James Fenn, Dublin, upholder.

85, 390, 60656   Mary Wilson (seal)

547 ROBINSON, JOHN, Dublin, plasterer and painter.

4 Jan. 1735. Narrate, 1 p., 9 March 1736.

" To his son Henry Robinson £50 payable out of his holding in Cuff Street devised to his son Joseph Robinson." Testator's son Anthony Robinson. Jno. Robinson, son to said Anthony. His [testator's] son George Robinson. To testator's son Joseph Robinson his pew in St. Peter's church, etc. His son William Robinson. His daughter Ann Grundy. Exors. his said daughter Ann Grundy, and Mr Joseph Rathborn and Mr Nichs. Manfield.

Holding in Cuff Street [Dublin]. Ground and houses in Garden Lane, Dublin. The holding wherein the testator then lived in St. Kevans Street [Dublin]. Holding in Golden Lane, Dublin, demised to the testator by the exors. of Wm. Howard, Esq. Holding in Digg Street leased from David Digges Latouche, Esq. Money borrowed from David Latouche, junr. His holding in High Street.

Witnesses : Jno. Annesley, Kevan's Street, Dublin, sadler, Philip Peel, Dublin, bricklayer, Benjamin Johnston, public notary, Dublin.

Memorial witnessed by : George Thomas, Dublin, gent., George Bambruck, Dublin, cordwainer.

86, 339, 60658   Ann Grindy (seal)
Ann Grundy als. Grindy,
one of the exors.

548 KING, WILLIAM, then of Douglas, Isle of Man.

29 Dec. 1736. Full, ½ p., 18 March 1736/37.

To be buried in Abby Boyle in Kingdom of Ireland. My mother. My sister. Francis Ormsby, Esq., of Willybrook, exor. All my real estate to Rt. Hon. Sir Henry King of the Kingdom of Ireland, Baronet. Annuity to Mrs Frances Lockwood. Money to be remitted to Mr Patt Savage, merchant, for discharge of my debts in this isle and funeral charge. Charles Smith my servant. Signed for William King by Geo. Hussey.

Witnesses : Patrick Savage, Dowglass, Isle of Man, merchant, and Margery Savage his wife, Charles Smith, servant to testator, Geo. Hussey, Dowglass, gent.

Memorial witnessed by : Charles Smith, Wm. Knox, Dublin, gent.

87, 94, 60726   Henry King (seal)

549 WRAY, SIR CECIL, Branston, Lincoln, Bart.

21 Jan. 1735. Narrate, ¾ p., 21 March 1736.

His wife Dame Mary Wray. His natural and reputed daughter Miss Anne Casey then living with him at Branston.

Castle, town and lands of Cathcannon, B. Coshma, Co. Limerick. The Rectory impropriate and the Glebe lands and tythes of the church and parish of Uregare, and the advowson of said parish of Uregar, B. Coshma, Co. Limerick. Town and lands of Clonanna, Lissleenbeg als. Lisseen, B. Puble Bryan, Co. Limerick. Ballynegaedy als. Ballygaedy, Casey, Liscanah, part of Ballynegaedy and Garrykettin, B. Coshlea, Co. Limerick. Greybridge (about 160 acres) als. Drohidiglissan, part of the lands of Rathmore, B. Coshma, Co. Limerick, and the other part of said lands of Rathmore in B. Small County, Co. Limerick. Messuage in Kilmallock, Co. Limerick and all other his lands etc. in said county of Limerick and elsewhere in said kingdom of Ireland.

Witnesses : Thos. Becke, Edwd. Litherland and Jno. Becke, all of Lincoln city, gents.

Memorial executed by : Dame Mary Wray, Hanover Street, Parish of St. George, Hanover Square, Co. of Middlesex, widow of testator, Hon. Jno. Selwyn, Cleveland Court, parish of St. James, Westminster, Esq., Thos. Farrington, Chiswelhurst, Co. Kent, who by said will are appointed guardians and trustees of said Ann Casey, now the wife of Rt. Hon. the Lord Vere Bertie, and by Lord Vere Bertie and Lady Ann Bertie. Memorial witnessed by : Thos. Adamson, Lincoln's Inn, Middlesex, gent., David Jones, of same, gent.

86, 357, 60743   Mary Wray (seal)
                                   J. Selwyn (seal)
                                   Thos. Farrington (seal)
                                   Vere Bertie (seal)
                                   Ann Bertie (seal)

550 MITCHELL, CALEB, Dublin, carpenter.

18 Jan. 1723. Précis, a few lines, 6 May 1737.

All his goods, chattles, houses, leases, interests, household goods and all other his worldly substance to his wife Rose Mitchell (extx.) and his sons Gay and Thos. Mitchell.

Witnesses : Patrick Magee, Dublin, perukemaker, Luke Butler, same, merchant.

Memorial witnessed by : Jno. Aston, Dublin, merchant, Chas. Meares, Dublin, gent.

86, 413, 61013   Rose Mitchell (seal)

551 HOUSTON, JOHN, Castle Stewart, Co. Tyrone.

13 Jan. 1734. Full, ¾ p., 12 May 1737.

To be buried in the parish church of Donoughhenry. My sister Alice Houston als. Alice Caulfield. My sister Jane Houston. My sister Grace Houston. My sister Elizabeth Houston als. Elizabeth Scott. My cousin Wm. Houston.

Wm. McCausland. Mrs. Elinor Johnston. £50 to poor of parish of Donoughhenry. Rev. and Hon. Chas. Caulfield and Wm. McCausland, attorney in Dublin, exors.

My estate of inheritance and all my leases and leasehold lands in the county of Antrim and real estate in this kingdom and elsewhere.

Witnesses : James Templeton, Stewartstown, Co. Tyrone, merchant, Jno. Campbell als. Dougall, Dungannon, Co. Tyrone, gent., Jno. Campbell, servant to said testator, now of Dublin.

Memorial witnessed by : Henry Chritchley, Bartholomew Delandre, Dublin, gents.

86, 428, 61091   Ch. Caulfield (seal)

552 CRUMP, JAMES, Dublin, merchant.

10 May 1735.   Narrate, ½ p., 16 May 1737.

His wife Catherine Crump. His dau. Mary Crump, his daughter Jane Crump (both unmarried). Sons John Crump, Patrick Crump, Nicholas Crump, Adam Crump. His brother Patrick Crump. Testator's wife Catherine, Richard Mathews, Dublin, gent., and Bartholomew Fletcher, Dublin, merchant, exors. His personal estate, goods and chattles.

Witnesses : Jos. Crump, grocer, Bryan Fagan, brewer, both of Dublin.

Memorial witnessed by : Michael Argent, Bartholomew Delandre, clerks to Wm. Parry, notary public, Dublin.

85, 494, 61141   Catherine Crump (seal)
                                                        her mark

553 PEARSON, THOMAS, Beamore, Co. Meath, Esq.

26 June 1736.   Narrate, ½ p., 18 May 1737.

His wife Jane Pearson, extx. His nephew Wm. Conolly. His sister Keating. His niece Coghill. His friends the chief Baron [Thomas] Marlay and Dr. Trotter. His servants Sam Cooper and Dorothy his wife. Rev. Mr Jno. Echlin. Mr John Shiell.

Lands of Calliaghtown, purchased from Lord Anglesea [situation not mentioned]. (Reversion of these lands to said Sam Cooper and Dorothy his wife after death of testator's wife). Tythes of Beamore. His real and personal estate in the city of Dublin. Houses on Usher's Quay, and in the lane leading to St. Catherine's church. His interest in Patrick Street and the house commonly called the Wheat Sheaf in Thomas Street. Hamon Lane [Dublin].

Witnesses : Rev. Steuart Wilder, Vicar of Julianstown, Co. Meath. Bryan Robinson, Dublin, George Taaffe, Drogheda, Doctor in Physic.

Memorial witnessed by : Jane Cooper, Beamore, Co. Meath, spinster, David Shiell, Dublin, gent.

86, 438, 61156   Jean Pearson (seal)

554 HAYES, EDWARD, Ballydowling, Co. Wicklow.
   23 March 1736/37. Narrate, 1 p., 7 June 1737.
His wife, exor. His mother Margery Hayes, widow. His brother
Andrew Hayes. Testator's eldest son John Hayes, exor. His son
Edward Hayes (under twenty three years). Daughter Sarah Hayes.
To his daughters Mary, Elizabeth and Ann £200 each on marriage.
His four daughters. His brother-in-law Mr Mathew Lucas, exor.
William Acton, Esq., overseer. His brother Thomas Hayes. £5 to
poor of parish of Wicklow. His wife during widowhood to be guardian
of his children that were under age.
   Holding of land in Ballyfree [Co. Wicklow] then enjoyed by testator's
said mother and brother Andrew. Lands of Killmullen. The house,
holding and lands of Ballydowling [Co. Wicklow]. Lands of Kill-
namanamore [Co. Wicklow] and Cappa [? Co. Wicklow]. The tan yard
outhouses and utensils thereunto belonging.
   Witnesses : " Said Thomas Acton, Esq.",[1] Thos. Parsons, sword
cutler, both of Dublin, Edwd. Byrne, servant to said John Hayes.
   Memorial witnessed by : Bartholomew Delandre, James Saunders,
clerks to Wm. Parry, public notary, Dublin.
87, 204, 61293   John Hayes (seal)

555 HOUSTON, JANE, Castle Stewart, Co. Tyrone, now in Dublin,
   spinster. 9 May 1737. Full, 1 p., 15 June 1737.
My sister Alice Caulfield als. Houston. My sister Grace Staples als.
Houston. £600 to be given to and amongst my sister Elizabeth Scott's
children. Hon. and Rev. Charles Caulfield, Rev. Thos. Staples, and
William McCausland, Dublin, gent., exors. Legacy to poor of parish
of Donaghenry.
   My real and personal estate. My right and interest of and to the
advowson or right of presentation of the parish church of Donaghenry
and all other parishes, rectories or vicarages.
   Witnesses : Hans Bailie, Dublin, merchant, George Houston,
Dublin, gent., Edward Sterling, Dublin, scrivener.
   Memorial witnessed by : Edward Sterling, James Hood, Dublin,
gent.
88, 11, 61371   Wm. McCausland (seal)

---

[1] Thomas Acton's name appears, both in transcript and original memorial,
as a witness but not otherwise.

556   WYNNE, Lieut. General OWEN, Hazelwood, Co. Sligo.
     3 Aug. 1734.   Codicil 28 Feb. 1736.   Narrate, ¾ p., 17 June 1737.

Niece Mary Wynne of Catherlagh. To Catherine Wynne, Dublin, £400 on marriage. His niece Katherin Wynne als. Folliott wife of his nephew Owen Wynne of Lurganboy, Co. Leitrim, Esq. Said nephew sole exor. Rev. Mr Eubele Ormsby. His servants John Baker, James Weir and John Clark. His real and personal estate.

Witnesses : Natl. Clemen[t]s, Dublin, Esq., Lieut. Lewis Folliott of Lieut. General Thos Pearce's Regiment of Horse, Thomas Cox, cornet in said regiment.

Codicil witnessed by : James Blair, Sligo, Co. Sligo, clerk, Peter Croghan, Rathconner, Co. Roscommon, Doctor of Physic, James Vallance, servant to said Owen Wynne of Lurganboy.

Memorial witnessed by : Bartholomew Delandre and James Saunders, clerks to Wm. Parry, Dublin, public notary.

84, 392, 61386   Owen Wynne (seal)

557   HUSON, Rev. NATHANIEL, Enniscorthy, Co. Wexford, clerk.
     4 July 1735.   Narrate, ¾ p., 18 June 1737.

His wife Sarah Huson, exor. His daughter Elizabeth Huson. His daughter Mary Cookman. Her son Nathaniel Cookman. His daughter JaneHuson, exor. Her son Nathaniel Huson. Rev. James Harvey and Richard Donovan, Esq., trustees.

His real estate and leasehold interests. Town and lands of Tomadilly, lease of lands of Ballyhill, leases of his houses and parks in Enniscorthy [? all in Co. Wexford]. Lands of Courtnacuddy and Ballyoriell, Co. Wexford.

Witnesses : Wm. Anderson, Dublin, gent., Joseph Landers, Henry Buckley, late of city of Dublin, notary public, deceased.

Memorial witnessed by : Thos. Drinkeall and Richard Rushworth, both of Enniscorthy, Co. Wexford, gents.

                                   Sarah Huson (seal)
                                   Mary Cookman (seal)
88, 23, 61419   Jane Huson (seal)

558   LYNAM, SARAH, Coleraine, Londonderry, widow of Richard Lynam late of said town, Esq., deceased. 5 Sept. 1736. Narrate, ¾ p., 4 July 1737.

Her son Richard Lynam, clerk (exor.), his said father Richard Lynam deceased. Her daughter Ann Church. Her tenement in New Row, town of Coleraine.

Witnesses : Richard Lynam, then apprentice or clerk to a merchant in Coleraine, Fredk. Curtis, same, merchant, Patrick McCormick, Dublin, gent.

Memorial witnessed by : Patrick McCormick, Hugh Carmichael, gent., clerk to said Patk. McCormick.

86, 501, 61527 Richd. Lynam (seal)

559 HUGHS, MAURICE, Galway, burgess.

4 May 1736. Full, 1 p., 19 July 1737.

My daughter Anne French als. Hughs. Edmond French her only son and heir. Rev. Wm. Little of Galway, clerk, Alexander Lynch of same, gent., and Thos. Holland, of same, alderman, trustees.

My house that I now live in, in town of Galway (mortgaged to reps. of Rev. Dr. Feilding Shawe, late of Galway, deceased).

Witnesses : Erasmus Irwin, Galway, alderman, William Hinde, Galway, alderman, Alexr. Reed, Galway, yeoman.

Memorial witnessed by : Erasmus Irwin, Morgan Connor, Galway, gent., Thomas Coigly, servant to Denis Daly of Raford, Co. Galway, Esq., Miles McDonagh, servant to Peter Daly of Dublin, Esq.

Anne French (seal)

87, 279, 61622 Alexr. Lynch (seal)

560 AYLMER, SIR GERALD, Donadea, Co. Kildare, Bart.

25 April 1735. Narrate, ¾ p., 8 Aug. 1737.

His daughter Lucy Aylmer. His second daughter Elizabeth Aylmer. In default of issue of his daughters his lands, tenements, hereditaments and all other his real estate etc. to the use of Rt. Hon. Henry Lord Aylmer Baron Balrath, then to Hon. Mathew Aylmer, eldest son of said Lord Aylmer, Hon. Henry, second son of said Lord Aylmer, Hon. John, third son of said Lord Aylmer, failing whose issue to the use of Sir Andrew Aylmer of Balrath, Bart. and to his heirs for ever being Protestants.

R

Witnesses : Mark Whyte, gent., one of the attornys of H.M. Court of Exchequer in Ireland, John Edwards and Francis Keating, both of Dublin, gents.

Memorial witnessed by : Mark Whyte, Boleyn Whitney, Dublin, Esq.

87, 299, 61700   L. Aylmer
                                          (Dame Lucy Ayl-
                                          mer widow of Sir
                                          Gerald   Aylmer,
                                          and guardian to
                                          his children)

561 ANGLESEY, ARTHUR EARL OF
        18 Feb. 1735. Full, 1¼ p., 1 Sept. 1737.

My cousin Charles Annesley, son of my uncle Charles Annesley deceased. My dear cousin Fras. Annesley, Esq., of Portugal Row, Lincoln's Inn Fields, Co. Middlesex, exor. My cousin Fras. Wingate of Harlington, Bedfordshire, Esq. My nephew Robt. Gayer, Esq. Ann Green, daughter of my late cousin Dorothy Green deceased. Mr Jno. Green, brother of said Ann Green. £14 to be laid out pursuant to the will of my brother James late Earl of Anglesey for erecting a monument in the church of Farnborough, Co. of Southampton.

The Hon. Dixie Windsor. The Hon. Brigr. Andrews Windsor. Rev. Mr Archdeacon Gooch. Thos. Scott, keeper of my park in the Co. of Wexford. Mr Martin Collis, one of the recds. [? an agent] of my estate in Ireland.

The park of Knockengarrow orse. Knockgrenon near Camolin, Co. Wexford, and the mansion house and keepers lodge by me there built to Chas. Annesley. Dwelling house in Bletchingdon, Co. of Oxford, wherein Brig. Edwd. Jones lately lived, to Mrs Dorothy Combe. A dwelling house in Bletchingdon wherein Jno. Perrin now lives to Mrs Eliz. Watkinson. My real and personal estate in Great Britain and Ireland. My lands in parishes of Bletchington and Hampton Poyle, Co. Oxford.

Witnesses : Richd. Shuttleworth, Garthrop, Co. of Lancaster, Esq., Thos. Lister, Gisburn Park, Co. of York, Esq., Thos. Barsham, Inner Temple, London, gent.

Memorial witnessed by : Henry Adam, Inner Temple, gent., Thos. Barsham.

89, 21, 61889   Fra. Annesley (seal)

562 STERLING, WILLIAM, Adamstown, Co. Meath.
15 March 1733. Préeis, a few lines, 3 Oct. 1737.
His nephew Marcus Barnes. His leasehold interest in Adamstown, his English lease of Tankardstown, his lease of Athgaine [? all in Co. Meath].
Witnesses : John Stanley, Thady McCan, Elizabeth Hughes, spinster, all of Adamstown.
Memorial witnessed by : William Cosgrave, Charles Street, Dublin, gent., Edward Sterling, Dublin, public notary.
87, 332, 61932   Mar. Barnes (seal)

563 PARSONS, WILLIAM, Saint Johns, Co. Wexford, gent.
7 Sept. 1736. Précis, ¼ p., 27 Oct. 1737.
His mother Judith Parsons (sole legatee and extx.). His real and personal estate.
Witnesses : Jack Hatton, Dublin, gent., Margaret Malone, widow and William Franklin, yeoman, both of St. Johns, Co. Wexford.
Memorial witnessed by : Jack Hatton, Robert Clifford, Wexford town, apothecary.
88, 155, 62040   Jud. Parsons (seal)

564 STEWART, GEORGE, Red Bay, parish of Laid, B. of Glenarm,
    Co. Antrim, gent. 12 April 1730. Narrate, part in full, ¾ p.,
    7 Nov. 1737.
My only beloved son Francis Stewart. I confirm marriage articles perfected 1 Jan. 1712 with my wife Sheely McAulay. My brother John. My said wife and my friend Mr Patrick O'Hagan of Bay, exors. All my real estate in parish of Laid.
Witnesses : Randle McDonnell and Coll McDonnell, both of Lagg, Alexander Stewart, Gortaclee, all in parish of Laid, gents.
Memorial witnessed by : Alexr. Stewart, George Eaton, Chancery Lane, Dublin.
88, 167, 62083   Fran. Stewart (seal)

565 CONNER, DANIEL, Bandon, Co. Cork, gent.
26 Jan. 1733. Narrate, part in full, 7 Nov. 1737.
Father Daniel Conner, exor. My only son Daniel Conner. My brother Wm. Conner, exor. My sister Jane Lapp.

Real and personal estate in England and Ireland. Town and lands of Sart and Bootes Town being my estate in Co. Kilkenny.

Witnesses : Ralph Clear, senr., Richard Clear and Thos. Burk, all of Bandon, Co. Cork.

Memorial witnessed by : Ralph Clear, senr., John Hart, Cork, gent.

87, 359, 62093   Willm. Conner (seal)

566 MATHEWS, EDWARD, Anakeragh, Co. Armagh, gent.

4 June 1734. Narrate, 1 p., 19 Nov. 1737.

His son Richard Mathews. His second son John Mathews. A debt due to the widow Ann Verner of Armagh.

Part of the townland of Agrologher, in parish of Loughgall, the two townlands of Anaghkeragh and Drominalduff, all in Co. Armagh.

Witnesses : Thomas Thompson, Cornamuckla, Henry Sinnaman, Ballyfodran, Thos. Johnson, Cornamuckla, all Co. Armagh, and Edward Mathews of Lisgarr, Co. Cavan, gent.

Memorial witnessed by : Said Edward Mathews of Lisgarr, John Scott, Dromgola, Co. Armagh, gent. Executed by John Mathews, son of testator, to whom said lands are descended by the death of Richard Mathews, brother of the said John.

84, 507, 62285   John Mathews (seal)

567 DOYLE, PATRICK, Bride Street, Dublin, dealer.

1 Jan. 1735. Précis, ¼ p., 2 Dec. 1737.

Wife Catherine Doyle als. Powell since deceased. His brother Daniel Doyle in the Co. Wicklow. His two nieces Mary Vardan als. Doyle and Alice Doyle. Aris Brass, merchant, Bride Street and Thos. Forstall, merchant, Church Street, exors. His lease in Bride Street, Dublin.

Witnesses : Nichs. Doyle, Dublin, cordwainer, Joseph Forstall, Dublin, mariner.

Memorial witnessed by : Nicholas Doyle, Will Devall, public notary, Dublin.

89, 115, 62370   Aris Brass (seal)

568 KING, JOHN, Tubberbryan, Co. Tipperary, gent.

25 Jan. 1734. Narrate, 1 p., 17 Dec. 1737.

His estate of Tubberbryan and real and personal estate to his niece Jane Harrison, sister of Joseph Harrison of city of Dublin, attorney-at-law, and her heirs, failing whom to said Joseph Harrison and his heirs, or to Richard Croker, second son to Edward Croker, Dublin, apothecary, Samuel Croker third son, Charles Croker fourth son, of said Edwd. Croker, on condition that said Jane Harrison, Joseph Harrison, Richard Croker, Samuel Croker and Charles Croker when they and each of them and their several heirs male and female shall come to possession of said lands of Tubberbryan shall take upon them the surname of King.

Witnesses : Richard Pope, Clonbrick, Co. Tipperary, gent., Wm. Edge, Tipperary town, merchant, John Murphy, Ballygiddan, Co. Tipperary, yeoman.

Memorial witnessed by : Richd. Pope, Thomas Pope, Tubberbryan, yeoman.

90, 5, 62495   Jane King (seal)
                             (Jane Harrison)

569 KNOX, ANDREW, Rathmacknee, B. Forth, Co. Wexford, Esq. 31 July 1737. Narrate, 2 pp., 31 Dec. 1737.

Articles dated 27 June 1719 made before his marriage with his then wife Mary Knox als. Grogan now his widow. Other articles made by the testator on the marriage of his only daughter with John Grogan of Johnstown, Esq. His grandson John Grogan. Such of the younger sons of his daughter as shall inherit his real estate shall be called by surname of Knox. Testator's wife Mary Knox, John Grogan his son-in-law and Rev. James Harvey of Killane, clerk, exors. Richard Row of Ballyharty, Co. Wexford, Esq., and his said son-in-law John Grogan, trustees. Thos. Knox, eldest son of Berkley Sydney Knox, Esq., nephew of the testator. Tempest Knox, second son of said Berkely Sydney Knox and Elizabeth Knox daughter of said Berkley Sydney Knox.

Rathmcknee. Testator's slate house in parish of St. Iologe [Doologe] in town of Wexford. Testator was seized in fee of one moiety of the manor of Ballybrenan as well as of Rathmcknee in common with Charles Monck, Esq. Lands of Great and Little Rathmcknee, Moylestown, Rathjarney, Knockingall, Owenstown, Shortallstown. Part of Hobbinstown, Garlicks Lake and Cunigar Newtown and Gregorystown. The castle or mansion house of Rathmcknee. His lands of Ardci nrush (Ardianrush) als. Ardcandrush in Co. Wexford.

Witnesses : Robert Tench, Dublin, Esq., John Lamb, Dublin, clerk to said Robert Tench, Valentine Broder, Knockingall, Co. Wexford, farmer.

Memorial witnessed by : Robt. Tench, Valentine Broder.

87, 459, 62580   Jno. Grogan (seal)

570 SHAW, ROBERT, Galway, Esq.

20 Oct., 1737. Codicil 21 Oct. 1727. Narrate, 1½ p., 2 Jan. 1737/38.

His wife Alice Shaw als. Croasdaile. Reciting settlement dated 9 Nov. 1706 between Robert Shaw, senr., and Robert Shaw, junr., son and heir apparent of said Robert, senr., both of Newford, Co. Galway, Esqrs., on the one part, and Henry Croasdaile, Rinn, Queen's Co., gent. and others of the other part. His eldest son and heir apparent Thomas Shaw (exor.). His daughters Mercy Shaw and Elizabeth Shaw. His sons William Shaw, George Shaw, Croasdaile Shaw, John Shaw, Richard Shaw, Robert Shaw. David Power and John Disney, Esq., to be guardians of such children as were under age.

Town and lands of Cahirowen in liberty of Athenry, Co. Galway. Lands of Gortnalickey and Gortnacapah, West Liberties of town of Galway. A house in High Street, Galway. A lease from Capt. Hugh Montgomery of his estate in town of Athenry. His real and personal estate and leases in Co. Galway and county of the town of Galway.

Witnesses to will and codicil : David Power, John Giles, Loughrea, Esq., Matthew Kelleher, Coorheen, gent., both in Co. Galway.

Memorial witnessed by : Michael Argent and Bartholomew Delandre, clerks to Wm. Parry, Dublin, notary public.

88, 279, 62583   Thos. Shaw (seal)

571 CROFTON, GEORGE, Drumgrana, Co. Leitrim, gent.

2 April 1736. Narrate, ½ p., 6 Feb. 1737.

Profits from lands to his wife Ann Crofton als. Slack to commence after decease of Ann Crofton, testator's mother. His children [not named]. Lancelot Lawder, Kiltubrid, Co. Leitrim, Esq., Wm. Slack, Bealscarrow, said county, gent., and testator's wife Ann Crofton, exors.

Lands of Gortnara [Co. Leitrim] and Gortnanowell [? Co. Leitrim]. Part of Park [? Co. Leitrim] held from Mr Pierce Fitzgerald and part held from the Earl of Shelburne.

Witnesses : Patk. Raverty, Drumgrana, farmer, Fras. Dunlevy, Cloonsarran, Co. Leitrim, Doctor of Physic, Randal Slack, Bealscarrow, gent.

Memorial witnessed by : Randal Slack, Fred. Reynolds, Rosconis, Co. Leitrim, farmer.

90, 45, 62783   Anne Crofton (seal)

---

572 WILSON, FRANCIS, Tully, Co. Longford, Esq.

27 May 1737. Narrate, 1 p., 7 March 1737/38.

His wife Jane Wilson, exor. His eldest son Jno. Wilson. His youngest son Joseph Wilson. His eldest daughter Mary Wilson als. Hutcheson, wife of Mr Francis Hutcheson, then one of the professors of philosophy in the University of Glasgow. His second daughter Elizabeth Wilson als. Johnston, wife of Jas. Johnston, junr., of Tremount, Co. Down, gent. His third daughter Eleanor Wilson als. Arbuckle, wife of Jas. Arbuckle, Dublin, Doctor of Physic. His youngest daughter Catherine Wilson. His brother-in-law Rev. Jas. Johnson, exor. Testator's wife and said brother-in-law guardians of his son Joseph Wilson and daughter Catherine Wilson. Randal Adams, Dublin, Esq.

Lands of Tully, B. Granard, Co. Longford. Lands of Eskar, B. and Co. of Longford (subject to a chiefry of sixpence per annum payable to the Earl of Granard). Lands of Drumnacookie, Dalystown [? Co. Longford], Carrigduff, Bawn and Emloch.

Witnesses : Wm. Bruce, Alexr. Hutcheson and Gabl. Heatly, all of city of Dublin, gents.

Memorial witnessed by : Wm. Bruce, Jas. Thompson, Dublin, gent.

89, 247, 63047   Jane Wilson (seal)

---

573 LESLIE, JOHN, Tarbert, Co. Kerry, Esq.

30 Nov. 1735. Full, 1 p., 14 March 1737.

My daughter Lucy. My uncle George Leslie now of Ballyconnell, clerk, guardian of my said daughter Lucy until she is twentyone. Desires daughter Lucy to marry the eldest son of said uncle George. Mrs. Letitia Johnston of Kilmore, my father's sister. Her son Mr Francis Johnston. My niece Mary Rowan and my niece Sarah Rowan, daughters of John Rowan and my sister Sarah Rowan. Alexr. Clark, Robert Hamilton, Wm. Carrogam my malster, all now my servants. My friend Amos Vereker, Esq., of Limerick, Doctor of Physic. My real estate in Co. Kerry and Co. Cork.

Witnesses : Lan. Glanville, Nich. Glanville, Henry Longan.
Memorial witnessed by : Alexr. Nesbitt, Dublin, gent., Andrew
Geoghegan, Dublin, his clerk.
91, 17, 63103   Geo. Leslie (seal)

574 WRAY, ANGEL, Fore, Co. Donegal, widow of Wm. Wray, late
of Fore, Esq., deceased. 8 March 1732. Full, 2 pp., 20 March
1737.
Articles made by my late husband Wm. Wray on marriage of his
son Humphrey Wray with Ann Brooke. My daughter Isabella
Babington, wife of Richard Babington. My daughter Elizabeth
Sinclair. My daughter Marian Knox, wife of George Knox of Monimore,
Co. Donegal, Esq. My granddaughters Angel Wray, Sarah Wray,
Lettice Wray, Anne Wray. My grandsons Charles Wray, Henry
Wray, My son-in-law said George Knox of Monimore, exor.
Recites indenture dated 20 April 1732 made between testator on
one part and Henry Wray of Castlewray, Co. Donegal, Esq., and Wm.
Span of Ballyemacoole, clerk, of the other part concerning annuities
arising out of lands of Magherymenagh, Corcreggan, Fore, Bracky,
Clonemess [? Clonmass], Ballymore, Dunfanaghy, the marble and mill
quarrys, Rendrum, Cashell, Minode and Dunloey [? Dunlewy],
[? all in Co. Donegal].
Witnesses : Fredk. Stewart, Danl. McMongil, Bernd. Knox.
Memorial witnessed by : Giffard Nesbitt, Esq., and Alexr. Nesbitt,
gent. both of Dublin.
90, 100, 63131   Geo. Knox (seal)

575 BADCOCK, BENJAMIN, Dublin, cooper.
1 Oct. 1737. Narrate, ½ p., 7 April 1738.
His wife Bridget Badcock, exor. His eldest son Joseph Badcock.
His second son Benjamin Badcock. His daughter Elizabeth Badcock.
His daughter Mary Badcock. Wm. Laban, Dublin, tanner, exor.
His house in Temple Bar, suburbs of Dublin, wherein Wm. Carlisle
then dwelt, his house adjoining wherein John Aughy then dwelt.
House in Essex Street in said suburbs whereof George Harford is in
possession, and house adjoining.
Witnesses : George Williamson, Dublin, carpenter, Barnaby
Gunning, Dublin, victualler, Laurence Bryne, Dublin, gent.

Memorial witnessed by : Batholomew Hefferan, Dublin, peruke maker, Wm. Montgomery, Dublin, gent.

91, 39, 63213   Bridgett Badcock (seal)
                                          (her mark)

576 MASON, JOHN, Waterford, Esq.

1 Oct. 1735. Narrate, ¾ p., 18 April 1738.

His only son Aland Mason. His [? testator's] sisters Henrietta Alcock als. Mason, Susanna Mason, Mary Mason. Henry Alcock, eldest son of his sister Eliz. Alcock als. Mason, deceased. Jno. Boyd, son of his sister Urith Boyd als. Mason, deceased, Jno. Sheppard, son of his sister Hannah Sheppard als. Mason, deceased. His brother Henry Mason, Esq.

His real estate in Co. of Waterford, county of the city of Waterford and Co. of Kildare, Queen's Co., the Co. of Cavan and city of Dublin.

Witnesses : Jno. Barker, Waterford, gent., Arthur Mason, Waterford, cordwainer, Danl. Taylor, Waterford, notary public.

Memorial witnessed by : Adam McCoole, Waterford, yeoman, Wm. Stranger, Waterford, yeoman.

89, 297, 63286   Mary Mason (seal)
                                         a devisee

577 WALCOTT, JOHN, Croagh, Co. Limerick, Esq.

27 March 1730. Narrate, 1 p., 2 May 1738.

His wife Elenor Walcott. A settlement to her dated 22, 23 Dec. 1712. William FitzGerald, Sixmilebridge, Co. Clare, Esq., and Charles Smith, Newcastle, Co. Limerick, Esq., trustees. His brother William Walcott. John Minchin, eldest son of his cousin Edward Minchin of Glanahilty, Co. Tipperary, Esq. Charles Minchin third son, Humphrey Minchin fourth son, Francis Minchin fifth son and Wallcott Minchin sixth son of said Edward Minchin. Paul Minchin of Ballynakill, Co. Tipperary, Esq. Persons in possession of estate to take surname of Wallcott.

His wife to enjoy the mansion house of Croagh, and lands called Clonegraige, the Pigeon's close, the wood als. Killadam, and the Raheens including the mount and cony warren.

Witnesses : William Acton, Limerick, clothier, Samuel Hulett, Limerick, gent., William Smith, Limerick, gent.

Memorial witnessed by :   William Smith, Humphrey Minchin, Dublin, gent.

88, 497, 63440   Jon. Minchin (seal)

578   PUTLAND, SISSON, Little Barkamstead, Hertfordshire, Esq.
18 Feb. 1737.   Narrate, ¾ p., 13 May 1738.

His mother Meriell Putland. His brother Heron Putland then in America. To each of his two daughters £500 [brother's daughters].[1] His brother George Putland, exor. His sister Martha Putland, exor. His sister Hester Gape, her husband Wm. Gape, Esq. To his brother Geo. Putland all his moyety of the profits arising out of the Pell Office in Ireland. His nephew Thomas Putland of Dublin. His cousin Thos. Skellern [Skellion].[1]

Mary Wilks. Legacy to Margaret Lindar and furniture etc. of the house he then lived in in Spring Garden. His servant John Moreton. Two houses on Ormond Quay, Dublin.

Witnesses : Mary Kempenfelt, city of Westminster, spinster, Alex. McCarthy, of same, Esq., John Elliot, London, gent.

Memorial witnessed by : William Noy, George Sparks, Dublin, gents.

91, 112, 63570   Geo. Putland (seal)

579   TAYLOR, BERKELEY, Ballynort, Co. Limerick.
Not dated.   Narrate, ¾ p., 8 July 1738.

His wife. His son Wm. Taylor.

His farms and lands of Derintubrid, his share of farm of Knockcoolkear. All his houses in Cork. Town and lands of Castlecor, Ardtemple, Ballymcpierce, Knockballymartin North and South[2] Ballydradin, Dromeenagore, Coolvaghan als. Coolmachain, Lackillia als. Lackill, part of Ballyhasty, Rathnagard, Mechanan, Glaunfaney, Drumsachane, Dwargin [? Duarrigle], Gurtigeen, Coultefeune, Cuilehane, Rathroe, Lyrevihane, Cleawragh, Gurtefinogy, and Killeen, Ballintubber and Ballyphillippeen, all in Co. Cork, and any other farms and lands he was seized of in Co. Cork.

---

[1] Sisson Putland died without issue 22 March 1737. *Betham's Will Pedigrees*, Genealogical Office, mention a cousin Thomas Skellion.

[2] Presumably N. and S. Knockballymartin.

Witnesses : John Minchin, Dublin, Esq., John Moffit, Dublin, gent., George Moore, Dublin, public notary.
Memorial witnessed by : John Minchin, John Wallis, Dublin, gent.
92, 125, 64117   Wm. Taylor (seal)

580 SMITH, Rev. JOHN, Galtrim, Co. Meath, clerk.
      15 July 1737. Narrate, 1½ p., 22 July 1738.
His wife Judith Smith. His eldest son John Smith. His second son William. His third son Peter Smith. His daughter Elizabeth Smith. His daughter Judith Smith. His wife Judith Smith, his brother-in-law Adam Newman of the city of Cork, Esq., and Rev. Benezer Murdock of Killpadder, exors., and trustees.
Confirms his marriage settlement whereby £60 annuity or rent charge was to be paid to his wife per annum out of his estate of inheritance of Ballymore, Co. Cork. Town and lands of Killpadder, Co. Cork. Rest of his personal estate.
Witnesses : Lancellot Fisher, senr., Ballsoone, Co. Meath, gent., Mary Flin, servant to said Judith Smith, Lancellot Fisher, junr., Dublin, gent.
Memorial witnessed by : Lancellot Fisher, senr., James Saunders clerk to Wm. Parry, Dublin, public notary.
92, 150, 64203   Wm. Smith (seal)

581 HUDSON, ELIZABETH, Dundalk, Co. Louth.
      21 July 1738. Précis, ¼ p., 3 Aug. 1738.
Her sister Susanna Brady als. Hudson. Thomas Wynne, Dundalk, merchant, and Thomas Brady, her brother-in-law, exors.
Her real and personal estate, viz : one half of the Goal Castle, the tenement in possession of James Gudding in Dundalk, the field on south side of the mill race of Dundalk in possession of Thos. Allen, grazier. Concerns bequeathed to her by her father Thos. Hudson, late of Dundalk, deceased.
Witnesses : Joseph Vavasor, merchant, Rev. David Burches, clerk, Jno. Hill, taylor and Eliz. Hill his wife, all of Dublin.
Memorial witnessed by : James Saunders and Bartholomew Delandre, clerks to Wm. Parry, Dublin, notary public.
89, 496, 64256   Susana Brady als. Hudson (seal)

582 SHIRLEY, Hon. ROBERT, Spring Garden within the Liberty of Westminster, Esq. 11 July 1738. Précis, part in full, ½ p., 8 Sept. 1738.

My sister Lady Stuarta Shirley. My Irish estate is subject to two mortgages by me made to Mrs Frances Duport deceased for £3,500 and to George Edwards, junr., for £1,500 [situation not mentioned].

Witnesses : Josiah Cooper, Nathaniel Templeman, Benjamin Collinson.

Memorial witnessed by : Josiah Cooper, Hutton Perkins, Lincoln's Inn, Middlesex, Esq.

91, 337, 64413   S. Shirley (seal)

583 STEUART, WILLIAM, parish of St. George, Hanover Square, Middlesex, Esq. 31 May 1726. Narrate, 1 p., 14 Nov. 1738.

His wife Elizabeth, exor. (who hath since intermarried with Henry Rowe of the parish of St. George, Bloomsbury, Esq.). His nephew Col. John Steuart. Testator's nephew James Steuart, exor.

His lands, tenements and hereditaments in the counties of Westmeath, Longford, Catherlogh or elsewhere in the kingdom of Ireland. Lands near Loughlinbridge, Co. Catherlogh.

Witnesses : Christopher Arnold, London, banker, Peter Webb, London, jeweller, Daniel Reading, London, gent.

Memorial witnessed by : Christopher Arnold, Robert Harrison, Middle Temple, London, gent.

                                            Js. Steuart (seal)
                                            Hen. Rowe (seal)
93, 80, 64904   Eliz. Rowe (seal)
                                            (Elizabeth Steuart now
                                         · Rowe, relict of testator)

584 OWEN, HENRY, Ballenedrumny, Co. Meath, Esq. 11 May 1738. Précis, ½ p., 5 Dec. 1738.

His wife Mary. His nephew Henry Owen of Killmore, Co. Monaghan, exor., son of his brother Edward Owen.

His estates of Ballenedrumny and Woodtown West, Co. Meath. Galtrim, Boycetown and Mitchellstown and all other his estates.

Witnesses : Edwd. FitzSimons, Doctor of Physic, Thos. Potterton Rathcormick, farmer, Walter Walsh, Athboy, innkeeper, all in Co. Meath.

Memorial witnessed by : Brab. Noble, Bartholomew Delandre, both of Dublin, gents.

90, 415, 65134   Hen. Owen (seal)

585 FARRELL, JAMES, Killmore, Co. Roscommon, Esq.
    25 July 1738. Codicil 18 Aug. 1738. Full, 3½ pp., 27 Jan. 1738/39.

Wife Jean Farrell als. Blake. My brother-in-law Peter Daly of Quansbury and my kinsman Denis Daly of Raford, both Co. Galway, Esqrs., trustees and exors. (revoked in codicil). In default of issue male or female of my own . . . estates etc. . . . to John Kelly, junr., second son of my nephew Jno. Kelly of Clonlyon, and his heirs ; they are to assume surname of Farrell and take the coat of arms of Farrell. Richard Caddell eldest son of my sister Cecila Caddell als. Farrell by my brother-in-law Thos. Caddell ; Robert Caddell, second son of said sister Celia. Denis Kelly the youngest son of my brother-in-law Jno. Kelly of Clonlyon deceased. My sister Anstas Kirwan als. Farrell, her husband Richard Kirwan. My nephew Arthur French (trustee) ; my nieces Margery and Rose French, sisters of said nephew. My nephew Patrick French their brother. My nieces Fras. Kelly and Hellen Kelly, two of the daughters of my brother-in-law John Kelly. My nephew John Kelly their brother. Bridget Nettervill, daughter of my brother-in-law Patrick Nettervill. Edmd. Nettervill, Esq., (a trustee named in codicil). My sister Rose Farrell. Great loss sustained by my poor kinsman James Costelloe, brother to William Costelloe of Tullaghan, Co. Mayo, in his long lawsuit with my late mother.

All my estate in the counties of Galway, Roscommon and Sligo. My estate in the north of Ireland in the counties of Down and Monaghan. Lease of houses and plots in Meeting House Lane [Dublin].

Witnesses : Richd. Shillen, merchant, Patrick Missett, wool draper, both of Dublin, Myles McDonough, clerk to Peter Daly, Dublin, Esq.

Codicil witnessed by : Thos. Caddell, Herbertstown, Co. Meath, gent., Rich. Caddell, Dublin, linen draper, Elinor Caddell his wife.

Memorial witnessed by : James Saunders, Bartholomew Delandre, clerks to Wm. Parry, Dublin, public notary.

                                    John Kelly (seal)

93, 283, 65475   Celia Caddell (seal)

586 TACKABERRY, ELIZABETH, Ballynabanoge, Co. Wicklow, widow. 12 Sept. 1735. Précis, ½ p., 31 Jan. 1738.

Her son Nathaniel Tackaberry. Her real estate of town and lands of Ballynabanoge in parish of Arklow, B. of Arklow, Co. Wicklow.

Witnesses : Chas. Dickenson, Michl. Headon, and Saml. Dickenson, all of said parish, farmers.

Memorial witnessed by : Michl. Headon, Isaac Walsh, Dublin, gent.

90, 447, 65494   Nath. Tackaberry (seal)

587 ST. LEGER, MARY, Cork, widow and relict of John St. Leger, late of city of Cork, Esq. 8 Sept 1735. Narrate, ½ p., 31 Jan. 1738.

Her daughter Barbara St. Leger. Her daughter Elizabeth St. Leger, extx.

The plowland of Rahagrough, B. Kinalea, Co. Cork, and residue of her real and personal estate.

Witnesses : Rev. St. John Brown, Kinsale, Co. Cork, Peter Lucas, Cork, merchant, Robert Wallis, Cork, public notary.

Memorial witnessed by : Andrew Nash, Dublin, gent., John Ellis, Cork, gent.

94, 97, 65508   Barbara St. Leger (seal)

588 FRENCH, JAMES, Dublin, Esq.

11 Feb. 1737. Narrate, ¾ p., 1 March 1738.

His wife Anne French als. Godfrey. His brother Robert French, Esq., Capt. Rowley Godfrey and Thomas Kingsburry, Esq., Doctor in Physic, exors.

His personal estate. Lands of Ballynduff and Sheehee, Co. Galway. A house lately belonging to his father Martin French, Esq., deceased in the city of Galway, now in the possession of his elder brother Robert French of said county, Esq.

Witnesses : Ann Godfrey, Letticia Godfrey and Lullum Batwell.

Memorial witnessed by : Lullum Batwell, George Murray, Dublin, gent.

94, 162, 65771   Tho. Kingsburry (seal)
                                 Anne French (seal)

589 EDWARDS, HUGH, Castlegore, Co. Tyrone, Esq.

12 Oct. 1737. Narrate, 1½ ., 2 March 1738.

His wife Ann Edwards. His eldest daughter Olivia Edwards. His daughters Jane and Elizabeth. His brother Thomas Edwards. Trustees : Henry Cary, Dungiven, Co. Londonderry, Esq., Rowley Hill, Wallworth, said county, Esq., Hen. Mervyn, Trelick, Co. Tyrone, Esq., Wm. Hamilton, Dunnemanagh, Robt. Steuart, Steuart Hall, and James Richardson, Springtown, Esq., all in said county.

All his manors, lands, tenements and hereditaments in county of Tyrone and elsewhere. His house of Castlegore with the demesnes and farm thereunto belonging. His lease of Ballylannes.

Witnesses : Robert Cross, merchant, Samuel Ewing, merchant, Charles McManus, gent., all of Londonderry.

Memorial witnessed by : Peter Hamilton and Bartholomew Delandre, Dublin, gents.

94, 163, 65772   Tho. Edwards (seal)

590 WADE, JOHN, Cloonybreny, Co. Meath, Esq.

7 Sept. 1730. Narrate, 1 p., 6 April 1739.

His nephew Clotworthy Shields son of his late brother-in-law Michael Shields, Esq., deceased. His nephew Robert Shields of Wyanstowne, Co. Meath, Esq. His nephew Henry Shields, brother of his said nephew Robert Shields of Wyanstowne, Esq. His sister Mrs Elizabeth Beckett, wife of his brother-in-law Wm. Beckett, Esq. His nephew and godson John Daniel, eldest son of Mr Bridges Daniel. His niece Mrs Dorothy Cooke, wife of Thos. Cook of Dongillane, Esq. His niece Mrs Elizabeth Daly, wife of Major Abel Daly [Dally].[1] Michael Philips, son of Mr Thos. Philips.

Manor town and lands of Cloonybreny and Dyamore, Co. Meath, The town and lands of Hamlinstowne, Martinstowne, Ardglasson, Crossakeele, Crevagh, Drumanallister, Smithstown, Dogstowne, Piringstown, Gylleastowne, Dyamore, Gibbonstowne, Seraghstowne and Herbertstowne, Co. Meath. Danestown, Co. Dublin. Lands of Cloonestown, all his part of the town and lands of Batterstown otherwise Warrenstowne, and Woodcockstowne, Co. Meath. Proudstown, Clownestowne otherwise Clavenstowne, Loganhall, Tullamedan, Co.

---

[1] Abel Dally was Town Mayor of Galway. *Betham's Will Pedigrees*, Genealogical Office.

Meath. His house in Trim, Co. Meath. Kilcooley, Co. Meath. Silloge, Co. Meath. Wrightstowne, Monkeland, Great Finglastown otherwise Parkstowne and Greenbatter, Co. Meath. Ballygeeth, Co. Meath. Moynaloey, Co. Meath.

Witnesses : Richard Fenner, Michael Mitchell, Wm. Marshall, Wm. Fenner, all of Dublin, gents.

 Memorial witnessed by : John Falkiner, Kevans Street, Co. Dublin, Esq., Wm. Cuthbert, Dublin, gent.

90, 513, 65974   J. Daniell (seal)

591 CONYNGHAM, WILLIAM, Slane, Co. Meath, Esq.

 10 Oct. 1738. Codicil, not dated. Narrate, 2 pp., 12 April 1739.

His wife Constance Conyngham otherwise Middleton, extx. His brother Henry Conyngham. His aunt Mrs Catherine Conolly. His aunt Jane Bonnell. His aunt Mary Jones. His cousin Roger Jones, Elenor Jones his wife, Richard Jones his son. His cousin Richard Conyngham. His cousin Henry Conyingham.

James Howison, Dublin, Esq., Wm. Fenner, Dublin, gent., trustees. Col. Robert Dalway. Gabriel Johnston, Esq. Mr Andrew Fisher. Joshua Johnston, Esq. His servant Wm. McClure. His servant Bartholomew Cloud. His old servant Patrick McGuary. Legacies to poor of parish of St. Paul, and parish of St. Ann, Dublin. £200 " for the more effectual carrying into execution the Rev. Dean Swift's scheme for erecting and endowing a proper house for the reception of idiots and lunaticks and such like " or to Mercer's Hospital in Dublin.

His lands in B. Boylagh and Bannagh, Co. Donegal. Lands called The Point, Co. Donegal. His real estate in Manors of Maghriemore and Port Dungloe. Leasehold interests in Dublin city. Lands and a house in Manor of Slane leased by testator to John Blakely, gent. Mrs Anne Dixon, Dublin, widow.

Witnesses : Rev. John Maxwell, Slane, Co. Meath, clerk, Roger Jones, Slane, gent., Patrick Smith, Drogheda, apothecary, Phillip Purcell, Dublin, gent.

Codicil witnessed by : John Maxwell, Joseph Walsh, Faganstown, Co. Meath, gent., Roger Jones, Richard Fenner, junr., Dublin, gent.

Memorial witnessed by : John Maxwell, Richard Fenner.

95, 147, 66005   C. Conyngham (seal)

592 CROFTON, ANN als. WEBB, Lurgan, Co. Leitrim.
Not dated. Précis. ½ p., 10 May 1739.
Her son Duke Crofton, exor. Her son and daughter Warren. Lands of Park, Co. Meath. Lands farmed from Mr. FitzGerald [situation not mentioned].
Witnesses : Sarah O'Neill, wife of Charles O'Neill of Erew, gent. Henry Trumble, Mohill, gent., both in Co. Leitrim, Benjamin Meacom, servant to said Duke Crofton.
Memorial witnessed by : Crofton Warren, Dublin, gent., James Saunders, clerk to Wm. Parry, public notary.
94, 237, 66130   Duke Crofton (seal)

593 TALBOT, CHARLES, Curragheloe, Co. Wexford, Esq.
28 April 1739 [? 1730]. Narrate, ¾ p., 14 April, 1739.
His daughter Ann McAllen als. Murphy als. Talbot. His daughter Mary Burtonwood als. Talbot. His daughter Elenor Higinson als. Talbot. His daughter Elizabeth Redmond als. Talbot. His son Jno. Talbot. "To each of his grandchildren by his grandson Clifton Talbot lately deceased one shilling." His son Waller Talbot. Wm. Talbot of Ballynemony, William Browne of Ballyoriell, exors.
Witnesses : Walter Synnott, Ballaghbleake, George Annesly, Killpatrick, Cornelius Kenny of Corclough, all in Co. Wexford, gents.
Memorial witnessed by : Geo. Annesley, Walter Synott.
95, 207, 66188   Wm. Talbot (seal)

594 GRAYDON, ALEXANDER, Killishe, Co. Kildare.
17 Aug. 1732. Narrate, 1½ p., 22 May 1739.
His son Thomas Graydon. His daughter Jane Graydon. His son Richard Graydon. His grandson Alexr. Graydon son of said Richard Graydon. His son George Graydon, exor. His daughter Catherine Graydon. His daughter Avis Graydon.
Lands of Greenhill, Ballymee and Corbally. His lease of Killishee and Swordwallstown and the wood of Killishee. His estate of freehold in the Naas [? all in Co. Kildare].
Witnesses : James Savage, Dublin, gent., Joseph Landers, then of the same, gent., but now public notary, Henry Buckley, Dublin.
Memorial witnessed by : James Savage, Joseph Landers.
93, 460, 66341   Geo. Graydon (seal)
S

595 MAXWELL, ROBERT, Fellows Hall, parish of Tynan, Co.
    Armagh, D.D. 29 Dec. 1731. Narrate, ¾ p., 28 May 1739.
  His wife Ann Maxwell, extx. His nephew Robert Maxwell Leavense.
His nephew Capt. Robert Maxwell of Colledge Hall. His nephew John
Maxwell of Falkland.
  " The four towns of lands purchased from the late John Hamilton of
Callydon, Esq." [situation not mentioned]. His College leases.
  Witnesses : Wm. English, Armagh, notary public, James Gillmer,
Monoony, gent., both in Co. Armagh, John Elliott, then servant to
testator.
  Memorial witnessed by : James Smith and Bartholomew Delandre,
Dublin, gents.
  94, 298, 66419   A. Maxwell (seal)

596 WARREN, CHRISTOPHER, Dublin, upholder.
    26 March 1739. Narrate, ¾ p., 30 Feb. 1739/40.
  His wife Elinor Warren, exor. His brother Patk. Warren, exor.
His sister Mary Doyle als. Warren. His sister Rose Kean als. Warren,
her husband. His brother Michael Warren, gent. His sister Mary
Carter.
  Walter Codd, Dublin, merchant, and his wife Catherine Codd. Mary
Carroll, Dublin, wife of Christopher Carroll, her mother Mary Plunkett,
widow. Mrs Elizabeth Walkison als. Cooper.
  Witnesses : Bartholomew Fletcher, Dublin, linen draper, Margt.
Hand, wife of Wm. Hand of Stoneybatter, Co. Dublin, brewer, Jno.
Devall, Dublin, gent.
  Memorial witnessed by : James Davidson, Dublin, gent., Henry
Humphrey, clerk to George Mo[o]re, public notary in Dublin.
  93, 479, 66436   Elinor Warren (seal)

597 RUCK, JAMES, " citizen and mercer of London."
    2 Feb. 1737. Précis, ½ p., 6 June 1739.
  His three sons James Ruck, Wm. Ruck and George Ruck. Lanas
etc. both in England and Ireland and elsewhere.
  Witnesses : John Lightfoot, John Henry Merttins, junr., and
Richard Cholmeley, all of Threadneedle Street, London, gents.

Memorial witnessed by : John Henry Merttins, junr., Benj. Cook.
94, 322, 66521   James Ruck (seal)
                                  (James Ruck of London,
                                  one of the said devisees)

598 WALKER, JOHN, Smithstown, Co. Meath, gent.

29 June 1736. Narrate, ½ p., 26 June, 1739.

Thos. Shepheard, Dublin, merchant, Wm. Moore, Julianstown, gent., trustees. His sister Jane Shepheard, wife of said Thos. Shepheard.

Dawsland, parish and barony of Duleek, Co. Meath. Tythes of Killune, Co. Meath, expectant on the death of Mrs Catherine Draycott. Lands of Pillstown, parish of Colp, Co. Meath. Lease of Killtrogh, parish of Colp, Co. Meath, granted to him by Draycott Talbott, Esq., for 61 years from 1702. Leases of town and lands of Smithstown, Co. Meath.

Witnesses : Rev. Steuart Wilder, Vicar of Julianstown, Diocese of Meath, Julius Allen, Armilghton, Co. Meath, lately of Smithstown, yeoman, Patk. Kennedy, Julianstown, Co. Meath, smith.

Memorial witnessed by : Steuart Wilder, James Maculla, notary public.
94, 352, 66656   Jane Shepheard (seal)

599 SWIFT, MEADE, Lynn, Co. Westmeath, Esq.

5 Aug. 1738. Narrate, ¾ p., 28 June 1739.

Confirms marriage settlement 9 Jan. 1728 made on his then wife Frances, (extx.). His son Michael, his son Godwin (both under 21 years). His son Alexander. Said Alexander [Swift] and William Delgardno, Rahinn, Co. Westmeath, gent., to be exors. if said Frances should marry again. His son Thomas. " To his sons John Theophilus and Meade 5/- apiece." His three daughters Susanna, Mary and Elizabeth. Edward Thompson, clerk, vicar of Mullingar, Co. [? West] Meath, and Andrew Johnston, Littlemount, Co. Fermanagh, trustees.

Lands of Lynn, Co. Westmeath and his estate in the city of Dublin. Lands of Clonguff, Co. Westmeath.

Witnesses : Hugh Wilton, Catherinstown, Co. Westmeath, Esq., David Jones, Clonmoyle, said county, gent., Robert Johnston, Dublin, gent., one of the attornies of H.M. Court of Exchequer.

Memorial witnessed by : Robt. Johnston, John Pageitt, Dublin, gent.

94, 356, 66668   Frances Swift (seal)

600 INGOLDSBY, HENRY, Carrtown, Co. Kildare, Esq.

28 July 1731. Full, 8½ pp., 2 May 1739.

My wife Catherine Ingoldsby als. Phipps. My daughters Catherine (eldest) and Frances (second). To daughter Catherine £3,000 when 18 years or day of marriage. Arthur Blenerhassett and William Smyth, Dublin, Esqrs., trustees. My aunt Barbara Smyth. My cousin Mary Blenerhassett and my cousin Sarah Russell daughters of my aunt Buckworth deceased, and my cousin Mary Blenerhassett als. Pope daughter of my aunt Pope, deceased. My cousin Ralph Smyth son to said Barbara. My worthy friends and relations Major George Sawyer, London, Wm. Smyth and Arthur Blenerhassett, Dublin, Esqrs. exors., (said William Smyth to be guardian of testator's daughters).

Mary Cavenagh my wife's maid. Elizabeth Atkinson. Bryan McGuill my butler. John Williams my apprentice. My housekeeper Elizabeth Barry. Samuel Plant my now present steward at Carrtown.

My castles, towns, lands, tenements and hereditaments and all other my real estate. My dwelling house in Mary Street, Dublin.

Witnesses : Rev. Robert Bligh, Co. Cork, clerk, Bryan McGuill and John Mitchell, then servants to testator.

Memorial witnessed by : Bryan McGuill, Wm. Crookshank, Dublin, gent.

94, 361, 66698   Art. Blenr. Hassett (seal)

601 MALONE, HENRY, Litter, King's Co, Esq.

30 June 1739. Narrate, 1 p., 14 July 1739.

Reciting marriage articles 1736 made between Richard Malone of Baronstown, Co. Westmeath, Esq., and the testator concerning the marriage of Ann Malone the testator's youngest daughter with Richard Malone the younger, third son of said Richard Malone. Mary Malone, wife of testator, mentioned in another deed of same date. Said Richard Malone of Baronstown, trustee.

Manor of Cadamstown and Lordship of Ely O'Carroll and territory at Fircall being his estate of inheritance, and all other his real estate in King's Co. Two denominations called Coughes being part of the Manor of Cadamstowne. Fee farm lease of the Glebe and rectorial tythes of the parish of Litter under the title of Mr. Percy.

Witnesses : John Fergus, Dublin, Esq., Doctor in Physic, James Magan, Dublin, apothecary, Walter Barrett, Dublin, gent.

Memorial witnessed by : John Lewis, servant to said Richard Malone, Walter Barrett.

94, 386, 66811   Richd. Malone (seal)
                                                 of Baronstowne

602 BROWNLOW, WILLIAM, Brownlowsderry, Co. Armagh, Esq. 18 Jan. 1732. Full, part narrate, 3 pp., 11 Sept. 1739.

My wife the Lady Elizabeth Brownlow extx. and guardian to my children. My eldest daughter Elizabeth Brownlow now Lady Vesey. My second daughter Mary Brownlow. My third daughter Anne. My fourth daughter Lettice. My fifth daughter Isabella. (If estate of Brownlowsderry should descend to any of these daughters and their husbands they are to take name of Brownlow and use the Brownlow's coat of arms). My son Wm. Brownlow. My cousin McCormick. My sister Ann Ford. My cousin James Clinton. Thos. Clinton. My cousin Anne Barnaby, to her sister Dynes £10 which her husband owes me. My cousin Sarah Courtney als. Walsh. £10 to each of my cousin Arthur Jones's daughters. Henry O'Neill.

My estate of Richmond, Co. Armagh. My estate in Co. Monaghan and Louth. My house at St. Stephen's Green, Dublin. My estate of Brownlowsderry. Estates in counties of Louth and Monaghan which had lately come to him by death of his brother Philemon Brownlow, Esq.

Witnesses : Nicholas Merrifield, Dublin, gent., Christopher Weldon, same, gent., Felix Bingham, same, servant to testator.

Memorial witnessed by : Christopher Weldon, Richard Magenis, Dublin, gent.

95, 465, 67155   Elizth. Brownlow (seal)

603 MATHEWS, ALEXANDER, Lurgan, Co. Armagh. 15 April 1724. Narrate, ¾ p., 7 Nov. 1739.

Wife Margt. His daughter Jane Bell, extx. John Nicholson, Robert Hodson, and Mordecai Barrow, all of Lurgan, merchants, overseers.

His house or tenement in Lurgan lately in the possession of John Dowglass. Lands etc. in Co. Armagh and Co. Antrim.

Witnesses : Abm. Hoyle, Wm. Hutcheson and John Lancaster, all of Lurgan, merchants.

Memorial witnessed by : Hugh Carmichael, Dublin, gent. Andrew Carmichael, Dungannon, Co. Tyrone.

96, 229, 67398   Jane Bell (seal)

604 ANDERSON, JOHN, Cantitrinell [? Cantytrindle, Co. Fermanagh]. 4 April 1738. Narrate, ½ p., 28 Nov. 1739.

To his brother William after his father's decease the tate of Dring for ever. Wm. Anderson the elder.

Witnesses : Jno. Kearns, Barbara McIlroy and Christopher Hetherington, all of Dring, Co. Fermanagh.

Memorial witnessed by : Christopher Hetherington, Robt. Johnston, Dublin, gent.

97, 131, 67625   Wm. Anderson (seal)

605 GRIFFIN, MARGARET, Dublin, widow.

2 June 1732. Narrate, ½ p., 4 Dec. 1739.

Her daughter Margaret Bennett otherwise Griffin, extx. Her house in Katherine Street, Dublin, held under Mr Jos. Litton. Her other houses.

Witnesses : John Bermingham, Skinner's Alley, in the Liberties of Thomas Court and Donore, Co. Dublin, narrow weaver, Nathaniel Thelwell, Pimlico, in the Liberties aforesaid, narrow weaver, Thos. Halgan, late of Ash Street, suburbs of city of Dublin, narrow weaver, deceased.

Memorial witnessed by : Thos. Walker, Dublin, distiller, Arthur Shepheard, Dublin, public notary.

98, 78, 67688   Margaret Bennett (seal)

606 WALLIS, HENRY, Drishane, Co. Cork, Esq.

29 Oct. 1734. Narrate, ½ p., 6 Dec. 1739.

His son and heir Thomas Wallis. His second son Henry Wallis. His grandson Henry Wallis. His grandson Geo Wallis. All his real and personal estate.

Witnesses : Rev. Stanley Craven, Mt. Leader, Co. Cork, clerk, Thomas Bryde, Millstreet, Co. Cork, innholder, Francis Hillgrove, Lackabane, Co. Cork, farmer.

Memorial witnessed by : Francis Hillgrove, Daniel McCarthy, Cork, gent.

99, 21, 67718   John Wallis (seal)

---

607 NEWMAN, DILLON, Dromineen, Co. Cork, Esq.

11 May 1733. Full, 2 pp., 14 Dec. 1739.

My son Charles Newman. My son Richard Newman, exor. My son Adam Newman (married). My son Thos. Newman. I gave . . . my daughter Elizabeth Dunscombe 1,200 guineas on her marriage . . . my daughter Susanna Graham £800 on her marriage . . . my daughter Dorothea White £1,100 on her marriage. My grandson Wm. Dunscombe. My grandson Richd. Dunscombe. My granddaughter Mary Dunscombe.

Lands of Ballygriggin als. Ballyregan, Donevally als. Dunevally, B. Fermoy, Co. Cork. Lands of Cloghanemore, Cloghanebegg, Lisangle, Corellis, Gortemucula and Drominagh, in B. West Carbury, Co. Cork.

Witnesses : Rev. Benezar Murdock, Killpadder, Co. Cork, John Strange, Dromehane, Co. Cork, gent., Geo. Foot, senr., Kellveliton, Co. Cork, gent.

Memorial witnessed by : Benezar Murdock, Wm. Thomas, Newberry, Co. Cork, gent.

96, 302, 67792   Richd. Newman (seal)

---

608 COLLES, DUDLEY, Collesford, Co. Sligo, gent.

30 Dec. 1736. Narrate, 1 p., 8 Feb. 1739.

Reciting an indenture tripartite 2 Jan. 1733 made between (1) said testator and Alice Prendergast als. Colles als. Perse, (2) Rev. Henry Wright, Loughrea, Co. Galway, clerk and Denis Daly, Raford, said county, Esq., and (3) Pierce Prendergast of Ramore, said county, gent. Articles of intermarriage 15 Nov. 1734 (made on said Dudley's intermarriage with his wife Dorcas Colles als. Birne) made between Bryan Birne of Creggs, Co. Sligo, gent. and said testator.

Anthony Colles, then living near Castleconnor, B. of Tierieragh, Co. Sligo.

Lands of Collesford, Maghrymore and Castlegall, Co. Sligo. Lands in Co. Wexford, to wit Ballybranon, Ballybrittas, Tumfarny, Carrickginnanee and Rathnoon.

Witnesses : James Crofton, Dublin, gent., one of the Attornies of His Majesty's Court of King's Bench in Ireland, Hugh Shiel, Doonally B. Carbry, Co. Sligo, physician, Gilbert Stanley, Drimcormick, B. Boyle, Co. Roscommon, gent.

Memorial witnessed by : James Crofton, Arthur Price, Hogg Hill, Dublin, apothecary.

94, 547, 68084   Phil. Birne (seal)
                                                       (a legatee)

609 CAIRNES, WILLIAM, Killifaddy, Co. Tyrone, Esq.
    15 Dec. 1739. Narrate, ½ p., 11 Feb. 1739/40.

His wife Lydia Cairnes, extx. His real estate in Manor of Killifaddy, Co. Tyrone, etc. to John Elliot, Morn, Co. Down, gent. (exor.) and his heirs male and female, failing such heirs to James Elliot, provided that John Elliot and they that succeed him in his real estate should be for ever thereafter surnamed Cairnes.

Witnesses : Andrew Bailie, Stewartstown, apothecary, David Johnstoun, Mullybeany, gent., and John Renwick, notary public in Clogher, all Co. Tyrone.

Memorial witnessed by : David Johnstoun, James Saunders, clerk to Wm. Parry, Dublin, public notary.

99, 95, 68102   John Eliot Cairnes (seal)

610 JOHNSTON, HUGH, Redemon, Co. Down, gent.
    20 Nov. 1737. Narrate, ¾ p., 15 Feb. 1739.

His wife Elizabeth, exor. His son Arthur Johnston. His son William, His daughters [? daughters of testator]. Mr James Trail, Marybrook. Mr David Boyd, Downpatrick, exors. and trustees.

Town and lands of Redemon, Crevycarnonas, Glasshouse and Donbegg, Co. Down. His interest in lands of Ballywillen, Clontagh, Dromgiven and moiety of Ballyhacamore, Co. Down.

Witnesses : Wm. McCormick, schoolmaster and Wm. Murdagh, farmer, both of Redemon, Samuel Lightbody, Killmore, farmer, all Co. Down.

Memorial witnessed by : Wm. McCormick, Wm. Murdagh.
99, 103, 68142   Elizth. Johnston (seal)

611 DOYLE, HENRY, Kilcashen, Co. Kildare, gent.
   12 Dec. 1739. Narrate, 1 p., 23 Feb. 1739/40.
His then wife Violetta Doyle, exor. His son George Doyle. His son
Wm. Doyle. His son Henry Doyle. His daughter Christian Doyle
(children of Violetta). His children Gart, Henry, Jno., Mary and
Elizabeth Doyle by his first wife Elizabeth Doyle deceased.
His farm of Kilcashen held from Jas. Dalyell, Esq. His interest in
farm etc. of Ballyvane, Co. Kildare.
Witnesses : Saml. Slicer, Jno. Ford, Henry Levingston and Jno.
Boyd, gent., all of Dublin.
Memorial witnessed by : Michael Argent, Jas. Saunders both of
Dublin, gents.
97, 247, 68187   Violetta Doyle (seal)

612 ROWLEY, PHILIP, Saggard, Co. Dublin, farmer.
   29 Aug. 1739. Narrate, ½ p., 8 March 1739/40.
His wife Bridget Rowley. His son Peter Rowley. His son Thomas
Rowley.
Farm of Carranbee [situation not mentioned]. His dwelling house
and concerns in Saggard.
Witnesses : James Fallan, Killald, Co. Mayo, gent., Dennis Hanlon,
Saggard, yeoman, Thomas Mathews, Saggard, weaver.
Memorial witnessed by : James Fallan, Wm. Nowland, clerk to
Thos. Mulock, Dublin, public notary.
99, 126, 68276   Petter Rowley (seal)

613 CRAGGS, JANE, wife of John Craggs, Cork city, gent.
   22 Dec. 1737. Narrate, 1 p., 8 March, 1739.
Her then husband the said John Craggs. Her sister Eliz. Boyle
[? als. Cartwright—see next abstract].
Dwellinghouse, garden, etc. situate without Water Gate of city of
Cork set by lease to her father John Cartwright late of said city, gent.
deceased, by Alderman George Wright. Holding in N.E. quarter of
city of Cork.

Witnesses : Elizabeth Warren, Cork, widow, Margrett Rickotts, wife of Josias Rickotts, Cork, mariner, Charles Berry, Cork, apothecary, Thomas Hill, Cork, gent.

Memorial witnessed by : Chas. Berry, Thomas Hill.

99, 127, 68279   John Craggs (seal)

614 CAREY, ELIZABETH orse. BOYLE orse. CARTWRIGHT, Cork city. 10 March 1738. Narrate, ¾ p., 8 March 1739.

Her relation Mr Thomas Cartwright of the Navy Office, London, exor. Her brother-in-law John Craggs, Cork, gent., exor.

Her real estate in Hannover Street, Cork, said holding being set by Alderman George Wright deceased to her father John Cartwright late of Cork, gent., deceased. Farm at Killigrohan. Holdings near Wisdom's Lane, Cork.

Witnesses : Mathias Smith, Cork, gent., Catherine Berry, wife of Charles Berry, Cork, apothecary and said Charles Berry.

Memorial witnessed by : Charles Berry, Thomas Hill, Cork, gent.

99, 128, 68280   John Craggs (seal)

615 JONES, ROBERT, Mountkennedy, Co. Wicklow, Esq.

16 Aug. 1739. Précis, ½ p., 20 March 1739/40.

His cousin Mrs Elizabeth Barker of Grafton Street, Dublin, extx. His real and personal estate.

Witnesses : Ambrose O'Neill, Esq., George Spence, brewer, John Evans, gent., all of Dublin.

Memorial witnessed by : Bartholomew Delandre, Dublin, gent., John Coppinger, Dublin, Esq.

98, 264, 68359   Elizth. Barker (seal)

616 NASON, WILLIAM, Cork, merchant.

31 March 1740. Narrate, ½ p., 23 April 1740.

His wife Huldah Nason and his brother Jno. Nason of Mellifontstown, Co. Cork, Esq., exors. His [testator's] son William Nason.

Lands etc. of Rahenitty orse. Rahenitigg and Disert, B. Barrymore, Co. Cork.

Witnesses : Joseph Deyos, Cork, merchant, Wm. Cumins, Cork, cooper, Richd. Kinefick, Cork, butter buyer.

Memorial witnessed by : Joseph Deyos, Wm. Cumins.

97, 323, 68523   Huldah Nason (seal)

617 JERVIS, JOHN, Rosscorroll, King's Co., gent.
3 March 1709/9. Narrate, ¾ p., 28 April 1740.

His eldest son Charles Jervis. His son John Jervis, exor. His son Martin Jervis. Testator's brother Wm. Jervis late of Battell, county of Sussex. His daughter Mary Kent. All his real estate in the kingdom of Ireland.

Witnesses : Randolph Nott, Dublin, Ebenr. Nott of same, bakers, John Brady, of same, hatter.

Memorial witnessed by : Richd. Cossiens (Cossens), Tullavin, Co. Limerick, gent., Jonas Percy, son of Francis Percy of Ballintemple, King's Co., gent.

99, 195, 68584   John Jervis (seal)

618 KANE, Colonel RICHARD, Carrickfergus, in province of Ulster and Kingdom of Ireland. 29 May 1735. Narrate, ½ p., 8 May 1740.

His cousin german John Dobbin, eldest son of his uncle James Dobbin deceased. Said Jno. Dobbin, since deceased, his sole exor.

His estate in and near Carrickfergus. The estate of Dromcashell, Co. Louth.

Witnesses : Rowley Godfrey, captain in testator's Regiment at Minorca, Rev. Alexr. Cornwall, chaplain to said Regiment, and Phineas Jno. Edgar, ensign in said Regiment, which said Regiment now lyes at Minorca and belongs to Brig. Reid.

Memorial witnessed by : Rowley Godfrey, Rev. Alexr. Cornwall.

97, 374, 68757   Arthur Craven (seal)
                                                  London, gent, exor. and
                                                  residuary legatee of said
                                                  John Dobbin

619 BARKER, RALPH, Kevins Port, county of the city of Dublin, gent. 9 May 1740. Narrate, 1½ p., 13 June 1740.

His nephew Thos. Barker, son of his brother Oliver Barker deceased. Wm. Barker, son of his brother John Barker deceased. His niece

Mary Blackburn als. Tate, daughter of his sister Geraldine Barker als. Blackburn als. Burby deceased. His niece Geraldine Blackburn, daughter of his sister Geraldine. His niece Mary Barker, daughter of his brother John Barker deceased.

Money owed to Mrs Elizabeth Denham. His servant Mary Linton als. Jones. His friend John Dexter, Dublin, gent., and Thos. Thomas, Kevins Port, Esq., exors.

Two leases from Wm. Usher Esq., of ground in and about Kevins Port mortgaged to Mrs Frances Norton.

Witnesses : Wm. Brownly, Dublin, apothecary, John Katherns, Dublin, public notary.

Memorial witnessed by : John Katherns, John White, Dublin, merchant.

98, 432, 69049   John Dexter (seal)

620 FORD, EDWARD, Island Bridge, Co. Dublin, Esq.

10 Sept. 1738.   Full, ½ p., 17 June 1740.

My wife Mary Ford, extx.   My brother Thos. Ford.   My sister Elizabeth Ford.   My estate and personal goods.

Witnesses : Wm. Bennett, Ter. Farrill and Elizabeth Cash, all then servants of testator.

Memorial witnessed by : Wm. Bennett, Thos. Ford, brother of testator, Jno. Scott, Limerick, gent.

97, 444, 69079   Mary Ford (seal)

621 HUTCHESON, FRANCIS, Bishop of Down and Connor.

17 April 1736.   Narrate, 1 p., 19 June 1740.

His wife Ann.   His son Thos. Hutcheson.   Samuel Hutcheson, senr., Esq., his brother, and the Rev. Samuel Hutcheson, junr., of Rasharken, Dean of Dromore, son of the said Samuel Hutcheson the elder [trustees].

His dwelling house and demesne lands in the town of Portglenone [Co. Antrim or Co. Londonderry], lands and house in Portglenone village, and the mill and lands in lease to Rev. Alex. Leslie and Francis Lorimar.   Lands etc. of Garvaghy and Mullinsallagh in Largry, Co. Antrim.   Glenone, Co. Derry.   Ballintaugh otherwise Ballinittry, Co. Antrim.   Ballybegg and Carnary [? both Co. Antrim].   The three town-lands of Ballyneveagh otherwise Staffordstowne, Killifad and Ballurvereagh in the Feveagh, Co. Antrim. House in Bow Street, Dublin. Lands of Drumaglish, Co. Down. His lands etc. purchased from Roger Haddock in Co. Down. The eight town and lands in the Feveagh, Co. Antrim, known by the names of Ardcloan otherwise Arttone, Bally-cloghan otherwise Ballyclogan, Ballyhirgan otherwise Ballylurgan, Derrygowan, Drumbo, Carnorn, Rahahan and Ballytamnaderry otherwise Tamnederry. Slevanagh, Drumra, and the farms in the occupation of Hugh Boyd and Quinton O'Cahan. Lands of Ballynefe in the Largy [? Co. Antrim]. Rents and profits of Ballyronan als. Ballyconelly [? Co. Antrim], Cregnakeeragh and Leinnekerry [? Limnaharry, Co. Antrim].

Witnesses : John Humfrey, Esq., Daniel Wright, and Francis Godfrey, gent., all of Dublin.

Memorial witnessed by : John Humfrey (Humphry), Alexr. Hamilton, Dublin, Esq.

96, 488, 69108   Saml. Hutcheson (seal)

                 (the younger)

622 PARSONS, DAME ELIZABETH als. ST. GEORGE, wife of Sir Wm. Parsons, of Parsonstowne, King's Co., Bart. 26 Nov. 1739. Narrate, 2½ pp., 25 June 1740.

Reciting indenture 22 March 1727 to which Wm. Parsons, second son of Wm. Parsons, Esq., deceased, who was the eldest son of said Sir William Parsons, was a party and a deed 7 Jan. 1728 mentioning property which by the death of Emilia Carleton als. St. George descended to the said Elizabeth Parsons the testatrix.

Piggott Parsons, third grandson of said Sir Wm. Parsons, George Parsons his fourth grandson, Thomas Parsons his fifth grandson and William Parsons his second grandson.

Witnesses : Rev. George Warburton, Castletown, King's Co., clerk, Rev. Robert Pinsent, Athy, Co. Kildare, clerk, George Head, Parsonstown, gent.

Memorial witnessed by : George Head, John Humphrey, Rushall, Queen's Co., gent.

99, 297, 69171   P. Parsons (seal)

                 (Pigott Parsons, third

                 grandson of said Sir

                 Wm. Parsons).

623 PORTER, EDWARD, Tulligg, Co. Cork, gent.
      17 Dec. 1735. Narrate, 1¼ p., 15 July 1740.
   His wife Ursilla Porter, extx. His brother Robert Porter. His brother Thos. Porter. His nephew Richd. Porter. His nephew Thos. Porter. His brother-in-law Alexr. Walton and his wife and children. His cousin Jno. Dorman, son of Richd. Dorman said John to take surname of Porter if he inherits testator's estate. Richard Dorman junr., son of said Richard, a like condition. Said Richard Dorman and Robert Atkins, Esq., overseers.
   His leasehold lands of Ballynaboy. His real estate in lands of Lissillea and the mills near Ballincassige, all in Co. Cork.
   Witnesses : Jno. Gillman, Curryheen, south liberties of Cork city, gent., Edidy Bay, Ballincranig, in the same liberties, spinster, David FitzGerald, Tulligg, yeoman.
   Memorial witnessed by : Jno. Gillman, Anthony Lane, clerk to Russell Wood, Cork, gent.
100, 2, 69336   Jno. Dorman (seal)

624 KELLY, DENIS, Dublin, formerly of Aghrane, Co. Galway,
      Esq. 1734. Narrate, 2½ pp., 6 Aug. 1740
   His wife Hon. Mary Kelly als. Bellew. His dear child Frances Arabella Kelly deceased. Kinsman (his cousin) John Kelly of Clonline, Co. Galway, Esq. The children of John Kelly late of Clonlyne, Esq., father of the said John Kelly (said John Kelly their brother). His kinsman Denis Daly of Raford, Co. Galway, Esq. His niece Helena Kelly als. Burke, to her eldest son Wm. Kelly £2,000 when 21 years. To his niece's eldest daughter Kate Kelly £1,000 when 21 years or on marriage. His niece's second son Denis Kelly. His niece's second daughter Margt. Kelly (unmarried). His niece's third and youngest boy—Kelly. The orphans of his kinsman Colla Kelly of Cornanarif. His kinswomen Sarah and Mary Kelly in Channell Row. To Peter Kelly then in Lord Dillon's Regt. in France £200 if living. Luke Kelly then or late in the Horse or Dragoons in England. His kinsman Francis Plunkett a surveyor who lately married his kinswoman Mary Nettervill. His godson Denis Kelly, eldest son of John Kelly of Clonlyne. The eldest daughter of the said John Kelly. " £20 paid by me to his eldest son Roger Kelly deceased at his going to Jamaica."
   Con Kelly in the mountain of Slinemurry. Allen Doyle son of old Nells. Bartle Kelly, son of Teigue Keogh Kelly, then with Bartle

Keogh perriwigmaker in Dublin. Wood sold to Alderman Evans of Kilkenny, and Mr Conny, their bonds lodged with Mr. McGuire of Ormond Quay. Said Denis Daly and John Kelly and his nephew Daniel Kelly of Turrock, Co. Roscommon, exors.

A real estate which formerly belonged to his father and other ancestors [situation not mentioned]. Real estate which the testator had purchased in counties of Louth, Meath, Galway and Roscommon. Lands of Bellagare, 900 acres Strafford's Survey. Clonruffe in half B. Killeghan, Co. Galway. Cartroncoila [? in said B.]. Leases he had from Edmond Donelan [situation not mentioned]. Lisnalane (Lisnalaune) [? Lisnalannow], B. Athlone, Co. Roscommon. "Arrears due to him on Lisnalane on [? to] Bryan McFarragh's heir. . . . £40 to said Bryan McFarragh's eldest son then living in consideration for any title . . . he might have to some acres in Knockbryan Gorue." Gortinelagh. Newtown and Ballyregan part of Castletown Bellew, Sherifs Park part of the same, Donoughmore, 834 acres in all purchased under Lord Bellew's Act of Parliament by Denis Kelly, Esq. Moiety of Thomastown, Little Mill, Dunbryne, in B. Roch, Co. Louth. Mooretown, Co. Meath.

Witnesses to will and schedule of lands therein recited : Theobald Dillon, Dublin, merchant, Michael Dillon his son, Laurence Saule, Dublin, merchant.

Memorial witnessed by : Michael Argent, Bartholomew Delandre, clerks to Wm. Parry, Dublin, public notary.

John Kelly (seal)

99, 341, 69450

Danl. Kelly (seal)

625 KELLY, DENIS, Aghrane, Co. Galway.

Codicils dated 24 May, 27 May 1740. Full, 2¼ pp., 6 Aug. 1740. Will (made some time ago) lodged in hands of my kinsman Denis Daly of Raford, Co. Galway, Esq., in which there are legacies etc. to Wm. Kelly, Catherine Kelly, Margaret Kelly and Denis Kelly my grand-nephews and grand-nieces. My grand-nephew James Kelly. Denis Kelly his brother. My niece Hellen Kelly [their mother]. My kinsman John Kelly of Cloonlyon, Co. Galway, Esq. The Rt. Hon. Lady Honoria Kelly. My niece Helen Kelly of Turrock. Denis Daly of Raford, John Kelly of Cloonlyon and Daniel Kelly of Turrock, Co. Roscommon, Esqrs., exors. Wm. Kelly my grand-nephew, the said

Daniel Kelly's (of Turrock) eldest son. Denis Kelly my grand-nephew, second brother to the said Wm. Kelly. My grand-nephew James Kelly, third brother to the said William.

Money lodged in Thomas Dillons & Cos. hands in Dublin. My lodgings in Surgeon Kelly's house. Mr Michael Dalton of Ratharrd (debtor). Money lent to said John Kelly for the use of Rt. Hon. Latitia Burke. Sir Thos. Taylor's mortgage. My tenants of Cloonruffe [Co. Galway]. My tenants of Tullymukenagh and Cloonakelleggy [? Cloonakilleg, Co. Roscommon]. My moiety of Thomastown, Little Mills and Dunbin in Co. Louth, purchased from Hon. Miss Bellew my wife's sister.

Witnesses : Dennis Farrell, Dublin, Esq., John O'Berne, Athlone, Co. Roscommon and Rickd. Burke, Ballinamore, Co. Galway, both Doctors in Physic.

Memorial witnessed by : James Saunders, Bartholomew Delandre, clerks to Wm. Parry, Dublin, public notary.

99, 343, 69451   Dens. Kelly (seal)
                                              (the exor.)

626   HOOPE, JOHN, Lurgan, Co. Armagh, merchant.
        20th day of second month commonly called April 1739, codicil
        25 April 1739. Full, 14 pp., 9 Aug. 1740.

Settlement made unto my son Edward Hoope upon his marriage with Sarah Willcocks. Settlement made to my son Robert upon his marriage with Sarah the daughter of James Lark of London. " My sons Edward Hoope and Robert Hoope deceased."[1] (" My son Edward Hoope deceased " mentioned in codicil). Henry Pemberton, Dublin, Robt. Clibborn, Dublin, merchant, my son-in-law John Clibborn of Mote, John Turner of Lurgan and John Handcock and Jacob Handcock of Lisburn, trustees. My daughter Abigail Strettell, Thomas Strettell her husband. My daughter Hannah Petticrew, John Petticrew her husband. My daughter Sarah Clibborn, John Clibborn her husband. My son Joshua Hoope (under age). My son James Hoope (a minor), apprentice to Robert Clibborn of Dublin. My three daughters Abigail Strettle, Hannah Petticrew and Sarah Clibborn and my sons James and Joshua Hoope. My father Robert Hoope by his last will left me £100 to be equally divided among all my children. My sister Sarah Walker,

---

[1] Robert Hoope's Will was proved 19 October 1737. *Betham's Will Pedigees.* Genealogical Office.

widow and relict of John Walker. My daughter Abigail Strettell's children. My son Edward Hoope's children. My son-in-law John Petticrew of Dublin, merchant.

Thos. Truman, Lurgan, linendraper. My servant Elizabeth Smith. James [? Averdue] junr. and James Adair [? testator's agents or managers of Dromanfy als. Cockhill, and the mills there].

Tenement in Lurgan wherein John Turner now lives ; another in which Samuel Barrow dwells subject to ground rent payable to William Brownlowe, etc. and to payment of £2 yearly for the ground rent of the Quakers Meeting House in Lurgan, my said trustees to keep the said Meeting House, front and back houses, garden, graveyard and gate and wall park always in good repair. My leases of Derricloan and Derrimore. My cozen Robt. Hoope, his farm in Kilmore, Co. Down is to devolve to me after the decease of my said cousin Robert and his present wife Ann. Lands of Derrycloan, parish of Aghagallan, Co. Antrim, Derrimore, (same parish and county). The house which I now live in in Lurgan and also that house which I bought which was Joseph Robinson's adjoining thereto, and land and lease of Aikins Park als. Hoope Hill [? in Lurgan] all held from William Brownlowe, also land in Aghneilvy [? Co. Tyrone]. My two thirds of the bleach yard held from John Usher of Bellymaceteer in the parish of Magheralin, Co. Down, by Jacob Turner for one third. Lands of Derinragibbugh (Derimagibbogh) and Dericarib and chief rent of Clanmackall all in Manor of Richmond, parish of Tartaraghan, Co. Armagh. All my boats and tackle. John Ralphston, [? tenant of] Dermia [see later— ? John Ralston of Derinra]. Lands of Clanchore, Dericaran (Derricarran) Derikeevan [Derrykeevan] and Derrykeeran in Manor of Richmond, parish of Tartaraghan, Co. Armagh, and Canoncal (Canoneal) [Canon-eill] and Timulkenny, parish of Drumcree in said Manor. House in town of Lurgan wherein Alex. Campbell now lives. Lands of Knock-nashane- [? Co. Armagh] held from Wm. Brownlowe leased to Robert Clarke of Lurgan. Firing for tenants out of Drumharriff moss [Co. Armagh], (William Brownlowe's tenants in Unshinagh to get their share out of the moss of Derrykevan or Derrykeran). Firing for my dwellinghouse, miller's house and kiln in Dromanfy als. Cock Hill in the manor of Richmond [Co. Armagh] to come out of Clanmacash "when any stop may happen " to Derykeevan. £5 to poor of people called Quakers belonging to the Lurgan Meeting. £5 to the Poor House Keeper and inhabitants in the manor of Brownlows Derry. I have running accounts in England with Jonathan Gurnal & Sons,

T

merchants in London, James Bolt of Bristol and Robert Fielding of Manchester.

An " Account of the rents and how the legatees are to pay " follows, ending with advice to his sons James and Joseph. The majority of the lands already listed above appear again in this account, but there is some additional information, as follows : John Turner to pay £5 half yearly for the tenements called Hoopes where he lives. Rents etc. for·the house and tenement where Samuel Barrow lives to be paid held yearly by Friends of the Meeting. Particulars of rents etc. out of Clanmakate. I hold from Thos. Geer beyond Charlemount a piece of land which was Alexander Mathews [situation not mentioned] . . . very bad and very dear. Lease of Aghnacloy [? in Lurgan], leased from Wm. Brownlowe. John Ralston and his wife to live in Derinra and take care of sons James and Joshua Hoope's affairs. Desires " best endeavors may be taken to continue and keep the Post Office [? in Lurgan] with the same care and faithfullness as I have held it for about forty years."

Witnesses : James Ogle, John Crooks, Lurgan, merchants, William Warren, Miragh, gent., Lawrence Bellew, agent to Mr Brownlowe.

Memorial witnessed by : James Thomas, Henry Chritchly, Dublin, gents.

100, 33, 69469   John Petticrew (seal)

627 STEUART, CHARLES, Dublin, Esq.

8 April 1740. Narrate, 1¾ p., 9 Oct. 1740.

His wife Sarah Steuart. A settlement made upon his first marriage. His daughter Rebecca (unmarried) ; her husband and children if she comes into possession of estates to take surname of Steuart. His son William Steuart. His brother-in-law Benjn. Gregory, clerk, his nephew Steuart Wilder, clerk, Leslie Corry, Esq., and testator's wife Sarah Steuart trustees and exors.

Monaghanoose [Co. Cavan], Dromenespick, Tonyfole [Tonyfoyle, Co. Cavan], Dromeir, lands of Drutamon [Co. Cavan] and Carnelinchy, Baillyburrow [? Bailieborough, Co. Cavan]. Houses in Thomas Street, Dublin. Carnagarve, Fartadreen, Lurganveel, Invergarroge [Invyarroge], Cordoagh, Cavett, Killnacreevy, Drumcro, Drumavaddy and Cornameighan, Co. Cavan. Mount Steuart, Dunmucky and chiefries in the county of Dublin. Gibstown, Co. Meath.

Witnesses : Wm. Hamilton, clerk to Benjamin Johnston, public notary, Dublin, Edward Sterling, public notary, Dublin, and said Benjamin Johnston.

Memorial witnessed by : Benj. Johnston, Ancketill Moutray, Lieut. in the Regt. of Foot commanded by Brig. Gen. John Guiess.

99, 400, 69753   Sarah Steuart (seal)

628 MADDEN, RICHARD, Fishamble Street, Dublin, merchant.
     4 March 1739. Full 1½ p., 20 Oct. 1740.

My son William Madden. My son John Madden. My son-in-law John Stones, of Dublin, chirurgeon, sole exor. My daughter Alice Stones, wife of said John Stones. My daughter Ann Wrightson, her husband Edward Wrightson. My grandson Richard Stones son of said John. My daughter Sarah Madden (unmarried).

My share or half part of the ship Surprize. Houses, lands etc. in Abby Street, Strand Street, Dame Street and Essex Street, Dublin. My holding in Fishamble Street, Dublin.

Witnesses : Terence Carroll, Dublin, vintner, James McCaddon, then clerk to Wm. Sumner, public notary in Dublin, and said Wm. Sumner.

Memorial witnessed by : Thos. Martin, Dublin, gent., Wm. Sumner.

100, 114, 69804   John Stones (seal)

629 WHEELWRIGHT, RICHARD, Clampclone, Queen's Co.,
     farmer. 15 Feb. 1727/8. Précis, ½ p., 12 Nov. 1740.

His wife Elizabeth Wheelwright (since also deceased), extx. His farm of Clampclone. His freehold in England lying in Co. of Cumberland and parish and town of Bridechurch.

Witnesses : Stephen McGachin, Burros, Queen's Co., John Whitley, lrey, said county, Joseph Tiffin, Ballyfin, said county.

Memorial witnessed by : Joseph Tiffin, Henry Whyte, Dublin, gent.

101, 84, 69971   Joseph Tiffin (seal)
                     (exor. to said Elizabeth W.)

630 KENNAN, THOMAS, Diswellstown, Co. Dublin, farmer.
     16 Dec. 1740. Codicil 26 Dec. 1740. Narrate, 1¼ p., 31 Dec. 1740.

Mary Bell otherwise Kennan his wife. His son-in-law Malcom McNeal and his daughter Christian Kennan otherwise McNeal. His grand-daughter Christian McNeal (under ten years of age). His son Thos. Kennan. His son Robert Kennan. Rev. Thos. Wall, vicar of Castleknock, and his son Thos., exors. His sons James, Andrew and Benjamin Kennan.

Lands of Diswellstown held from Simon Luttrell, Esq. To George Kennan his lease of Ashtown and Irishtown [Co. Dublin]. Lands of Astagobb [Co. Dublin] purchased from Abraham Sherigley, Sarah Sherigley, George Robinson and Ann Robinson his wife, and lease held from Dean and Chapter of Christ Church of the lands of Stagub otherwise Castagobb otherwise Astagobb [situation not mentioned. ? Co. Dublin]. Lands of Cornerstown, Co. Meath.

Witnesses : Jno. Price, nephew to testator, Pat. Keife, Diswellstown, labourer, Richard Rickisson, Dublin, gent.

Codicil witnessed by : Richd. Rickisson, Bartholomew Delandre, clerk to Wm. Parry, Dublin, notary public and said Wm. Parry.

Memorial witnessed by : Richd. Rickisson, Bartholomew Delandre.

102, 210, 70424   Thos. Kennan (seal)

631 MOODY, SAMUEL, Limerick, perukemaker.

15 July 1726. Précis, a few lines, 13 Nov. 1740.

To his mother Ann Deaves his lands etc. without West Water Gate in the county of the city of Limerick.

Witnesses : Jno. Rawlins, clothier, John Epwell, clothier, Joseph Evritt, perukemaker, all of Limerick.

Memorial witnessed by : Jno. Scott, Limerick, gent., George Bell, his clerk.

Jacob Deaves (seal)
Limerick, clothier

102, 268, 70713   Ann Deaves (seal)
his wife

632 MOODY, WILLIAM, Limerick, clothier.

15 July 1726. Précis, a few lines, 13 Feb. 1740.

To his mother Ann Deaves lands etc. without West Gate in the county of the city of Limerick.

Witnesses : Joseph Evritt, perukemaker, John Rawlines, clothier, John Epwell, clothier, all of Limerick.

Memorial witnessed by : Jno. Scott, Limerick, gent., George Bell, his clerk.

Jacob Deaves (seal)
Limerick, clothier
Ann Deaves (seal)
his wife

101, 212, 70714

633 BAMBER, RICHARD, Dublin, gent.
30 May 1729. Codicil 15 July 1731. Narrate, 2¼ p., 24 March 1740.

His eldest son Thomas Bamber, exor. His son Paul Bamber. His daughter Elizabeth Watkins. His grandson Richard Brown son of his then late daughter Hannah Brown deceased (if in possession of his real estate to take the surname of Bamber). His brother John Bamber. Nathaniel Kane, Dublin, alderman, and Ralph Card, Dublin, gent., trustees.

Town and lands Ardcaffe [Ardcalf], Faganstown, Braystown, Bryanstown, and Shalvanstown, B. Slane, Co. Meath and all other his lands in said county. Houses, holdings, etc. on West side of Caple Street and in Black Lyon Court, and North side Abby Street, suburbs of city of Dublin. His front house or tenement known by the sign of the Indian Queen in West side of Caple Street, leased from James Cottingham. A dwelling house in Caple Street, Simon Alcock, merchant, lessee. Three houses in Back Lane, Dublin. His houses in and about the town of Castledermot [Co. Kildare]. House in Eustace Street [Dublin].

Witnesses : David Woodside, cabinetmaker and Joseph Marriott, gent., both late of the city of Dublin, Thos. Hartley, Dublin, gent.

Codicil witnessed by : Margt. Campsie, late of Dublin, spinster, Michael Heynds, Dublin, coachman, Matt Quinn, late of the said city, butler to testator.

Memorial witnessed by : Robt Wilson, Denis Moore, both of Dublin, gents.

103, 133, 70944   Eliz. Watkins (seal)

634 PUREFOY, WILLIAM, Purefoy's Place otherwise Clonbullock, King's Co., Esq. 7 March 1740. Full, ½ p., 22 April 1741.

My cousin Wm. Purefoy of Clanivoe, King's Co., Esq., exor. My daughter Ann Purefoy. Mrs Hannah Talbot. Lands of Clonbullock otherwise Purefoy's Place.

Witnesses : John Taylor, Ahana, King's Co., gent., Thos. Watson, Deryganon, King's Co., gent., Richd. Homan, Purefoy's Place.

Memorial witnessed by : Richd. Homan, Mathew Pageitt, Dublin, gent.

102, 358, 71134   Wm. Purefoy (seal)

635 PUREFOY, WILLIAM, Purefoy's Place otherwise Clonbullock, King's Co., Esq. 17 April 1741. Narrate, ½ p., 22 April 1741.

His cousin Wm. Purefoy of Clonivoe, King's Co., Esq., exor. His daughter Ann Purefoy then in England. Lands of Clonbullock otherwise called Purefoy's Place, King's Co.

Witnesses : James Hickey, Purefoy's Place, parish clerk, Richd. Homan, Purefoy's Place, gent., Chas. Norton, Clonbullock, farmer.

Memorial witnessed by : Richd. Homan, Mathew Pageitt, Dublin, gent.

102, 358, 71135   Wm. Purefoy (seal)

636 BERNARD, CHARLES, Drinifilick, Queen's Co., gent.
17 March 1728. Précis, ½ p., 13 May 1741.

Devised £400 share and share alike among his younger children pursuant to the settlement made by Thomas Bernard, the testator's father.

Witnesses : Franks Bernard, Carlow, Co. Carlow, Henry Rudkins, senr., Well, said county, James Butler, Ballynekill, Queen's Co.

Memorial witnessed by : Wm. Doyle, Kilkenny, gent., Elizabeth Smith, Dublin.

100, 490, 71376   Mary Russell (seal)
                                             otherwise Bernard, one of
                                             the younger children of said
                                             testator.

637 ROCHE, GEORGE, Limerick, Esq.

13 June 1740. Codicil 4 Dec. 1740. Narrate, 1 p., 14 May 1741.

His wife Mary Roche, extx. Francis Bindon and David Bindon, both of Dublin, Esqrs., trustees. His son David Roche. His son Joseph Roche.

Towns and lands of Ballybigg, Co. Cork. Faranfierish [Farranferris] in county of the city of Cork. Several houses and tenements in city of Cork, and all other lands etc. in the city, the county of the city, and in the county of Cork.

Will and codicil witnessed by : Samuel Bindon, Templemongreld, liberties of city of Limerick, Esq., Ann Bindon, spinster, daughter of said Samuel Bindon, Francis Mold, then of said city of Limerick and now of Dublin, spinster.

Memorial witnessed by : Frances Mold, Thos. Gloster, Limerick, gent., Thos. Caffery, Dublin, yeoman.

100, 494, 71398 David Bindon (seal)

638 STEWART, JOHN, Loughgull, B. Dunluce, Co. Antrim, gent.

11 April 1738. Narrate, 1¼ p., 8 June 1741.

Alice Stewart otherwise McDonnell his wife. His brother William Stewart. His brother Henry Stewart. James Stewart of Carriferum, eldest son of Henry Stewart of Carriferum, gent. Wm. Stewart, son of said Henry Stewart. Henry Stewart, junr., son of said Henry Stewart, senr. John Stewart, fourth son of said Henry Stewart, senr. Robert Stewart, Stewart Hall, and John Stewart, Gortagill, Co. Tyrone, exors·

Lands of Knewell, Dundermitt, Drumnakilly, Drimalckel and Uttel. Corkey, Knockgallan, Carrifnegarry and Carriferum, in parishes of Dunaghy and Loughgeel [? Loughguile], B. of Killconway and Dunluce, Co. Antrim. His dwelling house of Carriferum.

Witnesses : Mathew Stewart, Stroan, Andrew Young, Corkey, both Co. Antrim, farmers, James Thompson, Ballinascreen, Co. Derry, gent.

Memorial witnessed by : James Thompson, David Graham, Clogh, Co. Antrim, yarn merchant.

103, 305, 71544 Ja. Stewart (seal)
(James Stewart, a devisee)

639 FOX, FRANCES, als. HERBERT, wife to Patk. Fox, Durrow, King's Co., the only surviving daughter and heir of Sir Edward Herbert, late of Durrow, Bart., deceased. 26 Sept. 1729. Narrate, 2 pp., 9 July 1741.

Her husband said Patrick Fox. Her cousin Bridget Fox. Reciting deeds of lease and release 28 July 1720 made between said Patrick Fox and Frances Fox als. Herbert his wife of the one part, and Brabazon Newcomen and Robert Clements, of Dublin, Esqrs., and trustees of her lands, of the other part.

Lady Jane Newcomen. Her god-daughter Frances Newcomen. Brabazon Newcomen and Robert Clements, trustees. Hon. Lady Hester Lambert. Her cousin Charles Lambert the elder, of Dublin, Gustavus Lambert, second son of said Charles Lambert. Elizabeth, Elinor, Mary, Emilia and Sophia Lambert, daughters of said Charles. Her cousin Elinor Lambert, sister of said Charles. Her cousin Philip Rawson, Esq., of Limerick. Her cousin said Brabazon Newcomen, Esq. Nathaniel Clements. Her cousin Phelix Coughlan of Cloghan, King's Co., Esq. Rev. Robt. Packenham, minister of Kilbeggan. Her cousin Frances Rawson, daughter of said Philip Rawson. Francis Salmon, son of her tenant John Salmon. Monument to be erected in parish church of Durrow. Herbert Rawson, third son of said Philip Rawson. Capt. Parker, holder of mortgage on part of her estate.

The woods of Doory als. Derrywoods. Impropriate Rectory and tythes of the parish of Durrow (Kilbride and Durrow), said tythes issuing out of town and lands of Tonycross, Ballyduffe, Munagh, Killbride, Ballykillmurry, Iragh, Ballydroghet [? Ballydrohid], Killisky, Ballynenagh, Ballycowen, Killadurrow, Agharny and Arden. Balleegbeg, King's Co. Killdangan, Ballybought and Tarah [Tara], King's Co.

Witnesses : Richard Hoyle, Dublin, Doctor of Physic, since deceased, Burdett Worthington, said city, gent., Bruen Worthington, then of said city, a public notary and since deceased.

Memorial witnessed by : John Scott, Limerick, gent., Thomas Stretton, servant to Mrs. Martha Rawson, widow of said Philip Rawson and mother and guardian of said Herbert Rawson, a minor.

103, 388, 71852   Mart. Rawson (seal)

640 SAVAGE, ROBERT, Chancery Lane, Dublin, gent.

30 March 1730. Full, 7½ pp., 13 Oct. 1741.

My wife Susanna Savage. My youngest son Robert Savage and my three daughters Mary Savage, Ann Savage and Susanna (Judith) Savage (under twenty four years). Maintenance for daughter Susanna Judith till she attain the age of twelve years. My eldest son Francis Savage (under twentyone years). John Digby, Landenstowne, Co.

Kildare, Esq., and Robert French, Dublin, Esq., exors. My brother Henry [Savage]. My sister Catherine [Savage]. My uncle John Moore of Drumbannagher, Co. Armagh, Esq., and my friend Joshua Cooper of Marcrea, Co. Sligo, Esq., trustees. William Knox, Sheep Street, Dublin, gent. Rev. Wm. French, Oakport, Co. Roscommon, clerk. My serving boy Peter Dowdall.

My house in Chancery Lane. Ballygauly, Co. Sligo, leased to John Audley. Annual payment or rent charge to Catherine Countess Dowager of Bellamont. My real and personal estate.

Witnesses : John Taaffe, Dublin, Esq., Patrick Aylmer, Dublin, Esq., since deceased, Bartholomew Brefoot, then clerk to said testator but now one of the attornies of the Court of Exchequer in Ireland.

Memorial witnessed by : Barw. Brefoot, Chas. Dempsey, Dublin, gent.

103, 500, 72317   Su. Savage (seal)

641 FAGAN, THOMAS, Johnstown, Co. Dublin, gent.

25 Aug. 1734. Codicil 9 Sept. 1734. Précis, ½ p., 6 Nov. 1741.

Residue of his real and personal estate to James Heffernan and Jno. Kennedy and appointed them and Margt. Fagan, exors. Codicil revokes clauses about James Heffernan.

Witnesses : Thos. Farren, Edmd. Connor and Patk. Missett, Newtown, Co. Dublin, husbandmen.

Codicil witnessed by : Edmd. Connor, Patrick Missett, and John Lahey, Dublin, gent.

Memorial witnessed by : Edmd. Connor, Jno. Meagher, Dublin, gent.

105, 45, 72422   Jno. Kennedy (seal)

642 LUKEY, ALICIA als. CROSS, Cork, widow.

19 May 1737. Narrate, 2¼ pp., 21 Nov. 1741.

Her nephew William Wallis, Esq. Henry Rugg, Esq., trustee. Her cousin John Gillman, Currykeen, Esq. Her cousin Ephenetus Cross, second son of Philip Hayes Cross of Cornody, Esq.

Mills commonly called Careen's Mills, Mr Fitton tenant. Tucker's concerns, John Raymond's holdings, Miles Jackson's concerns, all in city or suburbs of city of Cork, and all other her real estate.

Witnesses : Mary Farmer, widow of Saml. Farmer, Ballymacodagh, Co. Cork, gent., Henry Rugg, junr., apprentice to Danl. Knight, Cork, merchant, Robert Wallis, Cork, public notary.

Memorial witnessed by : Mary Farmer, Saml. Farmer.

101, 489, 72630   Wm. Wallis (seal)

643 ATKIN, REV. WALTER, Ballenleaden otherwise Leadentown, Co. Cork, clerk. 21 Oct. 1741. Full, 3 pp., 23 Nov. 1741.

My eldest son Rev. John Thomas Atkin, clerk, exor. His present wife. My grandson Walter Atkin. My second son Conningsby Atkin and Dorcas Roche otherwise Clarke " who is now sayed to keep in his house." My son Doctor William Atkin. My two daughters Barbara and Elizabeth (unmarried). My daughter Catherine Wydenham. My granddaughter Elizabeth Wydenham. My real estate of Ballenleaden otherwise Leadentown.

Witnesses : Rev. Atkin Hayman, Leadentown, clerk, James Hanning, Cloyne, Co. Cork, notary public, John Holland, Leadentown, yeoman.

Memorial witnessed by : John Holland, Anthony Lane, Cork, gent.

103, 560, 72661   John Thos. Atkin (seal)

644 THOMOND, HENRY EARL OF and VISCOUNT TED-CASTER. 14 Oct. 1738. Précis, ¾ p., 12 Dec. 1741.

Rt. Hon. Wm., Earl of Inchiquin and Robert French, Dublin, Esq., councellor-at-law, trustees. William Wyndham, Orchard Wyndham, Co. of Somerset, Bart., since deceased, and said Robert French, exors. All his castles, manors, lands, tenements and hereditaments in the Kingdom of Great Britain and Ireland.

Witnesses : William Spring, near Charing Cross in the parish of St. James, Westminster, Co. of Middlesex, goldsmith, Wm. Bradshaw, Soho Square, parish of St. Ann, said county, upholder, Richard Lahy, Gray's Inn, same county, gent.

Memorial witnessed by : Richard Lahy, Bryan Duffey, servant to said Robert French.

104, 260, 72371   Robt. French (seal)

645 FITZGERALD, GERALD, Pu[n]chersgrange, Co. Kildare, gent.
16 March 1738. Narrate, ¾ p., 16 Dec. 1741.
His second son Garrett FitzGerald. His daughter Susan FitzGerald.
His daughter Elinor FitzGerald. His eldest son Maurice. His second
son Garrett FitzGerald, his granddaughter Elizabeth Clarke and his
cousin Edmd. Coonan, Kilboggan, gent., exors.
Leasehold interest in the wood of Drumfree, Co. Kildare. His real
and personal estate.
Witnesses : Thos. Feaghry, Doctor of Physic, Andrew Geoghegan,
senr., and Andrew Geoghegan, junr., gents., all of city of Dublin.
Memorial witnessed by : Andrew Geoghegan, senr., James Saunders,
Dublin, gent.
105, 136, 72900   Garrett FitzGerald (seal)

646 STOTS, JAMES, Castle Lumney, Co. Louth, gent.
10 Oct. 1731. Narrate, 1 p., 24 Dec. 1741.
His wife Martha Stots. His nephew Plunkett Stots, one of the sons
of his brother John Stots of the Silvermines in the county of Tipperary. His sister Rachel Stots. His two natural daughters Mary
Stots and Bridget Stots (minors). His cousin Patrick Hill and his
friend Patrick Henderson and Richard Hansard, gent., exors. His
term of the Rath, Co. Meath.
Witnesses : George Beath, White River, weaver, Robt. Cary,
White River, weaver, Francis Hill, White River, weaver.
Memorial witnessed by : Patrick Henderson, Richd. Hansard.
101, 548, 72962   Patk. Hill (seal)

647 BOR, JOHN, Dublin, Esq.
10 Oct. 1741. Narrate, ¾ p., 9 Jan. 1741/42.
His mother Helena Maria Bor, extx. His brother Jacob Bor. His
brother William Bor. His brother Gerald Bor. Boleyn Whitney,
Dublin, Esq., and William Williams, Dublin, gent., trustees. His
lands, tenements, rents, reversions and hereditaments real.
Witnesses : Walter Barrett, Terence Kerin, James Mahony, all of
Dublin, gents.
Memorial witnessed by : Terence Kerin, Jonathan Callbeck, Dublin,
gent.
106, 122, 73008   Hellena Maria Bor (seal)

648 WORTH, WILLIAM, Dublin, Esq.
   20 Oct. 1719.   Narrate, ¾ p., 13 Jan. 1741.
His second son James Tynte otherwise Worth. His eldest son Edward Worth. His nephew Doctor Edward Worth. Rev. Doctor Christopher Lloyd.

Town and lands of Dunbell, Co. Kilkenny, part set to Lawrence Sweet, Esq., house and small garden set to Henry Parren, and part sold to Capt. Mathews. All the rest of his lands, tenements and hereditaments and other real estate.

Witnesses : John Usher, late of Dublin, Esq., deceased, John Moffitt, Dublin, gent., Garrett English, servant to testator.

Memorial witnessed by : John Moffitt, Daniel Bourne, his clerk.
104, 287, 73032   James Tynte (seal)

649 ELLIOTT, MARTHA, Tennisslatty, Co. Kilkenny, spinster.
   9 Oct. 1741.   Narrate, ½ p., 27 Jan. 1741/42.
Her only brother Richard Elliott of Tennislatty, gent. Her part of the lands of Benekerry and Busherstown, Co. Catherlough.

Witnesses : Lavinia Agar, Gowran, Co. Kilkenny, spinster, Oliver Roth, Gowran, Co. Kilkenny, apothecary, Thomas Houghton, Dublin, Esq.

Memorial witnessed by : Thomas Houghton, Will Justas, Dublin, gent.
106, 148, 73124   Richd. Elliott (seal)

650 READ, ELIZABETH als. FERRAR, Graigovin, Co. Kilkenny,
   widow. 24 July 1726. Narrate, ½ p., 5 Feb. 1741.
Her daughter Martha Drollinvaux als. Tripps, exor. Her grand-daughter Elizabeth Drollinvaux. Mr Hen. Briscoe, exor. Houses in city of Waterford.

Witnesses : Henry Lewis, late of Newtown, Co. Waterford, gent., deceased, Richard Young, late of Cloncunny, Co. Kilkenny, gent., deceased, Walter Power, Darragil, Co. Waterford, gent.

Memorial witnessed by : Richard Hinde, junr., John Field.
104, 328, 73209   Marth Drollinvaux als. Tripps
                                          (seal)

651   JACOB, MATHEW, senr., St. Johnstowne, Co. Tipperary, gent.
21 Oct. 1732. Codicil 31 March 1733. Full, 4½ pp., 20 Feb. 1741.
To be buried in churchyard of Killinan where my father is buried.
My two sons Mathew Jacob, junr., Esq., and John Jacob, gent., exors.
My second son Mathew Jacob, Council-at-Law, my third son John
Jacob. Mathew Jacob, eldest son of said John Jacob. Wm. Jacob,
second son of my said son John Jacob. Samuel Jacob, third son of my
said son John Jacob. My grandson Mathew Jacob, son of Samuel
Jacob deceased (unmarried and under 21 years). My granddaughters
Rebecca Jacob and Mary Jacob, daughters of said Samuel Jacob
(under 18 years). My eldest daughter Abigal Sankey als. Jacob. Her
eldest son Mathew Sankey. His brother John Sankey. His brother
Richd. Sankey. My brother-in-law John Minchin. My grandson
Mathew Latham, his father John Latham, gent. John Latham, brother
of Mathew. My grandson Wm. Latham.

John Minchin of Ballybeagh, Co. Kilkenny, gent., and John Perry
of Woodroffe, Co. Tipperary, gent., trustees. John Bagwell, Clonmell,
Co. Tipperary, merchant, holds a mortgage. John Latham, Meldrum,
Co. Tipperary, gent., and John Minchin, junr., Shangarry, Co. Tip-
perary, Esq., trustees. Mathew Lane of Killenale. Mr Rice Taylor.
William Power of Slainstowne.

Town and lands of St. Johnstown, Milltown St. John, part of
Couleagh, Ballylosky and Clonegawny [? Cloneygowny], Kilkennybegg
als. Kilkenny St. John, Glangault, that part of Ballingarry held by
James Butler, Ballaghboy, and Tenuknuck.[1] Town and lands of
Mobarnan purchased of the Widow Prince and Mr Epaphroditus
Marsh. Mortlestowne, Kilbreedy als. Kilbarry, part of Ballynenan,
part of Knockuragh now held by my niece Mary Miller, widow. Part
of Clonihea called Tirally, and Ballyrichard now held by Edmond
Miller and the lands held by Edward Grace from me. Town and lands
of Slainstown, Higginstowne, parts of Peppardstowne (Pepperstown),
Lismoynane, Kilmakovoge, Cappantallagery [Cappauntallegary], part
of Priestowne (bought of Francis Smyth deceased ; sums to be paid
to the eldest daughter of the said Francis Smyth's eldest sister "as
an acknowledgment of my kindness and love for her uncle said
Francis Smyth "). Town and lands of Jamestowne, Meldrum and
Kilstafard [? all in Co. Tipperary].

Witnesses to Will and codicil : Henry Sheppard, Fethard, Co.

---

[1] Probably equivalent to the modern Tonaknock, (e.g. in Co. Kerry), but I
have been unable to trace a place of this name in Co. Tipperary.

Tipperary, feltmaker, Edmd. Headon and Thos. Headon, both of St. Johnstown, said county, farmers, Philip Hackett, Killarlea, said county, gent.

Memorial witnessed by : Philip Hackett, John Murphy, servant to said Mathew Jacob of Mobarnane.

Mathew Jacob the younger (seal)
of St. Johnstown, Co. Tipperary, Esq.,
grandson and heir at law of testator.

106, 194, 73350   Mathew Jacob the younger (seal)

of Mobarnan, Co. Tipperary, Esq., second
son and surviving exor. of testator.

652 WHITNEY, THOMAS, Newpass als. Derrydown, Co. Westmeath, Esq. 30 April 1740. Narrate, ¾ p., 26 Feb. 1741.

His brother Boleyn Whitney, Esq., trustee and exor. His sister Ann Upton wife of Ambrose Upton, clerk. His brother Shuckburgh Whitney, Lieut. Colonel in H.M.'s service. Roger Martin, junr., son of Capt. Roger Martin of Stepney.

His castles, towns and lands of Newpass, Rathowen, Colemore, Colebegg, Win[d]town, Ballygarron, Ballydorey and all other his lands and hereditaments in Co. Westmeath.

Witnesses : Thomas Taylor and Joseph Brisco, both of London, gents., Patk. Makin, servant to testator.

Memorial witnessed by : William Williams and Alexr. Williams, Dublin, gents.

105, 180, 73405   Boleyn Whitney (seal)

653 POCOCK, EDWARD, Bristol, then of Killenure, Queen's Co. 20 Aug. 1736. Narrate, 1 p., 4 March 1741.

His grandfather Edwd. Hackett, Lydia Hackett his wife. Lydia Pocock (daughter of said Lydia Hackett), wife to Thos. Pocock, and mother of testator. Ground, premises etc. in Maudlin Lane, parish of St. James, Bristol, purchased by testator's grandfather Edwd. Hackett, left in trust by said Lydia Hackett to her daughter Lydia Pocock and Thos. Pocock, and at her decease to their children. Reciting that said Edward Pocock her eldest son [the testator], Robert Pocock and Andrew Pocock were then living, and that soon after Robert died, of full age, his share becoming vested in said Edward as eldest brother who purchased his brother Andrew's share and deposited the deeds in hands of Thos. Hackett in Bristol.

His cousin Anthony Sharp of Killenure, Queen's Co., his cousin Mary Sharp. His friend Wm. Glaister of Mountrath. Humphrey Hipwell, Killenure aforesaid.

Witnesses : John Robinson, sadler, James Morton, shoemaker, Edwd. Honnor, wigmaker, all of Mountrath, Queen's Co.

Memorial witnessed by : Edwd. Honnor, Jno. Humphrys, Dublin, gent.

105, 189, 73452   Wm. Glaister (seal)

654 MAUDSLEY, Lieut. JOHN, Killee, King's Co.

31 Oct. 1741. Narrate, 1 p., 4 March 1741/42.

His niece Elizabeth McClure. His son John Maudsley. His friend Thos. Granger, Dublin, Esq., trustee and his nephew Henry Maudsley exors. His house and concerns in manor of Thomas Court and Donore, Co. Dublin.

Names of witnesses to Will not recorded.

Memorial witnessed by : Christopher Dalton, Dublin, notary public, Thos. Gibbons his clerk.

107, 125, 73466   Hen. Maudsley (seal)

655 GORE, DAME ELIZABETH, widow of Sir Ralph Gore, Dublin, Bart. 12 May 1733. Narrate, ¾ p., 19 March 1741.

Rt. Rev. Edward [Synge] Lord Bishop of Cloyne and Hon. Henry Hamilton, Dublin, trustees, and guardians with her mother Jane Ashe and Hen. Brooke, Dublin, Esq., of her children and exors. Her younger children Ralph and Richard. Her second son Ralph Gore. Her third son Richard Gore. All her real estate in Co. of Limerick and King's Co.

Witnesses : Anthony Bury, Co. Tipperary, clerk, Nathaniel Clements, Dublin, Esq., Henry Buckley, late of Dublin, public notary, since deceased.

Memorial witnessed by : Chrisr. Bowen, Albert Cathers, both of Dublin, gents.

107, 160, 73596   Hen. Brooke (seal)

656 HUGGINS, JOHN, Glenarb, parish of Aghalow, Co. Tyrone.
   7 April 1741.   Précis, ¼ p., 23 April 1742.
   His son-in-law David Ferguson.   Town and lands of Kedie [situation not mentioned.   ? Keady, Co. Tyrone].
   Witnesses : Wm. Peebles of Rahachy near Carrantall, Co. Tyrone, a Dissenting clergyman, Wm. Maxwell, Guinea near Callidon, Co. Tyrone, gent., Robert Huggins, Glenarb.
   Memorial witnessed by : Wm. Maxwell, Hugh Carmichael, Dublin, gent.
   106, 283, 73771   Davd. Ferguson (seal)

657 ASTON, ANN, Dublin, widow.
   20 Jan. 1729.   Narrate, 1 p., 4 May 1742.
   Her daughter Ann Powell, exor.   Her cousins Jno. Powell and John Cook, trustees.   Her granddaughter Mary Powell.   Her grandsons George Powell, John Powell, Wm. Powell, Richard Powell, Robert Powell and Thos. Powell, exor.   Her cousin Mary Millburn als. Cook.
   Lease of lower end of St. John's Lane near Thomas Street in suburbs of city of Dublin, then in possession of Richard Hill, Hugh Wallace and others.   A house and stable in York Street, Dublin, then in possession of Rev. Dean Jeremiah Marsh.   The house wherein she then dwelt in Thomas Street, Dublin.   House in Capel Street, Dublin, wherein Edwd. Scott, merchant, then dwelt.
   Witnesses : Jonathan Maughan, late of Dublin, apothecary, deceased, Mark Ferrall, Dublin, brewer, Nicholas Simpson, apprentice to said Jonathan Maughan.
   Memorial witnessed by : Mark Ferrall, Forbes White, clerk to Jno. Kathrens, Dublin, public notary.
   105, 264, 73813   Thos. Powell (seal)

658 THOMAS, ANNE, wife of Anthony Thomas, Galway, gent.
   10 Feb. 1741.   Narrate, ½ p., 17 May 1742.
   Her former husband Mr Wm. Small.   Her daughter Sarah Small (unmarried and under 18 years at time of testatrix's marriage with Anthony Thomas).   Her brother George Gilchrist.   The then present Lord Chan[cello]r, Chas. Gerry and George Gilchrist her brother and Anthony Thomas, exors.

Witnesses : Elizabeth Price, Galway, widow, Elizabeth Surridge, wife of Fras. Surridge of Dunmore, Co. Galway, gent., George Gilchrist, Dublin, gent.

Memorial witnessed by : Elizth. Devall, wife of Wm. Devall, public notary in Dublin, and said Wm. Devall.

105, 291, 73958   Geo. Gilchrist (seal)

659 CUFFE, THOMAS, Dublin, Esq.

27 April 1738. Narrate, a few lines, 17 June 1742.

My wife Grace Cuffe als. Tilson. All my real and freehold estate.

Names of witnesses to Will not recorded.

Memorial witnessed by : Christopher Dalton, notary public, Dublin, Thos. Gibbons, his clerk.

108, 11, 74225   Grace Cuffe (seal)

660 RYLANDS, Lieut. NICHOLAS, Col. Groves Regt. of Foot now in Dublin. 13 Jan. 1726/7. Full, ½ p., 10 July 1742.

My wife Ann Cowling als. Rylands, extx. My brother Richard Rylands and my sister Margaret [? Rylands]. All my estate both real and personal. All my Spanish pay and arrears due to me.

Witnesses : Jas. Belcher, Dublin, Esq., Thos. Morse and Geo. Callcott, Dublin, gents.

Memorial witnessed by : Kene Perceval, Dublin, clerk, Paschall Wilson, Dublin, scrivener.

107, 349, 74439   Ann Rylands (seal)

661 MIDDLETON, BARNABY, Dublin, merchant.

19 March 1741. Narrate, ¾ p., 17 July 1742.

His son Rev. Hector Middleton, clerk. His son John Middleton. John Bertand, Dirty Lane, merchant, and Arthur Lamprey, wax chandler, exors.

Two houses on N. side Dame Street, Dublin, one set to Mr Gowers the other to Mr Tudor. Ground and house on City Quay in Parish of St. Mark, Dublin. House on N. side of King Street, Dublin wherein Capt. Bonvillette now lives. Two houses in Crow Street, Dublin, one set to Mr Arbuckle the other to Mr Palliser.

U

Witnesses : John Willson, Georges Lane, Dublin, brushmaker, Chas. Couse, said place, hosier, Benj. Pineau, Dublin, gent.

Memorial witnessed by : Rev. Warter Wilson, Dublin, clerk, James Morris, Dublin, writing clerk.

108, 38, 74505   Ann Middleton (seal)
                                    a legatee

662 KIERNAN, ROBERT, Co. Dublin, gent.
        2 July 1741. Narrate, 1 p., 10 Aug. 1742.

His wife Susanna Kiernan. The widow and fatherless children of Mr Linan of Duleek, Co. Meath, deceased. His sons James and Robert Kiernan. Legacy to his eldest daughter Elizth. Kiernan when 20 years, and to his younger daughter Suzanna Kiernan when 17 years. Rev. Henry Ware, Vicar of Balrothery, Co. Dublin, Rev. John Antrobus, Prebend of St. Michan's Dublin, and his wife Suzanna exors.

Lands of Blackhall, the Mill of Little Ballbrigen [Balgriggan], Co. Dublin. His two houses in Church Street [? Dublin], a settlement of them made on him by his mother Elizabeth Kiernan in her lifetime.

Witnesses : John Brown, Edward Bassett, Samuel Brown, all of Balrothery, Co. Dublin, gents.

Memorial witnessed by : John Brown, Patrick Forman, Dublin, gent.

106, 452, 74664   Robt. Kiernan (seal)
                             one of the devisees in said
                             Will.

663 PETER, WALTER, Drumcondra Lane, county of the city of
        Dublin, merchant. 11 Feb. 1741. Narrate, ½ p., 10 Sept. 1742.

His wife Rebecca. His son David Peter, exor. His daughter Margt. Sumner. His daughter Rebecca Peter, her mother said Rebecca Peter. His son Thos. Peter.

His estate and interest in Drumcondra Lane, Co. Dublin. Holdings on Blind Quay, Copper Alley, Pembroke Court and Castle Street [Dublin] ; Willlam Street, Jervis Street and Chequer Lane, in the county of the city of Dublin. Fishamble Street, Dublin.

Witnesses : Mark Synott, Drumcondra Lane, Esq., Stephen Robinson, Dublin, vintner, Charles Meares, Dublin, public notary.

Memorial witnessed by : Stephen Robinson, Wm. Sumner, public notary in Dublin.

109, 34, 74802 Dad. Peter (seal)

664 HEATLY, DANIEL, Dublin, gent.

12 June 1740. Narrate, ½ p., 22 Sept. 1742.

His nephew Daniel Heatly, exor. His nephew Isaac Heatly. His sister Alice Bingly [? testator's or Isaac's sister]. His nephew Thomas Heatly Destournell. His nephew Wm. Heatly. His niece Elizabeth Corry. His servant Mary Davis exor.

His messuages or tenements in the Bagnio Lane in the county of the city of Dublin. Messuage, house or tenement on Temple Barr where the office was then kept, another wherein Mr Robert King then lived, another formerly in possession of Daniel Lament [? Laurent]. His house in Essex Street then in the possession of James Campbell.

Wiitnesses : Alexander Stephens, instrument maker, Paul Parker, grocer, Thomas Martin, gent., all of city of Dublin.

Memorial witnessed by : Paul Parker, Philip Collins, Dublin, gent.

106, 497, 74863 Danl. Heatly (seal)

665 BATH, CHRISTOPHER, Charles Street, Dublin, gent.

Feb. 1739. Narrate, ½ p., 22 Sept. 1742.

His only child Susanna Bath. His mother Mrs Jane Bath. Joseph Bath, son of his uncle Peter Bath. Remainder to his sister Flynn's eldest son and his heirs, he and they calling themselves Bath ; for want for male issue to her eldest daughter she calling herself Bath and her children as aforesaid. Mrs Esther Quinn of Thomas Street. John Bath of Church Street, gent. John Bath of Sheep Street, gent.

All his estate in Drogheda. His title to town and lands of Painstown and elsewhere. Lease of a house he had from Robert Ramsay to Jane and Mary White [situation not mentioned]. Appointed Capt. Humphry Browne and Susanna his wife[1] guardians to his said child and exors. with his mother and said Esther Quinn.

Witnesses : Laurence Keary, James Redmond, both of Dublin, staymakers, Mary Keary, then of Drogheda, since deceased.

Memorial witnessed by : Laurence Keary, James Saunders, Dublin, gent.

106, 508, 74904 Easther Quinn (seal)

---

[1] Probably Susanna Browne as *Betham's Will Pedigrees*, Genealogical Office, show that the name of Christopher Bath's wife was Anne.

666 BOWEN, NICHOLAS, Bowensford, Co. Cork, Esq.
　　24 Jan. 1728. Narrate, 1 p., 6 Nov. 1742.
His eldest son Wm. John Bowen. To his three daughters Sarah, Mary and Constance £300 each on marriage. To his son Nicholas £600 etc. when 21 years. John Bowen of Killbolane. Stephens Bowen. Henry Bowen of Glanicomane. Nicholas Bowen, brother to said Henry Bowen. Philips Bowen. David Power, Cooreheen, Co. Galway, Esq., Rev. Geo. Chiney [Chinnery], Midletown, Co. Cork, exors.
　　His real estate in kingdom of Ireland. The two Ballynahas. Delliggimore, Moneykenastea and Knockagh als. Clonny, B. of Orrery and Killmore, Co. Cork.
　　Witnesses : David Quin, Glanduff, Co. Limerick, gent., John Collins, Bowensford, gent., Lewis Moore, servant to testator.
106, 532, 75054   D. Power (seal)

667 KENT, JOHN, Roscrea, Co. Tipperary, Esq.
　　30 Nov. 1736. Narrate, ½ p., 16 Nov. 1742.
His cousin George Despard, exor. or his cousin Edwd. Despard or his cousin Lambert Despard. His cousin George Tew. £50 a year to his Mo [? Mother]. Legacy to his sister Despard after the death of her husband. His uncle Henry Kent. His sister Margt. Kent.
　　All his estate in Roscrea and Ballinveny [Co. Tipperary]. Lands of Kilnasinally [? Kilnashanally, Co. Tipperary].
　　Witnesses : John Frank, merchant, Hopton Butler, apothecary, Vizer Bridge, gent., all of Roscrea.
　　Memorial witnessed by : Vizer Bridge, John Humphrys, Rushall, Queen's Co., gent.
107, 508, 75184   George Despard (seal)

668 CROSBIE, WILLIAM, Tubrid, Co. Kerry, Esq.
　　19 Jan. 1738. Précis, ½ p., 24 Nov. 1742.
Arthur Crosbie, Ardfert, Co. Kerry, Esq.   ·
　　Town and lands of Ballicarbery, Baslicane and Begginis, Ballinvoher, Emily, Gortbregogy, Glanahiry, Glaunnlanes, Rathduffe, Ballyandry, the Derrygormans, Ballinpleminig, Ballintagart, Tane, Cloundonogan, Killknedane, Cahirdiane, Sheans and Knockanaulart, Balligarrett, Killtinbane and Tonekilly, Carrigfrehane, Castlelogh, Arda[g]h,

Dromeadrislig, Turk, Gortacunigg and Fartew and all his lands and tenements within the town and signory of Castle Island, the two Killikills and Ardconnell, in Co. Kerry.

Witnesses : Domk. Rice, Rathkenny, Co. Kerry, farmer, Patk. Plunkett, servant to testator, Wm. Scannell, Tralee, Co. Kerry, clerk.

Memorial witnessed by : Patk. Plunkett, Domk. Rice, Mathew Scannell, servant to said Arthur Crosbie.

107, 530, 75263   Artr. Crosbie

669 BUTLER, JAMES, Dublin, Esq.

30 Dec. 1734. Narrate, 2 pp., 25 Nov. 1742.

His wife Ann Butler (sole extx). Reciting that his dear brother Lord Newtown[1] devised to testator a rent charge out of his lands in Co. of Cavan and Fermanagh with remainder to Mrs Ann Butler, testator's wife.

His nephews the Hons. Humphrey Butler, Thos. Butler, Robert Butler, John Butler, and his niece the Hon. Judith Cramer als. Butler. His grand-nephew Brinsly Butler, eldest son of his said nephew Humphrey Butler. His brother-in-law Rev. James Stopford. His nephew Rev. Francis Glover and Mr Theophilus Glover. His two nieces Elizabeth and Ann Chettwood. His two servants John Laynge and Margaret Laynge his wife.

Town and lands of Newtown and Crevequin and all other his lands and estate in the counties of Roscommon and Longford. Jackstown Upper, Claragh, Mustard Garden, and the tythes of Killaghy and Lackany all in Co. Kilkenny. His ground, houses and estate in Chequer Lane and New Street, in the county of the city of Dublin. Lands of Knockanacrow als. Lackanally, B. I[d]ron[e], Co. Catherlogh. His house on St. Stephen's Green in which his brother the Rt. Hon. the Lord Viscount Lanesborough then lived, and two plots of ground one on either side of said house.

Witnesses : William Usher, Dublin, Esq., William Palliser, Rath-farnham, Co. Dublin, Esq., Rev. Dr. James King, Erratty, Co. Donegal.

Memorial witnessed by : William Usher, Rev. John Palliser, Rathfarnham, clerk.

106, 552, 75269   Ann Butler (seal)

---

[1] Probably Brinsley (Butler) Baron of Newtown-Butler. *The Complete Peerage* by G. E. C. states that he took his seat in 1725 as ''Lord Newtown '' and was created Viscount Lanesborough 1728.

670 ALLEN, JOSHUA VISCOUNT.
25 Jne 1730. Précis, a few lines, 10 Dec. 1742.

His real and personal estate in Great Britain and Ireland to Margaret Lady Viscountess Allen his wife, (extx.).

Witnesses : Frances Lady Countess Newburgh, Dublin, Mary Delaballa, Stillorgan, Co. Dublin, spinister, James Cullenan, of same, servant.

Memorial witnessed by : Mary Delaballa, Stillorgan, spinister, James Cullenan, of same, servant, William Seddon, of same, farmer.

106, 556, 75397   M. Allen (seal)

671 SMITH, SAMUEL, New Ross, Co. Wexford, merchant.
3 May 1742. Narrate, ¾ p., 8 Feb. 1742/43.

His niece Mary Grubb, Waterford, widow. Wm. Weekes, eldest son of his nephew Richard Weekes, late of the city of Waterford, merchant, (exor.). His servants Mary and Catherine Brennan. Rev. Wm. Deniston, Waterford, clerk, and Mr Henry Allen, New Ross, trustees and overseers.

His house on the Quay of New Ross wherein Mr Henry Allen then dwelt. Lands of Coole, Finnock and Ballygow, Co. Wexford.

Witnesses : John FitzGerald, New Ross, gent., Wm. Cahill, of same, slater, Ambrose Bedford, of same, perukemaker.

Memorial witnessed by : John FitzGerald, Saml. Taylor, Waterford, gent.

109, 251, 75775   Wm. Weekes (seal)

672 ROSE, HENRY, one of the Justices of the King's Bench.
13 July 1740. Narrate, ¾ p., 10 Feb. 1742.

His two sons-in-law, trustees and exors. [William Gun and Will. Talbott]. His son-in-law William Gun. His daughters Sarah and Jane. His son George.

Henry Honahan owes testator sum of money on the mortgage of lands of Broghill. Lands of Connigar, Milltown, Creggs and East and West Creave, Tinis, Kilbradran, Lisbane, Ballydorlis, Ballyverneal, Rathnagore, B. Conelloe, Co. Limerick. Leases for years that he held in the county of the city of Cork, Co. Cork, Co. Limerick and Co. Kerry. Lands of Morgans and Coolnorane, Co. Limerick, contiguous to his son's estate. His house in Dublin.

Witnesses : Dennis Heayes, John Connor, Edmond Heayes, all then servants to testator.

Memorial witnessed by : Edmond Heayes, James Saunders, Dublin, gent.

108, 191, 75786   W. Talbot (seal)

673 STOAKES, JOHN, Tonnattygorman, Co. Fermanagh, gent.
     27 March 1741. Narrate, ½ p., 15 Feb. 1742.

His eldest son Robt. Stoakes. His son John Stoakes. His son Wm. Stoakes. His sons Robert and John Stoakes and Rev. Robt. Nixon, exors. Lands of Latgarr, Tonnattygorman and Carrardagh [? Co. Fermanagh].

Witnesses : Lant. Johnston, Uttan [Uttony], John Forster, Rathmoran, James Wallace and John Denny, both of Lisnamallart, all in Co. Fermanagh, gents.

Memorial witnessed by : John Forster, Edmund McGuire, Latgarr, Co. Fermanagh, yeoman.

111, 109, 75831   John Stoakes (seal)

674 ROBINSON, ANNE, Dublin, widow.
     21 Feb. 1742. Précis, a few lines, 25 Feb. 1742.

Her real and personal estate to her cousin Ann Veron Court otherwise Ann Veron Fawcett, wife of John Fawcett, Dublin, glass grinder.

Witnesses : Henry Dering, Esq., Rev. John Grace, clerk, Richd. Prest, public notary, all of Dublin.

Memorial witnessed by : Alexr. Gordon, painter, of Dublin, and Richd. Prest.

112, 1, 75931.   Ann Veron Fawcett (seal)

675 DOWNING, JOHN, senr., Broagh, parish of Tarmaneny [Termoneeny] B. of Lo[u]ghinsholin, Co. Londonderry, gent.
     25 Jan. 1733/34. Narrate, ¾ p., 2 April 1743.

His nephew John Downing of Ballydermot, Co. Londonderry, second son of his brother Adam Downing, Esq., deceased, exor. The half townland of Broagh.

Witnesses : Rev. John Spotswood, clerk, Alexr. Spotswood, gent., Margery Spotswood, spinster, of Ballyaghey, Co. Londonderry.

296 ABSTRACTS OF WILLS

Memorial witnessed by: Rev. John Spotswood, clerk, Andrew Spotswood, Ballyaghey, gent.

108, 243, 76200   John Downing (seal)

676 WARNER, ANNE, Cork, spinster.
　　4 Jan. 1742. Précis, a few lines, 20 April 1743.
All her real and personal estate to her aunt Mary Boles.
Witnesses: Swithin White and Nichs. Weekes, Cork, Esqrs., Thos. White, Cork, clerk.
Memorial witnessed by: Swithin White, John Wallis, Dublin, gent.

109, 382, 76273   Mary Boles (seal)

677 DOWLING, ANNE, Dublin, widow.
　　5 Jan. 1736. Narrate, 1½ p., 5 May 1743.
Her daughter Rachel Jane Edgeworth then wife of Richard Edge-worth, Esq. A devise made by her late husband Murtagh Dowling of yearly sum of £20 out of lands of Marshallstown and Corhistown, Co. Meath, to support four persons in the poor house in St. Peter's Parish. Luke Dowling, Dublin, stationer. Her son George Lovell. John Skeffington, Antrim, Esq., Robert Sandford, Castlereagh, Esq., trustees.
House in Grafton Street [Dublin] wherein testatrix then dwelt. Lands of Baconstown, Co. Kildare.
Witnesses: George Carter and Matthew Daniel, then clerks to Wm. Devall, public notary, Dublin, and said Wm. Devall.
Memorial witnessed by: Wm. Devall, Chas. [? Christopher] Dalton, Dublin, public notary.

109, 422, 76449   Geo. Lovel (seal)

678 DOWLING, ANNE, Dublin, widow.
　　Codicil 18 April 1743. Narrate, ½ p., 5 May 1743.
Her son Geo Lovell. Her daughter Rachel Jane Edgeworth. Rev. Cutts Harman trustee in room of Hon. John Skeffington deceased, named in her Will of 5 Jan. 1736. Marshallstown and Corhistown, Co. Meath.
Witnesses: Frances Harman, widow, Geo. Duant, surgeon, Christr. Dalton, public notary, all of Dublin.

Memorial witnessed by : Christr. Dalton, Wm. Devall, Dublin, public notary.

111, 251, 76450   Rachel Jane Edgeworth (seal)

679 DONNOVAN, JEREMIAH, Dublin.
28 May 1743. Full, ¼ p., 30 May 1743.

My most noble and generous friend the Rt. Hon. Chaworth Brabazon Earl of Meath. Mrs Anne Toole. Nicholas Clinton, city of Cork. My son Robt. Donnovan. My two worthy friends Sir C. D., Bart, and Richard Wingfield, Esq.

Town and lands of Little Bray, Co. Dublin. Balsarne and Black-ditch, Co. Meath. My estate in Back Lane and James Street [Dublin].

Witnesses : John Stones, chirurgeon, Hugh Shaw, apothecary, Wm. Toole, yeoman, all of city of Dublin.

Memorial witnessed by : John Stones, John King, Dublin, Esq.

112, 25, 76624   Nichs. Clinton (seal)

680 MOORE, ELIZABETH, widow of the Hon. John Moore, Dublin,
clerk. 19 May 1738. Précis, a few lines, 3 Oct. 1743.

My son John Moore. That part of my real estate which descended to me from my brother Porter.

Witnesses : Rev. James Stopford, Rev. John Pratt, both of Finglass, Co. Dublin, Thos. Stopford, Dublin, Esq.

Memorial witnessed by : George Howison, Dublin, gent., William Drury, Dublin, scrivener.

110, 313, 77438   John Moore (seal)

681 MAY, EDWARD, Mayfield, Co. Waterford.
23 Aug. 1723. Narrate, ¼ p., 4 Oct. 1743.

His wife Elizabeth May. Confirms settlement of his lands on his (eldest) son James May on his intermarriage. His daughter Elizabeth May.

Lands of Rocketscastle otherwise Mayfield, Gurtard, Woodrock and Coleroe, Co. Waterford.

Witnesses : Yelverton Dennis, Wexford, gent., Edward Morris, Ballyneirn, Co. Waterford, gent., Wm. Poer, Park, Co. Waterford, gent.

Memorial witnessed by : Wm. Power, John Fleming.

111, 436, 77443   Eliz. May (seal)

682 LAWLESS, JOHN, Loftus Lane, parish of St. Mary, Dublin.
14 Oct. 1734. Narrate, part in full, ¾ p., 21 Oct. 1743.
His wife Joanna Lawless, exor. My daughter Margt. Monaghan. Lawrence Monaghan my son-in-law. My brother Richd. Lawless. Catherine Harris my sister. Hugh Swift and Lawrence Swift my stepsons. Pat. Carr, Dublin, victualler, Henry McDaniell, Drumcondra Lane, gardener, exors.
The house he then lived in. Two houses in Cherry Lane [Dublin]. Two houses then in possession of Byrne and Keogh [situation not mentioned].
Witnesses : Thomas Mylear, brickmaker, Nicholas White, yeoman, Thos. Ward, schoolmaster, all of Dublin.
Memorial witnessed by : Michael Tobin, Dublin, yeoman, Hugh Swift, Dublin, dairyman.
113, 82, 77506   Joanna Lawless (seal)
                                          her mark

683 POWER, JOHN, Barrettstown, Co. Tipperary, Esq.
6 May 1734. Full, 3½ pp., 11 Nov. 1743.
My wife Elizabeth, exor. My daughters Rebecca, Elizabeth, Jane, Elinor, Martha (sums to be paid these younger children when respectively aged 21, or on marriage ; said Elizabeth their mother). My daughters Sarah, Bridgett, Avis and Margaret (all under 21 years). Their uncle Ambrose Congreve, Waterford, Esq., to be guardian of children if testator's widow marries again. My two youngest sons Richard and John. My eldest son Ambrose. My brother and sister Going. My cousin Stephen Moore of Clonmel. Stephen Moore, Moorepark, Co. Cork, Esq., Guy Moore, Abby, Co. Tipperary, and Rev. Joseph Moore (exor), of Clonmell, Co. Tipperary, clerk, trustees.
Barrettstown, Coleman, Redcity, Ballylomasny, Williamstown and Garransillagh [? all in Co. Tipperary]. The house in Clonmel wherein John Butler, cutler, dwells, another there in which Mrs Catherine Pourquire dwells. The Island near the town of Clonmell called Batty's Island, and lands of Tobberheeny, Co. Tipperary. Lands of Borrisnefarny [Co. Tipperary].
Witnesses : Richd. Clotterbuck [Clotterbooke], William Warren Lacy, Stephen Moore, notary public.
Memorial witnessed by : Stephen Moore, Gambell Dawson.
113, 110, 77647   Eliz. Power (seal)

684 DOBBYN, WILLIAM, Ballynakill, Co. Waterford, Esq.
3 Aug. 1739. Narrate, 1 p., 14 Nov. 1743.
Settlement made 7 Nov. 1730 by testator upon marriage of his son William. His three sons. His three daughters Mary, Elizabeth and Margarett. His sons Wm. Dobbyn, Ballymaclode, Co. Waterford, Esq., and Robert Dobbyn, city of Waterford, Esq., exors. His beloved friends Henry Mason, Nymph Hall, Co. Waterford, Esq., and Wm. Dennis, Waterford, clerk, Archdeacon of Lismore, trustees.
Town and lands of Cullen Castle, B. Middle Third, Co. Waterford, and Drumrosk, B. Gaultier, Co. Waterford. Lands, houses etc. in city of Waterford.
Witnesses : Stephen Downes, Samuel Taylor, both of Waterford, gents., John Smithwick, Abby Athasell, Co. Tipperary, gent.
Memorial witnessed by : Stephen Downes, Saml. Taylor.
110, 336, 77678   Margaret Dobbyn (seal)

685 ROTHERY, DOROTHY, Dublin, widow.
6 Sept. 1743. Précis, ¼ p., 16 Nov. 1743.
Her real and personal estate to Nathaniel Orpin son of John Orpin of Crane Lane, glazier. Said John Orpin exor.
Witnesses : John Micheles, Dublin, victualler, Wm. Rufus Chetwood and Chas. Meares of Dublin, gents.
Memorial witnessed by : Chas. Meares, Wm. Montgomery, Dublin, gent.
113, 127, 77701   Jno. Orpin (seal)

686 DONELANE, WILLIAM, Carrowcrurn [? Carrowcrin], Co. Galway, gent. 16 June 1740. Narrate, 2½ pp., 21 Nov. 1743.
His cousin David Power of Coorheen, Co. Galway, Esq. His eldest daughter Anne Donelane. His second daughter Catherine. His other three daughters Nelly, Molly and Helen Donelane. His second son Nicholas Donelane. His two youngest sons Peter and Edmond Donelane.
Cloghrosty, Lorrage [? Larraga, Co. Galway], and Cappacuna [? Co. Galway].
Witnesses : Peter Killkenny, Brian Killkenny, both of Loughrea, and Redmond Burke, Clonlea, Co. Galway, gent.
Memorial witnessed by : James Saunders, Robert Stafford, both of Dublin, gents.
113, 141, 77752   D. Power (seal)

687 WHEELER, RICHARD, Lyrath, Co. Kilkenny, Esq.

2 March 1735. Narrate, 1 p., 23 Nov. 1743.

His wife Rose Wheeler als. Brabazon, extx. His eldest daughter Marian. His eldest son. His second daughter Judith Wheeler, his third daughter Rose Wheeler, his fourth daughter Sarah Wheeler, his second son Oliver Wheeler, his fifth daughter Brabazon Wheeler (all under 21 years).

Lands of Lyrath St. Martins, Cloghlea, Nashtown, Killamery, Killtaalahan [Kiltallaghan] all situate in Co. Kilkenny. Garryvring in city of Kilkenny. Archersrath in Liberties of city of Kilkenny, and Fogsland in said city of Kilkenny.

Witnesses : Sarah Baxter, Kilkenny, widow, Arthur Helsham, Legattrath, in Liberties of city of Kilkenny, Esq., John Birch, Kilkenny, gent.

Memorial witnessed by : John Birch, Wm. Gregg, Irishtown near city of Kilkenny, notary public.

114, 26, 77782   Rose Wheeler (seal)

688 KING, DENNIS, New Row, Co. Dublin, brewer.

24 Feb. 1742, codicil not dated. Narrate, ½ p., 16 Dec. 1743.

His wife Arabella King and John Chamney, Shelelagh, Co. Wicklow, Esq., exors. Testator's son Henry King. His brother John King.

Witnesses : John Hemsworth, Dublin, Doctor of Physic, Thos. Cooley, Dublin, counsellor-at-law, Rev. Philip Cooley, Dublin, clerk.

Codicil witnessed by : Rev. Caleb Cartwright, D.D., and John King and James Semple both now servants or clerks to said Arabella King.

Memorial witnessed by : John King, Simon King, Dublin, gent.

110, 372, 77987   Arabella King (seal)

689 WALKER, SIR CHAMBERLAIN, Dublin, Knt.

13 Oct. 1730. Narrate, ½ p., 22 Dec. 1743.

His wife Dame Catherine Walker, guardian of his children, exor. His son Chamberlain Walker. To his daughter Catherine £800 when 18 years or day of marriage. His brother John Walker of Gurteen, Co. Kilkenny, Esq., and John Barrington, Castlewood, Queen's Co., Esq., exors.

All his lands, tenements and hereditaments or estate of inheritance in Queen's County, Co. Tipperary, Co. of Limerick or elsewhere.

Witnesses : Robert Savage, Dublin, gent., one of the Attornies of H.M. Court of Exchequer and since deceased, Saml. Taylor, Dublin, gent., then clerk to said Robert Savage and now one of the Attornies of said Court, Charles Dempsey, Dublin, gent., then likewise clerk to said Robert Savage. .

Memorial witnessed by : James Flack, Dublin, gent., one of the Attornies of said Court of Exchequer, Thomas Plowman, Athy, Co. Kildare, gent.

111, 545, 78029   Catherine Walker (seal)

690 MOORE, Rev. FRANCIS, Rahinduff, Queen's Co., clerk.

29 Dec. 1718. Narrate, ¾ p., 10 Jan. 1743.

His wife Katherine Moore. His daughter Katherine Moore, extx. Robert Weldon, Roscomerow, King's Co., gent., trustee.

Town and lands of Rahinduff, Queen's Co., mortgaged about the year 1695 to Hanover (Honour) Foley of Dublin by testator's father ; Thos. Whittley, Esq., was husband of said Honour Foley in 1698.

Witnesses : Robt. Pinsent, Athy, Co. Kildare, Esq., Edith Pinsent, his wife, Elizabeth Macoun, Rathinduff, Queen's Co., spinster, Edward Brown, Athy, Co. Kildare, gent.

Memorial witnessed by : Thos. Holt, Dublin, gent., Simon Foden, Dublin, gent.

114, 84, 78100   Ka. Moore (seal)

691 KEEGAN, ROBERT, Drogheda, dyer.

3 Oct. 1737. Narrate, ½ p., 16 Jan. 1743.

His wife Elizabeth Keegan. His youngest son Richard (under 21 years). His two daughters Margaret and Mary. His eldest son Robert Keegan. His second son John Keegan. Mr Henry Blackwell, Harristown, Co. Louth, gent. and his said wife Elizabeth [Keegan] exors.

His houses on the old Cornmarkett Hill. A field near the Yellow Batter then in the possession of John Clark [situation not mentioned]. His working tools and shop utensils ; a " press pleat " to son John.

Witnesses : Gerrald Aylmer, merchant, Joseph Lorey, weaver, Maurice McDaniell, gent. all of town of Drogheda.

Memorial witnessed by : Michael Argent, James Saunders, both of Dublin, gents.

110, 389, 78124   John Kegan (seal)

692 CROSBIE, WILLIAM, Tubrid, Co. Kerry, Esq.

Codicil 17 April 1742. Narrate, ½ p., 23 Jan. 1743.

His brother Maurice Crosbie, father of Thomas Freke Crosbie. His brother Arthur Crosbie, father of William Crosbie.

Witnesses : Dominick Rice, Rathkenny, Co. Kerry, gent., Danl. McCarthy, Ardfert, Co. Kerry, apothecary, Patrick Plunkett, then of Tubbrid, servant to testator, and now of Muckrus and servant to Edwd. Herbert.

Memorial witnessed by : Daniel McCarthy, Patrick Plunkett.

110, 396, 78165   Mau. Crosbie (seal)

693 STOYTE,·JOHN, the elder, Dublin, Esq.

20 March 1741. Full, 2¼ pp., 4 Feb. 1743.

My dear wife Ann Stoyte, exor. with son John. Settlement made by me and my son John 26 March 1740 (lands etc. to be vested in testator's right heirs " upon failure of issue male of my said son John and my son Edward Stoyte "). My said son Edward is since deceased. Francis Stoyte, Ensign in Major Gen. Howard's Regt. of Foot in Great Britain. My nephew John Minchin. My friend Lewis Meares, Dublin, Esq., trustee.

All my mannors, lands and tenements and hereditaments, that is to say town and lands of Glascorn, Ballykeeren, Street, Donamon and Corelly, Gurteen, Gainstown and Tyrellstown, Frevanagh, Pallish [Pallas], Ballycahin, in Co. Westmeath. Lenemarren otherwise called Knock and Thornhill, King's Co. Crackanstown and Blackwater, Co. Meath, and my houses, warehouses, etc. in Smock Alley, Dublin, and all other my lands. Leases which I hold from Lord Malton [situation not mentioned].

Witnesses : Edmond Meares, Dublin, merchant, George Meares and Charles Meares, Dublin, gents.

Memorial witnessed by : Lewis Meares, Dublin, Esq., Charles Meares, Dublin, gent.

110, 404, 78272   Jno. Stoyte (seal)

694 CALLAN, PATRICK, Dublin, gent.

30 March 1742. Précis, ½ p., 10 April 1744.

His grand-daughter Margt. Moore. His cousin John McDaniel. His daughter Barbara Callan.

Land he purchased in the Isle of Man. Lands of Gallanstown held by lease from late Sir Thos. Mollineux [situation not mentioned. ? Co. Dublin].

Witnesses : Henry Humphrey and Surdeville Taylor, clerks to George Moore, Dublin, notary public, and said George More.

Memorial witnessed by : Surdeville Taylor, Ambrose Keon, Dublin, gent.

114, 227, 78734　　　　　　　　　　　　Barbara Callane (seal)

695 KILDARE, ROBERT EARL OF

19 Feb. 1743. Narrate, 1 p., 13 April 1744.

His wife Rt. Hon. Mary Countess of Kildare, exor. His son James Lord Offaly. Lady Margt. FitzGerald, the said Earl's daughter.

Hon. Catherine Downes. Margt. Hall. The Hon. Richard Allen. Robt. Sandford, Esq., exor. Rev. Geo. Tisdall. Robert Downes, exor.

Lands in Co. Kildare. Estate and lands in Co. Down. His estate and lands of Carrtown, Co. Kildare. His dwelling-house in city of Dublin. Estate and lands in Co. Kildare, Co. Meath and Co. Louth.

Witnesses : James McManus, Maynooth, Co. Kildare, Esq., Edward Smyth and Ezekiel Nesbitt, Dublin, Doctors of Physic.

Memorial witnessed by : Ezekiel Nesbitt, Richd. Nelson, Dublin, gent.

115, 7, 78756　　　　　　　　　　　　M. Kildare (seal)

696 BRIGDALL, WILLIAM, Inch, Co. Clare, gent.

26 Sept. 1743. Narrate, 1 p., 14 April 1744.

His eldest son Wm. Brigdall. His second son Hugh Brigdall. His brother-in-law Richd. Gregg, guardian of testator's said sons till they respectively attain 21 years. Rt. Hon. Francis Burton, John Stackpole and Edmond Hogan, exors. His real estate.

Witnesses : Rev. Sumner Wilkins, Ennis, Co. Clare, clerk, John Buxton, Ennis, gent., Jos. Hehir, Ballyally, Co. Clare, gent.

Memorial witnessed by : Rev. Sumner Wilkins, John Power, Dublin, gent.

113, 410, 78769　　　　　　　　　　　　Rich. Gregg (seal)

697 BARRY, Hon. DAVID JOHN, Barryshall, Co. Cork.

2 March 1742. Codicil 9 Sept. 1743. Full, 1½ p., 18 April 1744.

My wife Margaret Barry, sole extx. My nephew Hon. John Barry.
" My well beloved Mrs Agnes Rogers daughter to my wife." My god-
daughter Miss Agnes Frankeland, daughter of Richard Frankeland,
Esq., of Cork, physician.

Daniel Hea. Legacies to poor of parishes of Timoleague and Castlelyons.

Lands of Ardneerusty, Ballymacorkan, Lactenafoy, Cabaragh,
Coolmountain, Dromree, Killvaultra, East Downeeny and West
Downeeny, all in B. Muskerry, Co. Cork. Mohona [Co. Cork] where I
now live, and Shenagh which I hold from my brother the Earl of
Barrymore. House in Timoleague called the Ganynoe or Fryar's House.
Mortgage which I have on lands of Ballintub[b]rid assigned to me by
Wm. Colburn. Lease of Donegal Island.

Witnesses : James Stewart, Timoleague, Co. Cork, gent., Roger
Heaney of same, yeoman, Daniel Hea, Barryshall, Co. Cork, gardener.

Memorial witnessed by : James Stewart, Roger Heaney.

110, 473, 78803 Margt. Barry (seal)

698 HOVENDON, THOMAS, Gurteen, Queen's Co., Esq.
20 April last past. Narate, 1½ p., 30 May 1744.

His wife Lancellette Hovendon. His eldest son John Hovendon.
His second son Pierse Hovendon (his youngest son). His eldest
daughter Mary Hovendon. His second daughter Jane Hovendon.
His daughter Lancellette. Dudley FitzGerald, Ballyavis, Queen's Co.,
guardian to said Pierse Hovendon during minority, and exor. with
Anthony Gale, Crottontegle, Queen's Co.

Gurteen, Ballylyhane, Towlerton and Teerernane in Queen's Co.
Ballickmoyler, Queen's Co., part of which was in possession of Richard
Hovendon.

Witnesses : Edward Folie, Fleet Street, Dublin, gent., James
Loughlin, Fleet Street, clerk to said Edward Folie, Denis Doran,
Aungier Street, Dublin, gent., Arthur Hovendon, Towlerton, Queen's
Co., gent.

Memorial witnessed by : Denis Doran, James Loughlin.

114, 309, 79060 Ed. Folie (seal)

699 BOND, EDWARD, Bondville otherwise Tullaghbrackitra, Esq.
13 Dec. 1742. Narrate, 2½ pp., 4 June 1744.

Edward Shand, clerk, Henry Bond, gent., and . . . [blank] exors. His sister Jane Roe, each of her daughters and her son Thomas Roe. Bond due by Thomas Roe, deceased, to be cancelled. His sisters Jane and Mary. His nephew Rev. Edward Shand. The children of his cousin Geo. Richardson deceased. His cousin John Bond, John Bond deceased, father of said John. His brother George Bond. His nephew Middleton Bond then at the College of Dublin. Henry Bond of Tullybrickitra, Co. Armagh, gent. His nephew John Pooler, his mother, and to each of his sisters £100 on marriage. " He [the testator] received about ninety pounds from George Grindall of money belonging to the children of his [John Pooler's] father Wm. Pooler, deceased."

His brother Walter Bond died in the year 1717 possessed by lease of the lands of Gartgonys [? Gortgonis, Co. Tyrone] long since expired. Lands of Ahanargale and half of Derimagoan (except the Island called Derinasool), also lands of Aghnacloy and Annaghagh, Lissdromard, Balletiran, and several tenements in and near town of Armagh. His brother's children and widow. Elizabeth, his brother's youngest daughter, Mary his eldest daughter. Edward Bond, second son of his brother George Bond.

To Thomas Campbell he bequeathed what he owed for what he laid out in barley to carry on a malt trade and Tobacco trade. Mrs Jane Smith otherwise Wilton, her father Mr Thos. Wilton deceased.

Deriliiagh [? Derrilla], Derryviny [? Derryveen] and Derryene, Derrylea, Egliss and Glengavelin, in manor of Clanticlew, Co. Monaghan. The four towns and lands of Cloghernagh, Mullaghlamphill, Dreen, Broughsloy and the water mill, Co. Tyrone. Lands of Drombee, Tulligarran, Tullinkekoll, Balliscandell and Tullyneagh, parish and county of Armagh. Tullinegall, Co. Tyrone. Grangemore, Co. Armagh. Derrylapan, Co. Tyrone. Woods of Dunmadigan, Co. Monaghan, Derrynoose. Leases of Dunemoney and Kilbracken, Co. Tyrone. Cladymore, part of Cladybegg [Co. Armagh], part of Tereniscobe. Drumcarr, Knockrainill, [? all in Co. Armagh], and houses in Irish Street, Armagh. Houses in city and suburbs of Dublin. Two houses on the corner of Carrion Row facing Charles Street bequeathed to Mary Kearny, merchant, during her life.

To Henry Bond[1] the town and lands of Tullabrackitra, Coolkill, Reencran, Mullinary and Unshog, Co. Armagh ; Cavancreery, Cullertragh, Killygold, Deericreevy, Knockagolis, Tategar, Ahnaglave, Taffan, Croghan and Mullaghaduff, lease of the six tates of Tehollan,

---

[1] *Betham's Will Pedigrees* show Henry Bond as the testator's natural son.

x

White Island and Cleary in Co. Monaghan, part of Cortyna, Agh-
magurgan, Co. Armagh. Carnevanaghan [situation not mentioned] to
said John Bond.

Witnesses : Thos. Faulkiner, gent., Thos. Bond, glazier, Thos.
Moore, all of city of Dublin.

Memorial witnessed by : James Blanchville and James Saunders,
Dublin, gent.

112, 465, 79188   Hen. Bond (seal)

700   READ, GEORGE, senr., Rossenarra, Co. Kilkenny, Esq.
     26 Feb. 1727. Précis, ½ p., 26 June 1744.

His third son Joseph Read, clerk. Seskin and Garrythomas, B. Kells,
Co. Kilkenny.

Witnesses : Henry Baker, Rathcullen, Co. Kilkenny, Esq., Thos.
Rake, Ballaghtobin, Co. Kilkenny, gent., John Moore, Callan, Co.
Kilkenny, yeoman.

Memorial witnessed by : Michl. McCarthy, clerk to Robt. Wallis,
Cork, public notary, and said Robt. Wallis.

115, 68, 79281   Joseph Read (seal)

701   JONES, HENRY, Drombegg, B. of East Carbery, Co. Cork, gent.
     7 Oct. 1738. Précis, ½ p., 5 July 1744.

His daughters Jane, Mary, Frances and Grace Jones, his son John
Jones (all under 21 years). His eldest son Edwd. Jones, exor.

Witnesses : Saml. Jervois, Brade, Co. Cork, Esq., Joseph Ledbetter,
Bandon, Co. Cork, Esq., Doctor in Physic, John Hungerford, Glandore,
Co. Cork, gent.

Memorial witnessed by : John Hungerford, Wm. Donovan, Reen,
B. of West Carbery, Co. Cork, gent.

114, 387, 79328   Edwd. Jones (seal)

702   ASHBORNER, RICHARD,[1] Dublin, merchant.
     25 June 1743. Narrate, 2¼ p., 10 July 1744.

Jas. Bibby, Co. Dublin, gent., trustee. His first cousin John
Ashborner, second son of his late uncle George Ashborner, late of Co.
of Cumberland, deceased. Richard Ashborner, eldest son of his
said uncle George Ashborner. Thos. Ashborner Parker, eldest son of

---

[1] This surname appears as Ashburner in Vicars *Index of the Prerogative Wills
of Ireland*, and in *Betham's Will Pedigrees*, Genealogical office.

his niece Ann Parker otherwise Thompson, wife of Paul Parker of Temple Barr, Dublin, merchant. Richard Parker second son, Isaac Parker third son. Wm. Parker fourth son, Paul Parker fifth son of said niece Ann Parker. Elizabeth Dulap[1] otherwise Ashborner daughter of his late uncle George Ashborner and wife of Robert Dunlap, Dublin, *upholder*. Said John Ashborner and said Eliz. Dunlap exors.

To Mary Malone otherwise Gernon, wife of Joseph Malone of Cork Hill, Dublin, hosier, he left his first wife's picture, etc. Susanna Hendrick, spinster. His tenant the widow Lyons. Andrew Craig, a poor lame man that lived on the Batchelor's Walk. Legacy to poor of St. Mary's Parish and St. Aude[o]n's parish. His servant Elizth. Brownrigg, her sister Mary Brownrigg. His sister Ann Thompson. Mary Ashborner his uncle George's youngest daughter. His niece Mary Brookbank otherwise Thompson. Dorothy Ashborner, his uncle George's widow. Samuel Gernon his first wife's son. His niece Ann Parker. His sister-in-law Susanna Burleigh.

Ground in Francis Street, Dublin, on which there was three or four houses built and the College of Dublin were his tenants. Two houses near St. Aude[o]n's Arch adjoining the Carpenter's Hall. Two houses, warehouses etc. on Merchant's Quay, Dublin. Ground in Chamber Street and Clothworkers Square. Ground fronting Dolphin's Barn Lane "joining to the water course that runs from Roper's Rest on which ground six new houses and the Anabaptist dipping Place did stand." Several leases in liberties of Thos. Court and Donore. Ground in Back Lane, Dublin. Holding on Hawkins Quay in parish of St. Mark's, Dublin. Holdings on Jervis Quay otherwise the Batchelor's Walk, Union Street and Abby Street, Dublin.

Witnesses : Stephen Robinson, Castle Street, Dublin, grocer, John Sumner, Dublin, confectioner, Wm. Sumner, Dublin, public notary.

Memorial witnessed by : John Kathrens, Dublin, public notary, Henry Steevens Reily his clerk.

117, 8, 79412   James Bibby (seal)

703 McDERMOTT, JAMES, Castleteheen, Co. Roscommon, Esq.

2 June 1744. Narrate, ¾ p., 20 July 1744.

His sisters Mary and Margaret McDermott. Sir Edward Crofton Moate, Co. Roscommon, Bart., Robt. Sandford, Castlereagh, Co

---

[1] *Betham's Will Pedigrees* mention Robert *Dunbar*, brother-in-law to John Ashburner. The will of Robert Dunbar of Dublin, *printer*, proved 1758, names his wife Elizabeth.

Roscommon, Esq., trustees. Patk. Curtis, Dublin, sadler, Mary McDermot his sister, and Edmond O'Flynn, Torlogh, Co. Galway, Esq., exors.

Lands of Kiltultoge [Co. Roscommon] and Garruclonagh purchased from Edw. Gardiner, Esq., and lands of Drumlogh, Annylough and Brenabegg purchased from Caaugh Fallon, gent., then in possession of Owen Connor, gent., [situation not mentioned]. Lands of Corgarrue [? Corgarrow, Co. Roscommon].

Witnesses : Richd. Wenston, Moneen, Co. Roscommon, gent., Jas. Horoghy, Kilbegnet, Co. Galway, Patk. Flynn, Dublin, merchant.

Memorial witnessed by : Patk. Flyn, Patk. Cruise.

117, 12, 79431   Sarah Dermott (seal)

704 PETTICREW, JAMES, Dublin, merchant.
　　　10 Oct. 1741. Précis, ½ p., 24 July 1744.

His son-in-law Francis Russell, Dublin, tobacconist, and Robert Petticrew, Dublin, merchant, trustees. His wife Ann Petticrew. His daughter Elizabeth Russell.

Hilltown and Knocktown, otherwise Ballyknock, Co. Wexford. The towns and lands called the three Ballykneens, Drinagh, Garroon, and Cloneheen in Queen's County [? all in Queen's Co.].

Witnesses : Thos. Smith, Dublin, hatter, Thos. Russell, then apprentice to said Francis Russell, Joseph Landers, Dublin, public notary.

Memorial witnessed by : Benjamin Johnston, public notary in Dublin, William Dixon his clerk.

112, 514, 79453   Francis Russell (seal)

705 CUFF[E], MICHAEL, Dublin.
　　　23 Aug. 1741. Narrate, ½ p., 7 Aug. 1744.

His wife. His daughter Mrs Elizabeth Packenham, her husband Thos. Packenham, Esq. His cousin James Cuff, Elm Hall, Co. Mayo, Esq. His cousin James Macartney. His dear friend and cousin Jno. Folliot, Esq. His wife, the Rt. Hon. the Earl of Kildare, Robt. Sandford, Castlereagh, Esq., and cousin James Cuff of Elm Hall, Esq., exors.

His estate, lands, tenements and hereditaments in Co. Longford, and city and county of the city of Dublin. Aungier Street and York

Street. His real estate in Co. Mayo, being already settled on hsi cousin James Cuff.

Witnesses : Paschall Wilson and Benjn. Higgins, clerks to Joseph Landers, late of Dublin, public notary, deceased and said Joseph Landers.

Memorial witnessed by : George More, Dublin, notary public, Surdeville Taylor his clerk.

117, 24, 79567   James Cuff (seal)

706 GILLAND, WILLIAM, Capperquin, Co. Waterford.

27 June 1744. Narrate, ½ p., 21 Aug. 1744.

His wife Catherine Gilland. His son Wm. Gilland. His daughter Mary Gilland. His son David Gilland. His daughter Fanny Gilland. Legacies to said sons when respectively aged 21, and to said daughters on respective marriages. The combing business to be carried on under the direction of his said wife and his daughter Mary and his brother-in-law Arthur Crafford.

His houses and holdings which he held under John Keane, Esq., [situation not mentioned. ? in Cappoquin].

Anthony Horn, his brother-in-law Arthur Crafford and his daughter Mary Gilland exors.

Witnesses : Richd. Musgrave, Esq., Thos. Bull, woolcomber, Joseph Horn, tallow chandler, all of Capperquin.

Memorial witnessed by : Michl. Argent, Robt. Stafford, Dublin, gent.

117, 31, 79580   Mary Gilland (seal)

707 HENRY, HUGH, Dublin, Esq.

30 May 1743. Narrate, 8 pp., 22 Sept. 1744.

His wife Ann Henry otherwise Leeson now of city of Dublin. His son and heir apparent Robert Leeson. Joseph Leeson, Dublin, Esq., and Denis Daly, Raford, Co. Galway, Esq., trustees. His second son Joseph Henry. His third son James Henry. His fourth son Hugh Henry. His fifth and youngest son John Henry. His daughters. His nephew Henry Mitchell, said Henry Mitchell's mother Jane Finlay otherwise Mitchell.

Lands of Clownings and part of Turnings, Co. Kildare. House in Henry Street, Dublin. Lands of Killowne otherwise Killowen, Raheen, Croghane, Lyrenearle, Monearle [? Lyre and Monea, both B. Decieswithin-Drum], Tinehalla, Killbrienill [Killbryan, B. Decies-without-Drum], Portanaboe, Brownswood, Crehannagh, Rath, Curroghbuolint-lea [Curraghballintlea] and Curraghnegarrygy, all in Co. Waterford. Liskfin, Tulloquain, Glangooll, Pointztown, Dromineer, Garrynagree, Carriggeen, Carrigballydrenan, Castleshelly [? Castlesheela], Garranefadda, Tuomoney, Garryduffe, Boytonsrath, Rathmacarty and Ballynehensey, all in Co. Tipperary. Cottrellsbuolly, Rathtutweny [Rathtuterny], Bohillough, Killalow, Fingarane, Tin[na]killy, Rossmore, Ballyline, Keppaheaden [Cappahayden], Shortalls Graige, all in Co. Kilkenny. Two third part of the tythes of parish of Carrick with the Glebe thereof situated in the several counties of Tipperary, Waterford and Kilkenny. Lands of Newcastle, B. Newcastle and Uppercross, Co. Dublin. Clonaghlys, Oldtown, Collinhill and Ballycommon, B. Salt, Co. Kildare. New Abbey, Nicholastown, Housetown, Cameclode [*Illegible, possibly Carneclode*], Knocklunsagh, Westerson, Newhays and Ballymanin, Co. Kildare. Ardrass, B. Salt, Co. Kildare. Beallaliand, Ballycorigan, Inchimore, Knockdromine, Inchibegg, Ballyda, Dromolohurty, Killenlessderry otherwise Killmucklessderry, Garryteneely, Iseland, Coolendorocory, Inchibriane, Ballymontony, Mynaghan, Killglassbryan, Ballyea, Roran, Curraghmore, Cragg, Anngholey [? Annaholty], Pollaghbegg, Colleveralls, Collen, Corticregane, Knockbullyrivick, Gortlegane, two Knockane, Accaricane, Coolecrosswood, Gortchane, Garrydonghan, Shurgadown, Ballykinloghy, Killimogknock otherwise Killmaccoge, Ferranaverly and Farrenmullhussey, all in B. Own[e]y and Arra, Co. Tipperary. Singland, the bog of Clincoe, in B. Conello and county of the city of Limerick. Ballilin, Vickerstown, commons of Curraghwherry, Derroughter, Derryeighter, Derrynehallow, Kincora, Wherry, Killoge McCloghy, Firebane, Ballyvillin, Ballyvora and Derricky, all in B. Garrycastle, King's Co. Brownstown, Dromlin, Rosseale and Baldongan, Baronies of Balruddery [Balrothery] and Nethercross, Co. Dublin. Sarney and Baytownpark, B. Dunboyne, Co. Meath. Tully, Brittas, Se[a]cash and Dungonnell and all his other lands in Co. of Antrim, with the rectorial tythes belonging to him in said county. Lands and house etc. of Straffan [? Co. Kildare].

Witnesses : John Farran, Thos. Hall, Richard Moore, all of Dublin, gents.

Memorial witnessed by : Loftus Jones, Dublin, Esq., Thos. Hall. Dublin, gent.

117, 70, 79712   Ann Henry (seal)

708 JELLETT, CATHERINE, Tullyard, Co. Down, widow.
25 June 1737. Precis, ¾ p., 9 Nov. 1744.
Her grandson Morgan Jellett. Her grand-daughter Sarah Jellett.
Her friend and kinsman John Stothard, Maheralin, Co. Down, Esq.
Lands of Tullyard, Co. Down.
Witnesses : Rev. John Standish, curate of parish of Maheralin, Co.
Down, Wm. Connor, Boteer, Jas. Wallace, junr., Tullyard, both of
Co. Down, weavers.
Memorial witnessed by : John Standish, Wm. Wynne, Tullyard,
gent.
116, 158, 79933   Morgan Jellett (seal)

709 TILSON, THOMAS, Dublin, gent.
7 May 1744. Narrate, 1 p., 28 Nov. 1744.
His wife Eliz. Tilson, extx. James Knight, Dublin, deceased, father
of said Thos. Tilson's wife. His eldest son James Tilson. His son
Oliver Tilson. His son Christopher Tilson. His daughter Alice Tilson
(under 21 years, unmarried). Debts due to testator from James and
Henry Tilson.
Lands of Bran(n)ockstown otherwise Brenockstown, Grangemore,
ye Gogstown otherwise Geganstown[1] and Rochstown, Co. Kildare.
Coldwells in Co. Kildare and Dublin. Ballyneclogh otherwise Bally-
necloghy, Co. Limerick. Clonbrin, Polloboy and Pollynecraige
[Pollaghnagraigue], King's Co. Tinnycross in and near Ballymore
Eustace, Co. Dublin [? Co. Kildare]. Westpanstown [? Westmanstown,
parish Rathcoole], Ballynakelly, Rathcredon otherwise Rathreding,
Newcastle, Co. Dublin.
Witnesses to will and memorial : Christopher Dalton, public notary,
Dublin, Jane Kyan, wife of Rev. John Kyan, Esker, Co. Dublin, clerk.
117, 163, 80137   Eliz. Tilson (seal)

710 GRUBY, WILLIAM, Dublin, tanner.
22 June 1744. Narrate, part in full, 1½ p., 24 Dec. 1744.
My wife Agnes Gruby, extx. My grandson William Gruby Barrow
(under 21 years). My daughter Agnes Barrow, extx. Isabella Barrow,
sister to said William Gruby Barrow. My two daughters Margaret
Maskew and Mary Falkener, exors.

---

[1] Gegan or Gagan is an anglicization of Mag Eochagain. The Gaelic form may
suggest an explanation of " ye Gog."

My houses and tanyard wherein I now dwell in St. James Street, Dublin.

Witnesses : John Towers, Dublin, tanner, Robt. Horner, Athy, Co. Kildare, farmer, William Stone, Athy, Co. Kildare, tanner.

Memorial witnessed by : William Brooks, Dublin, baker, Thos. Faulkner.

115, 238, 80352   Agnes Barrow (seal)

711 LEECH, WILLIAM, Coomb, Liberties of Thomas Court and Donore, [Dublin], gent. 23 Jan. 1743. Narrate, ¾ p., 17 Jan. 1744.

His wife Margt., exor. Edw. Godwin, Truck Street in the Liberties aforesaid, tallow chandler, trustee. Testator's son William Leech. His grandson John Harrison. Rev. Albert Nesbitt, Dublin, clerk, exor.

His holdings in Elbo Lane in the Liberties aforesaid.

Witnesses : Ann Harrison, wife of George Harrison, Esq., Cockermouth, Gt. Britain, distiller, Wm. Tuncks, the Coomb, Dublin, glazier, Arthur Shepheard, Dublin, public notary.

Memorial witnessed by : Arthur Shepheard, David Sayers, clerk to said Arthur Shepheard.

118, 188, 80447   Margrett Leech (seal)

712 TROTTER, WILLIAM, Drapers Court, Dublin, victualler. Not dated. Précis, ¼ p., 1 March 1744.

His wife Margret Trotter, extx. His son Jno. Trotter. His daughter Susanna Trotter. His real and personal estate.

Witnesses to will and memorial : James Moore, Dublin, joyner, Wm. Devall, public notary in Dublin.

115, 353, 80739   Margt. Trotter (seal)

713 MOUNTRATH, ALGERNON EARL OF
       26 July 1744. Narrate, 1¼ p., 2 March 1744/45.

His wife Diana Countess of Mountrath. His son Charles Henry Lord Castle Coole.

Robt. Coote, Esq., son of Chidley Coote, late of Killester, deceased. John Clephane, Doctor of Physic.

Adamstown, Gormanstown ¦and Ballygalla, B. Small-[county], Co. Limerick, then or late in tenure or occupation of Standis[h] Grady, Esq., and his under-tenants. His leasehold estate in city of Dublin.

Witnesses : William Smallbroke, Lincoln's Inn, Middlesex, gent., Thos. Heaton of same, gent., David Granger, servant to testator.

Memorial witnessed by : Thos. Heaton, Hutton Perkins, Lincoln's Inn, Esq.

116, 343, 80752   D. Mountrath (seal)

714 INGHAM, ROBERT, Dublin, cabinetmaker.

8 Dec. 1742. Précis, ¼ p., 23 March 1744.

To his wife Alice Ingham otherwise Harrison otherwise Frazer (extx.) all his real and personal estate.

Witnesses : John Botton [? Rotton], Dublin, cabinetmaker, Benj. Johnston, Dublin, public notary.

Memorial witnessed by : Andw. Preston, Dublin, joiner, Arthur Shepheard, Dublin, public notary.

115, 392, 80924   Alice Ingham (seal)

715 GORE, ARTHUR, Ballygarrett, Co. Carlow, Esq.

22 Dec. 1741. Full, 2 pp., 17 April 1745.

To be buried at the church of Aghade, Co. Carlow. My wife Mary Gore otherwise Echlin. My nephew Richard Gore (exor.), eldest son of my brother Richard Gore of Sligo, Co. Sligo. My nephew Francis Gore, brother to said Richard Gore. Henry Gore, son of my brother Francis Gore deceased. The eldest son of my brother Paul Gore deceased. The second son of my brother Paul. My nephew Francis Ormsby son to Col. Wm. Ormsby. Rev. Dr. John Echlin, brother to my said wife. My particular friend Richard Steele, Dublin, gent., exor. Mr Peter Owens, Tulla, Co. Carlow. Legacy to minister and churchwardens of parish of Aghade. Robert French, Esq., council-at-law, exor.

Wardhouse, Co. Leitrim. Craddockstown and Killdrina, B. Cranagh, Co. Kilkenny. Lisrivis, Co. Galway. Knockduffe, Co. Wexford. Gregnahoune, Queen's Co. House, town and lands of Ballygarrett, Co. Carlow.

Witnesses : Thos. Pollexfen, Dublin, Esq., Thos. Wetherelt and John Allen, Dublin, gents.

Memorial witnessed by : Thos. Wetherelt, John Allen.

120, 30, 81034   Richd. Gore (seal)

716 VILLIERS, HANNAH, Waterford, widow.[1]

22 Oct. 1744. Narrate, 2¼ p., 2 May 1745.

Her late husband George Villiers ; his will dated 20 Oct. 1720 proved in the Prerogative Court of Canterbury. He died in 1722. His three children by her, John his only son, Mary now married to Richard Weekes, and Elizabeth now married to Mathew Sankey. Her grandson Wm. Weeks. Her mother Elizabeth Frith, widow.

Rev. Wm. Denniston, Waterford, clerk, Eaton Edward, Esq., Doctor of Physic, trustees. Her said son John Villiers, her said son-in-law Mathew Sankey and her grandson William Weekes, exors.

Her real estate in parish of Hanbury in Staffordshire in Great Britain, and the Rectory or Parsonage at Hanbury. Lands of Sporthouse, Killbride, Monvooy, Turin, Ballyneclough and Clonfada, Co. Waterford, and Smartscastle, Co. Kilkenny. Her other lands in Gt. Britain, Ireland or elsewhere.

Witnesses : Nicholas Nash, Dublin, Esq., Thos. Osborne, Waterford, apothecary, Geo. Wakefield, Waterford, aledraper.

Memorial witnessed by : John Kelly, Theodore Cooke, Waterford, gents.

116, 397, 81091   Jno. Villiers (seal)

717 TUNCKS, LEONARD, parish of St. Andrew, Dublin, painter.

28 March 1744. Précis, ½ p., 4 May 1745.

His wife Mary Tuncks. His daughter Sarah Write. His cousin Richard Brown, London, weaver. Garrett Cavanagh and Peter Butterton, both of George's Lane, parish of St. Andrew, Dublin, exors.

His South Sea Stock and rest of his substance in Dublin.

Witnesses : Gerald Cavanagh, vinter, Dublin, Peter Butterton, upholder, Dublin.

Memorial witnessed by : Gerald Kavanagh, Robert Stafford, Dublin, gent.

118, 365, 81110   Mary Tuncks (seal)

---

[1] See abstract 723.

718 READ, RICHARD, Rossenarragh, Co. Kilkenny.
22 Jan. 1739. Narrate, 1½ p., 7 May 1745.
His daughter Martha and son John. His son Mathew. His son Richd. His eldest son George.
Lands in Co. Kilkenny. Killekebane [Killickabawn], Godswell meadow, and part of the Hill of the Downs, Co. Wicklow leased from Humphrey Mathews, Esq. Templelyon, Co. Wicklow. Lemonstown, Co. Kilkenny, leased "from James Staford, Esq., subject to his son George's option." New Churchtown and Smithstown, Co. Kilkenny. Unibeg, Co. Kilkenny. Cranareen [? Co. Wicklow]. Blackhall, Newtown, Great and Midle Rowans [Rowans Big, Rowans Little], Co. Dublin. Templelyon and Ballysallagh [? Co. Wicklow].
Witnesses : Thos. Baker, gent., Patk. Clahisey, John Walsh, yeoman.   id
Memorial witnessed by : Francis Evans, Dublin, gent., Dav Fleming, Dublin, writing clerk.
115, 435, 81123   Richd. Read (seal)

719 McCULLOH, JAMES, Dublin, Esq.
13 Feb. 1744. Narrate, 1 p., 13 May 1745.
His wife Mary McCulloh otherwise Ferguson. His nephew Mr Wm. McCulloh. His eldest daughter Margt. McCulloh. His second daughter Jane McCulloh.
James Stewart, Co. Antrim, Esq., and Charles Macartney, Dublin, merchant, trustees. To James Macartney son of said Charles Macartney £300 when 21 years. Alice Bowker of the Kingdom of Great Britain. His servant Alice Boyce £100 for her faithful service. James McCulloh of Piedmount, Co. Antrim, Esq., and his said nephew Wm. McCulloh exors. His real and personal estate.
Witnesses : John Treanor, Dublin, Edmd. Wall, Dublin, gent., Paschall Wilson, Dublin, scrivener.
Memorial witnessed by : Paschall Wilson, William Bigger, Dublin, gent.
116, 414, 81200   Wm. McCulloh (seal) ·

720 HARRIS, JOHN, Mountrath, Queen's Co., merchant.
17 Feb. 1742. Narrate, ½ p., 22 May 1745.
His wife and his son Joseph Harris exors.

Dwelling-house in the town of Mountrath which he leased from the Earl of Mountrath. His oil mill and Tuck Mills, and plots of land in Mountrath, leased from said Earl.

Witnesses: John Jones, innkeeper, Edwd. Jones, shoemaker, Edwd. Thompson, dyer and " prefer " all of Mountrath.

Memorial witnessed by: Benj. Johnston, public notary, Dublin, Mathw. Pageitt his clerk.

119, 45, 81290   Joseph Harris (seal)

721 CROFTON, SIR EDWARD, Moate, Co. Roscommon, Bart.
— Feb. 1741. Full, 2 pp., 1 June 1745.

My mother Dame Mary Crofton. My wife Dame Martha Crofton. Having as yet no issue. To be interred at the church of Killmaine in my family vault there. My cousin Oliver Crofton, Lissanougrow, Co. Limerick, Esq., trustee and exor.; his present wife. James Farrell and James Etheridge, two of my servants. Estates in remainder to my sister Catherine Crofton (unmarried); she and her husband to take names and arms of Crofton. Mr. James Cane, Dublin, gent. Legacy to Mr. Robert Mitchell of Moate aforesaid " in case he lives with me at the time of my death." Henry St. George, Woodsgift, Co. Kilkenny, Esq.

Lands, tenements, etc. particularly in Co. Roscommon, Co. Sligo and Co. Limerick.

Witnesses: Jno. Morrison, late of Dublin, merchant, deceased, Owen Dermott, late of Cork, servant, deceased, Thos. Branon, Dublin, late servant to Wm. Roan, Esq., council-at-law.

Memorial witnessed by: Thos. Branon, Saml. Wallace, Dublin, gent.

120, 39, 81372   Oliver Crofton (seal)

722 BUTLER, THOMAS, Ballyadams, Queen's Co., Esq.
17 May 1745. Narrate, 1½ p., 7 June 1745.

Wm. Butler, then residing at Killmoyler, Co. Tipperary, gent. His nephew Stephen Creagh [? Butler], then of Ballyadams, Queen's Co., gent., and James Butler of Newmarkett, Co. Clare, Esq., exors.

Lands, tenements and hereditaments etc. in Queen's Co., Co. Tipperary and elsewhere.

Witnesses : Edmd. Murphy, clerk to testator at Ballyadams, John Green, then servant and labourer to testator at Ballyadams, Thos. Barry, then and now servant to said Stephen Creagh.

Memorial witnessed by : Edmd. Murphy, James Loughlin, Fleet Street, clerk to Edward Folie, Fleet Street.

120, 42, 81408 Stephen Creagh Butler (seal)

723 VILLIERS, HANNAH, Waterford, widow.[1]
    3 Jan. 1744/45. Full, 2 pp., 8 July 1745.

My deceased husband George Villiers. By his will dated 20 Oct. 1720 he bequeathed to me and my mother Eliz. Frith, widow (since deceased) all his real and personal estate. He died in the year 1722. Said George left issue by me three children, John his only son, Mary now married to Richd. Weekes and Eliz. now married to Mathew Sankey. Said John hath proved an indiscreet and undutiful son. My grandson Wm. Weekes, Waterford, gent., eldest son of my said daughter Mary Weekes, he taking the name of Wm. Villiers. Rev. Wm. Dennison, Waterford, clerk. My son-in-law Mathew Sankey and my grandson Wm. Weeks, exors.

Sporthouse, Co. Waterford. My estate of inheritance in the parish of Hanbury, Co. Stafford. Lands of the two Killbrides, Monvoy, Turin, Killcop, Ballinecloughmore and Ballincloughbegg and Clonfada, in Co. Waterford. Smartscastle, Co. Kilkenny.

Witnesses : Eaton Edwards, Waterford, Esq., Isaac Nash and Robert Carew, Waterford, gents.

Memorial witnessed by : Robt. Carew, Oliver Keating, junr.

118   505, 81665 Eliz. Sankey (seal)

724 WYBRANTS, ROBERT, Dublin, gent.
    16 Feb. 1744. Précis, a few lines, 11 July 1745.

All his real and personal estate unto his uncle Rev. Robt. Fisher, Dublin, clerk (exor.).

Witnesses : Luke Vipond, Har[—] Harvey, Christopher Abbott, Dublin, gent.

Memorial witnessed by : Christopher Abbott, Anthony Funacanc. Dublin, gent.

118, 518, 81703 Robt. Fisher (seal)

---

[1] See abstract 716

725   SIMONS, ISAAC, Mountrath, Queen's Co.

9 Feb. 1744. Précis, a few lines, 17 July 1745.

His son Thomas, his kinsman Robt Fayl and his friend John Pim of Lackey, exors.

His freehold and farms of Derrycanton [Queen's Co.], Cranaghbegg, Cappah [? Queen's Co.]. His house and holdings in Mountrath.

Witnesses : James Horahan, Mountrath, grocer, Edwd. Honner, Mountrath, innkeeper, Edward Thompson, Mountrath, dyer.

Memorial witnessed by : Benjamin Johnston, Dublin, public notary, Wm. Dickson his clerk.

119, 104, 81755   Thos. Simons (seal)

                        son to said Isaac Simons.

726   FORSTER, DR. NICHOLAS, BISHOP OF RAPHOE.

4 Sept. 1742. Narrate, 3 pp., 22 July 1745.

Dr. George Berkeley, Lord Bishop of Cloyne, Rev. Robert Spence, clerk, rector of Donnaghmore parish, Diocese of Derry, Boleyn Whitney, Dublin, Esq., Councellor-at-law, Michael Hewetson, Coolbegg, Co. Donegal, trustees and exors. His niece Ann Berkeley, wife of said George, Lord Bishop of Cloyne. Elizth. Forster, daughter of George Forster, formerly attorney of the city of Dublin. Testator's sisters Jane Adair [and Ann Forster]. His nieces Ann Berkeley, Sarah Forster, Elizth. Spence, Mary Forster and Dorothy Forster all daughters of his late brother John Forster. His sister Ann Forster, his sister Jane Adair. His niece Dorcas Reynell. His nephew John Gay of Redmondstown, Co. Westmeath, Esq.

Lands of Baltrasney, Co. Meath, then in tenancy or occupation of James Reilly and Thomas Reilly. His lands of inheritance in Co. Armagh called Derryscolope otherwise Derryscolape [Derryscolsop], Kinary and Ardress. Reciting that by indenture of 1726 he had conveyed his right and interest in two tenements in St. Thomas Street, Dublin for the use of an English school in the town of Coolock, Co. Dublin for a certain term of years, and afterwards for the use of the Blue Coat Hospital in Dublin ; and also a house and two acres of land in Coolock for the use of the schoolmaster of said English School which was then in the possession of Mr Sheridan, schoolmaster. Lands of Coolock, Co. Dublin. Stephen Street and Ship Street, Dublin. Reciting that he had conveyed to the churchwardens of the parish of Raphoe a house in the town of Raphoe, known as the Vault House, and a piece of ground and garden belonging thereto for an almshouse. Lands of Mondowey, commonly called Upper Mondowey [Mondooey] then in the tenency or occupation of Charles Calhoune, Thos. Stewart, and Robert Stewart and Jno. Stewart or their respective undertenants, and Lower Mondowey, then in the tenancy or occupation of James Graham the younger, James Dredan and John Mackey or their respective undertenants, in B. Raphoe, Co. Donegal. Rents, etc. to the Bishop, Dean and Archdeacon of Raphoe for the time being and their successors for ever.

Witnesses : Gus. Stewart, Raphoe, gent., Rev. John Lamb, Raphoe, clerk, John Blackborne, Raphoe, public notary.

Memorial witnessed by : Francis Evans Dublin, merchant, John Somerville, Dublin, Batchelor of Arts.

115, 556, 81787   Boleyn Whitney (seal)

727 PRICE, MARY otherwise WRIGHT, wife of James Price, late of the city of Cork and then of Youghal, merchant. 22 Jan. 1742. Narrate, 1¼ p., 23 July 1745.

Thos. Shears, youngest son of her kinsman Henry Shears of Cork, Esq. Henry Shears, eldest son of said Henry Shears. Henry Shears the elder, exor. David John Shears, second son of said Henry Shears. Emanuel Pigott, Chetwind, Esq., Caleb Faulkner, Cork, merchant, trustees. Ballyburden, B. Barretts, Co. Cork.

Witnesses : Rev. Mathias Spread, Cork, clerk, Michl. McCarthy, clerk to Robt. Wallis then of the city of Cork but now of Dublin, public notary, and said Robert Wallis.

Memorial witnessed by : Mathias Spread, John Verdon, clerk to Anthony Lane, Cork, public notary.

116, 508, 81800   E. Pigott (seal)

728 KEILY, JOHN, Carrigleagh, Co. Waterford, Esq.

7 July 1745. Narrate, ¾ p., 24 July 1745.

His son John Keily of Knockalahirr ; his eldest son Richard Keily, his son John (under 21 years). His son Richd. Keily exor.

Lease of Knockalahirr [Knockalahara] and Clashnedarraff [Clashnadarriv] ; lease of Bewl[e]y, the two Knocknescaghs [Knocknaskagh Lr. and Up.]. House in Dungarvan wherein John Allen and his wife lived. Rest of his real estate.

Witnesses : David Roderick, Dungarvan, Co. Waterford, gent.,
Patrick Lyne, Dungarvan, innkeeper, Wm. Kennelly, clerk to John
Keane of Cappoquin, Esq.

Memorial witnessed by : Patrick Lyne, David Coughlan, Dungarvan,
yeoman.

120, 61, 81809   Rich. Keily (seal)

729 GLASCOCK, FRANCIS, Kilbride, Co. Kildare, gent.
         17 June 1745. Précis, a few lines, 5 Aug. 1745.
To his son James Glascock lands of Kilbride and Grangemore, Co.
Kildare.

Witnesses : Peter Coffey, Clancurry, Co. Kildare, farrier, Thomas
Glascock, gent., and Mathew Hughes, servant, both of Kilbride.

Memorial witnessed by : Michael Argent, Robt. Stafford, Dublin,
gents.

117, 546, 81896   James Glascok (seal)

730 STANLEY, SIR JOHN, Northend, in the parish of Fullam,
         Middlesex, Bart. 23 Dec. 1737. Codicil 31 Oct. 1739. Full,
         3¼ pp., 7 Aug. 1745.

My nephew Charles Monck, Esq., Henry Monck his eldest son.
Christopher Monck second son of my said nephew Charles Monck.
Thomas Monck another son of my said nephew Charles Monck. Wm.
Monck another son of my said nephew Charles Monck. My nephew
Henry Stanley Monck, Esq., My nephew Stanley Monck, Esq.
" . . . [blank] Stanley and . . . [blank] Stanley the two sons of my
late nephew Stanley Monck, Esq." My nephew William Monck of the
Middle Temple, London, exor.

Bernard Granville, Westminster, Middlesex, Esq., and Edward
Stanley of the Inner Temple, London, Esq., trustees. An annuity
payable to Alexr. Kellough, Co. Essex.

My real and personal estate in the Kingdom of Ireland, in Co. of
Dublin and elsewhere. My leasehold estate of Clonultah, Co. Tipperary.

Witnesses : Thos. Ward, London, banker, John Hughes, Inner
Temple, London, stationer, Richd. Mills, Inner Temple, gent.

Codicil witnessed by : John Hughes, Richd. Mills, Mesh, Steen,
Inner Temple, London, bookseller.

Memorial witnessed by : Campbell Craig, clerk to Chas. Caldwell, Dublin, Esq., Patrick Reading, Dublin, servant to said Chas. Monck.
120, 79, 81907   Charles Monck (seal)

731 KENNEY, ROBERT, Bristol, mariner.
8 April 1745. Précis, ½ p., 31 Aug. 1745.
To his wife Elizth. Kenney of Dublin (extx.), all his ready money belonging to or due unto him "more especially from the psers. and owners of the Shireness Privateer," and real and personal estate.
Witnesses : Jenkin Davis, Thomas Williams, both of Bristol, mariners.
Memorial witnessed by : Michl. Nowlan, victualler, Robt. Stafford, both of Dublin.
121, 47, 82001   Eliz. Kenney (seal)

732 DOGHERTY, JAMES, Tully, Co. Roscommon, gent.
29 Jan. 1743. Précis, ½ p., 26 Aug. 1745.
James Lawder the younger, Lowfield, Co. Roscommon, Esq. Exors.: John Harward, Portorny, Co. Roscommon, Esq., Wentworth Thewles, Dublin, gent., and Edmond Kelly, Churchborough, Co. Roscommon, gent.
His estate of Tully, B. Bal[l]intober, parish of Kilmore, Co. Roscommon.
Witnesses : George Cammell, Hugh Purcell, Owen Mulvey, all of Churchborough, Co. Roscommon, yeoman.
Memorial witnessed by : Owen Mulvey, John Lawder, Dublin, gent.
120, 153, 82180   James Lawder (seal)

733 WALCOTT, WILLIAM, Ballyvarragh, liberties of city of Limerick, Esq. 28 Oct. 1737. Full, 3½ pp., 2 Nov. 1745.
My wife Rebecca Walcott. Deed of 18 Aug. 1710 made with John Walcott, Esq., deceased, settling jointure of said wife. My good friends John Westropp, Atyflynn, Co. Limerick, Esq., and my brother-in-law Henry Miller of Tunagh, Co. Clare, gent., trustees. My cousin Bleany Walcott Brown, late of Ballyvarragh aforesaid, the youngest son of Thos. Brown of Ballyslattry, Co. Clare, Esq., deceased. Edmd. Brown, Ballyslatery, Co. Clare, Esq., eldest son to Thos. Brown of

Y

Ballyslatery, Esq., deceased. My cousin Thos. Brown, Limerick, merchant, third son of Thos. Brown of Ballyslatery aforesaid, Esq., deceased. My niece Dorothy Gough eldest daughter to my brother-in-law Hugh Gough, Garane, liberties of Limerick, gent. My father-in-law John Miller of Ballycasey, Co. Clare, gent., and Edmond Brown, Ballyslatery, Co. Clare, Esq., exors.

My dwelling-house, farm and lands of Ballyvarragh. Lands of Clonkeen, Killynegarriffe [Killeenagarriff], Ballyluskey, Cooltrommy, Carrahenne, Knocksentry and Carribegg, B. Clanwilliam, Co. Limerick.

Witnesses : Catherine Patton, Limerick, spinster, Richard Bunting, late of Ballyvarrain, liberties of said city of Limerick, farmer, James Armstrong, Ennis, Co. Clare, gent.

Memorial witnessed by : James Crowe, one of the Attornys of the Court of King's Bench in Ireland, James Armstrong.

119, 188, 82203   Blayney Walcott Brown (seal)

734 PHIPPS, SAMUEL, Dublin, linendraper.

1 Nov. 1745. Narrate, ¾ p., 6 Nov. 1745.

£50 which his mother owed him on account of the legacy left him by his father. His brother-in-law Mr John Fenn. £20 to the Blue Coat Hospital of Dublin. Legacy to poor of parish of St. Audeon's and St. Paul's. Mr Mathew Phelan. James Leasy. Mr Evans. Debt due to Mr Duff. Mr Robert Harding. His good friend Mr John Wilkinson, exor.

The house in Back Lane wherein said John Fenn then dwelt, and houses adjoining.

Witnesses : Rev. Boyle Travers, Dublin, D.D., John Kathrens, Dublin, public notary, Henry Steevens Reilly his clerk.

Memorial witnessed by : John Kathrens, Boyle Travers.

122, 57, 82215   John Fenn (seal)

735 FORD, JOHN, Ballyronan, Co. Wicklow, gent.

15 July 1745. Full, 1 p., 19 Nov. 1745.

To be buried in my parish church of Delgany near the bones of my dear wife Sarah Ford, and close to the graves of her daughters Mrs Hodgkinson and Mrs Elizth. Sherland who lie there by her.

To my friend John Darcy of Grangebeg, Co. Westmeath, Esq., all my leases to pay legacies etc. Elizth. Lady Dudley, wife of Sir William

Dudley, Bart. and daughter and heir of the last Sir Richard Kennedy, Bart., deceased. Robert Gilbert of Feathard, son of my sister Katherine Gilbert, widow, deceased. My niece Katherine Blake. Peter Gilbert, grandson of my said sister Gilbert. Mrs Katherine Savel, widow of Rev. Daniel Savel, clerk, and her daughter Mrs Sarah Murray. My nephew Innocent Cruise. My friend Mark Whyte, Esq., attorney-at-law. Dominick Ford of Ballyfadd, gent. Rev. Francis Corbett, D.D., rector of Delgenny. A flagon of silver for the service of the said church. My niece Angelina Cusack, wife of James Cusack, Dublin, merchant, sole extx.

Witnesses : Henry Preston, Radowns, Co. Wicklow, gent., John Farrell, Dublin, Doctor of Physic, Edward Sterling, Dublin, public notary.

Memorial witnessed by : John Morrison, Dublin, gent., Ed. Sterling.
121, 119, 82305   Mark Whyte (seal)

736   DEANE, THOMAS, Cork, Esq.
1 Oct. 1734. Narrate, 1¾ p., part in full, 13 Dec. 1745.
My grand-nephew Mathew Deane, Esq., eldest son of my nephew Sir Matw. Deane. Robt. Deane, second son of said nephew Sir Mathew Deane. His grand-nephew Thos. Deane. Edmd. Knapp and John Allen, trustees.

The house next westward of St. Peter's Church in Cork. Newtown, Curraghdown, Bohireen, Shanbally, Coolineapishy [Coolnapisha], Drommelia als. Dromell and Kilmore, all in B. Counagh, Co. Limerick. Drumra, B. Duhallow, Co. Cork.

Witnesses : John Harper, Saml. Perry and James Piersy, Cork, merchants, John Long, Cork, notary public.

Memorial witnessed by : Christopher Dalton, public notary, Henry Stearne, clerk.
121, 166, 82502   Robert Deane (seal)

737   GILL, THOMAS, Ballyboy, King's Co.
25 Nov. 1745. Précis, ½ p., 19 Dec. 1745.
His son James Gill, exor. His daughter Jane Gill.
Ground near the town of Ballyboy commonly called Loganisky. Houses and plots in town of Ballyboy.

Witnesses : Hugh Carroll, Derradolny, woolcomber, John Coonin, Ballyboy, joiner, Daniel Rogers, Frankford, schoolmaster, all in King's Co.

Memorial witnessed by : Louis Prichett, Dublin, perukemaker, William Hall, clerk to James Saunders, Dublin, gent.

119, 280, 82532   James Gill (seal)

738 McLORINON (McLORINAN), DANIEL, Tullyboy, Co. Londonderry, gent. 20 Feb. 1745. Full, ¾ p., 28 Feb. 1745.

My wife Mary McLorinon, exor. My daughter Mary. My daughter Ann. My daughter Catherine. My daughter Jeane. My only son Phillip McLorinon, exor. "Twelve shillings to the clergy to be divided between the Rev. Mr Morgan and my parish priest."

Witnesses : Jno. Savage, Co. Down, gent., Jas. March, Dublin, gent., Hugh McLorinon, Dublin, gent.

Memorial witnessed by : Hugh McLorinon, Robt. Blakely, Dublin, gent.

119, 388, 82933   Phillip McLorinon (seal)

APPENDIX

1. Copy of a memorial registered in précis form. Abstract No. 279 was made from the following original memorial.

Memorial No. 23570.

To the Register appointed for Registering Deeds Conveyances and Wills etc. A memoriall of the last Will and Testament of Esther Van Homrigh one of the daughters of Bartholomew Van Homrigh late of the city of Dublin Esq., decd. bearing date the first day of May One thousand seven hundred and twenty three Whereby (among several bequests therein mentioned) she Gave and Bequeathed all her Worldly substance whatsoever and all her Real and Personal Estate of wt. nature soever unto the Revd. Doctor George Berkeley one of the Fellows of Trinity College in Dublin and Robert Marshall of Clonmell Esq., their Heirs exrs. and adms. subject nevertheless and lyable to the payment of such Debts as she should owe at the Time of her Decease of her own contracting As also to the Paymt. of the Several Legacys in the said Will mentioned which said Will is witnessed by James Doyle Edward Thrush and Darby Gaffney all of the city of Dublin and the said Memorial is witnessed by Thomas Prior and John Young both of the city of Dublin gents

Geor. Berkeley

signed and sealed in the presence of   Tho. Prior

John Young

The above named Thomas Prior maketh oath that he saw the above named George Berkeley duly sign and seal the above meml. And that he this Depont. is a subscribing witness thereto And that the said Memll. was Delivered to William Parry Dep. Regr. on the 18th Day of June 1723 . . . . . .

2. Some signatures found at the Registry of Deeds.

Memorial No.	Year	Signature
11148	1718	Esther Johnson Re. Dingley
		[" Esther Johnson of the city of Dublin spinster " and Rebecca Dingley.]
52677	1733	Jonath Swift
		[Rev. Doctor Jonathan Swift, Dean of St. Patrick's, Dublin.]
201709	1774	Charles James Fox
		[second son of Henry late Lord Holland deceased.]
234256	1782	Henry Grattan
		[of Dublin, Esq. Marriage settlement with Henrietta Fitzgerald.]

314272	1795	T. Wolfe Tone
		[Theobald Wolfe Tone, of the city of Dublin, Barrister-at-law.]
321029	1796	Robt. Emmet
		[Robert Emmet junr., Dublin, Esq.]
396042	1806	Arthur Wellesley
		[Knight of the Most Honourable Order of the Bath a Major General in His Majesty's forces. (Created Duke of Wellington 1814)].
550432	1826	Maria Edgeworth
		[of Edgeworthstown, Co. Longford, spinster.]
583118	1832	Daniel O'Connell
		[Merrion Square, Dublin, Esq.]
20. 196	1884	General Charles Geo. Gordon, R.E., [signs as a witness. He was killed at Khartoum the following year].

3. Fees chargeable in the Registry of Deeds, Dublin, for searches made in office, including fees for searching in public room

Scale
£ s. d.

From every person making General Search in the Office without limitation of period, including the liberty of taking notes or abstracts each day 7 6

From every person making Searches in the Office in any one day, upon Names for any period not exceeding ten years, including the liberty of taking notes or abstracts, for each different surname 1 0
For every additional ten years or fractional part of ten years   6

For Common Searches made by the Office under a requisition, upon Names for any period not exceeding ten years for each different surname 3 6
For every additional ten years or fractional part of ten years   2 6

For every copy of an Abstract of a Memorial whether contained in a Certificate of Search or otherwise 1 0

Making Certified or Negative Search upon a requisition, upon Names, for any period not exceeding ten years, for each different surname required 6 0
For every additional year beyond 10 years   6

Requisition for an Official Search should be lodged by a Local Agent or Solicitor. The Organisation and Rules of this Department preclude the transaction of such business by correspondence.

INDEX OF PERSONAL NAMES

The numbers refer to the numbers of the Abstracts, "N" to a footnote, "Ap" to an entry in the Appendix. Names of Testators appear in Heavy Type.

A surname appearing in the Index does not necessarily appear also in the relevant abstract. See *Introduction* page x.

Abbott, Christopher, 724
Abbott, William, 442
Accling, Mrs., 9
Acton, Grace, 276
—— Thos., 276, 463, 554
—— William, 554, 577
Adair, Alexander, 226
—— James, 626
—— Jane, 485, 726
—— Patrick, 272b.
—— Robert, 423, 485
Adaire, William, 62
Adam, Henry, 561
Adams, Henry Humphrey, 541
—— Randal, 572
—— Robert, 527
—— Samuel 213
—— William, 481
Adamson, Thos., 549
Adcock, Anne, 216
—— Richard, 216
Addis, John, 468
Agar, James, 99
—— Lavinia, 649
Agnew, Patrick, 94
—— William, 401
Ahmuty, Samuel, 194
Aickin, Francis, 438
—— William, 438
Aland, Sarah, 87
Alcock, Alexander, 34, 87, 117, 155
—— Elizabeth, 576
—— Henrietta, 576
—— Henry, 87, 576
—— John, 155
—— Mary, 155
—— Richard, 695
—— Robert, 155
—— Simon, 155, 633
—— Thomas, 155, 581
Alcock, William, 155
Alcock, William, 87, 134, 144, 155
—— Mrs. John, 155
—— Mrs. Simon, 155
Alderne, Thomas, 121
Aldrich, Katherine, 44
—— William 44

Aldrige, Francis, 243
Aldwin, Wm., 176
Aldworth, Eliz., 371
—— Mary, 371
Alexander, William 113
Algane, Thomas, 270
Alkin, William, 123
Allam, James, 430
Allcock, Toby, 115
Allen, Ann, 297, 347
—— George, 347
—— Henry, 671
—— James, 62
—— Jane, 332
—— John, 373, 385, 531, 715, 728, 736
Allen, Joshua Viscount, 670
Allen, Julius, 598
—— Lord, 143
—— Margaret Viscountess, 670
Allen, Patrick, 297
Allen, Richard, 332
Allen, Richard, 167
—— Robert, 166
—— Stephen, 321, 484
—— Wm., 294, 394
—— Mrs. John, 728
Alleyn, Thos., 383
Allford, Henry, 243
Allin, Elizabeth, 397
—— Jno., 176
—— John, 184, 513
—— Robert, 397
—— Slater, 397
Altham, Ursula Dowager Baroness of, 193
Amerson, William, 546
Amory, Thomas, 143
Anbere, Isaac, 66
Anderson, Alexr., 367
—— Francis, 188, 189, 255
—— George, 367
—— James, 255, 501
—— Jane, 501
Anderson, John, 604
Anderson, Mary, 367,
—— Nicholas, 224
—— Roger, 237

Butler, Edmund, 49
—— Edward, 19, 44
—— Elizabeth, 199
—— Hopton, 667
—— Humphrey, 371, 669
—— Isaac, 407, 635
Butler, James, 669
Butler, James, 296, 636, 651, 722
—— John, 669, 683
—— Jos., 389
—— Judith, 296, *ib.*, 669
—— Luke, 550
—— Margaret, 231
—— Mary, 407
—— Piers, 458
—— Richard, 249, 375, 389
—— Robert, 669
—— Stephen Creagh, 722
Butler, Hon. Theophilus, 296
Butler, Thomas, 722
Butler, Thomas, 669
—— Wm., 389, 722
—— Mr., 396
—— Widow, 159
Butterton, Peter, 717
Buxton, John, 696
—— William, 417
Byar, Job, 52
Byrn, Mr., 20
Byrne, Carbury, 446
—— Charles, 104
—— Daniel, 203, 268
—— Denis, 96
—— Edward, 554
Byrne, Elizabeth, 463
Byrne, George, 463
—— Gerald, 272 B.
—— Gregory, 284
—— Thos., 206
—— Will., 356
—— ——, 682
Byrtt, Nathaniel, 278

C.

Caddan, Susanna, 490
Caddell, Celia, 585
—— Elinor, 585
—— John, 403
—— Richard, 585
—— Robert, 262, 585
—— Thomas, 585
Caddow, John, 52
—— Mary, 52
Cadogan, Lord, 139
Cadow, John, 97
Caffery, Thos., 637
Cahalane, Matthew, 112
—— Thady, 112

Cahalane, William, 112
Cahan, Robert, 229
Cahill, Cornelius, 228, 259
—— Jno., 525
—— Moses, 131
—— Patrick, 542
—— Wm., 671
Cairnes, Lydia, 609
—— John Elliot, 609
Cairnes, William, 609
Cairnes, Sir Alexander, 237
Calcut(t), James, 509, 515, *ib.*
Calderwood, Andrew, 195
—— Anna, 195
Caldwell, Andrew, 233, 286
—— Charles, 359, 730
—— Jean, 462
—— John, 315
—— Sir John, 462
—— Joseph, 277
—— Patrick, 315
—— Will., 389
Calenhoosen, Andres, 1
Calhoune, Charles, 726
Callaghan, Anthony, 441
—— Charles, 125
—— Daniel, 441
—— John, 410, 441
Callan(e), Barbara, 694
Callan, Patrick, 694
Callan, Patt, 420
Callbeck, Jonathan, 647
Callcott, Geo., 660
Callen, Patrick, 1
Calvert, Joseph, 471
—— Mary, 471
—— Mathias, 471
Camack, John, 214
Camby, Ann, 112
Cammane, John, 300
Cammell, George, 732
Cammock, Wm., 440
Campbell, Agnes, 255
—— Alexr., 626
—— Alice, 255
—— Andrew, 478
—— Catherine, 255
—— Charles, 122, 155, 256, 282, 347, 362, 394
—— George, 255
—— James, 664
—— Jane, 255
—— Jno., 551, *ib.*
Campbell, Josiah, 255
Campbell, Letitia, 255, *ib.*
—— Margaret, 255
—— Moses, 422
—— Samuel, 699
—— Thomas, 699
—— Mr., 409

z

F

Kelly, Frances Arabella, 624
—— Fras., 585
—— Helen(a), 624, *ib.*, 625
—— Hel(l)en, 585, 625, *ib.*
—— Henry, 366
—— Lady Honor_a, 625
—— Hubbart, 483
—— James, 585, 625
—— John, 36, 80, 496, 585 *ib.*, *ib.*,
      624, *ib.*, 625. 716
—— Kate, 624
—— Laughlin, 270
—— Luke, 624
—— Margt., 624, 625
—— Martha, 143
—— Mary, 527, 624, *ib.*
—— Michael, 49
—— Peter, 50, 624
—— Roger, 624
—— Sarah, 624
—— Teigue Keogh, 624
—— Wm., 624, 625
—— Surgeon, 625
——, ——, 624
Kempenfelt, Mary 578
Kempston, Ellinor, 276
Kempston, Grace, 276
Kempston, Grace, 276
—— Henry, 276
—— John, 276, *ib.*
—— Thomas, 276
Kemys, Charles, 521
Kendall, Charles, 496, 498
Kendall, Mary, 496, 498
Kenedy, Jane, 215
Kennan, Andrew, 630
—— Benjamin, 630
—— Christian, 630
—— George, 630
—— James, 630
—— Mary, 630
Kennan, Thomas, 630
Kennan, Thomas, 630
—— Robert, 630
Kennedy, Catherine, 361
—— Elizabeth, 69, 735
—— Howard, 69
—— John, 260
—— Jno., 542, 641
—— Lady Katherine, 69
Kennedy, Sir Richard, 69
Kennedy, Sir Richard, 735
—— Patk., 598
Kennelly, Morrice, 185
—— Wm., 728
Kenney, Elizabeth 731
Kenney, Robert, 731
Kenny, Cornelius, 593
Kent, Catherine, 338
—— Henry, 667

Kent, John, 368
Kent, John, 667
Kent, Jon, 207
—— Margt., 667
—— Mary, 510
Kent, Robert, 510
Kent, Robt., 368
Keogh, Bartle, 624
——, ——, 682
Keon, Amborose, 694
Ker, John, 201, 215, 245. 262
Kerin, Terence, 647
Kernan, Thos., 284
Kerr, Elizabeth, 291
Kerr, Geo., 478
—— John, 277, 291, 478
—— Mary, 47
—— Teeny, 291
Kerry, Knight of, 133
Kevan, John, 85
Kevan, Martha, 85
Key, John, 404
Kid, Elizabeth, 425
Kiernan, Elizabeth, 10, *ib.*, 662, *ib.*
—— Honoria, 10
—— James, 662
Kiernan, James, 10
Kiernan, James, 662
Kiernan, Robert, 662
Kiernan, Robert, 10, 662
—— Sarah, 10
—— Suzanne, 662, *ib.*
Kildare, Mary Countess of, 695
Kildare, Robert Earl of, 695
—— Earl of, 705
Killala, Bishop of, Charles [Cobbe], 222
Killaloe, Bishop of, 443, 513
Killingher, Caleb, 436
—— Sarah, 436
Killkelly, Brian, 686
—— Peter, 686
Killpatrick, James, 215
Kilpatrick, Mrs., 355
Kindall, Sarah, 143
Kinefick, Richd., 517, 616
King, Arabella, 688
—— Charles, 57
King, Dennis, 688
King, Elizabeth, 513
King, George, 288
King, Henry, 688
—— Sir Henry, 548
—— James, 57, 669
—— Jane, 568
King, John, 568
King, John, 57, 679, 688, *ib.*
—— Margarett, 288
—— Mary, 57
—— Mathew, 412
King, Robert, 57

Love, Christopher, 125
—— Herbert, 160
—— John, 287
—— Joseph, 95
—— William, 125
Lovell, George, 677   678
Lovett, Clotilda, 390
Lovett, Edward, 390
Lovett, John, 390
Low, David, 231
—— John, 35
Lowry, Galbraith, 422
—— James, 422
Lowry, Robert, 422
Lowry, Robert, 256, 422
Lowther, George, 107
Lowther, George, 107
—— Jane, 107
—— Marcus, 107
—— Nichola Sophia, 107
Lowton, John, 345
Loyd, Christopher, 237
—— David, 362
—— Edward, 436
—— Owen, 211
—— Richard, 436
Lucas, Jas., 13
—— Mathew, 554
—— Nathaniel, 35, 78, 116
—— Peter, 587
—— Samuel, 485
Ludlow, Henry, 285
—— Peter, 359, 427
—— Stephen, 81, 118
Luffkin, Roger, 13
Luke, George, 97
—— Samuel, 500
Lukey, Alicia, 642
Lukey, William, 29
Lumley, Henry, 404
Lumley, Henry, 192
—— Hugh, 404
—— Mary, 160
Lunell, Wm., 409
Lurcan, Bryan, 81
Luther, Charles, 361
Lutherberry, Margaret, 410
Lutherborrow, John, 78
Luttrell, Elizabeth, 139
Luttrell, Henry, 139
Luttrell, Henry, 139
—— Laurence, 16
—— Margaret, 139
—— Robert, 139
—— Simon, 139, 630
Lye, Mary, 125
Lynam, Sarah, 558
Lynam, Richard, 558, *ib.*
Lynch, Alexander, 559
—— Denis, 299

Lynch, Jonathan, 293
—— Marcus, 159
—— Margaret, 22
Lynch, Mary, 293
Lynch, Nicholas, 293
—— Patrick, 22
Lynch, Philip, 126
Lynch, Stephen, 23
—— Stephen Fitz Nicholas, 22
—— Thomas, 5
—— William, 293, 349
Lynchy, Renald, 403
Lyndon, Edwd., 326
Lyne, Cornelius, 184
—— Patrick, 728
Lyon, William, 130, 216
Lyons, Benjamin, 253
—— Colley, 195
—— Cornelius, 376
—— John, 434
—— Widow, 702
Lynot, Ulick, 473
Lysaght, Ann, 344
—— Arthur, 344
—— John 344
—— Mary, 344
Lysaght, Nicholas, 344
Lysaght, Nicholas, 46, 344

M.

McAllen, Ann, 593
Macan, Thady, 562
McArdell, Henry, 9
Macartan, Edward, 363
Macartney, Charles, 719
—— George, 110
—— James, 705, 719
McAulay, Sheely, 564
McAvahan, Michael, 308
McBride, James, 514
McCaddon, James, 628
McCall, John, 114
—— Samuel, 219
McCally, Allen, 493
McCamis, Jane, 243
McCamrick, John, 322
McCan [family], 447
McCarmick, George, 246
McCarrell, John, 440
McCarroll, Charles, 265
—— Christian, 265
—— Lessly, 265
McCarroll, Robert, 265
McCarroll, Robert, 265
—— Simon, 265
—— William, 265
McCartan, Felix, 79
McCarthy, Alex., 578

Nesbitt, Catherine, 195
—— Duke, 195
—— Elizabeth, 195
—— Ezekiel, 695
—— Frances, 77, 195
—— James, 195
—— Jane, 144, 195
—— John, 195
—— George, 195
—— Giffard, 574
—— Gifford, 195
—— Helen, 195
—— Lettice, 195
—— Margarett, 195, ib.
—— Thomas, 144, 195
—— Thomasin, 195, ib.
—— William, 195, 220
—— Mrs. Alex., 242
Nettervill, Bridget, 585
—— Edmd., 585
—— Mary, 624
—— Patrick, 585
Nevill, Capt., 174
—— Mr. 219
Newbold, Ann, 333
—— Anthony, 333
—— Catherine, 333
—— Frank, 333
—— Hannah, 333
—— Mary, 333, ib.
—— Robert, 333
Newbold, Thomas, 333
Newburgh, Brockhill, 197
—— Frances Countess, 670
Newburgh, Henry, 377
Newburgh, Henry, 377
—— Letitia, 377
—— Obadiah, 377
Newcomen, Arthur, 423, 462
—— Brabazon, 639
Newcomen, Charles, 462
Newcomen, Edith, 462
—— Frances, 462, 639
—— James, 462, ib.
—— Lady Jane, 639
—— Robert, 462
—— Sir Robt., 51
—— Sarah, 462
—— Thomas, 291, 316, 462
Newenham, Elizabeth, 341
—— Francis, 341
—— Robert, 341
Newenham, Thomas, 341
Newman, Adam, 441, 580, 607
Newman, Charles, 441
Newman, Charles, 125, 607
Newman, Dillon, 607
Newman, Dorothea, 607
—— Elizabeth, 607
—— John, 519

Newman, Ralph, 207
—— Richard, 441, 607
—— Susanna, 607
—— Thos., 607
—— Widow, 519
Newstead, Margt., 499
—— Robert, 499
Newton, Ambrose, 372
—— Bartholomew, 220, 316
Newton, Major-Gen. John, 90
Newton, John, 90
—— Martha, 90
—— Mary, 90
—— Thomas, 90
—— William, 90
——, 90
Newtown Butler, Brinsley (Butler),
    Baron of, 669 N.
Newtown Butler, Theophilus, Lord, 296
Newtown, Lord, 669
Nicholas, Henry, 9
Nicholls, Elinor, 438
—— John, 438
Nicholson, Anne, 17
Nicholson, Charles, 426
Nicholson, Christian, 17, ib.
—— Christopher, 17
—— Eliza, 367
Nicholson, Gilbert, 17
Nicholson, Gilbert, 17, ib.
—— James, 17
—— John, 17, ib., 603
—— Mary, 17
—— Thomas, 17, ib.
—— Wm., 367, 426
Nihil, Laurence, 443
Nihill, John, 487
Nixon, Abraham, 248
—— James, 21, 57, 305
—— Joshua, 248
—— Robt., 673
Noble, Arthur, 243
—— Brabazon, 363, 478, 584
—— Elizabeth, 243
Nolan, Zack, 400
Norcott, Alice, 516
—— Charles Hyde, 516
—— Dorothea, 516
Norcott, Edward, 516
Norcott, Frances, 516
—— Mary, 516
—— William, 516
Norman, Robert, 155
—— Thomas, 295
—— Alderman, 282
North, Edward, 157
—— Francis, 121, 157
—— Henry, 157
Northup, Mrs., 9
Norton, Anne, 71

Roche, Edward, 199
Roche, Edward, 199
—— Elizabeth, 199
—— Francis, 125
Roche, George, 637
Roche, James, 199
—— John, 125, 199
—— Joseph, 637
—— Mary, 637
—— Morish, 199
—— Philip, 518
Rochfort, Alice, 450
—— Ann, 450
—— Arthur, 450 ·
—— Baron, 195
—— Elizabeth, 450
Rochfort, George, 450
Rochfort, George, 359, 450, 472
—— Hannah, 450
—— John, 450
—— Robt., 450, ib.
—— Thomazin, 450
—— William, 450
Roderick, David, 728
Rodes, Edward, 159
Rodger, William, 385
Roe, Andrew, 78
Roe, Andrew, 35, 78
—— Anne Sophia, 78
Roe, Charles, 170
Roe, George 343
—— Isabella, 512
—— James, 78
—— Jane, 699
—— John, 78
—— Margarett, 78
—— Mary, 78, ib., 406
Roe, Richard, 406
Roe, Thomas, 170, 699
Roe, Vincent, 512
Roe, Vincent, 230
—— William, 78, 170
—— Mrs. Chas., 170
Rogers, Agnes, 29, 697
—— Christopher, 160, 238
—— Cornelius, 448
—— Corsley, 160
—— Daniel, 122, 737
— - Elizabeth, 238
—— Francis, 29, 160, ib., 185
—— Frances, 311
Rogers, George, 29, 238
Rogers, George, 29, 160, ib.
—— Hannah, 238
—— Hodder, 468
—— James, 109, 156
—— Jane, 238
—— Joseph, 11, 29
—— Katherine, 29
— - Lucy, 29

Rogers, Mary, 29, ib.
—— Maurice, 339
—— Noblet, 160, ib.
—— Richard, 160
Rogers, Robert, 160
Rogers, Robert, 11, 29, ib., 160, ib.,
ib., 238
—— William, 29, 160
—— Mrs. Joseph, 29
Rohd, Nicholas, 1
Rohd., Rachel, 1
Rolet, William, 93
Rollston, Arthur, 499
—— Michael, 499
—— Stephen, 499
Ronane, Widow, 132
Rony, William, 132
Rooe, Mary, 299
—— Robert, 451
—— Stephen, 299
—— Thomas, 299
Rooke, George, 74
—— Joseph, 74
Roper, John, 486
Roscrow, Thomas, 218
—— William, 218
Rose, Benjamin, 353
—— George, 418, 672
Rose, Henry, 672
Rose, Henry, 418
—— James, 95
—— Jane, 52, 672
—— John, 52
—— Joseph, 315
—— Sarah, 672
—— Thomas, 52, 172
—— William, 244, 294
Ross, Anne, 57
—— Hamill, 57
—— Henry, 133
—— Mary, 57
—— Robert, 57, ib.
—— Samuel, 166
—— Mr., 122
Rossell, Ann, 474
Rossell, George, 474
Rossell, George, 366, 535
—— Mary, 366, 474
Rossell, Samuel, 366
Rossell, Samuel, 474
—— Simon, 366
Roth, Oliver, 649
Rothery, Dorothy, 685
Rothery, Elizabeth, 124
Rothery, George, 124
Rothery, George, 124
—— Martha, 124
Rotton, Ann, 485
—— Jane, 284
—— Jno., 284

2 c

Skellern, Hugh, 76
—— [? Skellion], Thos., 578
Skinner, Charles, 65
—— Dorothy, 65
Skynner, P.G.P., 8, 9, 19
—— Pan Gran Parabow, 10
Slack, Ann, 571
—— Randal, 571
—— Wm., 571
Slater, Benjamin, 206
—— Elizabeth, 397
Slater, Luther, 397
Slatery, Matt., 418
Slicer, Saml., 611
Slingsby, Ellis, 139
—— Simon, 139
Sloan, John, 448
Sloane, James, 53
Sloane, William, 395
Sloane, Wm., 395
Sloper, John, 89
Small, Sarah, 658
—— William, 658
Smallbroke, William, 713
Smalley, John, 446
Smith, Abraham, 356
—— Ann, 88, 208, 477
Smith, Anthony, 356
Smith, Anthony, 356
—— Baptist 66, 184, *ib.*
Smith, Benjamin, 353
Smith, Benjamin, 338
—— Brent, 61, 438
—— Bryan, 155
—— Catherine, 184
—— Charles, 548, 577
—— Ed., 325
Smith, Edward, 141
Smith, Edward, 243
—— El za, 141
—— Elizabeth, 164, 184, 413, 456, 477, *ib.*, 580, 626, 636
—— George, 88
—— Hanna, 413
—— Henry, 141, 363
Smith, Hugh, 456
Smith, Hugh, 161
—— Isabella, 88
Smith, James, 413
Smith, James, 7, 413, 442, 595
—— Jane, 184,477, 699
—— Jeremiah, 455
—— Jno, 293, 342
Smith, John, 164
Smith, John, 580
Smith John, 10, 24, 128, 142, 144, 172, 183, 184, 204, 206, 208, 235, 237, 244 307, 347, 355, 376, 382, 397, 437, 440, 456, 479 512, 580
—— Joseph 325, 477 *ib.*

Smith, Judith, 580 *ib.*
—— Kath., 141
—— Letitia, 1
—— Luke 164,
—— Margaret, 88
—— Margery, 456
—— Margret, 456
—— Mary, 141, 208, *ib.*, 293, 338, 349, 413, 477
Smith, Mathias, 184
Smith, Mathias, 184. *ib.*, *ib.*, 614
—— Michael, 477
—— Michael Wilkinson 477,
—— Nathan, 413
—— Nathaniel, 348
—— Patrick, 207, 591
—— Peter, 580
—— Ralph, 442
Smith, Robert, 208
Smith, Robert, 273, 293, 456
Smith, Samuel, 671
Smith, Samuel, 519
—— Sarah, 141, 413
—— Simon, 148
Smith, Thomas, 382
Smith, Thomas, 88, 117, 204, 442, 456, 477, 704
Smith, William, 88
Smith, William, 16, 41, 101, 208, 368, 382, 477, 490, 491, 577, 580
—— Widow, 20
—— Mrs. Thos., 382
—— ——, 460
Smithers, Jonathan, 216
Smithwick, Alice, 101
—— Catherine, 101
—— John, 684
—— Sarah, 101
—— ——, 101
Smothergill, Teenny, 291
Smyth, Barbara, 600
—— Edward, 695
—— Francis, 651
—— John, 200
—— Ralph, 600
—— William, 232, 233, 600
Snell, Jonathan, 461
Solsberry, Henry, 97
Somervell, Elizabeth, 338
—— Quayle, 338
—— Thos., 57
Somerville, John, 726
Sotheby, James, 295
Souch, Wm., 208, 211, 254, 281
Southwell, Agnes, 418
—— John, 418
—— Henry, 311
—— Meliora, Dame, 311
—— Robert, 311
Southwell, Richard, 418

INDEX OF PLACE NAMES

399

2 D

Kinary, Co. Armagh, 726
Kincora, King's Co., 707
Kingsmilltown, Co. Dublin, 282
Kingstown, Co. Longford, 346
Kinkellew, Co. Roscommon, 115
Kinneliskys, Two, Co. Louth, 81
Kinsale, 80, 168
,, Ballincurry, 80
,, Barry Tisaxon, 405
,, Church Lane, 80
,, Cork Street, 80
,, Freer Street, 80
,, Hospital, 237
,, Key, The Old, 80
,, Killany, 405
,, Kippagh, 405
,, Low Street, 80
,, Low Fish Street, 80
,; Nicholas Gate, fields near, 519
,, Tisaxon, 405
Kinturlagh, Co. Galway, 22
Kinvarrra, Co. Galway, 22
Kippane, Co. Cork, 160
Kirilagh, Co. Cavan, 76
Kirklinton, Cumberland, 249
Knaghill, Co. Monaghan, 332
Kneestown, Co. Catherlogh, 108
Knewell, 638
Knights Acre, Co. Limerick, 311
Knochily, Co. Kerry, 173
Knock, Co. Down, 389
,, King's Co., 693
Knockabehony, Co. Fermanagh, 280
Knockabrow, ? Co. Meath, 241
Knockaclarigg, Co. Cork, 344
Knockagallan, Co. Antrim, 638
Knockagh, Co. Cork, 666
Knockagolis, Co. Monaghan, 699
Knockalahirr [Knockalahara, Co. Waterford], 728
Knockanacrow, Co. Catherlogh, 669
Knockanadine, Co. Kerry, 173
Knockanaulart, Co. Kerry, 668
Knockane, 489
,, Co. Cork, 344
,, Co. Tipperary, 118, 707
Knockanecorbally, Co. Cork, 394
Knockanegh, Co. Limerick, 207
Knockaneglass, Co. Tipperary, 118
Knockanegowly, ? Co. Meath, 241
Knockaneivriegh, Co. Tipperary, 73
Knockan[e]leigh, Co. Cork, 42
Knockanemota, Co. Wicklow, 284
Knockangrasse, Queen's Co., 87
Knockaninagh, Queen's Co., 509
Knockanleigh, Co. Cork, 42
Knockballinebough, Co. Limerick, 60
Knockballintorliss, Co. Limerick 60
Knockballlyclery, Co. Galway, 22
Knockballyclory, Co. Galway, 22

Knockballymartin, North and South, Co. Cork, 579
Knockballymeagher, Co. Tipperary, 179
Knockban, Co. Sligo, 222
Knockbegg, Co. Kerry, 173
Knockbogh, Co. Mayo, 222
Knockbrack, Co. Cork, 46, 487
,, Co. Kildare, 87
,, Co. Limerick, 311
Knockbryan Gorne, ? Co. Roscommon, 624
Knockbullyrivick, Co. Tipperary, 707
Knockcolumkill, Co. Down, 387
Knockcoolkear, 579
Knockdromine, Co. Tipperary, 707
Knockdromrooe, Co. Limerick, 487
Knockduffe, ? Co. Wicklow, 188
,, Co. Wexford, 715
Knockellan, Co. Galway, 22
Knocker, Co. Antrim, 272B.
Knockendarragh, Co. Wicklow, 467
Knockengarrow, Co. Wexford, 561
Knockering, 350
Knockgrenon, Co. Wexford, 561
Knockhowlin, Co. Wexford, 506, 507
Knockicoulea, Co. Cork, 186
Knockihernane, Co. Limerick, 47
Knockine, Co. Tipperary, 73
Knockingall, 569
Knockkea, Queen's Co., 87
Knockleagh, 492
Knocklunsagh, Co. Kildare, 707
Knockmanduffe, 29
Knockmeale, Co. Waterford, 132
Knockmore, Co. Kilkenny, 88
Knocknagrawly, Queen's Co., 87
Knocknahawly, Co. Cork, 186
Knocknamease, King's Co., 39
Knocknamohill, Knockmohill, Co. Wicklow, 284
Knocknamore, Co. Wicklow, 284
Knocknamuckley, Co. Armagh, 466
Knocknanirke, Co. Cork, 185
Knocknarr, Queen's Co., 87
Knocknashane, ? Co. Armagh, 626
Knocknaskagh Lr. and Up. (the two Knocknescaghs), Co. Waterford, 728
Knocknebolighshy, Co. Limerick, 288
Knocknecoghie, Co. Cavan, 76
Knocknenanagh, Co. Cork, 344
Knocknescaghs, the two. See Knocknaskagh Lr. and Up.
Knockneskennagh Great, Co. Limerick, 311
Knockneskibbole, Co. Clare 143
Knocknesnaly, ? Co. Clare, 321
Knocknetean, Co. Cork, 468
Knocknokeon, Co. Wexford 4
Knockonterush, ? Co. Clare, 321